PORTRAITS, PAINTER
PROVINCIAL ENG

'This book makes a compelling case for
ture to our understanding of the social and cultural history of early modern England . . . a richly rewarding read'

Catherine Richardson, *History*

'Tittler provides in this important monograph a valuable window into the production of painted portraits by a category of artist until now little-studied within the history of English art'

Helen Pierce, *IHR, Reviews in History*

'the stories embodied in the portraits examined . . . are extraordinary. This is an excellent book'

Kathryn Davies, *Journal of British Studies*

'The importance of Robert Tittler's new book for anyone interested in British art or the history of the Tudor and early Stuart periods cannot be overstated'

Tara Hamling, *The Burlington Magazine*

'The spread of iconic portraits in an increasingly Protestant society is a fascinating and paradoxical topic. This book is where further research must begin.'

David Rollison, *American Historical Review*

Portraits, Painters, and Publics in Provincial England, 1540–1640

ROBERT TITTLER

OXFORD
UNIVERSITY PRESS

OXFORD
UNIVERSITY PRESS

Great Clarendon Street, Oxford OX2 6DP

Oxford University Press is a department of the University of Oxford.
It furthers the University's objective of excellence in research, scholarship,
and education by publishing worldwide. Oxford is a registered trade mark of
Oxford University Press in the UK and in certain other countries

First published 2012
First published in paperback 2013

British Library Cataloguing in Publication Data
Data available

Library of Congress Cataloging in Publication Data
Data available

ISBN 978–0–19–958560–1 (Hbk)
ISBN 978–0–19–968596–7 (Pbk)

This one is for the grandchildren:
Daniel, Anna, and Nicholas Drozhzhin; Peter and Isabelle Tittler

Contents

List of Illustrations and Table

LIST OF ILLUSTRATIONS

TABLE

List of Abbreviations

BL	British Library
fo(s).	folio(s)
MS/MSS	Manuscript/manuscripts
NPG	National Portrait Gallery
ODNB	*Oxford Dictionary of National Biography*
STC	A. F. Pollard and G. R. Redgrave (eds), *A Short-Title Catalogue of Books Printed in England, Scotland, and Ireland, and of English Books Printed Abroad, 1475-1640*, 2nd edn (1986)
TNA	The National Archives

Preface

Along with its other objectives, this book concerns a cultural tradition and way of doing things that has historically flourished and endured in provincial more than in metropolitan England. It is largely about the interface between that provincial or regional experience on the one hand and the London-centred, cosmopolitan mainstream that has often been misleadingly taken to represent all of England on the other. Its academic genesis lies in my long-term meandering and sometimes idiosyncratic progression through a series of questions and answers about early modern England, and especially about its local and regional components. But it also emanates from my very first experience working in an English county record office, which was in Norwich, in the autumn of 1968.

I used to take my morning coffee, on my graduate student budget, in a pensioners' café run by St Peter Mancroft Church, just a hundred yards or so below the Record Office as it then was. The first time I entered this sort of Quonset hut of a room, I immediately noticed two things. *First*, all the men around me—and they *were* all men—looked to be at least 70 years of age, and so had been born in the late nineteenth century and came of age prior to the First World War. And *second*, they were all speaking a language almost entirely unintelligible to my inexperienced North American ear. It was the local patois of Norfolk and Norwich. BBC English had still not yet obliterated the local speech, and the two forms of the language—the local vernacular and the formal/polite—simply ran parallel to each other in a way that, to any current resident of, say, South London or inner city Glasgow, would still be entirely familiar.

That experience has stuck with me to the present, taking on new meaning as I began to explore the concept of regional versus national forms of cultural expression. Those central preoccupations of this book also require some explanation, and the definition of some of the key terms employed throughout. Anyone writing today about paintings or similar cultural genres must come to grips with questions of terminology. Especially since the intrusion of critical theory into social sciences and humanities scholarship, including the study of the history of art, sundry terms whose meanings were only recently commonly understood have now become considerably pre-empted by the theoretically inclined. Some scholars have now abandoned certain such terms altogether as having meanings that seem to them too contested to be useful. We approach the point where there are two parallel scholarly discussions, each often dealing with essentially the same subject matter and even saying the same things, but divided by the use or non-use of critical methodology and its linguistic usage.

Let me state at the outset that I write mostly as an empirically grounded historian, working from my accustomed perspective of social, political, and economic history, rather than as an art historian grounded in aesthetic principles and connoisseurial training. I work with archives as well as images, and not from the images alone. I investigate and reconstruct the progress of events, causation, and consequences. I search for explanations. Much of what I do may be seen as constructing narratives and telling stories. I play by the rules of the second, hard-copy, edition of the *Oxford English Dictionary* (and of the marquis of Queensbury as should be required in the aftermath) and not, for the most part, by the latest catchword of deep theoretical discourse. I shall be delighted if this book makes some contribution to the understanding of its subject by all who may wish to read it, but save in deliberately addressing some of the questions raised by two or three particular theoretical discussions, I do not enter it very far into the lists of critical discourse.

I still take the word 'art' in its conventional senses, implying 'the application of skill to subjects of taste', and to 'the principles of a special science'. I acknowledge its reference to 'the skill in displaying itself in the perfection of workmanship'.[1] All of these meanings were uncontested and in common circulation prior to the 1640 terminal date of this study. But I also include a meaning that enjoyed only restricted usage prior to the late nineteenth century, which is art as 'the application of skill to the arts of imitation and design' and, as John Evelyn put it in 1668, also as something that entailed the idea of 'the perfection of painting demonstrated from the principles of art'.[2]

I take the word 'principles', common to two of these definitions, as critically important here. Those which Evelyn, one of the foremost connoisseurs of his day, would have had in mind would have been derived in part from classical notions of, e.g., perspective, proportion, the harmonious use of colour, and so forth, all of which were by his time (and for nearly a century before his time) described in sundry widely circulated treatises on that subject. Just as, by Evelyn's time, architecture had become something of an academic subject emanating especially from humanist scholarship of the previous century, so had the more refined aspects of painting. Most of Evelyn's contemporaries will not have referred to it as 'art' in its full modern usage, but they will have recognized the more refined and polite painting when they saw it; they will likely have lionized the painter particularly adept at producing it; and they may well have rushed to obtain and display it in their homes.

'Craft', often seen as the opposite of art, bears very similar dictionary definitions, but I distinguish it from 'art' here by its general innocence of formal, academic principles, its reliance on traditional and often locally specific methods and techniques of manufacture, the quotidian and utilitarian nature of its application, and by its exclusive derivation from the hands-on experience of the workshop rather than from any formal mastery of academic principles. (Niklaus Pevsner's famous dictum, that 'A bicycle shed is a building; Lincoln Cathedral is a work of architecture',[3] has some distinct resonance for the medium of paintings as well.)

Yet though they may be distinguished in these ways, art and craft should not be demarcated as irrevocable dichotomies. I see them instead as existing on a broad

1 *Oxford English Dictionary* [hereafter *OED*], vide 'art', especially I, 4–6.
2 As cited in *OED*, 'Art', I.6, example 1.
3 Niklaus Pevsner, *Outline of European Architecture*, 7th edn (Harmondsworth, Middlesex, 1968), 7.

continuum of skill, refinement, purpose, and imagination. At one end of that continuum we have the work of craft: often crudely worked, regionally specific, and deeply traditional in its form and production. This (taking another term especially from architectural history and also from literature and language) I refer to as the vernacular. And at the other end of that continuum lies the polite or formal, terms that suggest quasi-academic, classically rooted, and widely recognized principles, and a substantial degree of refinement. Each of these polarities applies as well to characteristics beyond the purely visual. As we'll see in the pages that follow, these include issues of, e.g., training, materials, marketing, patronage, and contexts of production which are social, economic, sometimes political, and often geographic in nature. Though the discussion that follows often dwells upon the extremes of that continuum rather than the middle ground, one should not lose sight of this metaphor and its applicability to the subject as a whole in what follows.

Most who take on the challenge of writing an academic book about portraits and painters will have been launched into the field with an appropriate formal university training in the subject, and nurtured by thesis supervisors with similarly appropriate expertise. I, by contrast, have no formal academic training in art history, having been reared instead, and many years ago, as an historian per se of early modern England. My research experience lies mostly, inter alia, in investigating questions about English politics and society, local communities, and the visual aspects of political culture in that era. My mentors in art historical issues found me well along in life and career and have not suffered the burdens or the obligations of getting me through doctoral training and helping me find employment. But they have nonetheless mentored with the best of them, remaining as helpful, patient, and encouraging as any supervisor could be. Christy Anderson has been a continually constructive and encouraging trail guide since conversations at Yale in 1998, and a patient, candid, and honest reader of some draft material. Tarnya Cooper's encouragement, advice, friendship, and good company in visiting provincial portrait sites have been indispensable throughout, and undoubtedly extended my shelf-life as a working historian well past its widely anticipated 'best before' date. Anne Thackray has been a valued and wise sounding board and sometime research collaborator. Karen Hearn, Maurice Howard, Jo Kirby-Atkinson, Joanna Woodall, Charles Phythian-Adams, and Kathryn Davies have been generous with their time and wisdom in responding to specific questions; Catherine MacLeod and Katherine Coombs equally generous with their encouragement. Lianne McTavish (who did her best to enlighten me about theoretical terminology) and Bronwen Wilson (who taught me, amongst other things, how to pronounce *gesso*) have contributed stern but nevertheless instructive reminders of the differences between what I do and what most academic art historians do. Concordia undergraduates allowed me to bring my ideas and research about portraits to the classroom between 2000 and 2006. Colleagues in the Making Publics project ('Making Publics: Media, Markets and Association in Early Modern Europe') based at McGill University, 2003–10, have been wonderfully tolerant of my mostly losing battles with critical theory, and patient recipients of several colloquia papers and essays produced from, or despite, that experience. Brian Foss afforded me valuable interchange with his wonderfully welcoming colleagues in the School for the Study of Art and Culture at Carleton University. Christy Anderson, Jo Kirby-Atkinson, and Charles Phythian-Adams gave generously of their time and expertise in reading chapters in draft. Charles Belanger and Sasha Drozhzhin offered valuable technical assistance in times of need.

Many others have provided valuable advice, access to particular paintings or archives, or valuable bits and pieces of research material. They include Robert Alexander (Point Park University), Michael Berlin, Susan Bourne and Tony Kitto (Towneley Hall), Nigel Cox (Gloucester Folk Museum), John Craig (Simon Fraser University), Henry French, Jane Whittle, and Mark Overton (University of Exeter); Elizabeth Goldring; Francis Gotto and Richard Higgins (Durham University Library Archives); Alan Hayward (Newcastle Record Office); Rica Jones (Tate Britain); Rhonda Kronyk (McGill University); Raewyn Passmore; Sophie Plender (National Portrait Gallery); Kenneth Reedie (Canterbury City Museums); Catherine Richardson (University of Kent, Canterbury); Stephanie Roberts (National Museum of Wales); Claire Titley and Wendy Hawke (London Metropolitan Archives); Joe Ward (University of Mississippi); Kathryn Whyte (Huddersfield Museums and Galleries); Helen Wicker (University of Kent, Canterbury); and Paul Yachnin (McGill University). Librarians at Concordia University (especially Melinda Reinhart, Wendy Knechtel, Luigina Vileno, Irene Fernandez, Sonia Poulin, and Chris James); at the Institute of Historical Research (especially Kate Wilcox-Jay); and at the Heinz Archive of the National Portrait Gallery (especially Paul Cox), have repeatedly offered invaluable assistance.

The generous scholars who have allowed me to read papers to their seminars or colloquia include Nancy Duff and Carol Payne of Carleton University; Ian Archer and Steve Gunn at Oxford; Roey Sweet at Leicester; Catherine Richardson at Kent and (with Kate McLuskie) at Stratford-upon-Avon; Phil Whithington at Leeds; Tania String and Catherine Hunt at Bristol; David Ormrod, Elizabeth Williamson, John Beckett, Pauline Croft, and Andrea Galdy in seminars of the Institute of Historical Research; William Sheils at York; Paul Yachnin, Brian Lewis, and Elizabeth Elbourne at McGill; Sally-Beth MacLean and Kim Yates at Toronto; and Tarnya Cooper, Catherine Daunt, and Caroline Pegum at the National Portrait Gallery. Even the best of friends and critics cannot save one from the infelicities and sheer wrong-headedness that inevitably find their way into the mix, and so I hasten to note that any such blots in this book are entirely my own. All sources were published in London unless specified otherwise.

Finally, I am enormously grateful for the financial support of the following institutions, without which this entire project would have yellowed with age on the drawing board. The Social Sciences and Humanities Research Council of Canada for both its Standard Research Grant and for its funding of the 'Making Publics' project, which also supported me in turn, and the Paul Mellon Centre for the Study of British Art have made this possible. I also thank Concordia University for offering me the post-retirement research office from which I work.

Robert Tittler
Montreal

1
Introduction

As the art historian and curator David Piper has famously noted, 'The British people were slow to show their faces'.[1] He might well have added that they were even slower to do so with the styles and technical accomplishment that could be found in much of the rest of western Europe in the sixteenth and early seventeenth centuries. The burgeoning of what we know familiarly as 'Renaissance Portraiture' with its widely understood and classically based subjects and aesthetic criteria, its secular as well as religious themes, its virtuoso creators who were rightly known as 'artists', and its coveted place in the material culture of its ambient society, came distinctly late to England. So did any notion of a theororetical framework for painting such as, e.g., Leon Battista Alberti had worked out in Italy long before.

Not until the 1540s, and the introduction of three-dimensional, classically derived, and naturalistic painting by Hans Holbein and a handful of other, almost entirely foreign-born or -trained, painters, did the fashion for such work, and the ability to produce it, even begin to emerge there. And not for several decades after did that more refined, theoretically informed, 'polite' portraiture become widespread beyond the court circle and senior aristocracy.

Until about the age of Holbein, and save for these elite circles, most English portraiture remained religiously oriented, relatively unrefined, and largely devoid of classical influences. It was produced by mere craftsmen, almost entirely anonymous to us, with their 'vernacular' and often highly regionalized approaches to visual depiction. It was by no means yet a coveted element in the ambient material culture of the day. Its status as 'art', and of its creators as 'artists', remained far over the horizon.

By about 1640 all this had changed. An English public for portraiture had clearly emerged, and it took in a much broader social base and wider geographic reach than ever before. That 'public' consisted not only of those who commissioned and purchased portraits, but also those who collected, copied, actively viewed, or talked and wrote about them, and even the trickle of gentlemen and ladies who took up portrait painting as a leisure-time activity. Portrait production, especially amongst native-English painters, had evolved in response to this active interest. Certain aesthetic and technical standards, including a significant recognition of classical theory and models, had come, if only recently, to be more widely understood and employed.

[1] David Piper, *The English Face* (1957; 2nd edn, 1992), 21.

That part of this story that concerned the development of technical and aesthetic proficiency from, e.g., Holbein to Van Dyck, and the canon of painters and paintings embraced in its telling, has been well established by the mainstream narrative of twentieth-century art history. The same may be said regarding the predominance of work produced in London, and especially by the foreign-born or -trained painters who had come to work there.

However, the process of forming a canon is one of exclusion as well as inclusion. In this case the excluded work consisted of that which failed to meet the aesthetic standards or connoisseurial judgment of those who have written the standard texts and launched the key gallery exhibits. Paintings of an 'inferior' aesthetic included most of those produced outside the London workshops of the mostly foreign-born or -trained, elite painters of the day. As late as 1978, the re-issued version of David Piper's summary of English portraiture cited only Nicholas Hilliard as standing out amongst native-English painters of the sixteenth century, and only William Dobson and Samuel Cooper in the first half of the seventeenth. George Gower and William Segar received but a single mention each; John Bettes, William Larkin, and Robert Peake none at all.[2] While a few skilled English painters came to be identified for the first time, other portraits and their creators rapidly fell by the wayside of scholarly interest. Their painters, when known, may have been mentioned in passing, but these works themselves attracted little or no scholarly attention and were less frequently displayed in any but local galleries and museums of art. In consequence, the received, mainstream narrative of 'Tudor and early Stuart portraiture' recognized only a carefully selected part of the portrait production of that era, much of it by the likes of, e.g., Holbein, Guillim Scrots, Gerlach Flicke, Hans Eworth, Paul Van Somer, Cornelius Ketel, Marcus Gheeraerts father and son, the Jan de Critzes, Cornelius Johnson, Daniel Mytens, and of course Peter Paul Rubens and Anthony Van Dyck. The very tag of 'Tudor and early Stuart Portraiture' (as opposed, for example, to 'Portraiture in Early Modern England' or 'English Portraiture, *c.*1500–1640') itself suggested a genre irrevocably dominated by the foreign-born and—as 'Tudor' and 'Stuart' refer to dynasties—ties to the crown and court circle.

This need not have been the case. Ellis Waterhouse's extremely influential *Painting in Britain 1530–1790*, first published in 1953, concentrated overwhelmingly on royal and courtly portraiture of an appropriate aesthetic accomplishment. But he was aware of and did allude to some provincial and lesser known painters, bringing at least the names of the 'equally unknown' Edward Bellin, John Carleton, 'one Heskett', Charles Barker, and especially John Souch to the printed page.[3] Much of the same may be said of Eric Mercer's chapter on painting in his widely read volume in the 'Oxford History of English Art'. Though Mercer persisted in what now clearly appear as mis-impressions about the 'absolute monarchy' of the Tudors, he did see that Tudor portraiture rested on several foundations beyond the enhancement of state power. He made at least passing references to provincial

[2] Piper, *The English Face*, 44, 75.

[3] Ellis Waterhouse, *Painting in Britain 1530 to 1790* (1953); I have used the 4th edn (Harmondsworth, Middlesex, 1978), 62–3.

English painters like Sampson Strong of Oxford, and John Matthew of Nottingham.[4] Both scholars therefore recognized another dimension to the English portraiture of this era. Yet neither chose to pursue works whose aesthetic quality failed to fulfil conventional connoisseurial sensitivities. Ironically, the latest effort to produce a grand history of English art abandons both the teleological narrative and the canon of artists of which it was comprised. But while nearly losing sight entirely of such leading lights as Holbein or Gheeraerts, it offers relatively little on the native, provincial scene.[5]

Yet once we begin to seek out that other dimension—in the country houses especially of the middling landed elites and of their city cousins, on the walls of the ancient grammar schools and university colleges, in the halls of the London liveries or provincial guildhalls, and now in myriad and mostly provincial museums of local history and folklore—we form quite different impressions of English portraiture, and of English culture in general, in this formative era. Here we find what survives of the contemporary vernacular work produced by local and regional craftsmen: not 'artists' by any means and only rarely identifiable by any signature or by the appearance of painters' names in archival sources. More often than not such work lacks the single-point perspective, the appreciation of classical modelling, the subtlety of brushwork or palette, the emotional content, or much of a sense of perspective, bodily proportion, or other such naturalistic elements, to warrant display elsewhere.

By conventional, classically derived, aesthetic standards these works may be the black sheep of the flock, but they are also a legitimate part of the history both of English portraiture and of English society itself. They, too, were painted in response to the expressed requirements of specific patrons; they, too, were intended to fulfil particular objectives; and they, too, were often meant to be displayed in specific venues. While the connoisseur or the curator may perhaps wish to ignore them on aesthetic grounds, the historian must not be let off so lightly.

It must also be said that in its pursuit only of the high or refined end of the portrait continuum, and of the elite court painters working at that level, conventional scholarship required little exploration of wider contextual issues beyond the high politics and state-craft that supported much of that initially court-centred work. By the same token, the utilization of archival sources seldom went beyond the records of the royal household or household accounts of the landed elites. For almost all who contemplated the subject, the Public Record Office, as it was known, much less the country record offices of county and town, remained terra incognita.

The exceptions must be noted, for they were also the harbingers of a more holistic approach. Erna Auerbach very usefully and thoroughly trawled the

[4] Eric Mercer, *English Art, 1553–1625* (Oxford, 1962), Introduction, Ch. 4, and 152–3. Whether the elusive Sampson Strong was English-born remains somewhat problematical, but all his known works were carried out in the area of Oxford and Abingdon and none show the influence of foreign training.

[5] David Bindman (ed.), *The History of British Art*, 3 vols (London and New Haven, 2008), esp. vols 1 and 2.

accounts of the Tudor royal household to produce a catalogue of those who had been employed as painters, pioneering the use of archival sources by an English art historian as she did so.[6] But few of Auerbach's painters painted portraits as well, and they were of course all linked to the royal household and to the royal estates principally in London, Greenwich, and Richmond. Her 1964 biography of Nicholas Hilliard remains a seminal work, but one that strengthened the canonical tradition rather than looking beyond it.[7] William Gaunt's 1964 entry into Praeger's 'World of Art' series took a huge step backwards in declaring that 'The local centres of art having vanished [after the Henrician Reformation], the tendency of painting to be centralized in London and in the service of the court was affirmed', and 'the habit grew of using foreign painters'.[8]

The most influential scholar and curator of Tudor and early Stuart portraiture in the last quarter of the twentieth century must surely be Sir Roy Strong, who has been as prolific as he has been influential. Strong has certainly deployed his training in historical archives to excellent effect in many of his publications, even adding to Erna Auerbach's catalogue of painters of the royal household.[9] But the great achievement of his work has been further and exhaustively to illuminate for us the portraiture of the monarchy and the court scene in precisely that era from Holbein to Van Dyck.[10] Only in a later essay, not published in an art historical journal, do we find a recognition, albeit a very important one, of the value of studying regional portraiture as well as the more familiar mainstream.[11]

The prime attention paid in these works to portraiture as a preoccupation of the monarchy, court circle, and senior elites not only privileged the London scene above all others, but it left little room for the consideration of any socially or geographically wider patronage. Aside from Rachel Poole's seminal, early

[6] Erna Auerbach, *Tudor Artists: A Study of the Painters in the Royal Service and of Portraiture on Illuminated Documents from the Accession of Henry VII to the Death of Elizabeth* (1954).

[7] Erna Auerbach, *Nicholas Hilliard* (London and Boston, MA, 1961), see especially Ch. 8 in which the author briefly discusses some of Hilliard's contemporary court painters as well.

[8] William Graunt, *A Concise History of English Painting* (New York, 1964), 15.

[9] Roy Strong, 'More Tudor Artists', *Burlington Magazine*, 108 (1966), 83–5, reprinted in *The Tudor and Stuart Monarchy*, I. *Pageantry, Painting, Iconography* (Woodbridge, Suffolk, 1995), 147–53. Strong won a first in History under the tutelage of Professor S. T. Bindoff at Queen Mary College, London, in the 1950s, and had previously been inspired to study the Tudors in particular by the late Joan Henderson, who took her graduate training with Sir John Neale.

[10] A selected list would include the following: *Holbein and Henry VIII* (1967); *Tudor and Jacobean Portraits*, 2 vols (1969); *The English Icon, Elizabethan and Jacobean Portraiture* (New York, 1969); *The Elizabethan Image: Painting in England, 1540–1620* (1970); *The Cult of Elizabeth, Elizabethan Portraiture and Pageantry* (Berkeley and Los Angeles, 1977); and *The Tudor and Stuart Monarchy*, 3 vols (Woodbridge, Suffolk, 1995–8).

[11] Sir Roy Strong, 'Forgotten Faces: Regional History and Regional Portraiture', *Historical Research*, 78/199 (February 2005), 42–57: a brief but highly encouraging effort. Earlier interest in the local scene, chiefly concerned with cataloguing the holdings of country houses in particular shires whether or not the paintings were produced there, include Edmund Farrer, *Portraits in Suffolk Houses (West)* (1908); Frederick Duleep Singh, *Portraits in Norfolk Houses*, ed. Edmund Farrer, 2 vols (Norwich, 1928); John Steegman, *Portraits in Welsh Houses*, 2 vols (Cardiff, 1957–62). The currently produced series entitled *Oil Paintings in Public Ownership* provides comparable catalogues for the holdings of museums and galleries in particular counties.

twentieth-century catalogue of Oxford City and University portraits, Virginia Tillyard's pioneering 1979 MA thesis on the Norwich civic portraits of this era, and a few other brief studies in county history journals, one could until quite recently have formed the impression that English portraiture of this era remained an almost exclusively elitist, heavily London-based activity, carried out mostly by foreign-born or -trained painters. Even Poole failed to venture much beyond cataloguing, so that the implications of the very extensive evidence she compiled for the City and University went unrecognized for far too long. As for her catalogue itself, its appearance in a county historical society publication did not bring it to the immediate attention of an art historical readership. Tillyard's thesis remains unpublished, leaving a short essay in a county journal as its chief expression.[12]

The same conservative approach has applied to theoretical and methodological concerns, and to the largely canonical responsibilities of the public galleries and museums. The reception of critical theory, and the interdisciplinarity that it implies, has been well employed by art historical scholarship in many quarters, but (though this may not be the utter tragedy that some would make of it) it has yet to make much headway in the published scholarship or public exhibits of early modern English portraiture. As for methodology, the enduring tendency has been overwhelmingly and narrowly to privilege the painting and the painter over the ambient culture in which portraiture emerged. That relevant context is best revealed in the record office rather than the gallery, and the former has not always been the well-employed resource which it now becomes. More than half a century has passed since Auerbach's contributions, more than three decades since Mary Edmond's pioneering use of unpublished royal household accounts to identify craftsmen painters working for the Crown in London,[13] and nearly that long since Susan Foister's path-breaking, archivally based, exploration of portrait ownership as revealed in the wills and inventories recorded in the Prerogative Court of Canterbury and preserved in The National Archives.[14]

Little of this enduring conservatism stems from wanton neglect. Much of the explanation for it surely rests with the close connection between portrait scholarship and the burdens of curatorial responsibility. Local museums are typically so financially challenged that their curators have little time for research at all. Most prominent specialists in Tudor and early Stuart portraiture have traditionally been

12 Rachel Poole (ed.), *Catalogue of Portraits in . . . the University, Colleges, City and County of Oxford* (Oxford Historical Society Publications, vols 57, 1912; 81, 1926; and 82, 1926). See also ead. (ed.), *Catalogue of Portraits Exhibited in the Reading Room and Gallery of the Bodleian Library* (Oxford, 1920); Virginia Tillyard, 'Civic Portraits Painted for, or Donated to, the Council Chamber of Norwich Guildhall before 1687', MA Thesis, Courtauld Institute (1978); ead., 'Painters in Sixteenth and Seventeenth Century Norwich', *Norfolk Archaeology*, 37 (1980), 315–19.

13 Mary Edmond, 'Limners and Picture-Makers: New Light on the Lives of Miniaturists and Large-Scale Portrait Painters Working in London in the Sixteenth and Seventeenth Centuries', *Walpole Society*, 47 (1978–80), 60–242.

14 Susan Foister, 'Paintings and Other Works of Art in Sixteenth Century English Inventories', *Burlington Magazine*, 123 (1981), 273–82. Foister has also employed the archives of the Painter-Stainers' Company of London to fine effect in her 'Foreigners at Court: Holbein, Van Dyck and the Painter-Stainers Company', in David Howarth (ed.), *Art and Patronage in the Caroline Court: Essays in Honour of Sir Oliver Millar* (Cambridge, 1993), 32–50.

and are still full-time curators of major national galleries and museums. Whatever their personal research interests might be, they must keep public interests and budgetary considerations foremost in mind in launching their exhibits, and thus in the expenditure of their research time and effort. As that gallery-going public for Tudor and early Stuart portraiture has been particularly well groomed in recent years to celebrate anniversaries of, e.g., the death of Elizabeth I and the accession of James I in 2003, the accession of Henry VIII in 2009, and the controversies over Shakespeare portraits, curatorial attention necessarily remains devoted primarily to that canonical side of the subject.[15]

It must also be said that most of those few scholars who did recognize the importance of portraiture outside of London and did at least employ some archival sources in their pursuit—including Auerbach, Edmond, and Poole—were effectively barred by their gender from the major curatorial or senior academic posts that might have allowed them more of a pulpit from which to preach.

Despite these realities, younger scholars have now come regularly to spend research time in the record office, though material circumstances often restrict them to London-based sources. Many now regularly consider the broader social and economic context of their subject as well, tying it to such important issues as religion,[16] material culture,[17] or feminist studies[18] as they do so. Yet scholarly consideration of local and regional portraiture, or to portraiture of the lesser elites, or to portraits done by provincial craftsmen painters, remains in its infancy. Most of the scholarship on these subjects remains obscurely published, often in county historical journals of limited circulation.[19] Until this side of English portrait history comes more fully to be explored, we will continue to have only part of that story.

[15] This is most vividly the case with the National Maritime Museum's 2003 exhibit on 'Elizabeth', curated by David Starkey and Tarnya Cooper, and with a catalogue edited by Susan Doran; Cooper's 2006 'Searching for Shakespeare' exhibit at the National Portrait Gallery, with her edition of the catalogue of the same title; and 'Henry VIII: Man and Monarch', curated by Starkey at the British Library in 2009 with a catalogue by Doran. Closely associated major and national exhibits in recent years include Karen Hearn's 1995 'Dynasties: Painting in Tudor and Jacobean England, 1530–1630' at Tate Britain; Susan Foister's 'Holbein in England' at Tate Britain in 2006; and Hearn's 'Van Dyck and Britain' at Tate Britain in 2009.

[16] For example, Tarnya Cooper, '*Memento Mori* Portraiture: Painting, Protestant Culture and the Patronage of Middle Elites in England and Wales', PhD thesis, University of Sussex (2001); Tara Hamling and Richard L. Williams (eds), *Art Re-Formed, Re-Assessing the Impact of the Reformation on the Visual Arts* (Newcastle, 2007). I am grateful to Dr Cooper for allowing me to cite her thesis.

[17] For example, Catherine Richardson and Tara Hamling (eds), *Everyday Things in Early Modern England* (Farnham, Surrey, 2009); Kathryn Davies, *Artisan Art: Vernacular Wall Paintings in the Welsh Marches, 1550–1650* (Almeley, Herefordshire, 2008).

[18] See, for example, Susan E. James, *The Feminist Dynamic in English Art, 1485–1603: Women as Consumers, Patrons and Painters* (Farnham, Surrey, 2009).

[19] See Tillyard, 'Civic Portraits'; ead., 'Painters in Sixteenth and Seventeenth Century Norwich'; Mary Edmond, 'Bury St Edmunds: A Seventeenth Century Art Centre', *Walpole Society*, 43 for 1987 (1989), 106–18; Victor Morgan, 'The Norwich Guildhall Portraits: Images in Context', in Andrew Moore and Charlotte Crawley (eds), *Family and Friends: A Regional Survey of British Portraiture* (1992), 21–30; eid., 'The Dutch and Flemish Presence and the Emergence of an Anglo Dutch Provincial Artistic Tradition in Norwich, *c.* 1500–1700', in Juliette Roding, Eric Jan Slutter, Bart Westerweel, Marijke van der Meji-Tolmsa, and Eric Domela Nieuwenhuis (eds), *Dutch and Flemish Artists in Britain, 1500–1800* (Leiden, 2002), 57–72; Robert Tittler, *The Face of the City: Civic Portraits and Civic Identity in Early Modern England* (Manchester, 2007), especially Chs 1–3.

Clearly this historiographical lay of the land makes the time distinctly ripe for those not bound by curatorial obligations to apply new approaches well beyond traditional subjects, sources, and conceptual frameworks. This study approaches its subject from long-standing, archivally based, research interests in English local and regional history and society, and also in the role of visual culture in those contexts.[20] It considers local, regional, and often vernacular forms of culture not only from those perspectives (or from the serendipitous but thought-provoking experience of coffee-drinking and eavesdropping in Norwich), but also from close observation of analogous research projects devoted to similar cultural forms.

The work of the Records of Early English Drama (REED) project in particular has been especially influential. This Toronto-based research effort began in the mid-1970s systematically to retrieve and publish the archival evidence for all sorts of mimetic activity carried out outside the London metropolis from the earliest years to the closing of public playhouses in 1642. Though REED soon came to incorporate London dramatic activity within its research purview as well, the lion's share of its evidence pertained, and still pertains, to the provincial English experience.[21] Taken together, and amongst its other findings, REED's vast achievement has debunked for all time the assumption that provincial England remained largely devoid of theatrical activity after the Henrician Reformation: an assumption that calls so closely to mind Gaunt's naive observation about 'local centres of art having vanished' after the Henrician Reformation.

It has also been instructive to consider models of cultural development including, for example, the formation of 'standard' English speech, which exemplify the gradual privileging of certain cultural forms over others. Those models raise questions about cultural authority in its historical and social dimension, especially as it may have applied in such a critically important era as this one for the formation of a national, English culture in its diverse forms. They beg the question of how some particular conventions of style rather than others received such general acceptance as to become the mainstream conventions over wide geographic areas. One wonders whether cultural conventions, often first received from abroad, were adjusted to fit the English scene, and then disseminated to the rest of the realm through the agency of London as England's one true metropolis. That model closely parallels a long-standing thesis of economic historians, who saw London as an 'engine' of economic growth at this time.[22] It has also been enticingly suggested by Paul

[20] See, for example, Robert Tittler, *Architecture and Power: The Town Hall and the English Urban Community, c. 1500–1640* (Oxford, 1991), and Tittler, *The Face of the City*.

[21] See Audrey Douglas and Sally-Beth MacLean (eds), *REED In Review: Essays in Celebration of the First Twenty-Five Years* (Toronto, 1976), Introduction, and Ch. 1: Alexandra F. Johnston, 'The Founding of Records of Early English Drama'.

[22] This tradition stems mainly from two seminal essays: F. J. Fisher, 'London as an Engine of Economic Growth', first published in J. S. Bromley and E. H. Kossman (eds), *Britain and the Netherlands*, IV: *Metropolis, Dominion and Province* (The Hague, 1971), 3–16, and E. A. Wrigley, 'A Simple Model of London's Importance in Changing English Society and Economy, 1650–1750', *Past and Present*, 37 (July 1967), 44–70.

Hunneyball in regard to Palladian architecture,[23] and it certainly fits the traditional 'Holbein to Van Dyck' narrative of Tudor and early Stuart portraiture.

But is there a place in the historical reconstruction of 'mainstream' cultural conventions for the role of traditional, indigenous forms and practices as well: in what, for example, Lucy Gent has so usefully labelled 'Albion' as opposed to 'Classicism'?[24] The value of understanding both elements of that dichotomy, and of the relations between them, has certainly been suggested by the contributors to her essay volume, by historians of the English language, by REED's findings for English dramatic activity, and by those who see the continued influence of native-English, even vernacular, building in the architecture of this era and after.

That approach also bears a geographic dimension, and one that begs questions about cultural communication and assimilation for a geographically insular and relatively isolated nation like England. Cultural interfaces with the adjacent and even more isolated kingdom of Scotland, not to mention Ireland and Wales, remained limited to say the least, while religious and political considerations came seriously to hamper what should have been more fluid ties with the Catholic nations of the Continent in the culturally vibrant second half of the sixteenth century. Those circumstances lead us to ask what we might make of the cultural interface, not merely between London and the Continent, but especially between London and the provincial centres of the realm, places like Norwich, Chester, Canterbury, Newcastle, and Gloucester, with their deeply rooted, craft-based, and indigenous traditions of cultural expression. It further raises the issue of cultural relations between such provincial centres and their regional 'hinterlands'.

That issue of cultural authority also begs the question of how might we understand the motivations and interests of that informal, de facto, collectivity of people, referred to here as a 'public', in helping form that cultural mainstream.[25] In this context, the notion of a 'public' refers to nothing more complicated than a collectivity of people who come, in a voluntary, unregulated, and uncredentialized manner, to share an active affinity for a common interest. The object of such an affinity may include material objects, ideas, tastes, or fashions, all of which are embraced in the notion of portraiture. Such publics need not by any means be credentialized, self-aware, hierarchically or formally organized, or in any way restricted in the pursuit of their interests. They typically emerge in a relatively casual and spontaneous manner, but not by mere chance.

[23] Paul Hunneyball, *Architecture and Image Building in Seventeenth Century Hertfordshire* (Oxford, 2004).

[24] Lucy Gent (ed.), *Albion's Classicism: The Visual Arts in Britain, 1550–1660* (London and New Haven, 1995). In her own essay in the collection, '"The Rash Gazer": Economies of Vision in Britain, 1550–1660', Gent expresses the need to lift the 'heavy stone' of classicism and 'to talk of Albion's traditions' as well (377).

[25] Though the precise formulation that follows is my own, it draws upon extensive discussions within the 'Making Publics' research project, and especially from the contributions of the late Richard Helgerson. 'Making Publics: Media, Markets and Association in Early Modern Europe' is a 'Major Collaborative Research Initiative' funded from 2005 to 2010 by the Social Science and Humanities Research Council of Canada, and from 2004 to 2010 by McGill University, which also hosts the project. See http://www.makingpublics.mcgill.ca.

Members of a public for portraiture as understood here will obviously have displayed their affinity when they commissioned or purchased a portrait. But they will also have demonstrated that affinity simply by observing, copying, displaying, discussing, writing about, or even practising portrait painting as a leisure-time pursuit. Those who painted for a living, on the other hand, cannot be said to have a voluntary affinity for the metier. They must be seen as respondents to such a public and facilitators for it, but not, strictly speaking, as belonging to it. Yet as the other side of the patronal relationship, equally necessary in the process of public-making for portraiture, painters must also be considered at length.

The task at hand is to investigate the formation of a public for portraiture in the chosen era, the social composition and nature of that public, and the role of the painters who responded to it. It asks what sort of people would have comprised such a public, and what would have led them to that defining interest. It considers how the production of portraiture came to meet, and be formed by, that shared affinity. It recognizes that any such public for something as diverse as portraiture over the titular span of years will have considerable breadth in its membership, objectives, and geographic reach, and will admit of substantial variations in all these respects.

The same must be said about the portraits themselves produced in this same era. Those portraits have been considered here as existing along a wide continuum of technique and refinement, running from the formal, classically inspired, cosmopolitan, and (to borrow a term more widely applied to architecture) 'polite'[26] at one end to the native-English, 'vernacular'[27], portraiture being produced in provincial as well as metropolitan England at the other. It will examine the interface of both ends of that continuum with each other, along with the possibility that the constant interface of those extremes produced a distinctive 'English School' of portraiture during the period at hand.

In exploring these questions, the gentle invocation of two theoretical models, neither of which has much been brought to bear in any substantial manner on English portraiture of this era, has proven a useful guide. Jürgen Habermas's notion of the 'bourgeois public sphere' as a characteristic of early modernity, and Charles Phythian-Adams's concept of distinct regional societies, which I think of as cultural 'provinces' or 'hinterlands' in pre-industrial England, may both be highly controversial, but both prove helpfully germane to the task at hand.

In his provocative and path-breaking book, *The Structural Transformation of the Public Sphere*, first translated into English in 1989, the German philosopher Jürgen

[26] This term should be taken to denote those forms of cultural expression that reflect widely recognized, formal, and quasi-academic principles. In the words of the self-described 'paynter and architect' John Shute, writing in the 1560s, 'paynters', along with other artificers, would never 'obtayne any worthy praise at all' without 'sum acquaintance' of 'diverse rational artes'. John Shute, *The First and Chief Groundes of Architecture*, facsimile edn (1912), A.ii.v, cited in Mark Girouard, *Elizabethan Architecture, Its Rise and Fall* (London and New Haven, 2009), 57.

[27] This term should be taken to denote those forms of expression that are not based on formal, even quasi-academic, principles or training, and that tend to be rooted instead in local or regional traditions of craftsmanship.

Habermas proposed artistic taste as one of the key operative factors of an organized and inclusive public life.[28] In serving as an object of free choice and changing preference, art came to constitute a critically important element of that sphere. But Habermas situated his transformation of the public sphere in the eighteenth century: a chronology that has come frequently to be criticized by those who have seen it at work much earlier. One objective of this study must therefore be to assess the evidence for the emergence of artistic taste, and of a 'public' for portraiture that may have spawned such taste, prior to 1640.

Habermas's legacy also requires us to look carefully at the question of how publics are formed and of what sort of people they consisted. Given the intricate but fluid dynamic of early modern English society, it is unlikely that the emerging affinity for material and cultural genres like portraiture can be attributed to any single social group. It remains equally unlikely that different social groups sharing such an affinity would do so from quite the same perspectives.

As applied to portraiture, it soon becomes obvious that the intellectual, social, and political elites, with their more sophisticated and cosmopolitan outlook and greater affluence, came more quickly to appreciate a more formal and polite portraiture than their provincial (in both geographic and cultural senses of the term) counterparts. At its most distinctive, this polite end of the contemporary portrait spectrum may be known by its formally theorized, quasi-academic approach, in which formal rules governing, e.g., perspective, composition, colour, and other, often classically inspired, elements would have been mastered and deployed with a substantial technical competence. Much of this more sophisticated work will have been carried out by foreign-born or at least foreign-trained painters housed in their London workshops. Clearly it is this portraiture that we see reflected in our museums, galleries, and textbooks. It is this which constitutes the familiar canon of 'Tudor and early Stuart portraiture', just as the plays of Shakespeare and a handful of his contemporaries form the familiar canon of English Renaissance drama.

At the other end of the broad continuum of that portraiture we find paintings that are blatantly provincial (in both aesthetic and geographic senses of the term) and naive or 'vernacular' in provenance and appearance. The characteristic clientele for these works derived from what we have come to refer to as 'the middling sorts of people':[29] those somewhat lower down in the scales of affluence, social status, political authority, or cultural sophistication, and especially those whose life's experience unfolded well away from the London metropolis or even the vicarious experience of continental taste. The clientele for works of this sort rested not only

[28] Jürgen Habermas, *The Structural Transformation of the Public Sphere: An Inquiry into a Category of Bourgeois Society*, trans. Thomas Burger (Cambridge, MA, 1989), esp. 39–40.

[29] The notion is perhaps best described in Keith Wrightson, 'Estates, Degrees, and Sorts: Changing Perceptions of Society in Tudor and Stuart England', in P. J. Corfield (ed.), *Language, History and Class* (Oxford, 1991), 30–52, and id., '"Sorts of People" in Tudor and Stuart England', in Jonathan Barry and Christopher Brooks (eds), *The Middling Sorts of People, Culture, Society and Politics in England, 1550–1800* (Basingstoke, 1994), 28–51, and in the editors' 'Introduction' to the same volume. See also the critiques in Jonathan Barry, 'Review and Commentary: The State of the Middle Classes in Early Modern England', *Journal of Historical Sociology*, 4 (1991), 75–86, and H. R. French, *The Middle Sort of People in Provincial England, 1600–1750* (Oxford, 2007), Introduction.

with individual people, but also with numerous civic institutions that were quite distinct in their location and purpose from the court circle and London metropolis.

Demand for portraits from these diverse quarters largely fell upon local, almost always anonymous craftsmen, primarily trained in such traditional metiers as, for example, cloth painting or staining, glass painting, wood carving, heraldic painting, tomb masonry, metal working, and other such occupations. Paintings of that sort represent what Gent calls the traditions of Albion as influenced barely or not at all by the intrusion of classical forms or theories. They remained largely devoid of classically derived or naturalistic figurative representation, single-point perspective, three-dimensional representation, subtlety in brushwork or blending of colours. In addition, they seem often to have reflected the distinctive characteristics of a particular region.

When we turn our attention to this provincial portraiture we return to the questions provoked by the Norfolk pensioners of 1969. They lead us to wonder whether provincial English culture of this era was sufficiently cohesive and uniform as to allow us to consider it as a whole, or whether it was still so regionally fragmented as to preclude such an essentially national and implicitly teleological approach. They lead us to ask about the communication of cultural forms and ideas in this formative, post-Reformation, era.

One approach to this geographic element has been articulated in several successive versions by Charles Phythian-Adams, and that brings us to our second theoretical beacon. In an important and provocative essay of 1987,[30] and in a succession of refinements on the same theme produced since that time, Phythian-Adams has proposed that pre-industrial England might be divided into a certain number of 'cultural provinces', each of which presented a distinctive profile of cultural (social, economic, political, religious, etc.) forms and activities.[31]

The recognition of regionally distinct, traditional, and craft-based societies defined in part by physical boundaries and features, is neither novel nor confined to the post-Reformation era. He himself traces the origins of these regional societies to the patterns of settlement and conquest in the early centuries of the Christian era. Though they broke down under the pressures of industrialization and population re-distribution from the late seventeenth century onwards, we see their remnants in such classic, quasi-autobiographical accounts as George Sturt's recollections of the peasant culture of mid-nineteenth century Sussex or the lesser known but even more vivid account of fenland Cambridgeshire by Mary Chamberlain. It appears in such imaginative scholarly treatments as, e.g., Keith Thomas's

[30] Principally in Charles Phythian-Adams's, *Rethinking English Local History* (Leicester, 1987) and his 'Introduction: An Agenda for English Local History', in id. (ed.), *Societies, Cultures and Kinship, 1580–1850: Cultural Provinces and English Local History* (Leicester and London, 1993), 1–23.

[31] See also Charles Phythian-Adams, 'Local History and Social History', *Local Population Studies*, 51 (1993), 30–45; *Land of the Cumbrians: A Study in British Provincial Origins AD 400–1120* (Aldershot, 1996); 'Environments and Identities: Landscape as Cultural Projection in the English Provincial Past', in Paul Slack (ed.), *Environments and Historical Change: The Linacre Lectures 1998* (Oxford, 1999), 118–46; and 'Differentiating Provincial Societies in English History: Spatial Concepts and Cultural Processes', in Bill Lancaster, Diana Newton, and Natasha Vall (eds), *An Agenda for English Regional History* (Newcastle, 2007), 3–22.

Man and the Natural World or Simon Schama's *Landscape and Memory*.[32] But it has yet to be as fully employed in the investigation of English visual culture, especially for such an earlier period as this.

Phythian-Adams has argued that indigenous societies appropriated the features of their ambient landscapes for their cultural development, and that they did so from such an early time of settlement as to create deep and enduring configurations of cultural life. Such configurations typically include elements of social memory, language, and folklore, but they could also be applied to distinctive patterns of material production such as might be found in, e.g., agriculture or building. They may be reflected to a degree by county or diocesan administrative boundaries, and especially to the boundaries of landscape and physical features. For a variety of reasons, most of them having to do with the fragmentary nature of the evidence, Phythian-Adams's work serves us better as a conceptual inspiration than a precise model, but its underlying approach reverberates through what follows.

Certainly the notion of regionally distinct societies and cultures find support in myriad studies of comparable cultural genres. It receives strong affirmation from the many volumes of mimetic records thus far published by the Records of Early English Drama project, in which regional venues have been shown to receive the 'Renaissance drama' of Shakespeare and his contemporaries while simultaneously maintaining traditional, and often regionally specific, forms of mimetic activity. They resonate in the observation of, for example, regional speech by David Crystal and Paula Blank,[33] regional patterns of decorative art by Anthony Wells-Cole,[34] regional vernacular building by such pioneering authorities as R. W. Brunskill and Alec Clifton-Taylor,[35] regionally specific senses of the past by Daniel Woolf,[36] and a host of historians too numerous to name on regional patterns of popular religious belief or political affiliations both before and during the Civil Wars of the 1640s. But despite these intriguing possibilities, the study of English portraiture from a local and regional perspective remains largely to be undertaken. The time has come to put the question, and the chosen era at hand seems the most appropriate era at which to put it.

That era, running from *c.*1540 to *c.*1640, aptly embraces the canonical 'Holbein to Van Dyck' narrative of English portraiture. Holbein first stayed briefly in England from 1526 to 1528, but returned in 1532 and remained in London

[32] George Sturt [pseud. George Bourne], *Change in the Village* (1912), and id., *The Wheelwright's Shop* (Cambridge, 1923); Mary Chamberlain, *Fenwomen: A Portrait of Women in an English Village* (1975); Keith Thomas, *Man and the Natural World: Changing Attitudes in England, 1500–1800* (1983); Simon Schama, *Landscape and Memory* (1995).

[33] Paula Blank, *Broken English, Dialectics and the Politics of Language in Renaissance Writing* (New York and London, 1996).

[34] Anthony Wells-Cole, *Art and Decoration in Elizabethan and Jacobean England: The Influence of Continental Prints, 1558–1625* (London and New Haven, 1997), *passim.*

[35] R. W. Brunskill, esp. *Illustrated History of Vernacular Architecture* (1971; 2nd edn, 1978); *Vernacular Architecture of the Lake Counties* (1974; 2nd edn, 1978), and *Traditional Buildings of Britain: An Introduction to Vernacular Architecture* (1981); Alec Clifton-Taylor, esp. *The Pattern of English Building* (1972).

[36] Daniel Woolf, 'Senses of the Past in Tudor Britain', in Robert Tittler and Norman Jones (eds), *A Companion to Tudor Britain* (Oxford, 2004), 407–29.

until his death in 1543. Van Dyck came briefly in 1620–1, stayed a little longer in 1632–4, and for longer still from 1635 to his death, also in London, in 1641. Both in their own way brought to England entirely new approaches to painting; both connected English to continental painting more firmly and dramatically than anyone else of their respective generations; both plied their trade in London and amongst the court circle of their respective times.

Yet in a number of respects that same era provides an equally appropriate chronology for a revisionist and more broadly contextualized approach. An account devoted to the patrons of this era, the public that they helped to form, and the painters who supplied their needs, need not rely on a chronology determined by the presence merely of iconic painters. It has many additional reasons to adopt the same chronological framework. The first of those dates may mark the approximate time of Holbein's permanent settlement in London, but it also marks the approximate point of the break from the Roman Catholic Church and the advent of Royal Supremacy. It coincides with the start of the largest turnover of landholding in English history, and all the profound social and economic ramifications of that seismic transition. It marks the entrenchment of what we commonly refer to as the Tudor state, not in the strictest sense of dynastic succession, but rather in the firm establishment of a more potent and far-reaching royal authority and crown-centred bureaucracy than England had ever known. It forms the approximate beginning of a sustained and unprecedentedly rapid population growth and (at least for many) an economic prosperity to match it. It entails a strikingly spirited competition for social status and legitimation amongst an increasingly affluent segment of the population. Then, too, these years marked distinctive patterns of England's relations with other areas of Europe which profoundly influenced the nature of the portraiture being produced on its shores. While these contextual factors will be explored in subsequent chapters, suffice it to note here that they all served to contribute to the emergence of secular portraiture in the era at hand; they determined as well the form and shape which that portraiture would take in the century to come.

The terminal date of this study approximately coincides with the outbreak of the Civil Wars of the 1640s, and the accelerating tensions leading up to them, both having a pronounced impact on the supply and demand for portraiture. A case has recently been made for the continued consumption of luxury items, including paintings, amongst the landed elite in general.[37] But that is not to say that the *patterns* of such consumption continued unabated, or that those who produced paintings especially outside of London could necessarily sustain 'business as usual'.

Numerous royalists who formed part of the portrait-buying clientele fled abroad at this time. So did some of the elite painters and engravers, including Cornelius Johnson and Wenceslaus Hollar, on whom the more affluent patrons might ordinarily have relied. Many used the opportunity of exile to acquire paintings

[37] See, for example, Linda Levy Peck, *Consuming Splendor: Society and Culture in Seventeenth-Century England* (Cambridge, 2005).

abroad, to bringing them back with them on their eventual return,[38] or to act as dealers in acquiring and sending paintings back to their English employers at home. Cornelius Johnson himself actually spent much of the decade after his 1643 departure supplying English patrons with paintings from the Netherlands.[39]

Pitched battles may not have been fought in its streets, but London was severely affected by the war nonetheless, especially between 1643 and 1646. Many merchants and manufacturers did well by supplying the parliamentary armies in particular, but the overall effects of the war on London's population and economic activity were disruptive and deleterious. Many shops shut down for lack of custom and high taxation. Military service seriously depleted the intake of apprentices. The uncertainty of travel in and out of the garrisoned city caused irregularities of transport and sometimes shortages of food, clothing, and fuel, with prices rising accordingly. Droves of refugees fleeing areas of actual fighting for the relative safety of London exacerbated these effects.[40] Taken together, those realities cannot but have intruded on the normal activities of patrons and painters.

By the same token, of course, the towns and cities whence such refugees came, including sundry regional centres in which portraits had long been produced, now produced fewer. Many of those provincial centres and cathedral cities, including Carlisle, Exeter, Gloucester, Hereford, Leicester, Newcastle-upon-Tyne, Winchester, Worcester, and York, suffered extensive destruction on a scale that cannot but have interrupted the activity of patrons and painters. Other county towns and larger market centres like King's Lynn, Pontefract, Reading, Hull, Banbury, Bristol, Lyme Regis, Chester, Taunton, Axminster, Bridgwater, Bridgnorth, Portsmouth, and Faringdon suffered sieges and/or extensive fires to the same effect.[41] In one way or another, it is therefore hard to escape the conclusion that the 1640s interrupted the normal patterns of portrait production and consumption, making it a logical terminal point for this study.

What follows is therefore a revisionist approach in many respects, undertaken from an historical rather than curatorial or connoisseurial perspective, with a prevalent archival and empirical methodology, a largely provincial rather than metropolitan focus, and with a nod to particular theoretical constructs. This ought not merely to be taken as a desire to tell another side of a familiar story or to 'fill in the gaps' in well-worn narratives. It means as well to raise questions about such subjects as the regionality of cultural expression, the visual representation of power and status, the relationship between patron and painter, and the working lives of painters themselves.

[38] Peck, *Consuming Splendor*, 240–54.

[39] *ODNB*, vide 'Johnson, Cornelius', essay by Karen Hearn.

[40] Stephen Porter, 'The Economic and Social Impact of the Civil Wars upon London', in id., *London and the Civil War* (Basingstoke, 1996), 175–204; Ben Coates, 'Poor Relief in London during the English Revolution Revisited', *London Journal*, 25 (2000), 40–58.

[41] Stephen Porter, *Destruction in the English Civil Wars* (Stroud, Gloucestershire, 1994), Ch. 4 and esp. 68–71.

The work proceeds, in Chapter 2, with a fuller discussion of those very broad contextual factors that encouraged and shaped the role of publics and painters in the production of portraiture in this era. This embraces such considerations as the role of demographic growth, questions of social structure and mobility, the keen competition for social status and legitimation, the establishment of the Tudor state in its distinctively centralized and bureaucratic form, and the increasingly iconic image of the monarch. It also addresses the Reformation, in regard both to ecclesiastical organization and to its implications for religious belief and practice. Finally, it observes the ways in which England's place in Europe, and its policies governing that place, had their telling effects on the forms and shape of English cultural expression.

Chapter 3, 'Locating the Public', seeks to identify the emerging portrait public in its intellectual, social, and geographic dimensions. It begins by observing the intellectual impetus for some of the emerging interest in portraiture, especially amongst the intellectuals of the day. It then turns to the social and geographic extent of portrait purchase, commissioning, and ownership as a means of identifying and describing that public. The discussion reveals a much wider involvement, in both geographic and social terms, in portraiture than has conventionally been recognized.

The formation of that wider public required an appropriate and comparable response amongst those who produced portraits, especially in the provincial context. Chapter 4, 'Provincial Painters', examines the social and economic aspects of the provincial painters' occupation, implicitly comparing it with the experience of the elite, often foreign-born, painters working principally in, or outwards from, London. It considers the conventional distinction made between 'artists' on the one hand and craftsmen painters or painter-stainers on the other. It places considerable emphasis on the guild structure of such centres as Newcastle, Exeter, and especially Chester, including the roles of masters, apprentices, journeymen, and widows, and the nature of training imparted by that time-honoured system. It considers the price of portraits and the painter's income, his social status, and what can be learned of his workshop practice. The Chester circle of painters serves as an especially well-documented example of these issues, making an interesting comparison with a comparable cathedral city like Canterbury, which was closer both to London and the Continent.

Much of the distinctiveness of provincial portraiture rested with the relatively limited resources available to the provincial painter in contrast to those upon which his city cousin might easily draw. Those resources consisted of two kinds. The painter's supplies, especially of pigments but also of brushes and supports, are perhaps the most basic, but instructional and even intellectual resources must be considered as well. Chapter 5, 'Painters' Resources' discusses access to supplies, but also the circulation of training manuals and pattern books outside of London. Finally, it considers the cultural outlook of the provincial painter in relation to the contemporary 'world of learning' as it applied in London and continental Europe: a cultural outlook that brooked large in the content as well as the meaning of contemporary portraiture.

Access or lack of access to these resources, both material and cultural, figured substantially in the distinctions between one end of the portrait continuum and the other. The provincial and occupational context in which many provincial painters worked necessitated production on the vernacular, rather than on the formal and polite, end of the continuum. Denied easy access to the materials available in the great metropolis, and insulated from contemporary currents both of painting technique and the wider world view that could inculcate a more refined approach, provincial painters remained tied more firmly to traditional, indigenously rooted, forms and means of painting. One of the most distinctive of those traditional elements, and one particularly suited to the requirements of contemporary patrons, was the heraldic device, and the genealogical legitimacy that it conveyed upon the sitter. Though this may be found in portraits at all levels of skill and patronage, it seems most evident in the provincial portraiture of the middling and lesser elites than in the courtly portraiture of the nation's aristocracy, and much more prevalent in England generally than anywhere else in Western Europe. Chapter 6 therefore examines the place of heraldry in Tudor and early Stuart portraiture: the complex occupational interaction between heralds and painters, of heraldic devices and portraits themselves, and of the significance of heraldry to English portraiture in general.

Of course heraldry and heraldic devices were by no means the only common element in provincial portraiture. Chapter 7, 'The Provincial Vocabulary', deals with other symbolic elements commonly employed in provincial work, all of them emanating from the patron's aim to communicate particular images of himself and his family to the putative viewer. The discussion thus begins with the question of identities, and the importance of verisimilitude. It moves on to consider such image-forming elements as, e.g., clothing, inscriptions, furnishings, books and scrolls, weapons, and the whole range of memento mori imagery (including skulls, hourglasses and clocks, withered foliage, and figures of the macabre) that were so commonly employed as statements of personal identity.

The possibility of regional distinctions in provincial portraiture runs through much of the foregoing discussion, and the final chapter, 'Varieties of Regional Experience', considers that subject in its own right. It summarizes and further elucidates elements of regionality in provincial portraiture, and considers its importance in the rapidly forming mainstream of 'English School' portraiture. Taken together these considerations bring us to a fuller understanding of early modern English portraiture as a whole, and to a more nuanced appreciation of its economic, social, and cultural context.

2

English Portraiture in Context

One should not assume from the years embraced by the title of this book that secular, panel portraiture sprang out of nowhere in England around the year 1540 with Hans Holbein's prolific production of portraits and other visual images.[1] One form or another of portraiture had long been produced in England in mostly religious contexts. But Holbein arrived at a time when England was ready for his skills and experience. This happy coincidence of circumstance and genius applied to the Henrician monarchy and its court circle, and also to the humanists surrounding that circle who recognized the classical scholarship and continental experience that informed his work.[2] It percolated as well, albeit for different reasons, much further down into the strata of social status and wealth, and more widely into the provincial corners of the realm, than has often been recognized.

Our understanding of Holbein's influence and that of his successors, and of the burgeoning interest in secular portraiture per se, must be grounded in the circumstances in which painters worked and in the aspirations of those who patronized them. Leaving the working life of contemporary painters to a later chapter, these factors require us to consider here several critical issues that appear on what we might think of as the demand side of the patron/painter equation.

For most of the era at hand these factors of 'demand' still had little to do with the consumption of luxury items or the operation of a fully fledged consumer mentality, both of which remained somewhat anachronistic concepts right into the early decades of the seventeenth century. They included instead the urgent need for political legitimation of the Tudor monarchy and its court circle, and the multiple consequences of the Reformation in its formative decades. Changes in religious belief and practice, in England's relation to continental cultural activity, and in the implications for land-holding and social mobility of the dissolutions of monastic and fraternal institutions in the 1530s and 1540s, all come into play. Sweeping developments in population size and social structure, and the implications that they

[1] Holbein's versatility as a creator of diverse forms of visual imagery is best described in Susan Foister, *Holbein and England* (London and New Haven, 2004) and *Holbein in England* (London and New Haven, 2006), and observed in the Tate Britain exhibit 'Holbein in England' (2006–7).

[2] Susan Foister, for example, has commented on Holbein's wide travels, his grasp of architectural principles, and his association with wealthy and sophisticated patrons both in England and abroad. In addition to his close ties to Sir Thomas More, she has placed him in the company of such other humanists as John Leland and Sir Thomas Elyot. Foister, *Holbein and England*, 1; ead., 'Humanism and Art in the Early Tudor Period: John Leland's Poetic Praise of Painting', in Jonathan Woolfson (ed.), *Reassessing Tudor Humanism* (Basingstoke, 2002), 129–50; Sir Thomas Elyot, *The Book Named the Governor* (1531), ed. S. E. Lehmberg (New York, 1962), 52.

bore for local governing institutions and their legitimation in the same era, must also be considered.

To begin with the most familiar of such contexts, the deep-seated need of the Tudor monarchs to legitimize their rule remained a constant and vivid presence throughout their dynasty. That need emerged with Henry VII's accession by conquest, victory in battle at Bosworth Field in 1485, rather than by more conventional means of legitimate inheritance. It grew more vivid with Henry VIII's claim to supplant the papacy as head of the Church. It accelerated further with the accession of the boy-king Edward in 1547, and further still with the ensuing and vigorously contested succession of England's first reigning queen, the Catholic Mary, in 1553. And it reached a climax with the accession of England's second reigning queen, the protestant Elizabeth, whom many Roman Catholics at home and abroad considered to be the illegitimate child of a still legally married Henry VIII and his paramour. The political imperative created by those circumstances to legitimize Tudor rule, and thus to command the respect and loyalty of English men and women, required the creation of a highly polemical court culture: one that was lavishly visual, highly ceremonial, publicly displayed, and yet, especially in Elizabeth's hands, financially restrained. The pursuit of such a culture, especially in the long reigns of Henry VIII and Elizabeth, met with a success that defined English royal imagery forever after. It resounds loudly and strongly in the media productions and gallery exhibits of the present day.

The role of court portraiture as an intimate part of that cultural display has been well and widely documented, taking a central place in the familiar art historical canon.[3] The subsequent reproduction of royal imagery, by the Tudors of themselves and their predecessors, and by the early Stuarts of theirs, formed a viable (and sometimes literal) cottage industry throughout the decades to come. The creation and reproduction of woodcut portraits of the English kings even, e.g., as early as 1529,[4] the increasingly frequent copying and collection of royal portrait images, and the wide proliferation of the royal arms in private homes and parish churches (where they frequently displaced the rood in its traditional place atop the rood beam) throughout the subsequent era, speak to nothing less.

At least in broad terms, the religious context of the age is equally familiar, even if its complexity has not always been considered as a critical context for portrait production. That complexity obviously extended to the break from Rome, to the innovation of royal supremacy, and to the ensuing varieties of religious belief and

[3] Of recent works alone, see Christopher Lloyd and Simon Thurley, *Henry VIII: Images of a Tudor King* (1990); David Howarth, *Images of Rule, Art and Politics in the English Renaissance, 1485–1649* (Berkeley and Los Angeles, 1997); Maurice Howard, *The Tudor Image* (1995); Karen Hearn (ed.), *Dynasties: Painting in Tudor and Jacobean England 1530–1630* (1995) and the associated exhibit of the same name at Tate Britain (also 1995); Foister, *Holbein in England*, esp. Ch. 4, 'Holbein and Henry VIII'; ead., *Holbein and England*; Tatiana String, *Art and Communication in the Reign of Henry VIII* (Aldershot, 2009); Kevin Sharpe, *Selling the Tudor Monarchy: Authority and Image in Sixteenth Century England* (New Haven and London, 2009); and the many publications of Sir Roy Strong.

[4] John Rastell, *The Pastyme of People: the Chronycles of Dyvers realmys and most specyally of the realme of Englond brevely co[m]pylyd* (*STC*, 20724, 1529.)

practice. But it went further even than that in its critical impact on the development of English portraiture. The implications of these events for England's relations with other European powers and their ambient cultures, and their less direct but nevertheless significant effect on English land-holding, social mobility, and local governance, must all be considered.

The dissolution of the monasteries and the break from papal authority in the 1530s (and, if we include the dissolution of the chantries and religious fraternities as part of the mix, the 1540s) created a critically important juncture: not only for the fundamental history of the nation itself and its religious belief and practice, but for the development of its portraiture. Added to successive acts of Parliament and such foundational writings as *The Book of Common Prayer*, these years in particular saw the effective evisceration of a religious culture deeply rooted, emotionally invested, mnemonically powerful, and highly visual. It gutted a millennium's accretion of popular beliefs and institutional foundations. It created deep and enduring fissures in what had long been a shared devotional culture with its attendant mimetic and visual expressions. Salvation by good works and pious bequests, and the intercessionary powers of the Virgin and 'all the saints in heaven' were now all proscribed by law. The very rafters of Christian obligation, resting on the foundations of the seven deadly sins and the ever-present fear of purgatory and hell, had been shaken loose. The attitudes, assumptions, behavioural conventions, and collective memories that had supported the ambient culture of pre-Reformation England now all came up for grabs.

In their place, and over the course of several decades, came a new, scripture and sermon-centred order in which the individual faced a great many more choices and perhaps fewer eternal consequences. English men and women of these generations felt compelled to re-examine their religious beliefs and practices as never before: either tenaciously and courageously to retain whatever elements of the old faith they could get away with or to weave their way through the myriad options opened to them in the search for reconfigured religious identities. These personal quests ensued amidst concerted but intermittently consistent government efforts to define and enforce new doctrines and approaches. They sometimes unfolded against the braying fury of iconoclasm, inspired particularly by Exodus 34:13: 'But ye shall destroy their altars, break their images, and cut down their groves'.[5] For much of the population, the beliefs and imagery of traditional, Roman Catholic worship were either destroyed or driven behind closed doors into the homes of the faithful.

These circumstances bore profound consequences for visual imagery of all sorts. On the one hand lay those few puritan zealots who opposed portrait images altogether as violations of the Second Commandment: 'Thou shalt not make unto thee any graven image, or any likeness of any thing that is in heaven above,

[5] King James version. On iconoclasm itself, see, for example, John Phillips, *The Reformation of Images: Destruction of Art in England, 1535–1660* (Berkeley and Los Angeles, 1973); Clifford Davidson and Anne Elizabeth Nicholas (eds), *Iconoclasm in Art and Drama* (Kalamazoo, MI, 1989); Margaret Aston, *England's Iconoclasts*, I: *Laws against Images* (Oxford, 1988), and ead., 'Puritans and Iconoclasm, 1560–1660', in C. Durston and J. Eales (eds), *The Culture of English Purianism, 1560–1700* (Basingstoke, 1996), 92–121; and Nigel Llewellyn, *Funeral Monuments in Post-Reformation England* (Cambridge, 2000), 259–69.

or that is in the earth beneath, or that is in the water under the earth'.[6] Though their efforts to destroy images and prevent more from being produced largely failed, they may well have had more of an influence on the production of, e.g., Elizabethan imagery, than we commonly recognize.

Professor Maurice Howard has suggested that not all of the visual distortions associated especially with portraits of Elizabeth stemmed from the painters' inability to project three-dimensional images on a flat surface. He observes that paintings such as Lord Henry Darnley and his brother Charles of 1562 present flat, two-dimensional figures, but place them in front of a three-dimensional background setting.[7] He proposes instead that realistic and life-like images might have seemed idolatrous to the protestant fundamentalist.

We might well find the same phenomenon exemplified in the works of Marcus Gheeraerts the younger (1561/2–1636). A comparison of his wonderfully sensitive and anatomically accurate 1594 portrait of Captain Thomas Lee (Fig. 2.1), a paragon of contemporary naturalistic portraiture at its peak, with the bizarre proportions of, e.g., his *c.*1592 'Ditchely Portrait' of Elizabeth suggests no less (Fig. 2.2). Some other portraits of the Queen by other painters—the 'Armada Portrait' of *c.*1588, the 'Ermine Portrait', the 'Rainbow Portrait' amongst the most familiar—display even greater fantasy than this. In many cases, paintings that looked crude or anatomically unnatural certainly did accrue from a lack of skills: sometimes a cigar is indeed just a cigar! Yet Howard's explanation must be taken into account to explain these highly stylized royal portraits and others like them.

However, in most cases, and even amongst the more mainstream puritans, a modest number of English men and women surprisingly far down the social ladder utilized portrait imagery to articulate statements about personal belief just as vividly, if sometimes at greater personal risk, than ever before. Some of the resulting images came out looking more life-like than others, but the objectives behind their creation remained much the same. This common dilemma of belief and identity must be seen as one of the imperatives of the sort of self-fashioning seminally described by Stephen Greenblatt, and as common to many national experiences in the world of Renaissance and Reformation Europe.[8]

One common preoccupation in this broad effort of self-definition emerged from the personal wrestling with the notion of death and salvation, a discourse in which what we know as memento mori portraiture came to play an important role.[9] With its imagery of hourglasses and clocks, skulls and skeletons, this common rubric indicated both the sitter's mortality and his/her humility before God. The entire

[6] King James version.

[7] Maurice Howard, 'Art and the Reformation', in Tim Ayers (ed.), *The History of British Art 600–1600* (New Haven and London, 2008), 234.

[8] Stephen Greenblatt, *Renaissance Self-Fashioning from More to Shakespeare* (London and Chicago, 1980).

[9] Tarnya Cooper, '"Frail Flesh, as in a Glass": The Portrait as an Immortal Presence in Early Modern England and Wales', in Mary Rogers (ed.), *Fashioning Identities in Renaissance Art* (Aldershot, 2000), 197–212; ead., '*Memento Mori* Portraiture: Painting, Protestant Culture, and the Patronage of Middle Elites in England and Wales 1540–1630', unpublished PhD thesis, Sussex University (2002). I am greatly indebted to Dr Cooper for allowing me to read and cite her thesis.

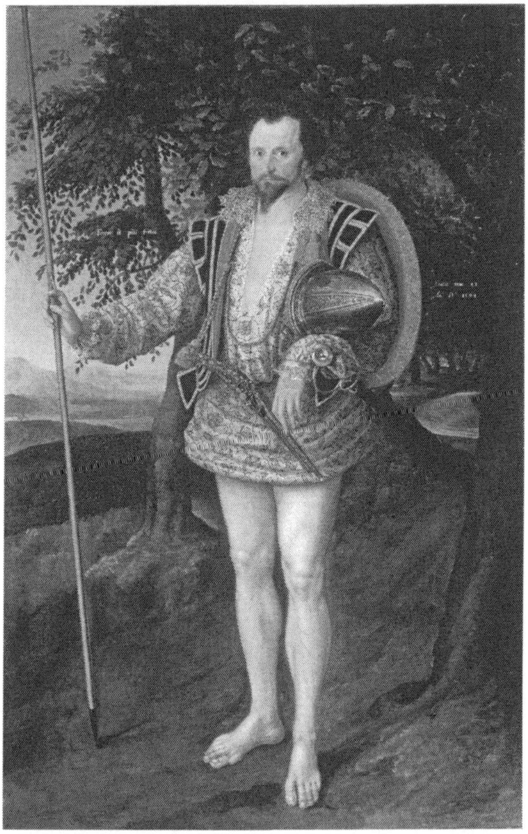

Fig. 2.1. Marcus Gheeraerts the younger, *Captain Thomas Lee*, oil on canvas, 90¾" × 59⅜" (1594). © Tate, London, 2011.

tableau made a case for the subject's worthiness, not only to have a portrait of him or herself (a controversial issue in Renaissance Europe generally),[10] but also for salvation itself.

Such devices also suggested the contrast between the living, mortal body, which would die and decay, and the eternal person, whose image would endure on panel or canvas forever.[11] This implicit claim to immortality may well have served as something of a post-Reformation surrogate for the traditional anniversary and obit prayers for the dead, and the periodic reading out from the parish bede roll the names of the departed souls. Both traditions had allowed the parish to retain in its collective memory the 'virtual' presence of the deceased. Both followed from the

[10] Joanna Woodall, 'Status Symbols: Role and Rank in Seventeenth Century Netherlandish Portraiture', *Dutch Crossing*, 42 (Autumn 1990), 34.

[11] Cooper, 'Frail Flesh', 197–8; Llewellyn, *Funeral Monuments*, 340.

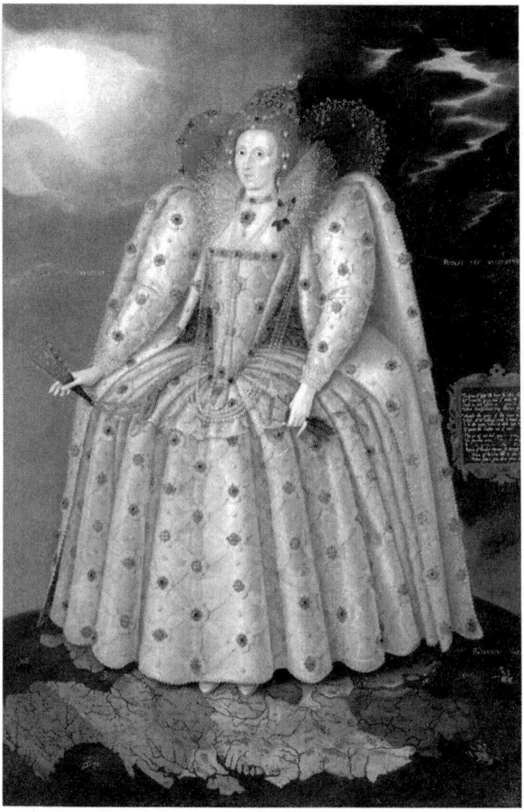

Fig. 2.2. Marcus Gheeraerts the younger, *Elizabeth I* (*The Ditchley Portrait*), oil on canvas, 95" × 60" (*c.*1592). © The National Portrait Gallery, London.

pre-Reformation notions of purgatory and salvation through prayer and good works. And both were emphatically undermined after the 1530s.[12]

Yet the desire to be remembered, and to have one's actual appearance remembered by his or her descendants, did not always come directly in religious guise. Thomas Whythorne, who commissioned no fewer than four portraits of himself during his lifetime, noted that many people commissioned portraits 'to leav with their frendz, especially with their children, [so that] thoh their fatherz be dead yet may thei see what matter of favor thee had'.[13] And the painter Gerlach Flicke inscribed on a self-portrait of 1554 the tag 'Such in appearance

[12] Susan Brigden, 'Religion and Social Obligation in Early Sixteenth Century London', *Past and Present*, 103 (May 1984), 67–112; Eamon Duffy, *The Stripping of the Altars: Traditional Religion in England, c. 1400–1580* (London and New Haven, 1992), 327–37.

[13] James M. Osborne (ed.), *The Autobiography of Thomas Whythorne* (Oxford, 1961), 134.

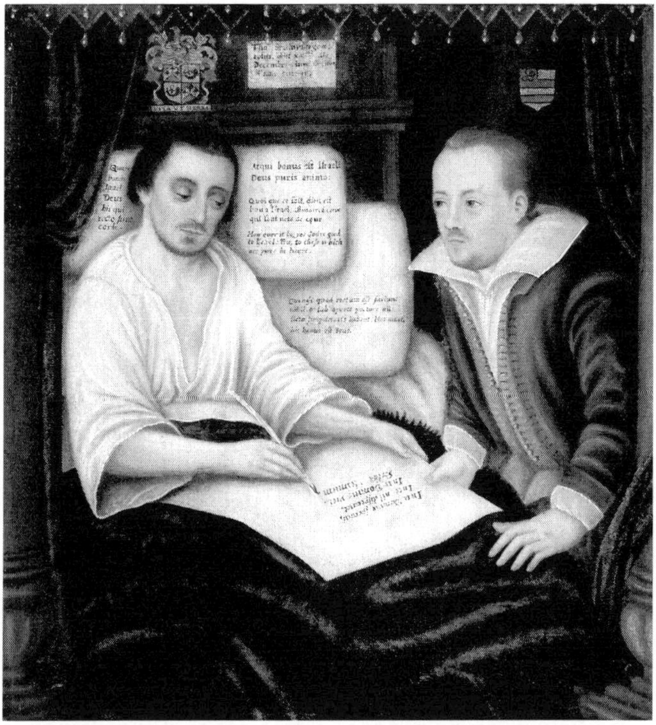

Fig. 2.3. Anon., *Thomas Braithwaite Making His Will* (1607), oil on canvas, 66 cm × 58.5 cm. By kind permission of the Abbot Hall Gallery, Kendal, Cumbria.

was Gerlach Flicke when he was a painter in the City of London. This he painted from a mirror for his dear friends that they might be able to remember him after his death'.[14]

In the same vein, some portraits were commissioned to record the memory of the sitter before he departed for a dangerous journey. Richard Madox commissioned one of himself from John Bettes before leaving for Brazil in 1582.[15] And of course portraits too numerous to count were done for funeral monuments of various types. An anonymously painted portrait of the Essex gentleman Thomas Braithwaite provides an intriguing twist to the notion of commissioning a portrait before death. This 1607 painting shows Braithwaite at age 31, on his deathbed, writing his will, with a friend witnessing the event: this extraordinary tableau recorded

[14] Flicke, *Gerlach Flicke and Henry Strangwish*, oil on paper laid on panel, 3½" × 4¾" (1554), NPG. Translated from the Latin and cited by Eric Mercer, *English Art, 1553–1625* (Oxford, 1962), 165.

[15] Lorne Campbell, *Renaissance Portraits* (London and New Haven, 1990), 213. Such journeys, even to more proximate destinations, often caused such considerations on the eve of departure. In the case of the London Painter-Stainer John Kelsey, an anticipated trip to the Netherlands caused him to sort out his will, in which he left various paintings to five different legatees, including the painter Robert Peake and his wife, Elizabeth; LMA MS. 9171/17/251 (1589).

the sitter's appearance, but also attested to the validity of the will being composed (Fig. 2.3).

Though memento mori portraiture prevailed especially amongst protestants, it should not be assumed that Catholic recusants simply abandoned the portrait image, or even traditional images of the sort that became proscribed during the Reformation. Though they had certainly to be wary of using portrait imagery as objects of worship, they did still employ portraits as affirmations of their continuing allegiance to the old faith. It has been suggested that portraits of Catholic subjects and of Catholics themselves continued to be produced and valued as surrogates for the more obviously proscribed icons of their faith. Catholic resistance itself could serve as a direct motivation for the production of such portraiture. Such paintings as the 1593 'Towneley Family at Prayer' in Towneley Hall, with its lengthy inscription reciting the persecution of the paterfamilias John Towneley, perpetuated the memory of Catholic sufferings, thus acting as a binding force for the English Catholic community (Fig. 2.4). Anthony Babington commissioned a portrait of

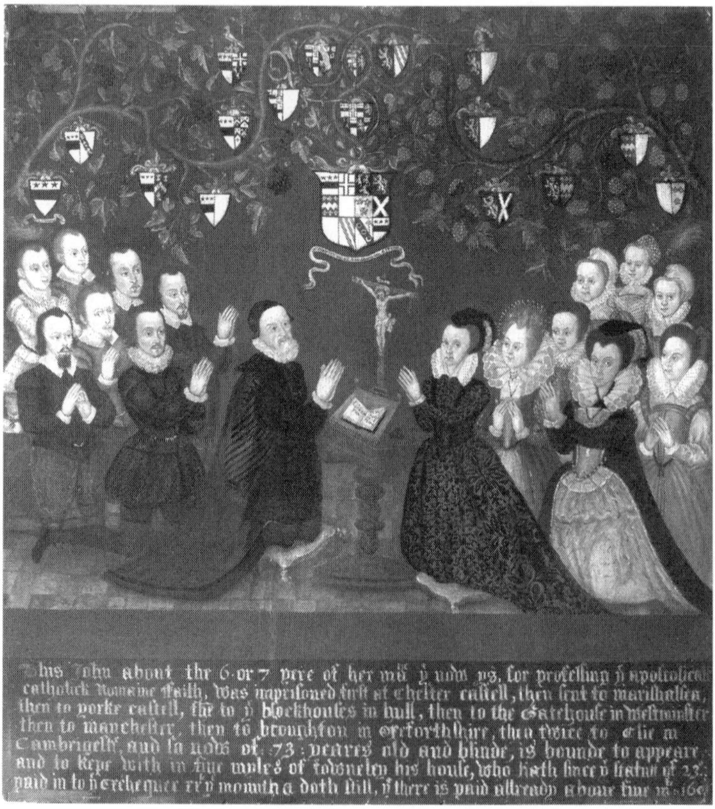

Fig. 2.4. Anon., *The Towneley Family at Prayer*, oil on panel, 35" × 40" (1593). © Towneley Hall, Burnley Borough Council.

himself and five of his fellow conspirators at the time of his infamous plot against Elizabeth in 1586, with an inscription celebrating what he saw as an heroic act. Not surprisingly, it was seized by the authorities, who proceeded to proclaim that the faces of the six companions be copied and distributed throughout the city of London so as to bring further ignominy upon them: another unintended boost for the martyr appeal.[16] As we will see in ensuing chapters, certain painters, both the famous like Van Dyck and the lesser known like John Souch of Chester, received most of their commissions from Catholic families and thus perpetuated the record of such dynasties in portrait form.

Of course, in the early years of the Reformation, or in that intriguing interlude of Mary's reign, combinations of Catholic-inspired and other portraits were still entirely common, and could be found depicting sitters surprisingly far down in the social order. In addition to money to say masses for his soul, Anthony Gilbert, a Somerset yeoman, had three portraits to leave in his will of March, 1555/6: one of the Virgin hanging 'at my beddes hedde', one of Edward VI, and one of Dives, the classical personification of wealth. Each invoked a different cultural base: traditional Catholic belief, loyalty to the Tudor line, and contemporary social discourse.[17] But as time went on and as protestantism in one form or another became more entrenched and enforced, the going got tougher for holding, e.g., portraits of the Virgin.

The Reformation also bore other important if less direct consequences for portrait activity in these years. Thirty years after Holbein settled in London, in the age of religious wars in France and the Low Countries, protestant England became a natural haven especially for Dutch, German, French Huguenot, and Flemish refugees. They came in droves, sometimes briefly to sojourn, often to settle. They brought with them vitally important and first-hand understandings of contemporary continental visual culture, especially of a Northern European and distinctly classical stripe, to a relatively insular, culturally isolated island nation. Though these immigrants were often resented, and their patronage contested, by many amongst their native-born English competitors, they were also admired by others. No lesser light than Nicholas Hilliard recognized the importance of this immigration to his art. '[O]f truth', he wrote in his *Treatise on the Arte of Limning*,

> all the rare siences [*sic*], especially the arts of Carving, Painting, Goldsmiths, [and] Imbroderers, together with the most of all the liberall siences came first unto us from the Strangers, and generally they are the best, and most in number.[18]

[16] Annabel Patterson, 'Catholic Communities and their Art', in Nicholas Howe (ed.), *Visions of Community in the Pre-Modern World* (Notre Dame, IN, 2002), esp. 113–15; Clark Hulse, 'Dead Man's Treasure: The Cult of Thomas More', in David Lee Miller, Sharon O'Dair, and Harold Weber (eds), *The Production of Renaissance Culture* (Ithaca, NY, 1994), 190–225; and Campbell, *Renaissance Portraits*, 209.

[17] F. W. Weaver (ed.), *Somerset Medieval Wills (Third Series) 1531–1558* (Somerset Record Society, 21, 1905), 176. The figure of Dives was often invoked in contemporary social and economic discourse following the 1496 published edition of *Dives et Pauper*, attributed to Henry Parker; *STC*, 19,213.

[18] Nicholas Hilliard, *A Treatise Concerning the Arte of Limning* (*c.*1600), ed. A. F. Kinney and Linda Bradley Salamon (Boston, MA, 1983), 19.

Religious considerations of the Elizabethan era also encouraged a Tudor foreign policy that moved England away from the Catholic states of Europe, France, the Italian states, and the Hapsburg empire in particular, with their distinctive, classically based, and religiously driven culture and traditions. The Elizabethan government saw England's natural alliances as resting instead with Dutch-, German-, and French- (at least in regard to the Huguenots) speaking lands.

Throughout Elizabeth's long reign these realities privileged the subject matter and decorative vocabulary of northern and protestant rather than southern and Roman Catholic visual culture. Those approaches also provided models of inspiration for that handful of Englishmen (including Nicholas Hilliard, William Segar, Robert Peake, George Gower, William Larkin, and both Rowland and Nicholas Lockey) who joined their foreign-born confreres in serving the elite patrons of the late sixteenth and early seventeenth centuries.

The dominance of foreign painters in Tudor courtly and aristocratic circles would continue and flourish in even broader terms under the more receptive foreign policy and open-minded patronage of the first two Stuarts. The likes of Anne of Denmark, Charles I, and the convent-educated Henrietta Maria, with her entourage of French painters and other visual craftsmen, opened the gates to wider contact with French and Italian visual culture. In addition, travellers and collectors like the earl and countess of Arundel, Inigo Jones, and others swarmed to southern and Catholic Europe to take in what had long and largely been denied their parental generation.

The Jacobean generation included some native-English painters who had come to prominence under Elizabeth, but foreign-born or -trained painters like the de Critzes, Isaac Oliver, Cornelius Johnson, Daniel Mytens, and others (some of whom were native-born but all of whom painted in a distinctly continental mode) remained at the top of their profession. They were succeeded in Charles's reign by such virtuosi as Rubens and Van Dyck, bringing an entirely new dynamic to the English scene. The best and best known of these émigré painters replicated the experience of their elite predecessors in finding their patronage at court, where they produced politically potent and highly polemical imagery of the monarchs, court circle, and senior aristocracy.

These are the directions in which the formal, polite, and cosmopolitan portraiture of the day responded to patrons' preferences. But by no means does it describe the course of portraiture as it served patrons of lesser status, income, or sophistication, or those in provincial rather than metropolitan England. And by no means does it take account of the lesser skilled, native-born, and often provincial painters who catered to the rest.

For that matter, neither the need for legitimation and other functions of the portrait image or portrait ownership itself stopped at the palace door or the castle moat. Whether couched in terms of religious, social, or political identities or in other such terms, myriad patrons of lesser status and meaner circumstances nevertheless experienced similar needs. And, in general terms, the more modest the patron's social status, the more likely were such requirements to be met by native-English painters of local provenance, insular outlook, and modest skills.

The Reformation played its part for these patrons as well, at least insofar as it brought about sweeping social changes that bore substantially on every level of society. The dissolution of the monasteries in the later 1530s, and of the chantries, fraternities, and other lay religious organizations in the 1540s, precipitated the largest turnover in English landed property at least since the Norman Conquest. Over the course of ensuing centuries that property came to be sold off by the crown to landlords who were often newly risen to that status, or who used such purchases to further their advancement in landed society. The resale process reverberated through several generations, as the initial recipients sold off or otherwise alienated their properties in subsequent decades. Throughout it all, great fortunes were frequently made, and the rails of social advancement remained well greased for a very long time to come.

Coupled with these elements of social and economic change, the same era also saw the first sustained rise in population since the early fourteenth century. Between 1540 and 1640 the population of England nearly doubled, from roughly three million to roughly five and a quarter million people.[19] The precise chronology of that population growth has long been the subject of debate, but few would argue that it had yet to begin by *c.*1540. By no means did population growth mean greater prosperity for all. The ensuing century was not without its economic setbacks, especially in the 1550s, 1590s, and 1620s, while an approximate six-fold increase in the price of consumer items between 1500 and 1640[20] left its mark in a genuine and distressing level of poverty, rootlessness, and unrest amongst substantial elements of the population. But the general economic growth of the era also created unprecedented opportunities for increased industrial, commercial, and agricultural production. Manufacturers, merchants, and agricultural producers often made substantial fortunes, moving rapidly through the ranks of social respectability as they did so. Social aspirations seemed readily obtainable for many, and both upward and downward mobility became hallmarks of the age. These circumstances made England perhaps the most socially and economically mobile nation in all of Europe.

While the barriers that served to divide one rank of English society from another had always been more porous than in most other parts of Europe, they become even more so during the sixteenth century and beyond before tightening up again towards the end of the seventeenth. At least in those same middling and upper reaches of the pyramid, the rungs on the social ladder remained closely spaced and easily breached.

At the same time, the stakes of social advancement for all socially mobile individuals became more visible and more abundant. Office holding itself, from parish to parliament, proliferated as an essential component of both the Tudor state

[19] E. A. Wrigley and R. S. Schofield, *The Population History of England, 1541–1871* (1981), Table A3.3, 531–4.

[20] Based on E. H. Phelps Brown and S. V. Hopkins, 'Seven Centuries of Prices of Consumables, Compared with Builders' Wage-Rates', *Economica*, NS 23 (1956), Fig. 1, 'Price of a Composite Unit of Comestibles in Southern England, 1264–1954', 299.

and its society. Armigerous status—the right to a coat of arms—imparted a formal recognition of a certain gentility, while the creation of knighthoods, and then baronetcies from 1611, accelerated steadily throughout the era. Many a Restoration-era baronet could thank his yeoman or shop-keeping grandparent for his place and his estate.

These factors provided an ideal breeding ground for a social competition of particular intensity. In a time-honoured pattern, those sitting nearer the top were little loath to grease the pole beneath them, an attitude that merely steeled the resolve of those climbing at their heels. Those emerging from the yeomanry to the gentry, through the sundry orders of gentle status (gentleman, esquire, and knight especially), and from the gentry to the peerage; those at the top threatened by the encroachment, real or imagined, of the parvenu; those who moved from urban and mercantile or industrial occupations to the more traditionally acceptable niche in rural society; and those who moved into mayoral office and found themselves at least temporarily having to command the allegiance and cooperation of their accustomed friends and neighbours, all grasped for every confirmation of status that they could summon. Along with fashionable clothing, heraldic devices, country houses, wands of office, and extensive genealogies (Elizabeth had one of her descent from Adam and Eve while others did as well as they could), portraiture provided an obvious, accessible, and inexpensive weapon in this fierce competition. Lawrence Stone said it best in noting that

> noblemen and gentlemen wanted above all formal family portraits, which take their place along with genealogical trees and sumptuous tombs as symptoms of the frenzied status-seeking and ancestor worship of the age. What patrons demanded was evidence of the sitter's position and wealth by opulence of dress, ornament, and background.[21]

But noblemen and gentlemen were not alone in those aspirations, or in their consequent interest in portraiture. Many a merchant, master craftsman, professional, and even aspiring yeoman, shared the same interests.

An integral part of the portrait's role in social legitimation lay in its ability to record (and thus to enshrine in the perpetual memory of panel or canvas) the leaps made from one rung to another. The occasional, commemorative portrait celebrated such milestones as, e.g., marriage in all its social dimensions, the pregnancy and parenthood which marked generational succession, the attainment of civic or guild office, the establishment of a country house, the granting of arms, and similar stages in the *cursus honorum* of contemporary society.

Given those circumstances, portraiture easily became a bone of contention between adjacent status groups. Merchants and others associated with the urban environment had a particular burden with which to contend. In a world still governed by the chivalric and aristocratic values of landed society, the city itself, fuelled by merchant enterprise at an early stage of capitalism, had long been considered as a sordid, greedy, and dangerous venue, its denizens capable of all

[21] Lawrence Stone, *The Crisis of the Aristocracy, 1558–1641* (Oxford, 1965), 712.

sorts of malicious or immoral behaviour.[22] John Weever, for example, though not a nobleman himself, spoke for many in descrying the tendency of mere merchants to imitate their betters, whereby 'in some of our epitaphs more honour is given to a rich quondam tradesman or griping usurer, then [*sic*] is given to the greatest potentate entombed in Westminster'.[23] A writer of 1598 rued the fact that 'every Citizens wife that wears a taffeta kirtle and a velvet hatt . . . must have her picture in the parlour'.[24] Much the same sentiment came through the pages of perhaps the most widely read discourse on painting of its time: Giovanni Paolo Lomazzo's *Trattato dell'Arte della Pittura*, as translated and edited for an English audience by Richard Haydocke in 1598.[25]

Such carpings attest to the notoriety of portraiture amongst the socially insecure, but they did nothing to impede its growing popularity. Sentiments both for and against did, however, help shape the volume and content of portraits being produced. Upwardly mobile, middling sorts of people came to covet portraits in greater numbers with each decade. Some of them, like Whythorne, opted first for portraits of themselves or their families. Others, like our Somerset yeoman Anthony Gilbert, preferred images of particular kings or queens or classical heroes whose glory they thereby appropriated in the effort to enhance their own. And of course many patrons acquired both kinds, associating themselves with celebrity as they did so. To the same ends they frequently added coats of arms to the scene to which they might (or, as was the case with John Isham of Lamport Hall and many others, might not!) be officially entitled by the College of Arms.[26]

However, the signal characteristics of a gentleman had much more to do with the perception by others than with any firm legal boundaries such as might apply in such contemporary societies as, e.g., France or Venice. The truth of William Harrison's dictum, that one who could 'live ydlely and without manuell labour,

[22] On the negative or ambiguous image of the English merchant of this era see, e.g., Alexander Leggatt, *Citizen Comedy in the Age of Shakespeare* (Toronto, 1973); Laura Stephenson O'Connell, 'Anti-Entrepreneurial Attitudes in Elizabethan Sermons and Popular Literature', *Journal of British Studies*, 15 (1976), 2–20; John McVeagh, *Tradeful Merchants: The Portrayal of the Capitalist in Literature* (1981), *passim*; Keith Wrightson, *English Society, 1580–1680* (1982), 27–31; Richard Grassby, *The Business Community of Seventeenth Century England* (Cambridge, 1995), 29–36; and Lawrence Manley, *Literature and Culture in Early Modern London* (Cambridge, 1995), Ch. 2.

[23] John Weever, *Ancient Funeral Monuments* (1631), 10–11, as cited in Llewellyn, *Funeral Monuments*, 17.

[24] Cited in Mercer, *English Art*, 165, from Anon., *Queen Elizabeth's Entertainment at Mitcham* (1598), 27.

[25] Giovanni Paolo Lomazzo, *Trattato dell'Arte della Pittura, Sculptura, ed Architettura*, 3 vols (Rome, 1844), ii.367–8, as cited in Joanna Woodall, *Portraiture, Facing the Subject* (Manchester, 1977), 77; Richard Haydocke, *A Tracte Containinge the Artes of Curious Paintinge* (Oxford, 1598). See also Campbell, *Renaissance Portraits*, 209–10.

[26] See Figure 7.2. Isham's Lamport portrait of *c.*1567 appears to have been created to mark his elevation to mastership in the Mercers' Company in that year, and moved to Lamport a year or two later as he moved into his new country house. But it had not yet been awarded by or registered in the College of Arms even by 1568. Anne Sutton, *The Mercery of London* (2005), 479 and n. 18; Ian Doolittle, *The Mercer's Company* (Leeds, 1994), 37. My thanks to Peter O'Donoghue, Bluemantle Pursuivant, for affirming this for me and to Tarnya Cooper for showing the portrait to me at Lamport. The issue of heraldry and portraiture will be discussed more fully in Ch. 6 below.

and thereto is able to beare the port, charge, and countenance of a gentleman . . . he shall be reputed as a gentleman',[27] meant that evidence of conspicuous expenditure proved more important even than the accumulation of the wealth on which it could be based.[28]

All the more important, then, to be portrayed as acting the part. In composing the tableaux of their portraits, strivers of the middling ranks thus began by the latter decades of the sixteenth century freely to ape, e.g., the education (as indicated by the inclusion of books), furnishings, and clothing of their betters. The affectation of elegant clothing in particular proved a vivid, and much resented, characteristic of the era. It became even more so when the Tudor sumptuary laws were allowed to lapse after 1604, and with the lavish, elegant, and cosmopolitan sartorial standards of the early Stuart court.[29] With some obvious and intriguing exceptions, as noted in Chapter 7 below, the striving merchant cum gentleman usually preferred to employ imagery indicating how he spent his money rather than how he earned it, so that, for example, the objects of charitable donations or country estates appear more frequently than scenes of the counting house or the merchant ship.

Legitimation, of course, remains a broad concept, covering many issues. Status might be attained in myriad ways. Some merely wished to trumpet their heritage as landowners, ranging from the ambitious yeoman to the great lords of the realm, and to establish their credentials, as Stone noted, by flaunting as ancient a family lineage as could be contrived. Others took pride in other attainments: their scholarship or piety, mercantile acumen, hospitality, office holding, military service, personal fecundity, families and friends, loyalty to the crown, and the personal appearance of themselves and their loved ones for the recollection of future generations. Still others strove to use the portrait to proclaim moral or civic virtues, an imagery often, as in the case of the Yorkshire yeoman John Kaye and many a civic portrait, conveyed through the use of lengthy didactic inscriptions.[30] As we'll see at greater length in Chapter 7, all these objectives came to be articulated, indeed, promulgated, by the portrait image itself and by the inclusion of such other elements as mottos, props, clothing, coats of arms, and even particular types of frame.

[27] William Harrison, *The Description of Englande* (1577), 128–9.

[28] Linda Levy Peck, *Consuming Splendor: Society and Culture in Seventeenth-Century England*, (Cambridge, 2005), 7–9; Keith Thomas, *The Ends of Life: Roads to Fulfilment in Early Modern England* (Oxford, 2009), 114–15.

[29] 1 Jac. I, *c.*25, 'An Acte for Continuing and Reviving of Diverse Statutes and for Repealing of Some Others', *Statutes of the Realm*, ed., A. Luders, T. E. Tomlins, and J. Raithby, 11 vols (1810–28); N. B. Harte, 'State Control of Dress and Social Change in Pre-Industrial England', in D. C. Coleman and A. H. Johns (eds), *Trade, Government and Economy in Pre-Industrial England* (1976), 132–65 and esp. 148–9; Maria Hayward, *Rich Apparel, Clothing and the Law in Henry VIII's England* (Farnham, Surrey, 2009), Ch. 1. As Harte points out, subsequent efforts even to propose a restoration of these acts in ensuing decades came to little.

[30] In addition to the portrait of himself (see below, pp. 61–3 and Figs. 4.2 and 4.3) plus one of his wife, John Kaye, an esquire of Woodsome, Yorkshire, commissioned two more 'tables' with genealogical reconstructions. His moral tenets, evidently the prime purpose of that image, appear in captions held by the several figures surrounding his own. Tolson Museum, Huddersfield, ref. nos. KLMUS 1990/399; KLMUS 1990/398; KLMUS 1990/398a; and KLMUS 1990/399a. I am grateful to Kathryn White for providing images of these paintings. See also J. T. Cliffe, *The Yorkshire Gentry from the Reformation to the Civil War* (1969), 97.

To this list of motivations for the growing popularity of portraiture one might also consider the contemporary tendency towards intellectual curiousity and the growing importance of cultural sophistication in the definition of a gentleman. As intellectual accomplishment came to rival military prowess as a valued aspect of social and political standing, and as humanistic studies made their way from the Continent to England in the early sixteenth century, such paintings became an important medium for intellectual and cultural exploration. Again the appearance of Holbein in England symbolizes a watershed in English cultural and intellectual life. Holbein had travelled widely; he had come to know, studied under, or corresponded with many of the illustrious men, artists, and others of his time. His role in exemplifying those activities, and in drawing upon them in his visual imagery, may not be as significant as his oeuvre itself. But in producing that work he helped bring the contemporary notion of gentility to England in his time. Many others amongst the foreign painters and associated craftsmen who settled in England then and thereafter perpetuated the importance of these sorts of contacts and experiences. And like the audience for, e.g., Richard Hackluyt's compendia about the exploration of the New World, their innovative contributions were avidly sought out by others seeking intellectual and cultural access to the same breadth of experience.

As Maurice Howard has pointed out, we see that novel imagery most often in the depiction, e.g., of classical architectural details in the backgrounds of Tudor portraiture, even when sitters themselves in these same portraits are depicted more conventionally.[31] But we also see them as central to the subject matter itself. Hans Eworth's familiar and enigmatic 'Turk on Horseback' provides an early expression of this interest; the better known are the sundry versions of the 'Armada Portrait' showing Elizabeth looking westward across the Atlantic. Eworth's intriguing work derives from a series of woodcuts made by his friend and countryman Pieter Coecke Van Aelst, who had visited Constantinople and drawn scenes of local life.[32]

In these years and after, some English men and a few women joined in Continent-wide discussions of particular religious, philosophical, moral or cultural problems, the summarization of results, and the publication of compendia of knowledge from their collective experience. These compendia might have taken as their starting points works like Machiavelli's *The Prince* or *The Dialogues*, or Castiglione's *The Book of the Courtier*, both translated into English in the mid-century and both inspiring English works on similar themes. But eventually they also included observations and rules for the visual arts, as in Lomazzo's work, translated into English by Richard Haydocke in 1598.

[31] Susan Foister, 'Sixteenth-Century English Portraiture and the Idea of the Classical', in Lucy Gent (ed.), *Albion's Classicism: Visual Arts in Britain 1550–1660* (London and New Haven, 1995), 163–4; Howard, 'Art and the Reformation', 234.

[32] Hans Eworth, *Turk on Horseback*, oil on panel, 22⅜" × 19" (1549), private collection, but depicted and discussed in Hearn (ed.), *Dynasties*, 64.

These winds of cultural inspiration, sweeping westward across the English Channel throughout the period at hand, gradually brought that island and isolated nation more fully into the cultural world of Europe, albeit without compromising native-English perceptions in the process. Portraits will have been an integral part of that cultural shift: as material objects of cultural legitimation, as talismans of gentility, and as objects of collection rivalling the cabinets of curiosity that became so popular elsewhere by the end of the sixteenth century. Few will have matched Henry Percy, ninth earl of Northumberland, whose Petworth library by 1632 contained 64 chests of books, sundry maps and globes, a cupboard of mathematical instruments, and 78 paintings, many acquired in the 1580s.[33] But the particular connection among, e.g., portraits, maps, and books appears also to have been replicated in kind, if not in extent, amongst the middling as well as the uppermost rungs of contemporary society. Estate inventories of lesser gentry, urban master craftsmen, professionals, and people of similarly middling status, which record paintings, very often record books and/or maps as well.

Some portraits served as tokens of friendship. The Marian bishop and apologist John Christoferson wrote in 1554 of displaying friends' portraits so he would not forget them even after their death.[34] A generation later Launcelot Andrewes kept one of his friend Richard Mulcaster over his study door.[35] In 1608 that same Henry Percy gave a picture of himself as a token of friendship to Lady Hatton.[36] John Vernon, prominent Merchant Taylor of London, left in his will of 1611 the portrait of his close friend Sir Thomas Vavasour to that sitter, and a portrait of himself to his other friend James Scudamore.[37] The same may be said for Lord Howard of Bindon, who asked Robert Cecil, earl of Salisbury, in 1609 for a copy of his portrait for his gallery. This he described as 'lately made for pictures of sundry my honourable friends', so that 'it will greatly delight me to often in that place where I may see so comfortable a sight'.[38] Others served as tokens of romantic affection (as may be seen in many portrait miniatures), or even as pledges to matrimony.

The offering of portraits as gifts is sufficiently well known at the highest levels of politics and society, both internally and internationally, as not to require much explanation here.[39] But the practice undoubtedly extended further down in the

[33] Gordon Batho (ed.), *The Household Papers of Henry Percy, Ninth Earl of Northumberland* (Camden Society, 3rd ser., 93, 1962), 75 and 119. I am grateful to Professor Robert Alexander for bringing this to my attention.

[34] Llewellyn, *Funeral Monuments*, 337; John Christoferson, *An Exhortation to all Menne* (1554), sig. Uiii, as cited in Thomas, *The Ends of Life*, 203.

[35] Noted in Llewellyn, *Funeral Monuments*, 337.

[36] *Historical Manuscripts Commission, Reports of the Percy MSS., Sixth Report, Appendix I* (1877), 226.

[37] TNA PROB 11/129, (1611).

[38] Cited in Mark Girouard, *Elizabethan Architecture, Its Rise and Fall* (London and New Haven, 2009), 71.

[39] See, for example, Nathalie Z. Davis, *The Gift in Seventeenth Century France* (Madison, WI, 2000); Linda Levy Peck, *Court Patronage and Corruption in Early Stuart England* (1990); Felicity Heal, 'Recoprocity and Exchange in the Late Medieval London Household', in B. A. Hanawalt and David

social pyramid as well. Such gift giving also had an institutional dimension, as leading members of London liveries or, presumably, other civic worthies from London and elsewhere gave portraits of themselves to their institutions, so to celebrate both giver and recipient.

Other portraits served to commemorate important national and/or historical events, or historical figures whose accomplishments still resonated meaningfully in Tudor society. Though the Tudor monarchs did not employ painting to mark celebratory occasions as well or as often as in most other contemporary states, the well-known painting of the 'Meeting of Henry VIII and the Emperor Maximilian I' or Elizabeth's 'Armada Portrait', became iconic images of those events.[40] The same might be said of Holbein's *c.*1543 painting of Henry VIII granting a charter to the Barber-Surgeons of London, in which eighteen members of the company and attending courtiers plus the King himself were individually portrayed.

While these paintings record moments in the history of the nation, they also had their counterparts on the more local scene. When the director of Christ's Hospital, Abingdon, Francis Little, wished to celebrate the pre-Reformation origins of that charity in 1607, he commissioned and donated to it a double portrait of 'The Bridge Builders', Geoffrey Barbour and John Howchion, who had built the bridge over the River Thames upon which its finances depended.[41] And when, in a much more overtly political vein, supporters of the condemned puritan William Prynne rallied to his side as he was transported through Chester to his banishment in 1637, some of them commissioned the veteran local painter Thomas Pulford to run up several portraits of the martyr on short order to mark the event for posterity.[42] Local officials then confiscated and burned them.

This mnemonic function can be seen in individual portraits of civic and other figures, in which heraldic devices or other such imagery presented an element of familial continuity to the viewer. One such format takes the form of a literal family tree, in which miniature portraits of family members hang from branches as if they were apples. We see this device employed by such privileged and powerful persons as Elizabeth's Lord Keeper Sir Nicholas Bacon,[43] but also by such provincial gentry as the Towneleys of Towneley Hall in Lancashire (Fig. 2.4), and even by aspiring yeomen like John Kaye of Woodsome, Yorkshire.[44]

Some portrait series devoted to the memory and/or celebration of important figures were collected by individual patrons so as to suggest a personal affinity with

Wallace (eds), *Bodies and Disciplines: Intersections of Literature and History in Fifteenth Century England* (Minneapolis, MN, 1996), 179–98.

40 Anon., *c.*1545, *The Royal Collection* (cat. no. 20), as reprinted in Christopher Lloyd and Simon Thurley, *Henry VIII, Images of a Tudor King* (1990), 50–1; several versions survive, but cf. that version pictured in Hearn (ed.), *Dynasties*, 88.

41 Arthur E. Preston, *Christ's Hospital, Abingdon: The Almshouses, the Hall, and the Portraits* (Oxford, 1929), 49–51. The painting may still be seen in the Hospital's small hall.

42 Rev. Canon Blomefield, 'Puritanism in Chester in 1637, an Account of the Reception of William Prynne by Certain Inhabitants of the City of Chester', *Journal of the Architectural, Archaeological and Historic Society of Chester*, 3 (1885), 271–88.

43 Reproduced in Robert Tittler, *Nicholas Bacon: The Making of a Tudor Statesman* (1976), opp. 129.

44 Tolson Museum, Huddersfield, no. KLMUS.1990.398a.

the subjects, or with the civilizations that they exemplified. This practice may not, as Lucy Gent has pointed out, have happened as soon as it did elsewhere on the Continent,[45] but it does seem to have begun to occur in these years. As we would expect, it appears most visibly in the collections of the aristocracy. Among the seventy-eight paintings recorded in Northumberland's Petworth library in 1585/6, for example, were a dozen of Hercules's labours, and two dozen Roman emperors.[46] The viscounts Montague held at their seat at Cowdray in Sussex paintings of Henry VIII landing at Calais in 1544 en route to observing the siege of Boulogne, of the siege itself, of the coronation of Edward VI, and of Sir Anthony Browne serving as proxy for Henry VIII at the latter's marriage to Anne of Cleves. Browne, father of the first viscount, had been present at all three events, and the paintings commemorated that connection.[47] Portraiture is an implicitly mnemonic device to begin with, but these efforts suggest the extent to which contemporaries relied on it to record elements of the past and present for posterity.

Yet the urge to collect portraits suggesting affinity with historic figures doesn't end with the great families of the day. Between 1617 and 1622 alone the actor, impressario, and amateur painter Edward Alleyn (1566–1626), whose acquisitions form the core of the Dulwich Picture Gallery's collection today, purchased twenty-six portraits of kings and queens, twelve of the Sybils, and a set of fourteen pictures of the Twelve Apostles.[48] In the same vein, the Edwardian reformer Christopher Hales displayed such an effort in 1550 when he tried to purchase portraits of several contemporary continental protestant reformers. These he hoped to hang along with his own portrait, making sure as he did so that the series would be seen as talismans of association rather than objects of worship.[49]

Such efforts to collect an heroic series were just as likely to be undertaken in an official or institutional context. Collections of the kings and queens of England, of figures from Greek and Roman mythology, of bishops and archbishops, and even of captains of that military contingent known as the trained bands were all undertaken in these years.[50] William Stanley, sixth earl of Derby, was extremely upset in 1624 when he thought that the Chester herald painter Randle Holme the elder had

[45] See especially Lucy Gent, *Picture and Poetry, 1560–1620* (Leamington, Warwickshire, 1981), 3, who concludes her observation on French patronage with the comment that 'No comparable middle-class inventory can be found in England . . . The meagreness of pictures is emblematic of the reluctance of English society . . . to provide any but meagre patronage'.

[46] The twenty-four emperors were purchased in 1586 for twenty-four pounds the set, or a pound each. Batho (ed.), *The Household Papers of Henry Percy*, 75.

[47] Related in Michael Questier, *Catholicism and Community in Early Modern England: Politics, Aristocratic Patronage and Religion, c. 1550–1640* (Cambridge, 2006), 26–8.

[48] Susan Foister, 'Edward Alleyn's Collection of Paintings', in Aileen Read and Robert Maniure (eds), *Edward Alleyn: Elizabethan Actor, Jacobean Gentlemen* (Dulwich, 1994), 33; Desmond Shawe-Taylor, *Dulwich Picture Gallery: A Visitor's Guide* (Dulwich, 2000), 4; *ODNB*, vide 'Alleyn, Edward'.

[49] Described in Daniel Woolf, *The Social Circulation of the Past: English Historical Culture, 1500–1730* (Oxford, 2003), 189.

[50] Mercer, *English Art*, 165; J. Wickham Legg and W. H. St John Hope (eds), *Inventories of Christ Church, with Historical and Topographical Introductions* (Westminster, 1902), 261; G. M. Bevan (ed.), *Portraits of the Archbishops of Canterbury* (1908); *Historical Manuscripts Commission, Sixth Report*, Appendix I, 226–7; John Ingamells, *The English Episcopal Portrait, 1559–1835: a Catalogue* (1981), 14–16; Tarnya Cooper, 'The Enchantment of the Familiar Face: Portraits as Domestic Objects in

misplaced and/or altered the portrait series of the barons of the Exchequer of Chester. He described the series as having been established under the first earl of Leicester, and then having devolved through his own family as they held that office to his own time.[51] Bishop Robert Sherborne of Chichester (1508–36) had the local painter Lambert Barnard do a series on the bishops of Chichester and its ecclesiastical predecessor, the diocese of Selsey, as well as a series on English monarchs and another on the 'Heroines of Antiquity', all just before the break from Rome.[52] Universities and their colleges also undertook such collecting. As early as the 1560s Peterhouse, Cambridge, commissioned a series of founders' portraits on panel, which eventually reached twenty-five in number.[53] But the grandest scheme in the entire university world must be the frieze of 202 portraits of intellectual and cultural forebears painted as frescoes in the Bodleian Library in the years 1618–20.[54]

A final consideration must be given to the emergence of a civic portraiture. Here the footprints of the Reformation, in the form of the monastic and fraternal dissolutions, may also be detected by the careful observer, but the need for legitimation, albeit of a political rather than a personal nature, again comes first. Just as population growth began to have its effect on many of the market towns and provincial centres of the realm, the monastic and other dissolutions removed the administrative jurisdiction of myriad lay religious and ecclesiastical bodies over particular civic government and social institutions. The consequent vacuum in civic governance fed contemporary fears of increased crime, rootlessness, and unrest in these communities. Schools and charitable institutions that had disappeared overnight were sorely missed. These and similar phenomena placed added expectations on the remaining instruments of urban governance.

Elizabethan and Jacobean England', in Tara Hamling and Catherine Richardson (eds), *Everyday Objects: Medieval and Early Modern Material Culture and Its Meanings* (Farnham, Surrey, 2010), 166–70.

[51] William, sixth earl of Derby to Randall Holme the elder, 16 September 1624; Chester Record Office MS. ZM/L/6/166.

[52] L. F. Salzman (ed.), *Victoria History of the County of Sussex* (1935), iii.112, 132–4; Brian Stewart and Mervyn Cutten (eds), *Chichester Artists, 1530–1900* (Canterbury, 1987), 2; Anon., *Oil Paintings in Public Ownership in West Sussex* (2005), 140–6; Witt Library, Courtauld Institute of Art, vide 'Barnard, Lambert'; Mary Hobbs (ed.), *Chichester Cathedral: An Historical Survey* (Chichester, 1994), 82–4; E. Croft-Murray, 'Lambert Barnard: An English Early Renaissance Painter', *Archaeological Journal*, 113 (1957), 108–25; J. Woolfson and D. Lush, 'Lambert Barnard in Chichester Cathedral: Ecclesiastical Politics and the Tudor Royal Image', *Antiquaries Journal*, 87 (2007), 259–80.

[53] Robert Tittler, *Face of the City: Civic Portraits and Civic Identity in Early Modern England* (Manchester, 2007), 43–4; Robert Willis, *The Architectural History of the University of Cambridge*, 3 vols (Cambridge, 1886, ed. John Willis Clarke; repr. 1988), i.63–7; R. J. Sklaer, 'The Panel Portrait of Andrew Perne', *Peterhouse: A Record* (vol. for 1997–8, published 1999), 38 and 41; S. Rees Jones, 'Five Portraits from Peterhouse, Cambridge' (Courtauld Institute of Art Research Report no. 152 [typescript], 1951). I am grateful to Ms Susan Pratt for retrieving this typescript for my use.

[54] Tittler, *Face of the City*, 44–6; J. N. L. Myers, 'The Painted Frieze in the Picture Gallery, *Bodleian Library Record*, 3 (1950–1), 82–90; E. Clive Rouse, 'Further Notes on the Painted Frieze and Other Discoveries in the Upper Reading Room and the Tower Room', *Bodleian Library Record*, 5 (October 1956), 290–308; M. R. A. Bullard, 'Talking Heads: The Bodleian Frieze and Inspiration, Sources, Design and Significance', *Bodleian Library Record*, 14 (April 1994), 461–83.

In response to these concerns, many towns sought in this era greater political authority from the crown. Coupled with that quest was the need to augment local financial resources which would facilitate the expanding role of the local administration. The dissolution of the monasteries and chantries, with its snowballing effect on transfers of land, provided the perfect opportunity for such acquisitions. Towns of the period from about 1540 thus clamoured for that legal authority that would not only enhance their authority, but which would also finance it through the acquisition of income-producing property. Always concerned with law and order, and compelled to rely ever more on those 'small knots of reliable men' to ensure order in particular communities, the crown was only too happy to comply.

The middle decades of the century thus saw the acquisition of such powers conveyed by several legal devices, but especially by an unprecedented spate of borough incorporation. In the first fifty-five years of Tudor rule (1485–1540) only thirteen boroughs gained formal incorporation. Between 1540 and 1560 the pace quickened dramatically to forty-nine, and by the end of the century under consideration here (1540–1640) no fewer than 149 boroughs gained incorporation, with seventy-two being re-incorporated with enhanced powers. Up to about the mid-Elizabethan era, most incorporations were chiefly intended to confer legal and fiduciary powers on local officials and thus to clarify the status of local political authority. But from that time to the end of the era, many new incorporations, and almost all *re*-incorporations, were intended further to enhance the role of smaller and more exclusive ruling groups within each town, so that the basis for local oligarchy that might do the crown's bidding became more firmly established.[55]

Local office holding served as a coveted perk and a reward for loyalty. It also represented a keen personal challenge for most who undertook it. A typical pattern saw a well-regarded resident of a town or hundred tapped by his fellows to serve as, e.g., mayor or alderman, or tapped by the crown to serve as JP or constable of a hundred, for a limited period of time, which could, in the case, e.g., of mayors, be but a single year. That abrupt and short-term accession to authority over one's fellows obliged one to step out from the fabric of the local community and apart from friends, neighbours, and relations, and to exercise administrative, even judicial, authority over them for a short time, before returning to their ranks.

This common experience required great diplomacy in order to be effective, and in order for the incumbent to live happily ever after with his neighbours. It also required that degree of political charisma upon which the effective exercise of political authority must rest. As anthropologists have long understood, such charisma is more frequently contrived and manufactured than naturally possessed. Those contrivances included as many props and visual symbols of authority as could be mustered to support the effort. Clifford Geertz, for example, spoke of the 'limousines and conferences' of modern times, but also of 'crowns and coronations' of past times. Upon these trappings, including robes of office, badges and emblems, wands

[55] Robert Tittler, 'The Incorporation of Boroughs, 1540–1558', *History*, 62/204 (February 1977), 24–42; id., *The Reformation and the Towns in England: Politics and Political Culture, c. 1540–1640* (Oxford, 1998), 87–96, 161–76, and 188–95.

of office, particular furnishings, and other such accouterments, myriad local officials like borough mayors or guild and livery company masters came to depend.[56]

In these circumstances, portraiture provided a convenient, accessible, and not terribly costly means of enhancing that charisma. And following the term in office, it could be either transferred to the personal residence or left in the civic hall for the perpetual memory of the local community. In consequence, a *civic* portraiture emerged especially in those institutions in which local authority had been formally fortified, and in which the need for legitimation grew accordingly.[57] Such portraits of mayors and aldermen were often commissioned during their time in office, thus enhancing the stature of their sitters. But as a means of creating loyalty to the community itself, and thus encouraging order and deference in its residents, many portraits were commissioned to depict local heroes, officials and benefactors especially, from past ages. In this aim the new civic portraiture may be seen as part of the greater interest in, and exploration of, 'local knowledge' that swept through much of Western Europe in this era,[58] though the emergence of the written local history must be the closest cultural analogue in the English experience. Whole pantheons of civic authorities were rehearsed in works like John Stow's *Survey of London*, particular worthies were 'portrayed' in works like Thomas Heywood's *If You Know Not Me, You Know No Body*, or, to turn to provincial histories, in Henry Manship's *History of Great Yarmouth*.[59]

Some were even semi-folkloric heroes or heroines, Dick Whittington of London or Lady Godiva of Coventry, for example, whose images were invoked as a way of emphasizing the 'ancientness', and therefore the legitimacy, of current authority.[60] Parallel to that development in the corporate boroughs and cities of the realm were analogous subsets of civic portraiture commissioned for, e.g., university colleges, provincial guilds and London livery companies, and grammar schools, the latter often the post-Reformation successors to schools formerly run by the local abbey, monastery, or religious fraternity.

All these essentially polemical images held up founders and benefactors as role models for current and future emulation. They employed pointedly symbolic imagery to emphasize those civic virtues most pertinent to the particular organization. These typically included prayer books in the hands of the religious; other texts for the intellectuals and academics; mayoral robes and wands of office for the borough leadership; and similar robes for livery company and gild masters. And in

[56] Clifford Geertz, 'Centers, Kings and Charisma: Reflections on the Symbolics of Power', in Joseph Ben-David and Terry Nicholas Clark (eds), *Culture and Its Creators* (Chicago, 1977), 152.

[57] The following paragraphs are largely based on Tittler, *Face of the City, passim.*

[58] See, for example, Alix Cooper, *Inventing the Indigenous: Local Knowledge and Natural History in Early Modern Europe* (Cambridge, 2007).

[59] Charles Lethbridge Kingsford (ed.), *John Stow: A Survey of London Reprinted from the Text of 1603*, 2 vols (Oxford, 1908); Tittler, *The Reformation and the Towns*, 279–94; id., 'Henry Manship: Constructing the Civic Memory in Great Yarmouth', in *Townspeople and Nation: English Urban Experiences, 1540–1640* (Stanford, CA, 2001), 121–39.

[60] Tittler, *Face of the City*, 62 n. 42; Thomas Sharpe, *Illustrative Papers on the History and Antiquities of the City of Coventry* (Birmingham, 1871), 219; R. A. Clarke and P. A. E. Day, *Lady Godiva: Images of a Legend in Art and Society* (Coventry, 1982).

an age fraught with discontinuities of one sort or another, these portraits often served as mnemonic devices to link the present and future to whatever elements of the past it remained politic to recognize.

Many of these themes will be re-visited and explored at greater length in subsequent chapters, but taken together, they all point to portraiture in most of this era as more a function of polemic than of politesse, valued more for its subject matter than for its aesthetic qualities or the reputation of its creators. Those creators frequently remain anonymous craftsmen of modest skills and refinement rather than the usually foreign-born or -trained, court-connected, virtuoso painters of the day.

However, towards the latter years of the sixteenth century the collecting activities of men like the earl of Leicester or John, Lord Lumley, and patronage by the likes of Francis Walsingham and Robert Cecil, served as harbingers of change. With the accession, not so much of James I himself but of his much more sophisticated wife Anne of Denmark, and the sensitivities of the future Charles I, English sensibilities at least at the highest levels began to change. Charles's consort, Henrietta Maria, brought a coterie of refined continental painters and other artists to the English court. The well-established generation of Daniel Mytens, Isaac Oliver, and Cornelius Johnson, whose work was already widely coveted, soon yielded pride of place to the likes of Rubens and Van Dyck in the court scene. The fame garnered by these living virtuosi and a small handful of their predecessors made their works ever more potent status symbols of the age—the 'limousines and conferences' of their time—and the competition for their ownership grew ever more intense.

Some measure of this change may be gauged by noting that, nearly three generations after his death, Holbein gained a posthumous fame and notoriety in England that was arguably greater than he had enjoyed in his own lifetime. 'I was told last night', wrote Lucy Harrington, countess of Bedford to Lady Jane Bacon in 1618,

> that your father-in-law was like to die but that he had some pieces of painting of Holbein's which I am sure as soon as Arundel hears he [will] try all means to get, but I beseech you entreat Mr. Bacon . . . to lay hold of them beforehand for me . . . for I am a very diligent gatherer of all I can get of Holbein or any other excellent Master's hand. I do not care at what rate I have them for price . . . and when Mr. Bacon come to London he shall see that though I be but a late beginner I have a pretty store of choice pieces . . . and be not curious to think I may pay too much, for I had rather have them than jewels.[61]

Needless, perhaps, to say, the aspirations expressed in the countess's desperate plea remained well beyond the reach of most portrait patrons at any time prior to 1640. For that substantial tranche of the emerging portrait public drawn from the middling and less affluent sorts of people, and especially those without ready access

[61] Lucy, countess of Bedford, to Lady Jane Bacon, cited in A. C. Edwards (ed.), *English History from Essex Sources* (Chelmsford, 1952), 34–35; see also Karen Hearn, 'A Question of Judgment: Lucy Harrington, Countess of Bedford as Art Patron and Collector', in Edward Chayney (ed.), *The Evolution of English Collecting* (London and New Haven, 2003), 221–39.

to the London market, such considerations of foreign, classically derived influence or of the fame of particular court painters were of little consequence. One may well wonder how portraits came into the possession of, e.g., Somerset yeomen, minor Worcestershire gentry, or Lincolnshire merchants' widows. That some such people certainly did own paintings, including portraits, in these years can no longer be ignored. Their identity and geographic distribution forms the core of Chapter 3. The kinds of painters whom they found to supply their needs stand in sharp contrast to the elite London painters of the day. Their identity and occupational organization forms the core of Chapter 4.

3

Locating the Public

The previous chapter has suggested reasons for which some people, below as well as within the ranks of the court circle and aristocracy, developed an affinity for portraiture in the era at hand. That discussion begs questions about the intellectual and cultural makeup, size, geographic location, configuration, and social status of the emerging public that they comprised. This chapter takes up these questions, and aims to locate the portrait public in the society and space of that time.

We naturally enough assume that a public defined by a common interest in a particular class of material objects would be most easily identified through a consumer demand for that product. In the era under the lens here, it would appear to follow that such demand percolated socially downwards from the crown, court circle, and beyond, and spread geographically outwards from the London metropolis to the rest of the realm. While these are not entirely erroneous impressions, they fail to consider alternative possibilities. In fact, though the most obvious manifestation of an emerging portrait public may well be consumer demand, in the form of commissions for new portraits and purchases of portraits already completed, it fails to tell the whole story. Just as the interest in luxury automobiles remains far more widespread as a subject for contemporary discourse than their actual purchase, the ranks of those interested in portraiture far exceed those who purchased a painting. Other activities also marked that interest. The lower visibility of such interests may make them more difficult to describe in detail or quantify, but they must be considered.

One such interest came from the contemporary 'Republic of Letters', in which the achievements of certain Greek and Roman painters, and the status of painting as a genteel pursuit, were heralded in humanist writings of the sixteenth and early seventeenth centuries. Discussion of some of the implications of England's participation in this vibrant intellectual milieu has been saved for the consideration of the mental world of the painter in Chapter 5. Yet the intellectual inclinations of the emerging English portrait public, and the social aspirations of that clientele, seem worth exploring here.

The importance of classical imagery in royal portraits of this era seems incontrovertible. Depictions of Elizabeth as, e.g., Virgil's Tuccia the Virgin, Diana, or Astraea,[1] or the widespread appearance of classical architectural detail in both royal

[1] Frances Yates, 'Queen Elizabeth as Astraea', *Journal of the Warburg and Courtauld Institutes*, 10 (1947), 27–82; Elizabeth W. Pomeroy, *Reading the Portraits of Queen Elizabeth I* (Hamden, CT,

and aristocratic portraits of the same era, speak for themselves. Yet the respect for classical imagery extended well beyond those rarified and courtly circles. Amongst those engaged with contemporary humanist scholarship an awareness of classical painters as heroic figures had become commonplace. Pliny's *Natural History*, widespread as a contemporary text, discussed classical painters and writers and quoted from their works. Well-educated Elizabethans will have known that Aristotle spoke highly of the visual arts: in a 1581 letter to his friend Abraham Ortelius, Richard Mulcaster cited Aristotle's defence of painting and drawing in the eighth book of the *Ars Politica*. By the late Elizabethan era such classical writers as Pliny and Aristotle made such figures as the painters Apelles and Parahesios, and the sculptor Polydorus, broadly familiar to educated men and women. Amongst the intellectuals of the day Sir Thomas More, Sir Henry Wotton, Richard Mulcaster, and of course Sir Thomas Elyot all extolled the virtues of painting, with Elyot especially eloquent in its defence as a gentlemanly pursuit.[2] The early Elizabethan herald and orthographer John Hart considered the art of portraiture so exemplary that he used it as a metaphor for proper writing in his best known treatise on the subject.[3]

Some of the reading public also acquired 'how-to' works on painting itself. Books by, e.g., John Shute, Nicholas Hilliard, Richard Haydocke (in his translation of G. P. Lomazzo), Henry Peacham, and others circulated amongst some of the middling gentry as well as the aristocracy, both within the London metropolis and elsewhere. Despite occasional lamentations to the contrary,[4] paintings and drawing (the words were often used interchangeably) did become a socially acceptable pastime by the opening years of the seventeenth century.

Amongst the Elizabethans, both Sir Thomas Smith at Hill Hall and Sir Henry Killigrew drew or painted as hobbyists in their time.[5] A generation later his lavish interiors and lush still lifes with portraits of his maids and others made Sir Nathaniel Bacon (1585–1627) the most familiar gentleman painter of his age.[6] His Buckinghamshire contemporary Sir William Borlase (1562–1629) also painted

1989), 46, *passim*; Andrew Belsey and Catherine Belsey, 'Icons of Divinity, Portraits of Elizabeth I', in Lucy Gent and Nigel Llewellyn (eds), *Renaissance Bodies* (1990), 11–35; Susan Doran, 'Virginity, Divinity and Power, the Portraits of Elizabeth I', in S. Doran and Thomas S. Freeman, (eds.) *The Myth of Elizabeth I* (Basingstoke, 2003).

2 Susan Foister, 'Sixteenth Century English Portraiture and the Idea of the Classical', in Lucy Gent (ed.), *Albion's Classicism* (London and New Haven, 1995), 167–8; Kathryn Davies, *Artisan Art, Vernacular Wall Paintings in the Welsh Marches, 1550–1650* (Almeley, Herefordshire, 2008), 9, 134, 147, 169, 187, and 200; Richard Mulcaster to Abraham Ortelius, April 1581, in J. H. Hessels (ed.), *Abrahami Ortelii... et virorum eruditoram ad candem et ad J. Colium Ortelianum... epistolae* (Cambridge, 1887), i.251; Sir Thomas Elyot, *The Book Named the Governor* (1531), ed. S. E. Lehmberg (New York, 1962), 52.

3 John Hart, *An Orthographie, conteyning the due order and reason, howe to write or paint thimage of mannes voice...* (2nd edn, 1569, *STC* 12,890), 1–2, 9, 27–8. See also *ODNB*, 'Hart, John'.

4 See, e.g., Sir George Buck, 'The Thirde Universitie of England or a Treatise on the Foundation of all the Colleges', published as an Appendix to John Stow, *The Annales or General Chronicles of England* (1615, *STC* 23,338), 987–8.

5 Edward Croft-Murray, *Decorative Painting in England 1537–1837*, I (1962), 28; Mark Girouard, *Elizabethan Architecture, its Rise and Fall* (London and New Haven, 2009), 51, 54.

6 Karen Hearn, *Nathaniel Bacon, Artist, Gentleman, and Gardener* (2005).

as a hobby. Borlase sent his portrait of his friend Ben Jonson to the poet as a gift with the short poem: 'To paint thy worth | If rightly I did know it | And were the best painter | halfe like thee, A Poet | Ben, I would shew it.'[7]

Amongst what one might refer to as 'urban gentry', Thomas Snelling (d.1623), alderman and mayor of King's Lynn and father to the better known miniaturist Matthew Snelling, seems also to have painted, as did his wife, Margaret, née Clarke.[8] His contemporary, William Whiteway, Recorder of Dorchester, took sufficient interest not only to have the itinerant French painter Jean Gagé do portraits of himself and his wife, but he also borrowed from that painter a copy of Peacham on the art of painting so as to copy long excerpts from it into his own commonplace book.[9]

Both Elyot and Mulcaster wrote on the education of the gentleman in an era when cultural sophistication had begun to replace military prowess as a required attainment. The importance that they placed on painting both encouraged and reflected its emerging place as an appropriate, genteel activity, its display in stately homes an anticipated form of entertainment. The long gallery of the country house became an ideal venue for such displays. Halls and parlours served as well in lesser houses, and even urban residences of the merchant elites had their analogue spaces. Some well-heeled aristocrats residing in some of the more isolated corners of the realm even supported a resident painter in their households, offering to make his services available to paint portraits of perspective guests as part of the entertainments offered in such visits.[10] It seems safe to assume that by the mid-Elizabethan era those who took a serious patronal interest in painting casually discussed the merits of specific painters with their friends, just as we know them to have discussed the merits of plasterers and masons for their homes.[11]

Perhaps our most revealing indication of this is the scene in Thomas Heywood's play, *If You Know Not Me, You Know No Body*, in which Alexander Nowell, Dean of St Paul's shows his guests through the picture gallery of his London townhouse.[12] Those guests included Sir Thomas Gresham, Elizabeth's agent in the Low Countries and founder of the Royal Exchange; Sir Thomas Ramsay, former sheriff and lord mayor of London; and his wife, Lady Alice, a major benefactor in her own right of Christ's Hospital and other causes. Amongst the portraits on display were those of the medieval lord mayors of London Sir John Philpot, Sir John Allen, and

[7] *ODNB*, vide 'Borlase, Sir William'.

[8] Mary Edmond, 'Bury St Edmunds: A Seventeenth Century Art Centre', *Walpole Society*, 43 for 1987 (1989), 111–12.

[9] *William Whiteway's Diary* (Dorset Record Society, 12, 1991), 134; BL. Egerton MS. 784, fo. 189; William Whiteway's Commonplace Book, Cambridge University Library MS. Dd.xi.73, fos. 23^r–8^v, 32^r–4^r. My thanks to Professor John Craig for retrieving this last reference for me.

[10] 6 November 1584, William, earl of Worcester to John Scudamore of Homelacy; TNA C.115/100/7373.

[11] See, e.g., Worcester to Scudamore as in note 10, and Anthony Wells-Cole, *Art and Decoration in Elizabethan and Jacobean England: The Influence of Continental Prints, 1558–1625* (London and New Haven, 1997), 70.

[12] Thomas Heywood, *If You Know Not Me, You Know No Body*, 2nd edn (1623, *STC*, 13,338), pt. II; Robert Tittler, 'Thomas Heywood and the Portrayal of Female Benefactors in Post-Reformation England', *Early Theatre*, 11/1 (2008), 33–52.

Sir Richard ('Dick') Whittington, plus the well-known benefactresses Alice Gibson and Agnes Foster. But though this is a work of fiction, the account itself is entirely plausible. Its role as a scene in the play required both setting and occasion in order to be familiar to the audience. Gresham, both Ramsays, and Nowell himself were actually the subjects of portraits in their own time, and Whittington at a slightly later time. By the very fact of writing about it as a commonplace scene in a play, as well as by the treatment he affords it, Heywood also affirmed that portraiture had become a common topic of conversation amongst people of reasonable but not necessarily extraordinary sophistication, and of mercantile and clerical as well as aristocratic or professional identity, by the turn of the seventeenth century.

However, when we have considered all these forms of interest, it is still the reality of consumer demand—a voluntary, uncredentialized, and wholly unregulated activity—that provides the most obvious and best documented manifestation of that emerging public for portraiture. In Heywood's play, Nowell was the consumer, as he would very likely have been in real life. His guests, all members of the London merchant and governing elite, would have been consumers as well.

If the public for portraiture outside the court circle and senior aristocracy consisted only of people like these it would have been a very small, constrained, and geographically limited public indeed. That makes it important to ask how widely these interests might by that time have spread elsewhere: to provincial centres and agrarian surroundings rather than the London metropolis, and to those of lesser social status, learning, or sophistication. How far, in other words, did this public extend, in all those dimensions, prior to 1640? However obvious and critically important that question might be, it remains difficult to answer, and virtually impossible to do so in any statistically precise sense. And of course it brings us back to that most visible form of public engagement, the commissioning and/or purchase, and ownership of the portrait itself.

Like all historical questions, the investigation of portraits remains at the mercy of the sources. Our first inclination in assessing the extent of portrait ownership might be to estimate the number of Tudor and early Stuart portraits that have actually survived from that period as a base from which to calculate the total produced. But problems with this approach quickly arise. The largest concentration of portraits from this time will have been in London, where they stood an excellent chance of being destroyed in the great fire of 1666. Those that survived, and others held elsewhere, may well have fallen victim to England's fluctuating and often humid environment, to the common vagaries of unstable materials—panels and pigments especially—and to other factors encouraging their physical deterioration. Social factors apply as well. The constant rise and fall of families likely to have commissioned them and the changing tastes that whisked the cruder portraits out of fashion and out of sight account for survival rates that are both numerically poor and socially skewed. Surviving portraits are more likely than not to be those created with more costly, stable, and well-prepared materials and held by wealthy and successful families who could safekeep and preserve them through the generations.[13] In sum, counting surviving portraits without additional, corroborative evidence remains fraught with risk.

Chances of estimating numbers and distribution improve somewhat when we turn to the archival record, some of which has only fairly recently been exploited. Of course the written record also deteriorates or goes missing, and the intricacies of those which survive have not always been recognized and respected. Nevertheless, a word about archival sources, especially household accounts, wills, and inventories, seems appropriate.

Household accounts are those records of payments and receipts kept for almost all manors and estates, usually by the lord's steward or bailiff. They can be nothing more than yearly totals, but landlords, and to a lesser extent tradesmen and merchants, began more diligently to keep them during the course of the sixteenth century. The fullest of such accounts record payments for material goods including paintings. A few of the very fullest tell us the cost of a painting, and an extremely small number even reveal the painter's name. But such accounts themselves, especially for those below the ranks of the senior nobility—men like the earls of Leicester and Arundel, who were the most prominent collectors of their time—remain rare survivals from the era at hand. Correspondence recording details of commissioning or purchase, much less receipts for payment, remain equally scarce.

In the face of these archival rarities, the determination of who owned what, and the associated questions of when and where they did so, must be carried out mostly by the study of wills and especially in those summaries of possessions found in probate inventories taken, as the term implies, after death. Other kinds of inventories were sometimes taken of the living subject's estate, as, for example, when a wealthy person felt the need to have a summary description of his moveable goods[14] or when a debtor sued for bankruptcy and had his estate inventoried against the obligation of outstanding debts.[15] But though these are very useful when and where they have survived, they are relatively few in number and often difficult to use. Probate inventories, by contrast and even prior to 1640, survive by the thousands.

By two statutes of 1529, 21 Henry VIII, *c.* 4 and *c.* 5, all estates including moveable goods exceeding five pounds in value had to be probated: wills filed and estates inventoried and recorded in the appropriate diocesan or sub-diocesan court. Wills of testators with properties in more than a single diocese, and therefore those which tended to be left by the more affluent members of society, had to be probated, and their wills and inventories registered, in the prerogative courts of Canterbury or York. Where they existed, municipal courts of orphans also listed

[13] For an elaboration of this theme, see Tarnya Cooper, 'The Enchantment of Familiar Faces as Domestic Objects in Elizabethan and Jacobean England', in Tara Hamling and Catherine Richardson (eds), *Everyday Objects: Medieval and Early Modern Material Culture and its Meanings* (Farnham, Surrey, 2010), 157–8.

[14] These have been very helpfully surveyed and listed in Maurice Howard, 'Inventories, Surveys and the History of Great Houses', *Architectural History*, 41 (1998), 14–29.

[15] Mostly listed in the form of 'extants for debts', as recorded in TNA, C.131 and C.239. I am grateful to Dr Tarnya Cooper for bringing these to my attention.

inventories of those who died intestate, but until after the Restoration these survive only (and spottily!) for London and a handful of provincial centres.[16]

On the face of it, wills and probate inventories sound like surefire tools for the identification of portrait ownership. Those who compiled the probate inventories were required by statute to 'make or cause to be made a trewe and perfyte inventory of all the goods catells wares marchaundyses as well movable as nott movable' of an estate, and to estimate the monetary value of each item listed.[17] Appraisers were drawn from the trustworthy members of the deceased's family or community. They often listed items in the order of the rooms where they were found. Added to what we know about the use and access to the common spaces in a household, such locational observations allow us to suspect who was or was not meant to see a portrait. This in turn casts some light on the owner's purpose in displaying it.

Yet as is often the case, things are not so simple. For one, not everyone wrote a will; not every estate required an inventory. Amongst women, whose property was considered part of a husband's estate if she were married, only widows and spinsters wrote wills or had personal estates to be inventoried. Neither were wills as commonly written, or as regularly registered, amongst the poorer segment of the society, a segment that probably amounted to 50 per cent of the adult population overall.[18] In addition, inventories cannot indicate which member (or even which generation) of a particular household acquired a painting, when they did so, or whether other paintings may have been sold off or given away prior to death and probate.[19] By the latter years of our period, exclusions could also arise for objects declared as heirlooms. Paintings that could be identified as having particular emotional or monetary value could be so declared. This designation allowed them to be earmarked for descent to particular members of the immediate family just as if they were non-moveable parts of the estate, and exempted from inventories.[20] They might then turn up in a will, but be missing from the inventory.

Nor can inventories reliably indicate the initial purchase price of a listed object. The monetary values assigned to inventoried goods are nothing more than the purely subjective and highly variable estimates of current market value of second-

[16] Charles Carlton, *The Court of Orphans* (Leicester, 1974), esp. Ch. 3, and, e.g., for London, the Common Sergeant's Books from 1586, LMA MSS. CLA/002/01/001 and CLA/002/03/001.

[17] 21 Henry VIII, *c.* 5 (1529); 'An Acte Concerning . . . the Probate of Testaments'.

[18] Mark Overton, Jane Whittle, Darron Dean, and Andrew Hann, *Production and Consumption in English Households 1600–1750* (2004), 22–6; Michael Zell, 'The Social Parameters of Probate Records in the Sixteenth Century', *Bulletin of the Institute of Historical Research*, 57 (1984), 107–13. Zell notes that a number of people with estates of less than five pounds left wills anyway, while some with larger estates failed to do so at all (109–12). But in such rural areas as Darlington, it has been estimated that testamentary activity of any sort ensued for only 27% of all deceased persons between 1600 and 1625: J. A. Atkinson (ed.), *Darlington Wills and Inventories, 1600–1625* (Newcastle, 1993), 3.

[19] The inventory of his picture collection taken by Lord Lumley's steward, John Lampton, in 1590 had a greater number of art works (255) than were listed in the inventory of 1609 (233): Lionel Cust, 'The Lumley Inventories', *Walpole Society*, 6 (1917–18), 21–8; Mary F. S. Hervey, 'A Lumley Inventory of 1609', *Walpole Society*, 6 (1917–18), 39.

[20] Richard Burn, *Ecclesiastical Law*, 6th edn, 4 vols (1797), IV.44, 303–4; William Blackstone, *Commentaries on the Laws of England*, 4 vols (1765–9), II.xviii and 427. I am grateful to Professor Mark Overton for the first of these references and for discussing this with me.

hand goods at a particular time and place, as estimated by the local amateurs who appraised them.[21] And most frustrating of all, both wills and inventories commonly camouflaged the presence of portraits by resorting in their descriptions to the amorphous category of 'pictures', so that we cannot always tell whether they were portraits at all, much less what their subjects or whom their painters might have been.

Despite these many cautions, both wills and especially probate inventories remain critically important sources. Ever since Susan Foister pioneered the use of probate inventories for art historical research three decades ago they have been the fundamental source for investigating the possession of such material objects as paintings,[22] just as they have been fundamental to some of the recent investigations of consumer behaviour and material culture in a slightly later period.[23]

Foister examined 613 inventories taken under the aegis of the Prerogative Court of Canterbury (PCC) between 1417 and 1588, classed in what is now The National Archives as PROB 2.[24] Most were of households in London or the Home Counties. She found that 63 of the 613 inventories contained references to what she defined as 'works of art', including pictures, hangings, and sculptures: slightly more than 10 per cent of her sampling, with the number increasing towards the end of her period. But of those 613 inventories, only 19 referred to portraits per se, which works out to 3 per cent of a whole sample, and a sample which, as we will see, applied only to a geographically and financially select tranche of all households in the general population. Though evidence remained lacking for the decades of the 1510s and 1540s, only one of those 19 inventories derived from before 1550.

Foister's study constitutes a landmark in archival research on portraiture for this period and remains enormously important. Yet as an effective sampling of portrait ownership in general, it has its limitations. Notwithstanding statutory requirements about the registration of wills and inventories, a disproportionately large number of those PCC inventories were of urban people: London liverymen, leading provincial merchants, lawyers, and the like. Few derived from households beyond London and the Home Counties: even many of those which should by law have been

[21] Zell, 'Social Parameters of Probate Records', 107–13; Peter Spufford *et al.* (eds), *Index to the Probate Accounts of England and Wales, 'A to J'* (British Record Society, Index Library, 1999), xlv–liv; Margaret Spufford, 'The Limitations of the Probate Inventory', in J. Chartres and D. Hey (eds), *English Rural Society, 1500–1800* (Cambridge, 1990), 139–74; L. C. Orlin, 'Fictions of the Early Modern Probate Inventory', in H. S. Turner (ed.), *The Culture of Capital: Property, Cities and Knowledge in Early Modern England* (New York and London, 2002), 51–83; Overton *et al.*, *Production and Consumption*, Ch. 2. I am grateful to Richard Hoyle and Catherine Richardson for their observations on this issue.

[22] Susan Foister, 'Paintings and Other Works of Art in Sixteenth Century English Inventories', *Burlington Magazine*, 123 (1981), 273–82.

[23] Examples include Carole Shammas, *The Pre-Industrial Consumer in England and America* (Oxford, 1990); Lorna Wetherill, 'The Meaning of the Consumer Revolution in England and America in the Late Seventeenth and Early Eighteenth Centuries', in John Brewer and Roy Porter (eds), *Consumption and the World of Goods* (1993), 206–17, and *Consumer Behaviour and Material Culture in Britain, 1660–1720*, 2nd edn (1996); Overton *et al.*, *Production and Consumption*; and H. R. French, *The Middle Sort of People in Provincial England, 1600–1750* (Oxford, 2007).

[24] Foister, 'Paintings and Other Works of Art', esp. 279–80 and Appendix I.

registered in the archdiocesan court of Canterbury were registered in more convenient or accessible diocesan courts instead. And given the many thousands of pre-1640 wills and inventories that survive, it remains a relatively small sample upon which to construct broader conclusions about portrait ownership in general. One of the very most industrious investigators of inventories as sources for material culture has found that PCC wills and inventories were recorded more infrequently and less reliably prior to the Restoration and certainly prior to 1640.[25]

Since Foister's pioneering study both the availability and use of inventories as sources for the possession of material goods has increased dramatically. New sources have been made available in The National Archives for the Prerogative Court of Canterbury. Thousands of wills and inventories have been catalogued and examined, a few of them now indexed and digitalized, in specific diocesan collections outside London and the Home Counties.[26] The scholarly interest in 'consumerism' and in material culture of the past few decades has further encouraged these developments.

The numbers alone of surviving wills and inventories make it virtually impossible to conduct a systematic survey of the appearance of pictures, much less portraits, for the era at hand. But a core sampling of archival evidence, compiled from borings through the social strata and drilled at widely scattered and contrasting parts of the realm, does offer some intriguing suggestions about the possible size, social distribution, and geographic profile of the public for secular paintings, and portraits, as they emerged in this era.

First, they allow us at least to speculate about numbers. Pictures, much less portraits, are listed only in a very small proportion of surveyed inventories from this era. Foister's finding that 10 per cent of the inventories households contained 'works of art' may not be too far from the norm of socially and financially comparable households inventoried elsewhere. But the predominant element in that broad category in both her survey and others consisted of wall hangings (often painted, sometimes embroidered), which were indeed common in virtually all inventory collections. The approximate 3 per cent which were labelled as portraits seems very high when compared with findings elsewhere for the same period. No other sampling examined thus far has come close to this figure. Much of the explanation for this high incidence of picture possession no doubt lies in the preponderance of inventories in her sample left by the wealthier sort of people and from its emphasis on London and the Home Counties: the most affluent, sophisticated, and densely populated part of the entire realm, and the one in closest proximity to court.

Of the diocesan, as opposed to archdiocesan, evidence that has been systematically examined thus far, the next highest proportion of inventories listing pictures

[25] Overton *et al., Production and Consumption*, 22.

[26] A number of these had been edited and published even as far back as the mid-nineteenth century, but they were often selected rather than comprehensive in their coverage, indexed only by testator's name, and not as widely utilized for purposes of assessing consumption until relatively recently. For a new and complete list, see Simon Jervis, *British and Irish Inventories: A List and Bibliography of Published Transcriptions of Secular Inventories* (2010).

and/or portraits occurs in Kent. Given its standing as one of England's most prosperous and densely settled counties, obviously very proximate to London and providing a well-trod pathway for émigré painters arriving in England en route to London, this should not surprise us. Mark Overton's team at the University of Exeter, surveying some 8,000 inventories recorded in the diocesan courts covering Kent and Cornwall in the period 1600–1750, estimates that roughly 50 per cent of all households were inventoried. Of this proportion, 2 per cent of 1,160 households owned 'pictures' in Kentish parishes in 1600–29, rising to 6 per cent of 753 Kentish households from 1630 to 1659.[27]

Ipswich probate inventories from the years 1583–1631, where 6 out of 71 published household inventories listed pictures, reflects another fairly affluent and sophisticated region, and one with similar, if smaller scale, links to the Continent.[28] But in striking contrast to such affluent areas as Kent, Ipswich, and the Home Counties, Overton's study found virtually *no* pictures in Cornish households prior to the mid-seventeenth century.[29] Some other sparsely settled or relatively remote areas also yielded low numbers: 2 households with 'pictures' out of 92 in the Stockport area, both post-1613; none in 307 selected inventories from rural Yorkshire; and but 1 out of 58 wills and inventories in the Darlington area.[30]

These small samplings suggest that the overall proportion of picture-owning households in the nation as a whole remained quite small. Bare-faced and perhaps foolhardy speculation based on a broad reading of published and some unpublished wills and inventories conservatively suggests that not much more than 1 per cent of all inventoried English households held 'pictures' during the era at hand: a third of what Foister found in PCC wills to 1582 and half the proportion that Overton found in affluent Kent for 1600–29. It seems even more foolhardy to estimate what proportion of pictures were easel portraits. Risks multiply even further when one attempts even a rough estimate of the proportion of households in the earlier decades of our study, when the registration and survival of inventories were so much thinner and inconsistent than they would become.

Notwithstanding all of these cautions, it may still be worth considering that if we accept the commonly understood figures of 4.1 million people estimated to have lived in England in 1600, and the average household size of 4.5 people, there would

[27] Overton *et al.*, *Production and Consumption*, Tables 5.4, 22–6, 111, and A1.2, 180. I am grateful to Mark Overton, Henry French, and Jane Whittle for discussing their work with me in Exeter in December 2009.

[28] Michael Reed (ed.), *The Ipswich Probate Inventories, 1583–1631* (Suffolk Record Society, 22, 1981), 38, 70–1, 75, 100, 110–11, and 112.

[29] Edwin George and Stella George (eds), *Bristol Probate Inventories, Part I, 1542–1650* (Bristol Record Society, 54, 2002), 18, 64, 67, 81, 89–91, 110, 112–14, and 117–18.

[30] C. B. Phillips and J. H. Smith (eds), *Stockport Probate Records*, 2 vols (Record Society of Lancashire and Cheshire, 1985), 124 and (1992) 131; Hartley Thwaite (ed.), *Abstracts of Abbotside Wills, 1552–1688* (Yorkshire Archaeological Society Record Series, 130, 1902); Peter C. D. Brears (ed.), *Yorkshire Probate Inventories, 1542–1689* (Yorkshire Archaeological Society Record Series, 134, 1972); Elizabeth K. Berry (ed.), *Swaledale Wills and Inventories, 1522–1689* (Yorkshire Archaeological Society Record Series, 152, 1998); J. A. Atkinson *et al.* (eds), *Darlington Wills and Inventories, 1600–1625* (Surtees Society, 201, 1993).

have been some 911,000 (rounded figure) English households in all at that time.[31] If 50 per cent of them (approximately 455,550) were inventoried, and 1 per cent of that number held pictures, there would have been 4,500 picture-holding and inventoried English households *c.*1600. Of the 50 per cent that would *not* have been inventoried, it is estimated that 40 per cent were too poor, and therefore unlikely to have held pictures anyway. But it is also estimated that the most affluent 10 per cent, those most likely of all to hold portraits, were exempted or had their wills probated not in the diocesan courts, which have been more thoroughly surveyed, but in the Prerogative Courts of York and especially Canterbury.[32]

On questions like, e.g., how many 'pictures' noted in inventories would have been portraits, or how many picture-owning households will have held more than one portrait, it remains far too difficult even to speculate. It also remains impossible to estimate the number of civic bodies that held portraits. Though such bodies were far more likely than individual households to hold portraits by 1600, and more likely as well to hold more than one each, they were not regularly inventoried. Most of these figures are of course entirely speculative, but they do point to the possibility of several thousand easel portraits held in England by 1600, with the number accelerating rapidly thereafter, probably to over 10,000 by 1640, as both the population and the 'habit' of portrait ownership within that population continued to grow.

Next come questions of geography. Kent, of course, is exceptional in its location. Its example does little on its own to challenge the natural assumption that the affinity for portraiture spread outwards from London and the southeast over the course of the era at hand. But as we learn from samplings taken elsewhere, a similar receptivity towards portrait patronage and production pertained right along the east coast and inwards to towns and cities along the major rivers. The dating of portrait acquisition amongst individual (as opposed to institutional) patrons remains far too speculative even to contemplate, and therefore rules out any meaningful analysis of this geographic distribution over time. Yet a pin-stuck map of portrait locales produced by the core sampling of archives does offer some enticing suggestions. Moving northwards along the east coast from London, centres like Ipswich,[33] Norwich,[34]

[31] E. A. Wrigley and R. Schofield, *The Population History of England, 1541–1871* (1981), 208 and 532.

[32] Overton *et al.*, *Production and Consumption*, 22–6.

[33] Reed, *Ipswich Probate Inventories*, 110–12; John Blatchley, *The Town Library of Ipswich* (Woodbridge, Suffolk, 1989), 1 and 9.

[34] Virginia Tillyard, 'Civic Portraits Painted for, or Donated to, the Council Chamber of Norwich Guildhall before 1687 with Documentary Evidence relating to the Artistic Background of the City', unpublished MA thesis, Courtauld Institute (1978); ead., 'Painters in Sixteenth and Seventeenth Century Norwich', *Norfolk Archaeology*, 37 (1980), 315–19; Victor Morgan, 'The Dutch and Flemish Presence and the Emergence of an Anglo-Dutch Provincial Artistic Tradition in Norwich, *c.* 1500–1700', in Juliette Roding, Eric Jan Sluijter, Bart Westerweel, Marijke van der Meij-Tolmsa, and Eric Domela Nieuwenhuis (eds), *Dutch and Flemish Artists in Britain, 1550–1800* (Leiden, 2002), 57–72; id., 'The Norwich Guildhall Portraits: Images in Context', in Andrew Moore and Charlotte Crawley (eds), *Family and Friends: A Regional Survey of British Portraiture* (1992), 21–30.

Grimsby,[35] York,[36] Durham,[37] and Newcastle[38] all show significant portrait ownership by the opening of the seventeenth century. The same may be said of some centres proximate to the south coast like Exeter,[39] or the west coast like Chester.[40]

Somewhat surprisingly, Henry French has also found considerable evidence of portrait ownership in a sampling of Lancashire parish inventories, amounting, in a slightly later period, to a much higher incidence than even samplings in Essex and Suffolk.[41] Though such inland centres as Leicester,[42] Worcester,[43] Bury St Edmunds,[44] and Coventry[45] exhibit such activity at least by the 1610s, port towns, or towns well connected to them, seem to predominate. Overton's findings of virtually no portrait ownership in Cornwall to the end of our period seems

[35] Robert Tittler, 'Regional Portraiture and the Heraldic Connection in Tudor and Early Stuart England', *British Art Journal,* 10/1 (2009), 3; A. C. Wood (ed.), *Memorials of the Holles Family, 1493–1656* (Camden Society, 3rd series, 55, 1937), 125.

[36] Of John Harrison, dated 1563 (York Art Gallery YORAG 1129), Mary Denton (by George Gower) dated 1573 (YORAG 1137), and William Wooller, *c.*1597 (Merchant Adventurers' Hall, seen on site, 7 December 2006). My thanks to Caroline Worthington of the York Art Gallery for showing me the first two.

[37] Anon., *Wills and Inventories from the Register at Durham,* II. *1580–99* (Surtees Society, 38, 1860), 65, 66, 318, 337; Durham University Archives MSS. DPRI/1/1610/H16/2, DPRI/1613/B4/3, DPRI/1/1620/F1/1, DPRI/1/1620/A2/2, DPRI/1/1620/B5/2, DPRI/1635/C1/3, DPRI/1640/C9/2, and DPRI/1640/J1/4. The latter set derives from a sampling of the first twenty inventories, listed alphabetically by name, registered at ten-year intervals from 1600 to 1640, or 160 in all.

[38] Anon., *Wills and Inventories from the Register at Durham,* 134; Durham University Archives MSS. DPRI/1573/P1, DPRI/1597/B3/1, DPRI/1618/L5/2, DPRI/1616/B3/6; Tyne and Wear Archives Service, Newcastle, MS. NC/F/1/1/10 fos. 305^{v}, 306^{r-v}.

[39] Hugh Lloyd Parry, *The History of the Exeter Guildhall and the Life Within* (Exeter, 1936), 152–4; 'Exeter Corporation Act Book no. 5', Devon County Record Office, Exeter Branch, 172, 432.

[40] Robert Tittler and Anne Thackray, 'Print Collecting in Provincial England Prior to 1650: The Randle Holme Album', *British Art Journal,* 9/2 (Autumn 2008), 3–11; eidem, 'Cultural Relations between London and the Provincial Towns: Portraiture and Publics in Early Modern England', in Bronwen Wilson and Paul Yachnin (eds), *Making Publics in Early Modern Europe: People, Things, Forms of Knowledge* (Abingdon and New York, 2010), 123–38; Robert Tittler, 'Faces and Spaces: Displaying the Civic Portrait in Early Modern England', in Catherine Richardson and Tara Hamling (eds), *Everyday Objects, Medieval and Early Modern Culture and Its Meanings* (Farnham, Surrey, 2010), 179–90; id., 'Regional Portraiture and the Heraldic Connection', 3–10; Sally-Beth MacLean, *Chester Art: A Subject List of Extant and Lost Art Including Items Relevant to Early Drama* (Kalamazoo, MI, 1982).

[41] French, *The Middle Sort of People,* Table 3.2a. French's sample lumps pictures and maps together in a single category, and covers the years 1625–79, and thus does not lend itself to any more precise figures for pictures, let along portraits per se.

[42] James Thompson, 'The Herrick Portraits in the Guildhall, Leicester', *Transactions of the Leicestershire Architectural and Archaeological Society,* 2 (1870), 43–54; Mary Bateson (ed.), *Records of the Borough of Leicester,* 3 (1905), 64, 241, and 263; Helen Stocks and W. H. Stevenson (eds), *Records of the Borough of Leicester,* 2 (Cambridge, 1923), 377; Leicester Museum and Art Gallery, *Catalogue of Local Portraits* ([Leicester], 1956), 4–12.

[43] Malcolm Wanklyn (ed.), *Inventories of Worcestershire Landed Gentry, 1537–1786* (Worcestershire Historical Society, NS, 16, 1998), 124, 135, 142, 153, and 167.

[44] Edmond, 'Bury St Edmunds', 106–18; Margaret Statham (ed.), *Accounts of the Feoffees of the Town Lands of Bury St Edmunds, 1569–1622* (Suffolk Record Society, 46, 2003), lii and 239.

[45] Herbert Art Gallery, site visit; Mary Dormer Harris (ed.), *The Register of the Guild of the Holy Trinity, St Mary, St John the Baptist, and St Katherine of Coventry* (Dugdale Society, 13, 1935), 4, 14, 30, 42, 46, 64, 68, 74, 91, 104, 108; Birmingham Public Library, Aylesford Collection, *passim*; Ronald A. Clark and P. A. E. Day, *Lady Godiva: Images of a Legend in Art and Society* (Coventry, 1982), *passim.*

exceptional and anomalous, and certainly so for a coastal shire in which at least two ports, Fowey and Falmouth, engaged in at least modest trade with continental Europe throughout the era.[46]

Another perspective on the geographic distribution of portraits in this era derives from the observation of those acquired not by individuals at all, but rather by civic institutions such as towns and cities, charitable institutions, London livery companies, and even Oxford and Cambridge colleges in the period at hand.[47] Such institutions also strove for the legitimation that could be conferred by portraits of their founders, benefactors, and exceptional leaders. They, too, could employ the vocabulary of the portrait to emphasize the aims and aspirations of their particular fellowship. Many such institutions also kept fuller and more systematic accounts of their expenditures, even to the point where chronological patterns of acquisition may be detected.

As we might anticipate, the evidence certainly affirms the early appearance of portraiture in London, especially amongst its livery companies. The inauguration of this institutional portrait tradition appears to have been Holbein's 'Great Painting' of *c.*1540, which recorded Henry VIII granting its charter to the Barber Surgeons Company. But curiously, this portrait statement does not appear to have been followed up any time soon thereafter by other livery companies. The Grocers had obtained a portrait of one of their worthies, Thomas Lovell, sometime shortly before 1566/7, and the Cutlers one of Mrs Margaret Craythorne in 1569. But even as leading London merchants by the score had come to the habit of portraiture in their personal lives by the middle of the sixteenth century, no other company portraits seem to have been acquired before the very last years of the century, when the Haberdashers hung five such paintings in 1598. All the rest of which record has survived came in the seventeenth century, thirty-eight of them being recorded in twelve different livery companies between 1600 and 1640.

By curious and striking contrast, portraits amongst the Oxbridge colleges not only appeared much earlier, but proliferated more rapidly. Portraits of Lady Margaret Beaufort at Christ's College Cambridge, Elizabeth Woodville of Queens, and possibly Bishop John Alcock of Jesus seem likely to have appeared by 1510. These early college portraits provide a link between *pre*-Reformation donors' and founders' portraits in quasi-ecclesiastical settings and *post*-Reformation, secular portraits, in what had become more secular settings. Corpus Christi Oxford had one of its founder, Richard Fox, by 1532, and two more of him by 1604. Christ's Cambridge acquired a second Beaufort portrait in the 1530s, and four more appeared there or elsewhere in the University by 1598. Trinity Cambridge received one of Henry VIII as a gift in the 1560s. That same decade saw the first nineteen of an eventual portrait series of twenty-five founders and benefactors completed at

[46] Overton *et al.*, *Production and Consumption*, Table 5.4, 111. A. L. Rowse, *Tudor Cornwall*, (London and New York, 1969), 69–76.

[47] The following five paragraphs derive from Robert Tittler, *The Face of the City; Civic Portraiture and Civic Identity in Early Modern England* (Manchester, 2007), Chs. 2 and 4, and Appendix A, 'Civic Portraits Painted or Acquired, 1500–1640'.

Peterhouse. By the end of the century Cambridge and its colleges had at least forty-two portraits, including the large Peterhouse series, and Oxford but twelve, though Oxford colleges would make up for lost time in the early decades of the seventeenth century.

Amongst charitable institutions, and so far as can be determined, only a handful acquired portraits prior to 1600, most of those being London-based. But towns and cities came to possess significant numbers of 'civic' portraits prior to the seventeenth century and their acquisition of such works accelerated rapidly thereafter. Bristol will have commemorated the Thorne brothers, Nicholas and Robert the younger, with portraits of each possibly by the mid-1520s and certainly by 1536. Norwich acquired one of Alan Percy in 1549: one of approximately nineteen (imprecise dating accounts for the uncertainty of timing) acquired by that city before the turn of the seventeenth century. Also before that date we have further acquisitions in Bristol plus one or more each in Chester, Coventry, Dover, Exeter, Leicester, Lichfield, Oxford (City), Reading, Salisbury, and possibly (based on conjectural dating) Gloucester and Winchester. After 1600 the numbers of both venues and portraits increase rapidly, a perception too vivid to be explained by a better survival rate of either documentation or portraits themselves.

In sum, and taking the evidence of both personal and institutional portraits together, the critical importance of London's role cannot be denied. But it also looks as if the metropolis cannot have been the sole point of distribution either for portraits themselves—many of those done elsewhere were obviously done by local craftsmen—or for the public affinity for portraiture emerging in these years. The hub-and-spokes model for relations between London and provincial England traditionally favoured by most economic and even some architectural historians thus seems to have its limitations when applied to portraiture.[48] There are many reasons for this.

Residents in or near the south and east coast ports will have benefitted from their close continental contacts in acquiring the taste for portraits, hosting the painters who painted them, and more readily obtaining many of the supplies required to produce them. Cathedral and university centres, both of them likely to have been less culturally insular than many other parts of the realm, were also early to collect portraits. All such communities were likely to have long-standing, direct, and active economic and/or cultural links with continental centres as well as with London.

In addition, the significance of the substantial numbers of protestant refugees who came over to such centres, especially from the protestant Dutch- and German-speaking areas of northern Europe from the 1560s, looms very large. The largest number did of course come and settle in London, though they often passed through

[48] F. J. Fisher, 'The Development of London as a Centre of Conspicuous Consumption in the Sixteenth and Seventeenth Centuries', *Transactions of the Royal Historical Society*, 4th series, 30 (1948), 37–50, and 'London as an Engine of Economic Growth', in J. S. Bromley and E. H. Kossman (eds), *Britain and the Netherlands*, IV: *Metropolis, Dominion and Province* (The Hague, 1971), 3–16, both frequently reprinted; and E. A. Wrigley, 'A Simple Model of London's Importance in Changing English Society and Economy, 1650–1759', *Past and Present*, 37 (July 1967), 44–70; and Paul Hunneyball, *Architecture and Image-Building in Seventeenth Century Hertfordshire* (Oxford, 2004).

other areas on their way. In addition, there were substantial 'stranger' settlements in numerous other towns of the south and east coasts, all of them contributing to local production of material objects such as paintings.

English merchants and travelling gentlemen had long admired continental portraiture. Many will have had their portraits painted abroad at a time when no such comparable craftsmanship pertained in England. Edward Grimston had sat for the Flemish painter Petrus Christus as far back as 1446,[49] the courtier and sometime MP Sir John Astley had his portrait done in Italy just before he returned to England to take up a seat in parliament for St Albans in 1555.[50] Sir William Drury had Daniel Van Den Queecborne paint him while on military service in the Netherlands in or about 1587.[51] Sir Thomas Gresham famously did so in Antwerp and perhaps elsewhere on several occasions.[52] Many others followed suit throughout the period. Their example fostered both an affinity for portraiture and a standard of production widely to be emulated by friends and neighbours back home.

Needless to say, not all areas of portrait activity enjoyed such contacts to the same extent. The cultural hinterland anchored by the city of Chester, of which more will be said in a later chapter, included southern Lancashire, most of Cheshire, northern Shropshire, and both Flintshire and Denbighshire. Much of this area lay proximate to the sea, but not to the continental ports or to the Dutch and protestant diaspora so influential in eastern and southern England at the same time.[53]

Even then, some foreign influence made its way, at least in the last years of the sixteenth and on into the seventeenth century. Anthony Wells-Cole has remarked on the appearance of continentally derived, classical details in several otherwise isolated venues: in the north range of Sir Piers Leigh's Lyme Park *c.*1570, in cartouches of Sir William Brereton's Brereton Hall of 1586, and of a frieze at Crewe Hall *c.*1615–36.[54] And though a persistent and painful hernia made it virtually impossible for him to travel to London even for the coronation of Charles I, which, as a deputy herald, he was obliged to attend, Randle Holme the elder collected continentally derived figurative prints and drawings in his own right. This collection, to which his son and namesake added considerably, still exists, and more will be said about it below. But suffice it to say for now that it must have formed a valuable teaching tool for the several Cestrian apprentices taken on by Holme father

49 David Piper, *The English Face*, 2nd edn (1992), 21, plate 13.

50 NPG, no. 6768; *ODNB*, vide 'Astley, John'; S. T. Bindoff (ed.), *The House of Commons, 1509–1558*, 3 vols (History of Parliament Trust, 1982), I.345–6.

51 Oil on canvas, Yale Centre for British Art, acc. no. B1973.1.15; Ellen Chirelstein, 'Emblem and Reckless Presence: The Drury Portrait at Yale', in Gent (ed.), *Albion's Classicism*, 291.

52 These including portraits by William Scrots and Antonis Mor. *ODNB*, vide 'Gresham, Thomas'; Carew Hazlitt, *The Livery Companies of the City of London* (1892), 182.

53 Julian Treuherz, 'New Light on John Souch of Chester', *Burlington Magazine*, 139/1130 (May 1997), 299–307; Tittler and Thackray, 'Print Collecting in Provincial England', 3–11, and eidem, 'Cultural Relations', 123–38; Tittler, 'Regional Portraiture and the Heraldic Connection', 3–10; *ODNB*, vide 'Souch, John'.

54 Wells-Cole, *Art and Decoration*, 22, 34, 64, 66, and 68.

or son, some of whom become prominent local portrait painters in their own right.[55]

In sum, and though the proportion of portrait-holding households remains quite small (perhaps something like the number of stamp-collecting households in England today), extant portraits in about 1600 may likely be numbered in the low to mid-thousands and perhaps even to 10,000 by 1640. Portrait acquisition seems geographically, if unevenly, widespread throughout most areas of the realm by those years, and London was by no means the only point of its inspiration or distribution. The most remote and rural areas and small towns form the general exceptions to this distribution pattern, though even many of those show some portrait ownership by the last decades of this study.

Finally we come to the social composition of the emerging portrait public. That also appears to be much broader by the latter years of this era than one might have assumed. Here it proves useful to call to mind Lawrence Stone's classic observation about the craving for portrait ownership in this era. He was undoubtedly correct to identify 'noblemen and gentlemen' as those who 'demanded . . . evidence of the sitter's position and wealth by opulence of dress, ornament, and background' and thus formed a core constituency of the portrait-owning public.[56] But in a work specifically about the aristocracy, he perhaps understandably overlooked portrait ownership amongst other groups: townspeople (provincial as well as metropolitan), professionals, even some yeomen, and especially women.

Women certainly did take an active interest in portraiture in this era, as admirers, patrons, and collectors. It is indeed hard to imagine that at least some of the collections documented in males' wills and inventories were not assembled at least in part by their wives, the female role effectively obscured by the fact that only widows and spinsters made wills of their own. Lucy Harrington's striking letter to Lady Jane Bacon[57] stands as a vivid testament to the fervour with which certain paintings could be coveted and collected by women as well as men. And in an era when men married younger women to begin with and were usually outlasted by them in the end, some of the paintings identified in their inventories had to have been acquired by those women rather than by their husbands. (In the case of Margery Belassis of Murton, Co. Durham, who outlived her esquire husband by 43 years and left several pictures at her death in 1587, the likelihood remains very high indeed!)[58]

The patronal role of queens and aristocratic women, spanning the entire era from Margaret Beaufort (1443–1509) to Lady Anne Clifford (1590–1676), remains

[55] Derby to Holme, 16 September 1626, Chester Record Office, MS. ZM/L/6/166; BL. Harleian MS. 2001; Tittler and Thackray, 'Print Collecting in Provincial England', 3–11; *ODNB*, vide 'Holme, Randall'.

[56] See p. 28 above. Lawrence Stone, *The Crisis of the Aristocracy, 1558–1641* (Oxford, 1965), 712.

[57] See p. 38 above. Lucy, countess of Bedford, to Lady Jane Bacon, cited in A. C. Edwards (ed.), *English History from Essex Sources* (Chelmsford, 1952), 34–5.

[58] Anon. (ed.), *Wills and Inventories from the Registry at Durham, Part II* (Surtees Society, 38, 1860), 315 and 318.

sufficiently familiar as to require little belabouring here.[59] These efforts reached a crescendo in the early seventeenth century at the hands of Aletheia Howard, the countess Arundel, who travelled widely on the Continent with her husband, Thomas, the fourteenth earl, and the successive queens Anne of Denmark and Henrietta Maria, both of whom came from royal courts sophisticated in the visual arts. But that activity extended to those of lesser status as well.

Though our evidence for this thus far comes largely from London-based and/or rather elite sources, some women undoubtedly commissioned portraits of their husbands or friends. These they kept for their own admiration and sometimes later presented them to institutions to which their spouses had enjoyed a connection. Elizabeth, Lady Middleton, may have commissioned the 1628 Cornelius Johnson portrait of her husband, Sir Hugh, which she gave to his Goldsmith's Company after his death.[60] In 1612 Dorothy Wadham, co-founder of Wadham College, Oxford, commissioned the portraits of Philip Bisse (1540–1613), founder of the College library, in gratitude for his service.[61] Lady Margaret Savile may have commissioned the portrait of her husband, Sir Henry, which she gave to Oxford University in 1622, paying for silk curtains to protect it and for its installation as she did so.[62] Joyce Frankland, née Trappes (1531–87), the wealthy widow of a London liveryman, went much further than that. She commissioned portraits of her parents, Robert and Joan Trappes, to be set up in the chapel of Gonville and Caius College, Cambridge, to which she also left a major benefaction, and several of herself to be set up in Brasenose and Lincoln Colleges, Oxford, and Emmanuel College, Cambridge. That of her father has been dated to 1554; the others were commissioned in her will and completed after her death (though it is unclear whether that intended for Lincoln College was ever completed).[63]

Some women of far lesser status, well before the end of the sixteenth century, also cherished portraits of their husbands and marked them out for specific bequests in their wills. The wife of Thomas Cony (1529–1611), a wool merchant and Merchant Stapler from Bassingthorpe, Lincolnshire, kept a portrait of her husband in the intimacy of her chamber up to her death in 1564.[64]

Stone's assessment remains right on target in noting the social range of portrait ownership amongst 'noblemen and gentlemen'. J. T. Cliffe has found that, in Yorkshire, obviously a very large county with both urban and very rural areas and a wide range of wealth, a substantial number of shire gentry owned paintings, and

[59] A general, if inflated, summary may be found in Susan James, *The Feminine Dynamic in English Art, 1485–1603* (Farnham, Surrey, 2009), 32–45.

[60] *ODNB*, vide 'Middleton, Hugh'; Sir Walter Shelburne Prideaux, *Memorials of the Goldsmiths' Company*, 2 vols (1896), I.159 and plate opp. p. 186, mis-dated to 1631.

[61] Oil on panel, 75" × 40", R. M. Poole (ed.), *Catalogue of Portraits in . . . the University, Colleges, City and County of Oxford*, 3 vols (Oxford Historical Society Publications, vols 57, 1912; 81, 1926; and 82, 1926), [hereafter Poole, *Catalogue*], III.211.

[62] Oil on canvas, 86" × 50", Poole, *Catalogue*, I.xiv and 32.

[63] *ODNB*, vide 'Frankland, Joyce'; Heinz Archive, NPG, vide Frankland; II.247–9; oil on panel, 25" × 20½", Poole, *Catalogue*, II.247–9. Several copies of these were also made after her death.

[64] James, *Feminine Dynamic*, 112.

presumably portraits, by the opening years of the seventeenth century.[65] Those owners included the shire's most prominent families of the sort who, for example, comprised the quorum on commissions of the peace or sat as MPs. Sir Thomas Gargrave, member of the Council of the North and eventually speaker of the House of Commons, had a portrait done of himself as relatively early as 1570.[66] But such relatively minor gentry as Sir Maugher Vavasour and his wife of Weston, Sir Matthew Boynton and his family of Barmston, and Sir Richard Cholmley of Roxby also owned paintings within our period. Several minor gentry of Worcestershire left upwards of ten pictures in a single room by the 1610s.[67] And lesser gentry strove to have their families painted in these years even in the Welsh counties of Flintshire and Denbeighshire.[68]

Just how far down the scale of status and affluence the ownership of portraits extended remains difficult to tell. As we have seen, inventories are the best source for such information but will not usually have been made for estates worth less than five pounds. Yet panel portraits remained surprisingly inexpensive right to about the 1610s, when those painted by the elite practitioners of what was coming to be seen as 'art' began to treble and quadruple in price. Even then crude works by lesser painters and painter-stainers could still be had for modest sums. Before that time a medium size portrait on panel or canvas could often be had for one to three pounds plus the cost of a frame and transport as required. Their resale value up to that time usually amounted to but a few shillings as estimated by those charged with evaluating estates after death.

Inventory evidence now allows us to extend the range of portrait owners identified by Stone even down occasionally to the yeomanry. Yeomen were much more likely to have commissioned the even less expensive wall paintings than panel portraits. Wall paintings in the Welsh Marches, for example, could be had for anywhere between a penny per square yard and five shillings for a larger and more elaborate scheme, with no outlay required for frame or transport. (Wall portraits were also reasonably common amongst the better off; they should not be thought of exclusively as the poor man's portrait.)[69]

However, some yeomen also commissioned and/or held panel portraits well before 1640. We have already noted that the Somerset yeoman Anthony Gilbert of 'Estecockes' (East Coker) held portraits of Edward VI, the Virgin, and the figure of

[65] J. T. Cliffe, *The Yorkshire Gentry from the Reformation to the Civil War* (1969), 97 and 108.

[66] *ODNB*, vide 'Gargrave, Sir Thomas'.

[67] E.g., Giles Nanfan, Esq., of Birtsmorton, with ten 'pictures' in his parlour in 1614; Thomas Folliatt of Pirton, Esq., who left ten in his parlour in 1617; Sir Thomas Bigge of Lenchwick who left eleven in his dining chamber in 1621; and Leonard Jefferies of Earl's Croombe, Esq., who left seven in his parlour and several elsewhere in 1629. Interestingly, none of this group who held pictures held fewer than this (Wanklyn, *Inventories of Worcestershire*, 124, 135, 142, and 152–3).

[68] See the discussion of painting in the Chester hinterland in Ch. 8 below.

[69] Kathryn Davies, *Artisan Art, Vernacular Wall Paintings in the Welsh Marches, 1550–1650* (Almeley, Herefordshire, 2008), Chs. 2–3 and p. 78. Not counted as 'moveable goods', they do not figure in household inventories.

Dives at his death *c.*1556.[70] Given their subject matter, these may have been bought off the peg on a trip to London rather than commissioned. But, as noted in the previous chapter, the rising yeoman and would-be industrial entrepreneur John Kaye of Woodsome near Huddersfield (1530–94) had very crude portraits done of himself (Fig. 4.2) and of his wife, Dorothy (Fig. 4.3), in 1567, along with putative family coats of arms on the back of one and a 'family tree', on which relatives hang from branches like apples, on the reverse of the other.[71] By the end of his life Kaye had certainly made his mark, but it is worth pointing out that this shows Kaye still very much on the near side of establishing his fortune. Other such acquisitions amongst the yeomanry must have been done at the same time. Milburgha, widow of the yeoman Henry Russell of Little Malvern, Worcestershire, left a 'table' of Henry VIII in her will of 1575, apparently acquired since Russell's death in 1560.[72] The Lancashire yeoman Henry Hesketh of Rufford left no fewer than thirty pictures, at least some of them likely to have been portraits, in 1620.[73]

Portrait ownership amongst people of such modest social standing appeared in urban as well as these agrarian milieux. By the mid-Elizabethan years what were most often described as 'pictures', portraits amongst them, began to appear in merchants' and professionals' inventories well outside the London metropolis. They appeared ever more frequently thereafter. The Canterbury sergeant-at-law and sometime MP William Lovelace left at least twelve portraits as early as 1577.[74] Inventories recorded for the diocese of Durham yield, inter alia, two portraits held by Edmunde Parkynson of Newcastle in 1573, thirteen 'pictures' including at least one portrait (of himself) held by the well-travelled merchant Ralph Cole of Newcastle and Gateshead in 1585, and one held by John Baxter of Newcastle in 1597.[75] York merchants were similarly portrayed, as early as 1563 and probably earlier still. Norwich inventories reveal such ownership by the hosier Roger Kilham (one, in 1593), the grocer George Downing (seven in 1617), Downing's widow, Susan (four in 1625), the brewer William Sumpter (one in 1628), plus assorted 'scholars', widows, gentlemen, and women who may have been spinsters.[76] Nicholas Meredith, chamberlain of Bristol, left upwards of forty-five pictures, some of them termed 'old' and therefore perhaps in his collection for quite a while, in his estate of 1639.[77]

70 F. W. Weaver (ed.), *Somerset Medieval Wills, Third Series, 1531–1558* (Somerset Record Society 21, 1905), 176.

71 Tolson Memorial Museum, Huddersfield, ref. KLMUS 1990/399 and 399A and KLMUS 1990/398 and 398A.

72 Wanklyn, *Inventories of Worcestershire* 50, as cited in James, *Feminine Dynamic*, 112.

73 Cited in Owen Ashmore (ed.), *Household Inventories of the Lancashire Gentry, 1500–1700* (Transactions of the Historic Society of Lancashire and Cheshire for 1958, 1959), 73.

74 TNA PROB 2/404B, 1577; Foister, 'Paintings and Other Works of Art', Appendix I, 281–2.

75 Durham University Library MS. DPRI/1573/P1; Surtees Society, 33, 1860, 134; and DPRI/1597/B3/1.

76 Norwich and Norfolk Record Office Probate Inventories 10/372, 28/130, 32/86, 34/184, 22/87, 28/108, 30/33, 36/141, 14/68, 41/183, and 43/193, all cited in Tillyard, 'Painters in Sixteenth and Seventeenth Century Norwich', 315–18.

77 D. M. Livock (ed.), *City Chamberlain Accounts in the Sixteenth and Seventeenth Centuries* (Bristol Record Society, 24, 1966), 172–4.

Clerics constituted another social or at least vocational group within our public, even from the mid-sixteenth century. The social structure of portrait owning amongst the clergy pretty well replicates that which pertained to the laity, running as it did from the elite down to the lower middling rungs. Other clerical collections may have reflected a lingering affinity for the religious imagery now largely proscribed by the sundry acts and admonitions of the Reformation. Some reflected an admiration for major theologians and fellow church officials; still others echoed a need to emphasize ecclesiastical continuity, at least amongst office holders, in an age of Reformation and patent *dis*continuity.

As early as the 1530s Bishop Sherborne of Chichester famously commissioned Lambert Barnard to paint a series of no fewer than fifty-seven roundel portraits of his predecessor bishops of Selsey and Chichester from AD 675 to 1536. The inventory of Matthew Parker's goods taken at Lambeth in 1575 listed thirty-six portraits, including those of seven bishops and seven reformed theologians. The archbishops of York's Bishopsthorpe Palace contained twenty-six pictures, including numerous portraits, by the end of the sixteenth century.[78] And a 1634 inventory of Canterbury Cathedral notes thirty-two portraits, chiefly of leading theologians, bishops, and statesmen of the previous century.[79] Even then that document omitted a portrait series of the deans of Canterbury, which would also have been present at that time.[80]

Trawling at lower depths in the ecclesiastical hierarchy also yields its catch. Like the possessions of the Norwich cleric Richard Bracket surveyed in 1635, these portraits were also often of religious or biblical figures.[81] Isabelle Rood, widow of the appropriately named Durham prebend John Rood, left *The Last Judgment of Solomon*, along with the Queen's arms and three maps in her estate inventoried in 1582. Considering his occupation, the painting was probably her husband's acquisition.[82] The Ipswich clerics Richard Rainsford and Jude Allen had their inventories taken in 1631. Each kept both books and pictures in their studies, though none of these objects have been identified by subject or medium.[83] Robert Hutton, Parson of Houghton-le-Spring, Co. Durham, left 'pictures and mappes about the parlour' and '9 pictures in frames' (and thus most likely to have been portraits) in the great chamber at his death in 1610.[84] Thomas Palmer, Vicar of St Mary Redcliffe and St Thomas in Bristol, also left a multitude of pictures, but these, alas, also remain unidentified.[85] Finally, Archdeacon William Morton of

[78] John Ingamells, *The English Episcopal Portrait 1559–1835: A Catalogue* (1981), 14–16.

[79] J. Wickham Legg and W. H. St John Hope (eds), *Inventories of Christchurch Canterbury, with Historical and Topographical Introductions and Illustrated Documents* (Westminster, 1902), 261.

[80] Roy Strong, 'Portraits of the Deans of Canterbury in the Cathedral', *The Canterbury Chronicle*, 65 (1970), 102–11.

[81] Tillyard, 'Painters in Sixteenth and Seventeenth Century Norwich', 318.

[82] Anon. (ed.), *Wills and Inventories from the Registry at Durham* (Surtees Society, 38, 1860), II.65.

[83] Reed, *Ipswich Probate Inventories*, 110–12.

[84] Durham University Archives, MS DPRI/1/1610/H16/2.

[85] George and George, *Bristol Probate Inventories*, 117–18.

Durham left in his will of 1620 some twenty portraits.[86] These included, inter alia, 'virtual' images of Bacchus and Venus, perhaps suggesting a suppression of personal sensuality imposed by his office.

Though obviously anecdotal and unsystematically compiled, this sort of evidence provides one more indication of portrait ownership as a point of pride amongst the intellectually assertive or economically acquisitive, and especially (as Stone saw clearly a generation ago) as a strategic asset in the constant battle for social legitimation amongst competing social groups. In addition, it allows us to see the decades prior to the Civil Wars, and certainly prior to the Restoration, as also exhibiting the beginnings of the consumerist behaviour amongst middling sorts of people—women as well as men, urban as well as landed, provincial as well as metropolitan—which has conventionally been attributed to that later era. Picture owners amongst the middling sorts of people must still be considered harbingers of those things to come, but they were certainly in place (and being both noticed and resented by their social superiors) by the start of the seventeenth century.

The same early signs of consumerist behaviour may be seen in the activities of the towns and cities to which these people were attracted for the purpose of commissioning or purchase of portraits and other luxury items. Though provincial centres of portrait production may be fewer in number and their painting activities carried out on a smaller scale, centres like Chester, Gloucester, Norwich, Canterbury, Newcastle, and York certainly came to provide those services by the early years of the seventeenth century and sometimes before. They, too, serve as harbingers, especially of what has long been known as the 'English Urban Renaissance' conventionally dated from the latter decades of the seventeenth century.[87]

In sum, the portrait-owning public to 1640 may have remained numerically small as a proportion of the whole population. The activity of its members in these years surely foretells, even if they do not yet constitute, a consumer revolution. Yet that public proves far more socially diverse and geographically widespread than one has commonly assumed for this era. While it may have been an exaggeration to complain in 1598 that 'now every citizen's wife that wears a taffeta kirtle and a velvet hatt . . . must have her picture in the parlour',[88] the breadth of portrait ownership and the social range of its sitters might well have given that impression to the socially insecure.

[86] He is not to be confused with the *Thomas* Morton who became bishop of Durham in 1632 and died in 1659; Diocesan Archives, Durham University Library MS. DPRI/1620/M7 and/M7/3; *ODNB*, vide 'Morton, bishop Thomas'.

[87] The seminal statement, from which an enormous literature has taken flight, is Peter Borsay, *The English Urban Renaissance: Culture and Society in the Provincial Town, 1660–1770* (Oxford, 1989), esp. Part IV, 'Society'.

[88] Anon., *Queen Elizabeth's Entertainment at Mitcham* (1598), 27, cited in Eric Mercer, *English Art, 1553–1625* (Oxford, 1962), 165, and Lena Cowen Orlin, *Locating Privacy in Tudor London* (Oxford and New York, 2007), 146.

4

Provincial Painters

Even in the late Elizabethan years some of the most fashionable London-based painters had begun to think of themselves as professionals and gentlemen, practitioners of a liberal art rather than mere craftsmen. George Gower, the scion of an armigerous Yorkshire gentry family to begin with, based his claim to gentility more on his skill in the art of painting than on his family lineage. This he proclaimed not only by painting a self-portrait, but by including in it the device of a balance beam in which his painter's calipers on one side outweigh his coat of arms on the other.[1] Hilliard, son of an Exeter goldsmith, made a similarly emphatic claim for the gentility of elite painters in his *Treatise on the Arte of Limning* written *c.*1600.[2] But nothing remotely like that would have been claimed by, or accorded to, the rank and file of provincial painters at any time during the period at hand.

This chapter examines the provincial painters' occupation from the economic and social perspective. The following chapter examines the material resources and the cultural outlook which these painters typically brought to their work. Both together aim further to illuminate the painters' occupation in provincial England at this time. They draw out the distinctions between both the occupational structure and the practice of painting as experienced in provincial as opposed to metropolitan England, and also between the polite and vernacular ends of contemporary painting. Neither chapter, on the other hand, considers that small handful of gentleman painters, men like Sir Nathaniel Bacon,[3] Henry Gibbs of Kent,[4] and Sir William Borlase,[5] who flourished in provincial parts, often producing very refined works, but who painted as a hobby and not as an occupation.

To begin with the occupation itself and even aside from the hobbyists, not all who painted were 'painters' by either training or occupational affiliation. Some surviving

[1] George Gower, 'Self-Portrait', 1579; oil on panel, 23¼" × 19½"; private collection. *ODNB*, vide 'Gower, George'. See also Joanna Woods-Marsden, *Renaissance Self-Portraiture: The Visual Construction of Identity and the Social Status of the Artist* (London and New Haven, 1998), 5, *passim*.

[2] Nicholas Hilliard, *A Treatise Concerning the Arte of Limning* (*c.*1600), ed. A. F. Kinney and Linda Bradley Salamon (Boston, MA, 1983), 15–17; Ellen Chirelstein, 'Emblem and Reckless Presence: The Drury Portrait at Yale', in Lucy Gent (ed.), *Albion's Classicism: The Visual Arts in Britain, 1500–1660* (London and New Haven, 1995), 287–8; Clark Hulse, *The Rule of Art, Literature and Painting in the Renaissance* (Chicago and London, 1990), 121–3.

[3] See esp. Karen Hearn, *Nathaniel Bacon, Artist, Gentleman and Gardener* (2006).

[4] Karen Hearn, 'An English Gentleman Painter, Henry Gibbs', *Burlington Magazine*, 140 (February 1998), 99–101.

[5] J. C. Davies, *A History of Borlase School* (Aylesbury, 1932), *passim*; TNA, PROB 11/156; *ODNB*, vide 'Borlase'.

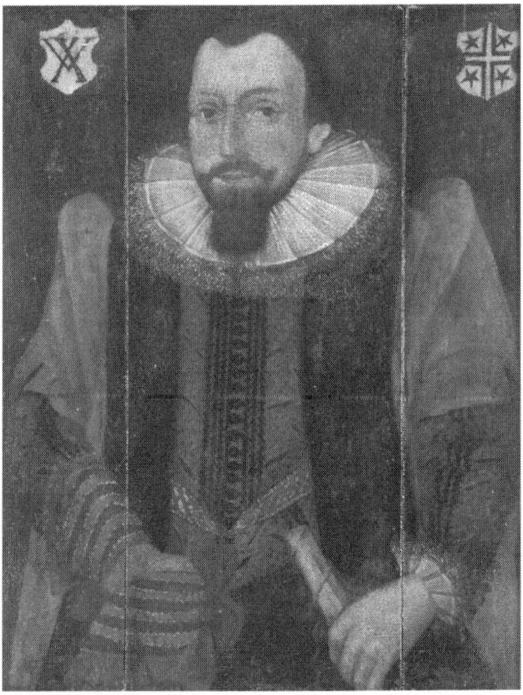

Fig. 4.1. Anon., *William Atkin, Mayor of King's Lynn* (early 17th c.). © King's Lynn and West Norfolk Borough Council.

portraits are so crude as to raise the possibility that they may have been done by people formally trained in some other craft occupation. The portrait of William Atkin, mayor of King's Lynn (Fig. 4.1),[6] the intriguing and remarkably crude 1567 portraits of John Kaye, Esq., of Woodsome, Yorkshire (Fig. 4.2), and his wife, Dorothy (Fig. 4.3),[7] and many of the wall painting portraits in this era fit into this category. Though their creators would have transgressed local guild monopolies in so doing, craftsmen like plasterers, masons, or glaziers would often have been able to produce work of this sort.[8] Certainly the continuing efforts of freemen painters everywhere to keep other building craftsmen from painting speak to the frequency

[6] To be seen in Trinity Guildhall, Kings Lynn.

[7] See above, p. 57.

[8] Kathryn Davies, *Artisan Art: Vernacular Wall Paintings in the Welsh Marches, 1550–1650* (Almeley, Herefordshire, 2008), 67–70, and see, e.g., the London Company of Painter-Stainers' petition against the intrusion of plasterers, joiners, bricklayers, glaziers, and upholsterers, who were allegedly painting 'pictures, counterfeits [a contemporary synonym for portraits], arms, and ensigns' to the empoverishment of the painters themselves and in violation of the monopoly granted the Company in its charter of 1573. Examples may be found in the petition of 15 November 1575 to the Queen, BL. Lansdowne MS. 20, fo. 22^{r}, and *Painter-Stainers* v. *Mason et al.*, TNA, STAC 5/P52/15 (18 October, 36 Elizabeth). The statute 'For the Redress of Certain Abuses and Deceipts used in painting' of 1603 (1 Jac. I, *c.* 20), took aim especially at the intrusion of the plasterers.

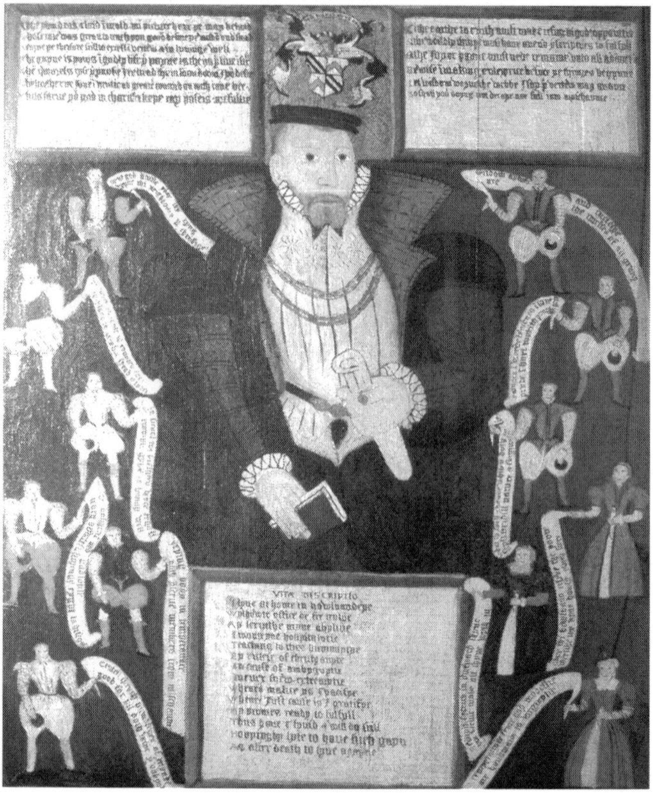

Fig. 4.2. Anon., *John Kaye of Woodsome* (1567). © Kirklees Museum and Galleries.

of such occupational intrusion. Some such crude work will also have been done by some of the many former apprentices to the painters' trade who, as we'll see below, failed to serve out their training.

Yet most painters in most provincial communities, especially those towns and cities with a reasonably formal governing structure, mirrored their metropolitan, native-English counterparts by training and working within a guild system or at least a well-established freemanry. Here the putative ascent from apprentice to journeyman and then to master comprised the conventional career ladder. Painters' guilds, or amalgamated guilds that formally included painters, operated in a number of the larger provincial centres during this time. Chester, where the painters had been grouped by a charter of 1536 with the glaziers, embroiderers, and stationers,[9] and Newcastle, where they were grouped by a charter of 1536 with the goldsmiths, plumbers, pewterers, and glaziers,[10] present the best documented

[9] A Painters' Company is recorded as early as the 1430s, but costs of producing the annual Chester pageants and Midsummer play, amongst other factors, encouraged their amalgamation with other companies at this time. BL. Harleian MS. 2054, fos. 88^{r}–9^{v} and copy, 156^{v}.

[10] Tyne and Wear Archives Service [hereafter TWAS] MS. GU.GP1/1, 1536.

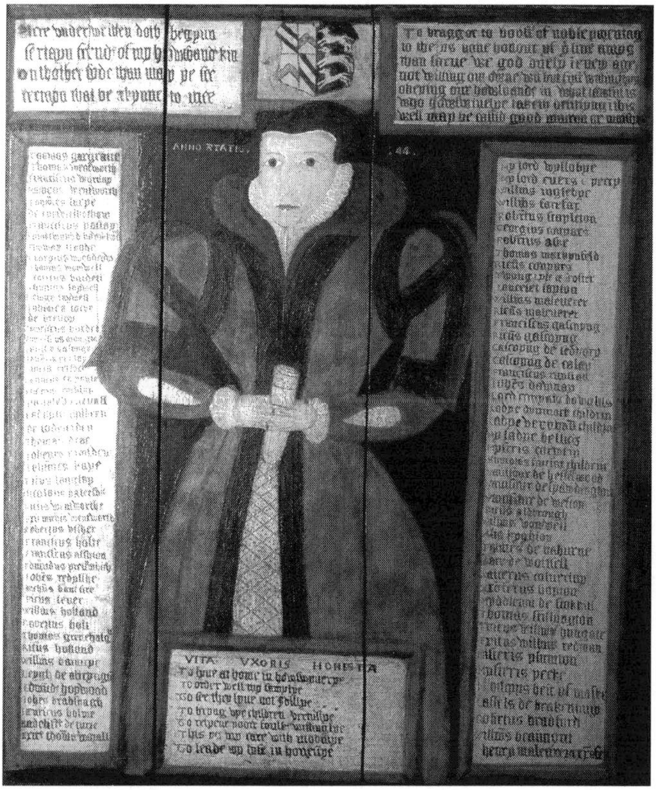

Fig. 4.3. Anon., *Dorothy Kaye of Woodsome* (1567). © Kirklees Museum and Galleries.

examples. But painters joined with the joiners, glaziers, and carpenters in Exeter (1586);[11] with cardmakers, saddlers, and masons (1444) and then with the carvers (1529) in Coventry;[12] with the goldsmiths, pewterers, plumbers, potters, and glaziers from 1532 in Durham;[13] and (informally and unaccountably!) with the saddlers in Shrewsbury.[14] In the absence of such occupationally specific guilds, the freemanry itself (variously labelled) served many of the same functions of supervising apprenticeship, regulating labour, defending privileges and monopolies, and providing general supervision so as to maintain that formal career pattern in a particular urban community. In either case it was membership in the freemanry,

[11] Wallace T. MacCaffrey, *Exeter, 1540–1640: The Growth of an English Country Town*, 2nd edn (Cambridge, MA, 1975), 87.

[12] R. W. Ingram (ed.), *Records of Early English Drama, Coventry* (Toronto, 1981), 16, 130, and 134.

[13] The guild itself, whose records survive only from 1699, came informally to be called the Plumbers' Guild, effectively camouflaging the painters' role to the casual researcher: C. I. Whiting, 'The Durham Trades Guilds, Part I', *Transactions of the Archaeological Society of Durham and Northumberland*, 9/2 (1941), 206.

[14] Davies, *Artisan Art*, 67. I am grateful to Dr Davies for bringing this study to my attention.

whether through apprenticeship, patrimony, or purchase, which supplied the credentials and permitted one to set up shop as a master painter or to work as a journeyman.

Of these three avenues to economic 'freedom' within the community, apprenticeship was the surest and most common. Those admitted to the freemanry or guild through patrimony or purchase were not necessarily trained in any particular craft. Their membership gave them the right to buy and sell at retail or engage in sundry other activities restricted to that body, but they did not necessarily have the skill or training to specialize in any particular production. Those without such specific occupational training would have found it more difficult to proceed up the ladder towards the status of an independent master with his own shop.

Apprenticeship was nevertheless often unsuccessful. The rates at which apprentices dropped out before completing the full term of their contract in sixteenth-century London averaged an astounding 60 per cent. It reached even higher levels elsewhere: between 75 and 85 per cent in a selection of provincial cities including Norwich, Bristol, and Salisbury in the sixteenth and seventeenth centuries combined.[15] Chester remains one of the very few provincial jurisdictions with sufficiently complete records to allow such a calculation. Such records show that only fourteen out of the sixty-three who apprenticed to the painters' trade between 1571 and 1635 eventually became freemen painters in Chester and members of that guild, making for a drop-out rate of 78 per cent. On average, it took just under eight years for them to complete that apprenticeship and become sworn as freemen, but some took as long as ten.[16] Edward Bellen (from 1624 to 1634) and John Souch (from 1607 to 1617) each served ten years while a number of others served seven, eight, or nine. Coincidentally or not, however, those like Bellen and Souch who served longest seem to have had the most flourishing careers.

In both metropolitan and provincial contexts, and not withstanding the experience of Souch and Bellen, the statutory seven-year regimen, re-affirmed in the landmark Elizabethan Statute of Artificers (5 Eliz., *c.* 4), often proved too rigorous, its tightly supervised life too chafing. Many apprentices felt capable of picking up sufficient work on their own after only four or five years. Escaping one's apprenticeship nevertheless constituted breach of contract. The price one often paid for it in provincial towns and cities was having to flee the jurisdiction. Flee they did,

[15] See Steve Rappaport, *Worlds within Worlds: Structures of Life in Sixteenth Century London* (Cambridge, 1989), 311–15; Ilana Kraus Ben-Amos, 'Failure to Become Freemen: Urban Apprentices in Early Modern England', *Social History*, 16/2 (May 1991), 41–65, and *Adolescence and Youth in Early Modern England* (London and New Haven, 1994), 130–1; Paul Griffiths, *Youth and Authority, Formative Experiences in England, 1560–1640* (Oxford, 1996), 330–5, and esp. 330 and n. 172; Keith Wrightson, *Earthly Necessities: Economic Lives in Early Modern Britain* (London and New Haven, 2000), 59.

[16] Based on Minute Books of the Chester Company of Painter-Stainers, Glaziers, Embroiderers, and Stationers, Chester Record Office MS. ZG 17/1 (*c.*1575–1621) and ZG 17/2 (*c.*1621 onwards), neither of which, unfortunately, has been paginated as of this writing. As the meetings were recorded sequentially for each year, references may be found for the year(s) in question. [Hereafter Chester MS. ZG/17/1 and/or /2.].

more often than not, to find their way as best they could on their own, outside the jurisdiction of local authorities.

For those who stuck it out to complete their apprenticeships, work as a journeyman was the anticipated next step. It often meant moving out from the master's residence in which an apprentice would have resided, working on a yearly contract for a set wage, and hoping to save up enough capital to set up as a master on one's own. Chester's experience with journeymen seems typical of the provincial and perhaps metropolitan experience. The forty painters admitted to full brotherhood in that City's Company of Painters, Glaziers, Embroiderers and Stationers in the period 1580–1650, including seven widows taking over their deceased husbands' businesses, employed a total of twenty-two journeymen. Some of those masters employed more than one journeyman, though very rarely at the same time. Edward Bellen employed five and Randle Holme the elder employed seven during the length of their careers. But only ten masters, a quarter of the whole, employed any journeymen at all. Virtually all the journeymen were hired for a year at a time, with few hired by the same master in a consecutive year. The exception was John Holme, hired on by his father, William, for five consecutive years from 1609 through 1613, but here the factor of paternal obligation played an obvious role.[17]

Table 4.1 Years in Which Journeymen Were Recorded in Chester[a]

Decade	Journeymen
1580–9	1
1590–9	6
1600–9	10
1610–19	14
1620–9	3
1630–9	5
1640–9	6–8

[a] Chester MS. ZG 17/1 and/2, *passim*

Journeymen tended to be hired at particular times, and more frequently in years of prosperity than in those such economically very difficult decades as, for example, the 1590s and the 1620s (Table 4.1). Masters could better afford to hire a journeyman in such good times, and general prosperity created the surges in demand for their work which necessitated extra help.

Journeymen also seem most likely to have been hired at two stages in their master's career. First, they were hired by young masters first setting up shop and perhaps needing a more experienced hand to help them through the early stages. Thus we have Bellen setting up in 1634 and hiring Henry Pincer in 1635; John Souch, setting up in 1617 and hiring Thomas Leigh the elder in 1618 and again in 1619. And second, they were hired by widows trying to keep a deceased husband's workshop going when they themselves lacked the training or experience required to

[17] Chester MS. ZG 17/1 and /2, *passim*.

run it alone. This certainly seems to have been the case with the Widow Dewsbury—the records omit her forename—in taking on Thomas Leigh the elder in 1615, three years after her husband's death.[18] Some of the Chester journeymen painters of this time had apprenticed in Chester, but just as many had not. We must presume that they had apprenticed elsewhere.

Thomas Leigh's life as a journeyman, and that of his son Thomas, are well enough documented to shed light on that whole group.[19] We may only guess at Leigh's origins, but he is most likely to have been a Cheshire man. The eight or nine (!) branches of this minor gentry/yeoman family made 'Leigh' (also spelled 'Legh' and 'Lee') a very common name and powerful extended clan in that shire. 'Thomas' was easily the most common forename for Leigh men: four of them were in the elder painter's age cohort and living in Cheshire in these years; another eight overlapped the painter's life-span at one end or the other.[20]

The journeyman painter 'Thomas Leigh' first comes to our notice when the Widow Dewsbury signed him on in 1615. She had presumably little to teach and much to learn from a journeyman familiar with the area and its clientele, suggesting that Leigh must have brought with him some sort of extended training, probably including a formal apprenticeship. Given that Leigh remained active at least until the 1640s, he must have been a young man, perhaps in his twenties (and therefore been born sometime before 1595) when she hired him. Whether the two proved incompatible, or she felt she could go it alone, or she couldn't afford to keep him, Leigh worked for Dewsbury for but a single year. Yet he remained in close enough touch with the Chester scene for John Souch to take him on in 1618 and 1619.

Leigh's work for Souch may either have facilitated a meeting of minds or provoked the beginnings of a pronounced rivalry, as both became well-established portrait painters catering to the same regional circle of gentry families. Leigh disappears from the radar screen for more than twenty years after he left Souch's workshop, but he must have remained in the region for at least some of that time. Here, like Souch, he accepted portrait commissions from many of the gentry, and especially Catholic Royalist gentry, of Cheshire and North Wales.

[18] Chester MS. ZG 17/1 and /2, *passim.*

[19] I am grateful to Ms Stephanie Roberts of the National Museum of Wales for bringing the portraits of both Leighs to my attention and sharing her knowledge of them with me.

[20] George J. Armitage and John P. Rylands (eds), *Pedigrees Made in the Visitation of Cheshire, 1613* (Record Society of Lancashire and Cheshire, 58, 1909), 142, 144–5, 148, 152; John Paul Rylands (ed.), *Cheshire and Lancashire Funeral Certificates, A.D. 1600 to 1678* (Record Society of Lancashire and Cheshire, 6, 1882), 124–6; J. P. Earwaker (ed.), *An Index to Wills and Inventories at Chester*, 2 vols (Record Society of Lancashire and Cheshire, 2, 1879 and 4, 1891), II.138; Thomas Malbon, *Memorials of the Civil War in Cheshire and the Adjacent Counties* (Record Society of Lancashire and Cheshire, 48, 1889), 241–2; George Ormerod, *The History of the County Palatine and City of Chester*, 2nd edn, 3 vols (1882), I.449, 451–64, 494–9, 581; III.659–64, 671–7, 892; Arthur Adams (ed.), *Cheshire Visitation Pedigrees, 1663* (Harleian Society, 1941), 63; J. P. Earwaker, (ed.), *East Cheshire Past and Present or, a History of the Hundred of Macclesfield in the County Palatine of Chester*, 2 vols (1877 and 1880), II.244; William F. Irvine (ed.), *Marriage Licenses Granted within the Archdeaconry of Chester in the Diocese of Chester* (Record Society of Lancashire and Cheshire, 54, 1909), vide 'Leigh, Thomas'; William F. Irvine (ed.), *A Collection of Lancashire and Cheshire Wills Not Now to be Found in any Probate Inventory, 1301–1752* (Record Society of Lancashire and Cheshire, 30, 1896), 103–4, 123–6.

To a remarkable extent the two painters shared a clientele and even family associations. Souch's portraits include a signed, double portrait of Robert Davies III, Esq., of Gwysaney (1606–66) and his wife, Anne Davies, née Mutton (1619–90).[21] Leigh painted duplicate, individual portraits of Robert[22] and Anne,[23] one for each of their respective families, as well as duplicates of Anne's sister Eleanor Mutton,[24] all in 1643. And in his double portrait of Sir Cecil and Dame Penelope Trafford, Souch was painting members of a family that had twice intermarried with the Leighs of Adlington, Cheshire. Margaret, daughter of Sir Edmund Trafford of Trafford, Lancashire, married Sir Vrian [*sic*] Leigh of Adlington (d.1627);[25] Mary, daughter of Sir Edmund Trafford of Osbarton, Notts., would marry Thomas Leigh of Adlington (1614–87), a Royalist lieutenant and future sheriff of Cheshire in 1662.[26] Whether Leigh used his extensive regional network of family and friends to bring work to his former master, or whether the two competed for that patronage, we will never know, but they certainly tilled the same field over the course of nearly a decade.

In any event, local records yield no trace of Leigh between the time he left Souch's employment in 1619, and when he reappeared in the area in 1642 and 1643. In the first year of his return the well-established Chester painter Edward Bellen, himself known as a portraitist, signed Thomas Leigh on as a journeyman . . . along with Leigh's son and namesake![27] Though the younger Thomas Leigh's career extends well beyond the chronological bounds of this study, it proves an even more illustrious one than his father's, extending to portrait painting in London, Shropshire, and elsewhere well into the 1660s. Even without the financial burdens of running a shop with its myriad overhead costs, not many journeymen could have come to enjoy similar advancement and success. But then, judging by his surviving works, few could have been as talented a portrait painter as the younger Leigh became.

The two Leighs indicate the extent to which even journeymen might at least in some, albeit exceptional, cases have painted portraits. Taken together, father and son did so in considerable numbers, over a long period of activity, over wide geographic areas, and at an admirable level of skill. Most journeymen would perhaps have aspired first to membership in a painters' guild or at least in the

[21] *Robert Davies and Anne Davies of Gwysaney*, 160 cm × 90 cm, private collection. Witt files, vide 'Souch'. The female figure has been misidentified in the Witt files as Robert's mother rather than his wife.

[22] *Robert Davies III of Gwysaney, Esq.*, National Museum of Wales, NMW A 20, 68. 8 cm × 59.0 cm, and *Robert Davies III of Gwysaney, Esq.*, private collection, 76.3 cm × 58.4 cm, both 1643. I am grateful to Stephanie Roberts of the National Museum of Wales for this information as well as that in the next two notes.

[23] *Anne Davies, née Mutton, of Gwysaney*, National Museum of Wales NMW A 21, 68.3 cm × 58.3 cm, and *Anne Davies, née Mutton, of Gwysaney*, private collection, 66 cm × 55.9 cm, both 1643.

[24] *Eleanor Mutton*, current location unknown, 69.9 cm × 57.2 cm, and *Eleanor Mutton*, private collection, 66 cm × 55.9 cm, both 1643.

[25] Armitage and Rylands (eds), *Visitation of Cheshire*, 144; Rylands, *Cheshire and Lancashire Funeral Certificates*, 124; Ormerod, *History of Chester*, III.660–2; Earwaker, *East Chester*, II.244.

[26] Ormerod, *History of Chester*, III.660.

[27] Chester MS. ZG 17/2, vide entries for 1642 and 1643.

freemanry of a corporate borough. Some succeeded in this effort despite being unable to claim membership by patrimony or apprenticeship. The Kentish portrait painter John Cawardan had already gained a strong regional reputation by the time he applied to become a freeman of Maidstone in 1637: a standing that would allow him to work unimpeded at his craft. After some deliberation, he was admitted for a fee of forty shillings.[28]

Many will have been content with steady, long-term employment in someone else's workshop. But as costs of setting up shop rose steadily, actual mobility through the ranks from journeyman to freeman/masters became more difficult in skilled crafts like painting even by the end of the sixteenth century. Only three former Chester journeymen painters in the period at hand, Thomas Chaloner in 1584, John Sidall in 1606 or 1607, and Thomas Robinson in 1612, were eventually admitted freemen and members of its Painter-Stainers' Company.[29] Other masters were presumably well enough off, or well enough supported by their families, to move directly from apprenticeship to the freemanry without the very slippery journeyman's rung in between.[30]

Most journeymen would not have been as skilled or fortunate as either Thomas Leigh. If the Chester experience is typical of other provincial communities, most provincial master painters took on very few journeymen or apprentices at any one time. In this they differed from their elite, metropolitan counterparts, whose portrait productions were often collaborative efforts of as many as four or five different hands, all working under the same master and in the same shop.[31] Provincial portraits are therefore much more often the product of a single hand. Even successful provincial painters like John Souch in Chester will have had no formal apprentices or journeymen working with them for much of the time.[32] For them, and even more so for those who had left their apprenticeships before completion, following the painters' trade could mean working more or less permanently in some small, rural community beyond the reach of guild or borough regulations, or as itinerants who moved constantly in search of work. Thus we find self-described 'painters' or 'painter-stainers' in such out of the way places as Leathley, Yorkshire;[33] Atherston, Warwickshire;[34] Inglescombe, Somerset;[35]

[28] Daphne Foskett, *A Dictionary of British Miniature Painters*, 2 vols (New York and Washington, 1972), I.197, citing BL. Stowe MS 243, fo. 212.

[29] Chester MS. ZG/17/1 and /2, vide entries for those years.

[30] Peter Earle has commented on the frequency with which families helped defray the start-up costs of a workshop in seventeenth-century London as well: Peter Earle, *The Making of the English Working Class, Business, Society and Family Life in London, 1660–1730* (1989), 108–10.

[31] My thanks to Dr Tarnya Cooper of the National Portrait Gallery whose 'Making Art in Tudor Britain' project has established this studio practice from its technical analyses of actual paintings, and who has kindly shared this information with me.

[32] The numbers and dates of apprentices and journeymen in Chester may be found in Chester Record Office MS. ZG 17/1 and /2.

[33] John Jennings, noted in a deed of 1577/8; TNA, E.210/10534.

[34] John Lakin, cited in 1552; Elizabeth Ralph and Nora M. Hardwick (eds), *Calendar of the Bristol Apprenticeship Book, 1532–1565 and Part II, 1542–1552* (Bristol Record Society, 33, 1980), 29.

[35] John Pereman, cited 1531; James Gairdner and R. H. Brodie (eds), *Letters and Papers, Foreign and Domestic, Henry VIII*, 15/689 (1896), 3–5.

Kelsale, Suffolk,[36] and Helhoughton, Norfolk.[37] None of these men, or most others like them, are known with any certainty to have done portraits, but none are known not to have done them either!

Other such marginally trained or un-credentialized workmen may have led itinerant lives, like Leigh, relying on employment as journeymen from time to time and working on their own between such stints. Those who were not thus employed, whether strangers from abroad or native-English craftsmen passing through, remained a continuing threat to the livelihood of provincial painters just as much as they did for the Painter-Stainers of London. The running battle fought against such interlopers frequently occupied the attention of Chester's Company of Painter-Stainers, Glaziers, Embroiderers and Stationers at the opening of the seventeenth century just as it did their London counterparts. It is probably only because of the unusually strong presence of painters in the civic government of Chester at that time—rare in itself—that the Company succeeded in bringing the city authority to enforce its monopoly against non-freemen painters.[38]

As unlikely as it may seem for a city so relatively remote from continental influences, some of that intrusion even appears to have come from 'strangers' from abroad, though it did so much later than in London and the southeast. In 1591 the Painters' Company agreed not to allow 'strangers' to work in Chester; in July 1600, it resolved not to employ them.[39] From time to time those who violated these ordinances were fined, but the practice seems to have continued. The elder Randle Holme, one of the leading and most respected members of that Company and a signatory to at least one of these ordinances, may have adhered to the spirit of these regulations, but not always to the letter. His employment of a Jacob de Villegrande, quite likely a 'stranger', in 1598, may have slipped between these ordinances.[40]

Of course some native-English provincial painters will not have been based so much in towns and cities, or even in villages. At least for a few years at a time a few were taken on as members of aristocratic households. Here they looked after their lord's picture collection, cleaning ('refreshing') particular paintings when required, making copies of pictures to present as gifts to others, or making copies for their lord from borrowed originals. Some assisted in the compilation of genealogies, using their painterly skills to embellish family trees on vellum and sometimes adding miniature portraits alongside entries on the family tree. Some also had

[36] Both Peter Stasey (d.1625) and his son John, both of Kelsale, are described as painters in Peter's will. East Suffolk Record Office MS. W61/203; Marion E. Allen (ed.), *The Wills of the Archdeaconry of Suffolk, 1625–1626* (Suffolk Record Society, 37, 1995), 106.

[37] Henry Rhodes, cited in 1556; Virginia Tillyard, 'Painters in Sixteenth and Seventeenth Century Norwich', *Norfolk Archaeology* 37 (1980), 317.

[38] In 1627, for example, two local plasterers were fined for painting their plaster work, a violation of the painters' monopoly; Chester MS. ZG 17/2, unpaginated, but vide entries for 1627.

[39] Chester MS. ZG 17/1, vide entries for 27 May 1591, and July 1600.

[40] *Op. cit.*, vide entries for 1598.

map-making or land surveying in their tool kit,[41] skills sets that even foreigners were quick to exploit. The mayor of Canterbury arrested one such stranger, Frances Desbronsweeke, in 1603, for claiming just such abilities.[42]

Some of these household painters will no doubt have done original portraits. But the frequency of such requests appears to have depended, inter alia, on the distance of the residential estate from the workshops of London and the frequency with which their landlords travelled there. In nearby Kent, as we'll see in Chapter 8, families like the Sidneys, the Oxendens, and the Derings often retained one or more painters at a time, employing them in these diverse capacities. But for the portraits of their own families, they sent to the nearby workshops of London where they could afford the services of, and had access to, the fashionable painters of the day. In 1626 Sir Edward Dering employed a Mr Rowley to 'trick in colours' part of the recently completed heraldic visitation of Kent, and to draw heraldic devices on his armour.[43] Later in the same year Dering paid for the services of the painter-stainers 'Kimby', 'Taylor', and 'Woodenot', all of whom seem likely to have been resident at Surrenden Dering for some of that time, to do heraldic work.[44] But at the same time he employed George Cottington of London, whom his bailiff recorded as 'Cuddington', to do his family's portraits,[45] and he would later commission the more fashionable and prestigious Cornelius Johnson to do more such portraits.

The further from London one lived, however (and despite the fact that some London-based painters travelled to take on commissions elsewhere), the more difficult it would often have been to rely on London-based painters, and thus the more likely the resort to local hands for portraits. Lord William Howard's seat at Naworth Castle in Cumberland was certainly such a place, but Howard (1563–1640) was not going to let his residence there disrupt his life-long interest in collecting books, manuscripts, and pictures. We find him employing and probably housing at least two painters, Charles Baker and Henry Heskett, there during the 1620s and 1630s. We cannot rule out the possibility that they may have

41 Examples include Thomas Geminus or Gemyny of London (fl. *c.*1540–62), one Grindall of Queen Camel, Somerset, (*c.*1573), and Richard Lyne of Lambeth and Cambridge (fl. 1570–98); Sarah Bendall (ed.), *Dictionary of Land Surveyors and Local Cartographers*, 2nd edn, 2 vols (1997), II.197, 217, and 326.

42 Richard Graunt, mayor of Canterbury, to Robert Cecil, 25 July 1603, *Calendar of the Manuscripts of the Marquess [*sic*] of Salisbury preserved at Hatfield House*, 15 (1930), 210.

43 Centre for Kentish Studies, Maidstone, MS. U 35/E4, fos. 50^{v} and 57^{r}. The reference is probably to Alexander Rowley, who had been admitted to the Painter-Stainers' Company of London in 1623, but was probably resident in Kent and perhaps at Dering's seat at Surrenden Dering, at the same time. Minute Book of the Painter-Stainers' Company of London, LMA MS. 5667/1/4.

44 'Kimby' must refer to Richard Kimby or one of his sons, John or Robert, all of whom were then or would soon become members of the London Painter-Stainers' Company. 'Taylor' is likely to refer to John Taylor, also a Painter-Stainer; Woodenot cannot be identified. J. H. Parker Oxspring, 'The Painter-Stainers and their Dispute with the Heralds', 3 parts, typescript (College of Arms MS. Her/BH, no date), I.28; LMA MS. 5667/1/29, 5667/1/39, and 5667/1/49 *et seq.*

45 Robert Tittler, 'George Cottington and the Dering Family Portraits of 1626', *Burlington Magazine*, 151 (April 2009), 208–11.

done original portraits or copies from borrowed originals during that time.[46] In 1544 the French painter Didier Bonayre dwelt with Edward Seymour, then earl of Hertford, at his Wiltshire seat at Wulf Hall, and may have travelled with him to and from France during that year.[47] And, painters being extremely rare on the ground thereabouts, the demand for portraiture from most of the Welsh counties—both geographically remote and economically not affluent—had partly to be met by sending to the larger border towns, Shrewsbury, Ludlow, and particularly Chester, for their paintings.[48]

Sometimes the resident household painter was indeed a local man, often referred to as such, and may have been asked at least to make copies of portraits. 'Whereas you doe offer that your mann shoulde doe the picture for mee I yelde your thanks', wrote William, third earl of Worcester from his seat at Raglan Castle in Monmouthshire to his friend John Scudamore of Holme Lacy in Shropshire in 1584. 'But I am of opinion [*sic*]', he added, 'that I have a very sufficient workeman here with me. Wherefore if yo wilbe soe good as to sende mee the picture rowled upp by this bearer I will cause my mann to Drawe ytt, and it shalbe salfye [*sic*] returned againe unto you wth thankes.' In a postscript he added the afterthought that 'yf yor comynge . . . my Paynter shall drae you allso'.[49]

Some and probably most of these resident painters will also have been admitted to the freemanry of some formally constituted urban community. Their sojourn in the well-supported country house by no means ruled them out for the benefits of such membership. The ability to act collectively against unlicensed competition, and thus to protect their common livelihoods, constituted one of the signal benefits of the freemanry or guild for painters and other craftsmen. Since admission to the freemanry and the involvement in its activities were usually matters of written record, the careers of these master craftsmen remain better documented. We have a much clearer idea of the painter's career at this level than of the apprentices or journeymen. Here again we meet a wide range of success, and an equally wide range of work, status, and remuneration. Aside from the additional occupations that many practised outside of painting altogether, a theme to be considered below, even the busiest and most successful painters took on a wide variety of work, often for quite modest, piecework, remuneration. Such tasks included what we would today refer to as house painting, as well as the more demanding and sometimes quite intricate decorative painting. At least some of the time it extended to the challenges of heraldic painting or, indeed, portraiture itself.

In the small port town of Dover, William Allen and John Whyman seem to have shared the borough's painting work in the first decade of the seventeenth century.

[46] Brian Stewart and Mervyn Cutten (eds), *Dictionary of Portrait Painters in Britain up to 1920* (Woodbridge, Suffolk, 1997), 85 and 148; Ellis K. Waterhouse, *The Dictionary of 16th and 17th c. British Painters* (Woodbridge, Suffolk, 1988), 121.

[47] William Page (ed.), *Letters of Denization and Acts of Naturalization for Aliens in England* (Publications of the Huguenot Society of London, 8, 1883), 75.

[48] Davies, *Artisan Art*, 67.

[49] William, third earl of Worcester, to John Scudamore, 6 November 1584; TNA MS. C.115/100/7373.

Between them, and no doubt amongst other commissions, they were paid by the borough to paint the 'post of correction' in the marketplace; the post and 'sawters' in the market cross; sundry parts of the new market house; the old column, pillars, and windows of the court hall; parts of the new custom house; the King's arms and those of the local magnate Sir Thomas Waller; and so forth, performing such work as their major occupation over the span of their working lives.[50]

Whether or not Allen or Whyman also received commissions to paint portraits of local people we will probably never know. But it remains more likely than not that portraits of the middling sort, far removed from London, will have been painted by men like them. In the meantime, such work as this, augmented as it must have been by private commissions, provided such craftsmen a modest but steady income. Allen and Whyman, and hundreds like them in towns and even villages throughout the realm, will have received less than a shilling for the smaller and up to three or four pounds in all for the larger jobs at the end of the sixteenth century. Almost any reasonably full set of civic or parish accounts record such payments, even when, as is usually (and frustratingly!) the case, the payees remain anonymous. Kathryn Davies has calculated the costs of most wall paintings, another source of work for the local craftsman, in terms of but a few shillings each as they were recorded in the Welsh Marches in the late sixteenth or early seventeenth centuries, with labour costs making up the lion's share of the total.[51]

However, the cost of actual paintings and especially portraits on panel or canvas, where labour costs would have been substantially higher, is much more difficult to determine, and especially so for paintings produced by native English painters. For much of continental Western Europe an art market may be said to have operated by at least the late sixteenth century and in some areas well before that time. The price range for the paintings of known 'artists' of the day were reasonably well established, as were the identities of those artists upon which such a range could in part be based. The trade in their works had become brisk, transnational, and integral to that European scene. To the extent that it fostered connoisseurship and the desire to collect amongst affluent and well-connected Englishmen, the Leicesters, Lumleys, and Walsinghams of the day, at least the demand side of that market extended more often to England as well. Agents sent by such collectors brought back key works that often still remain in British collections. That English portion of the market grew by leaps and bounds in the opening decades of the seventeenth century, when such connoisseurs as Anne of Denmark, Henrietta Maria, Charles I himself, and the earl and countess of Arundel became major international players and set the tone for others.

However, in most at least of the sixteenth century nothing of the kind pertained to England or English paintings outside the London metropolis or the ranks of such sophisticated and aristocratic collectors. Paintings produced by native-English

[50] Dover Chamberlains' Accounts, East Kent Record Office, MS. DO/FCA 4, fos. 55^{v}, 84^{v}, 89^{v}, 117^{v}, 119^{v}, 122^{r}, 123^{r}, 146^{v}, 148^{v}, 568^{v}, 570^{v}, 617^{r}, 640^{v}. I am extremely grateful to Dr Helen Wicker for retrieving this information.

[51] Davies, *Artisan Art,* especially Ch. 6 and Appendix.

craftsmen working the local scene and even the best native-English work being produced in London lacked that essential cornerstone of the 'international' market: the notoriety of a specific painter and the subsequent desire to collect his or her works. George Gower may have considered himself a gentleman painter, but no one outside of England clamoured for his works, and few outside of London will have done so either.

Without such an established market and the likelihood of an established (if necessarily broad) range of prices which such markets tended to establish, the investigation of the prices for English paintings becomes much more difficult. Household and civic accounts are the most useful sources for such references but, as noted in Chapter 3, inventories in particular must be considered with caution. They indicate nothing more than the appraiser's estimates of the sale value of a work at the time of appraisal: a figure that has little or nothing to do with the initial cost of a painting or the income derived by the painter for producing it.[52]

Payments must also be considered relative to the size of the work or the nature of the surface, whether board or canvas; to the rate of inflation, so that the actual cost of a painting can be seen against the cost of other consumer goods; and even to the number, cost, and availability of individual pigments employed in the painting. We must also consider that the price of a portrait did not always include payment for the painter's pigments or even the surface material, which were sometimes billed separately.[53] In addition, it is often impossible to tell whether the cost given for a painting was for an original or for a copy, the latter of course being much less costly, and often carried out by far lesser lights in the workshop hierarchy. Finally, the price of the painting only represents the painter's *gross* income. From this he had to subtract the wages of any journeymen and apprentices, the other overhead costs of his workshop, at least some and usually all of the costs of his materials, and such additional costs as were included in transport, communication, and so forth.

And yet, despite these sundry impediments, we do have sufficient evidence to suggest that in raw monetary terms the price of portraits in general, and thus the income derived from their production, remained fairly stagnant through at least the sixteenth century and into the opening years of the seventeenth. Considering that general tendency of paintings to become larger in size, and thus more costly to produce, over that time, the *relative* price of portraits may even have declined during that time. Christ's College, Cambridge, paid 60s. for a small painting of Margaret Beaufort in 1511/12 by the sometime court painter Maynard Vewicke.[54] Christ Church, Oxford, paid the same sum for a portrait of Thomas Cardinal

[52] See the editor's introductory explanation in Peter Spufford *et al.*, *Index to the Probate Accounts of England and Wales, Part I, A to J* (British Record Society, Index Library, 1999), p. xlv.

[53] Letter from Charles Bradshaw to Sir William More of Losely, *c.*1559–76, More/Losely Family of Losely Park, Historical Correspondence, 9 (1420–1642), Historical Manuscript Commission, *Seventh Report, Appendix* (1879), 667. In 1537 the second earl of Rutland paid the London painter-stainer Andrew Wright for painting his coat of arms on damask. Wright supplied the damask, and was paid specifically for it on top of the cost of the painting itself; Historical Manuscript Commission, *Twelfth Report*, Appendix V, v.4 (1905), 283.

[54] J. W. Goodison (ed.), *Catalogue of the Portraits in Christ's, Clare, and Sidney Sussex Colleges* (Cambridge, 1985), 35–6.

Wolsey, albeit by the provincial painter Sampson Strong and probably a copy, exactly a century later.[55] Both were oils on panel. University portraits in general during the first fifteen years of the seventeenth century ran between 13s.—for what were probably mere copies—of portraits of Martin Heton, Bishop of Ely, and Thomas Ravis, Bishop of London, both purchased by Christ Church, Oxford in 1609/10—and £13 6s. 8d paid to an anonymous painter by Cambridge University for a portrait of Prince Charles at roughly the same time.[56]

Though written contracts for the commissioning of a painting at this time are extremely rare, business arrangements that pertained to similar crafts at that time corroborate the suggestion that the patron probably paid for the painting either in two installments, one to seal the bargain and the rest on delivery of the completed work, or as a lump sum on completion. The former practice ensued when Sir Hamon Lestrange of Hunstanton, Norfolk, paid John Hoskins the elder £2 4s. in June 1617, and then the remaining balance of £1 16s. in September of the same year for portraits of himself and his wife. The latter ensued when Sir Edward Dering paid the whole lump sum of £25 to George Cottington for four family portraits in 1626.[57]

However, a major change in the gross cost of paintings at the high end of the scale seems to have occurred in the 1610s and 1620s. In these years the spirited and well-known court patronage of a small circle of elite painters by Anne of Denmark and then by Henrietta Maria and King Charles himself, along with the collecting activities of the earl of Arundel and other leading aristocrats, created a virtual craze for works of those favoured few. Lucy, countess of Bedford's desperate appeal to Lady Jane Bacon about acquiring her father-in-law's Holbeins speaks volumes about this rabid enthusiasm of the age.[58] Foreign-born or -trained painters like Jan de Critz the elder, Daniel Mytens, and Cornelius Johnson, or their English contemporaries like Robert Peake, William Larkin, and Isaac Oliver, were amongst the first to be so patronized and rewarded. They would be followed in turn by the even loftier likes of Peter Paul Rubens and then of Anthony Van Dyck, the first painters to be knighted for their celebrated virtuosity. By the 1620s painters of that ilk were easily able to command forty to sixty pounds for a single portrait, depending on its size, number of sitters, colour range, and so forth. Van Dyck regularly commanded the latter sum for full-lengths,[59] while Daniel Mytens, who suffered greatly from Van Dyck's competition, charged eighty pounds in 1628 for

[55] Oil on panel, 43" × 36¼", R. L. Poole (ed.), *Catalogue of Portraits in the Possession of the University Colleges, City and County of Oxford*, 3 vols (Oxford Historical Society Publications, vols 57, 1912; 81, 1926; and 82, 1926), III.4–5.

[56] Both are oil on panel, 29½" × 23½", Poole, *Catalogue*, III.17; Henry Bradshaw, 'On the Collection of Portraits belonging to the University before the Civil War' [1872], *Collected Papers of Henry Bradshaw* (Cambridge, 1889), 287.

[57] *ODNB*, vide 'Hoskins'; 'Edward Dering's Book of Expenses', Centre for Kentish Studies, Maidstone, MS. U 350 E4, fo. 57r.

[58] See above, Ch. 3, p. 38.

[59] For example, he received £444 for nine royal portraits in 1633, over and above his annual pension of £200 (Karen Hearn (ed.), *Van Dyck and Britain* (2009), 65–6).

'one great one of the Queen and the dwarf both in one peece' to be sent to Charles I's sister, Elizabeth, Queen of Bohemia.[60]

These few elite masters could make a very handsome living indeed by portrait painting alone. But though some of these, and especially the enormously prolific Johnson, could and did accept numerous commissions in provincial England, virtually no provincially based painter commanded anything near such reputation or prices in these years. Patrons demanding the finer work almost always looked to London if and when they could. Newcastle, for example, lacked neither for resident painters or patrons. Yet when its borough council wished to proclaim their loyalty to James I by commissioning a portrait of him for a new civic building on the bridge over the Tyne, they were willing to spend thirty pounds for the painting, but sent to London to have it done.[61]

In striking contrast, the bottom end of the market, especially but not exclusively outside the metropolis, does not seem to have risen at anywhere near the same rate. A huge gap in the cost of paintings, and in the income of different types of painter, opened up and grew ever wider with each passing year. All but the very elite of the profession seem to have received far less *real* income in the early Stuart era than in the early and mid-Tudor. The virtually equal cost of Strong's 1611 portrait of Wolsey and of Margaret Beaufort's a century earlier suggests no less. But even though the two works will not have been comparable in every respect, the cost of living, based on the price of a market basket of consumable items, is estimated to have risen some five-fold over the same era.[62]

The well-established, Oxford-based painter Richard Greenbury received only £4 for his portrait of Arthur Lake for New College, Oxford, in 1626/7; his equally well-known colleague Gilbert Jackson received but £3 5s. for his portrait of John, baron Mordaunt at Brasenose in 1638.[63] Given the relative obscurity of the sitters, neither portraits are likely to have been mere, and therefore less expensive, copies. And when the obscure London painter known only as 'Cooke' or 'Cocke' asked £5 a piece for portraying members of the Ironmongers Company in 1640, the Company demurred, noting that 'the Courte [the Company's ruling assembly] doe not hold them to be soe much worthe yet they will further inquire what other Companies payes for the like woorke'. Following such consultation with other companies they offered £3 5s. each instead. Cooke swallowed his pride, accepted the commission, and proceeded to paint five more portraits for the Ironmongers at the same rate.[64]

[60] Lord Chamberlain's Department, Miscellaneous Accounts, TNA, LC5/132, 29, 53, 110, and 148.

[61] The sum was payment 'in part for a more sum', and does not count the additional costs for bringing it from London and hanging it. Newcastle Borough Chamberlains' Accounts, TWAS MS. MD.NC/F/1/1/10, fos. 305–6.

[62] Based on E. H. Phelps Brown and S. V. Hopkins, 'Seven Centuries of Prices of Consumables, Compared with Builders' Wage-Rates', *Economica*, NS, 23 (1956), Fig. 1, 'Price of a Composite Unit of Comestibles in Southern England, 1264–1954', 299.

[63] Oil on canvas, 47" × 40½", Poole, *Catalogue*, II.153. and oil on panel, 30½" × 23½", ibid. I.247.

[64] Tittler, *Face of the City*, 86, from Ironmongers Company, Quarter Court Minutes, 29 April 1640, GH MS. 16,967/2, 306 and 318. 'Cooke' seems to have been Edward Cooke, described as a

Several factors may have contributed to keeping the cost of most painters' work at such a modest level. For one, these years saw the beginning of commercial print selling in London and elsewhere on a widely accessible level: a turning point marked by the opening, by John Sudbury and his nephew George Humble in 1603, of the first retail shop in England dedicated to the sale of prints.[65] With less expensive engraved images and even cheap woodcuts so much more widely available, many patrons of the middling and lesser ranks of society could satisfy their desires for pictures on the wall without the expense of an original or even a copied panel portrait. At the upper end of the scale the competition of foreign-born or -trained painters, and the lure of their more sophisticated work which could not yet be matched by any but a handful of English painters, must have induced the native English to keep their prices down in the hope of competing. Another force working to the same effect lay in the increased production in the Netherlands of copies and fakes of paintings by established Dutch painters, a trend dated especially to the establishment of the Peace of 1608. These were often detectable to the increasingly sophisticated Dutch portrait-public, and consequently dumped at reduced prices on the more innocent English.[66]

In addition, some of the steady increase in the retail sales of portraits, a practice that increased both supply and ease of access and kept prices low, must be attributed to the increased influx of Netherlandish painters fleeing the religious wars in their homeland from the 1560s. Scores of them made their way to protestant England and worked there at least temporarily thereafter.

It also remains true that almost all surviving references to the sale of paintings from this era concern paintings commissioned by the sitter or patron from the painter, or those purchased abroad by a well-heeled and affluent English collector or his agent. Yet there are tantalizing references to the retail sale of portraits that lay on hand in a painter's studio or shop and that had evidently not been commissioned beforehand. Some may have been the painter's own collected work and thus not for sale. Some may have been completed on commission and awaiting delivery. But some must also have been done for the retail trade without prior commission, available for sale off the peg. These uncommissioned works will have been intended for retail sale to the casual purchaser and will have portrayed subjects most likely to appeal to the broadest popular taste: images of kings and queens and biblical, folkloric or classical heroes, real or imagined. Even the court painter Robert Peake, who certainly will not have lacked for commissions by that time in his career, kept a

'picture drawer' in the Painter-Stainers' Company minutes of 1630, but may instead be Thomas Coke, against whom the Company issued a complaint in 1631 for painting without licence. Minutes of the Painter-Stainers' Company of London, LMA MS. 5667/2, 52 and 66.

[65] The shop was located at the sign of the White Horse, near Newgate, and remained there under successive owners for at least a century. Leona Rostenberg, *English Publishers in the Graphic Arts, 1599–1700: A Study of the Printsellers and Publishers of Engravings* (repr., New York, 1963), 2.

[66] Suggested in Anna Tummers and Koenraed Jonckheere (eds), *Art Market and Connoisseurship: A Closer Look at Paintings by Rembrandt, Rubens, and Their Contemporaries* (Amsterdam, 2008), Introduction.

shop ('neere Holborne conduit, next to the Sunne taverne') at which, and amongst other things, paintings will have been sold.[67]

This retail scene seems to have been established quite early in the period at hand. As he recorded in his autobiography written in the late 1560s, Thomas Whythorne, a young Oxford dropout looking for work as a music tutor in London, went into a painter's shop in about 1549, looked at sundry portraits in various stages of completion, and bought one of a comely woman playing a lute. Then in the same shop he commissioned one of himself playing the virginals.[68]

The reference is enormously revealing and important. It tells us that, at least in London, there were by 1549 at least some retail shops run by painters themselves where one could either commission an easel portrait or purchase one from stock on hand. Whythorne treats this as if it had been a normal occurrence at that time. By the latter years of our period paintings were also sold in London bookshops. The Painter-Stainers cited 'one Sherman a bookseller by the town dich' for so doing in 1632 in what seems to have become common practice.[69]

By the early seventeenth century, as attested to in a verse by the aptly named William Painter, the retail sale of paintings had moved to what sounds like a virtual open air market for such works along the Strand, just as one might see along Bayswater Road atop Hyde Park today: 'You curious painters | and you limners all, from Temple Barre | along to Charing Cross that your gay pictures | hang out on the wall'.[70] The verse refers to painters and limners, the latter term usually referring to portrait painters in general or miniaturists in particular.

Thus far lacking similar evidence of such retail sales elsewhere, we can only assume that in this as well the provincial scene lagged behind the metropolitan, and that off the peg sales may only have come to the major and more affluent provincial centres, perhaps Norwich, York, or Exeter, only in the very last years of the period at hand. But such a public display of paintings on offer from Temple Bar to Charing Cross meant an open, accessible, and no doubt highly competitive retail market which visitors from elsewhere in the realm could frequent and support. The Painter-Stainers' Company frequently complained about such displays.[71]

All of these factors will have pressed hard against the livelihood of provincially based painters, keeping prices down as they did so. Given such marketing competition, one can little wonder why the native-English painters of the Painter-Stainers' Company of London, and even their counterparts in Chester and elsewhere, lobbied so long and hard against the intrusion of foreign and unlicensed competition for portrait work. Richard Greenbury, along with George Cottington and a few other well-regarded and well-patronized portrait painters of their time,

[67] *ODNB*, vide 'Peake, Robert'.
[68] James M. Osborne (ed.), *The Autobiography of Thomas Whythorne* (Oxford, 1961), 20.
[69] LMA MS. 5667/1/73.
[70] William Painter, *Chaucer Newly Painted* (1623 edn, *STC* no. 19125–5), Prologue, unpaginated.
[71] E.g., LMA MS. 5667/1/73.

launched just such a campaign in the 1620s.[72] It was not the first and would not be the last effort of its kind.

For the provincial painter, the painting of portraits alone cannot by itself have been especially lucrative at virtually any time in the period at hand. Even the itinerant painter, spared the costs of guild-related dues and other fees, permanent workshops, and the overheads associated with them, will not have become a wealthy man at the level of established court painters like Cornelius Johnson or Daniel Mytens. It is unlikely that any provincial city or town could support those who painted portraits to the exclusion of all else, though certain painters, like Lichfield's Samuel Kirke[73] or Chester's John Souch,[74] gained a local, indeed, regional, reputation for that sort of work and were often called upon to do it.

In these circumstances, some painters eventually fell close to or even below the poverty line and were compelled to apply, when such remedies were available, for relief from their local guild or parish authority. Richard Hossell of Bicester left but £2 8s. 4d to his name, including but a single jerkin, when his goods were inventoried after his death in 1587.[75] More surprisingly (albeit perhaps idiosyncratically) even the well-established Newcastle painter William Robinson died poor. Robinson painted everything from barges to the royal arms and probably portraits as well, and frequently served as a steward to his company. He was also a herald painter and is additionally identified in his step-son's will as a painter and embroiderer. Like de Critz, albeit undoubtedly on a much smaller scale, he also regularly took on apprentices and the occasional journeyman. And yet with all this his probate inventory lists household goods worth but £10 1s. 10d, with 26s. 8d left to spend on coffins for himself and his wife.[76]

Diversification of employment therefore became a necessity for most painters, even for those at the very top of their profession and in metropolitan as well as provincial areas. Over the course of the era at hand, as the status of the elite painter developed from 'craftsman' to 'artist' and as the finest of portraits themselves began towards the latter years of our period to be seen, coveted, and collected as works of 'art', those at the top were able to specialize to a greater extent in, for example, the portrait painting on which their fame chiefly relied.

[72] Noted by Susan Foister, 'Foreigners at Court: Holbein, Van Dyck and the Painter-Stainers Company', in David Howarth (ed.), *Art and Patronage in the Caroline Court: Essays in Honour of Sir Oliver Millar* (Cambridge, 1993), 32–3, and described, inter alia, in LMA MS. 5667/1, 28, 61, 91, and 110. See also Cheshire Record Office MS. ZG 17/1, entries for 27 May 1591 and July 1600, unpaginated and ZG 17/2, for 1627, also unpaginated.

[73] Kirke or Kyrke painted portraits in Lichfield and elsewhere in Staffordshire from *c.*1614 to *c.*1632, giving way some time thereafter to his son Zacherie. NPG, Heinz Archive, vide 'Kirke/Kyrke', and letter from Robert Greisbrooke of Shenston, Staffs. To 'Mr Kirke in Lichfield', 23 March 1662, H. S. Grazeberooke (ed.), *The Heraldic Visitations of Staffordshire Made by Sir Richard St George and Sir William Dugdale* (1885), 156–7.

[74] *ODNB*, vide 'Souch, John'.

[75] M. A. Havinden (ed.), *Household and Farm Inventories in Oxfordshire, 1550–1590* (1965), 250.

[76] Court Books, Goldsmiths, Pewterers, Plumbers, Painters, and Glasiers' Company of Newcastle, 1598–1671, TWAS MS. GP2/1 (microfilm 1273/7) fo. 9^{v}, 10^{r}, 43^{v}; Newcastle Chamberlains' Accounts, 1635–9, TWAS MS. NC/F1/1/1/13, fo. 141^{r}. Probate Inventories, Consistory Court of Durham, Durham University Archives MS. DPR I/1/1636/R9/1 (1636).

Arrival at this high end of the spectrum of expertise and notoriety required the help of sundry journeymen and apprentices to do much of the 'heavy lifting' and even some of the finer work: priming panels or canvas, preparing pigments, painting backgrounds, drapery, or even more specialized elements of a portrait. Men like Jan de Critz the elder almost certainly had large workshops, which allowed them to take on a number of commissions at once, principally of portraits but also of a wide range of other work. Much of this he did for the crown in his capacity as Sergeant Painter after 1605, but he also did a great deal besides that.

In de Critz's case this sometimes meant the failure to meet deadlines for contracted work or even the prospect of shoddy work: indications of the volume of his commissions.[77] Employment in these workshops provided opportunities for journeymen who were unable to succeed as painters on their own, though some of them might simultaneously take on additional work outside their employer's shop.

However, painters like Robinson, well known locally but never amongst the elite, might well have undertaken work in such related crafts as glass painting, map-making, tomb painting, wall-painting, engraving, glazing, gilding, calligraphy, the construction and illustration of genealogical trees on vellum, and perhaps especially (as we will see at greater length in Chapter 6) the practice of arms or heraldic painting, which involved training and skills in both genealogical reconstruction and painting itself.

Particularly in the more remote areas where no guild existed to protect members from encroachment, interlopers from other crafts or unlicensed workers of any description are more likely to have been commissioned to paint. Some of their work, including images like the portraits of John and Dorothy Kaye noted earlier, extended to portraiture and especially to wall-painted portraits or tomb painting as well as decorative imagery. Some craftsmen seem even to have served as general contractors, providing a wide range of skills including painting. In Elizabethan Shrewsbury John Cley served in that manner, and he undoubtedly had his counterparts in other such communities.[78] Then as now, occupational versatility and family ties proved reliable bulwarks against hard times.

Given the same circumstances, by-employments and other sources of income *outside* the visual arts were also common amongst contemporary painters. Those who kept shops for the sale of their work may well have sold other things as well, including books, engravings, and maps. Peake's shop sold copies of Serlio's *Five Books of Architecture*, suggesting an arrangement with the printers who had produced the work to his order.[79] Some painters, especially members of the Painter-Stainers' Company of London but also some master painters in provincial centres,

[77] LMA MS. 5667/1/59; Sidney Young, *Annals of the Barber Surgeons of London* (1890), 508; Mary Edmond, 'Limners and Picture-Makers: New Light on the Lives of Miniaturists and Large-Scale Portrait Painters Working in London in the Sixteenth and Seventeenth Centuries', *Walpole Society*, 47 (1978–80), 163–70; *ODNB*, vide 'de Critz, John'; Robert Tittler, 'Three Portraits by John de Critz for the Merchant Taylors' Company', *Burlington Magazine*, 147/1228 (July 2005), 491–3.

[78] Davies, *Artisan Art*, 67, 102. John Cley's expertise extended from painting even to garden design and gardening; his business extended to his close relatives Jeffrey Cley and Jeffrey's son Humfrey.

[79] *ODNB*, vide 'Peake, Robert'.

were well enough off to earn income through rental properties. At the turn of the seventeenth century many reasonably well-established members of the Painter-Stainers' Company of London were able to leave in their wills sums of up to several hundred pounds in cash plus an entire house, often with workshop attached, and some lands in or, more often, outside of London.[80]

However, this experience also varied widely. Though provincial painters also pursued alternative careers, it is difficult to imagine that either they or their fellow craftsmen in London attained such levels of affluence. Thomas Poole, who worked for forty-two years (1600–42) as a member of the Painter-Stainers of Chester, also worked from time to time as a barber to make ends meet.[81] The London painter-stainer John Wisdom also practised medicine as an unlicensed surgeon from about 1542 to 1562.[82] While working as a painter on the coronation pageant for Anne Boleyn in 1531 the enterprising Ellis Carmanelle of London bought up Flemish paving tiles from merchants in Kilburn and sold them at a tidy profit to the royal works.[83] William Milles of Lavenham worked as both a painter and a glazier: a combination so common in some towns that they were sometimes listed as one occupation.[84] Francis Hickes worked in Worcestershire as a limner and translator.[85] Thomas Lambe worked in Yorkshire as a painter and embroiderer.[86]

Not all of these by-employments derived from economic necessity. Holbein himself held a royal licence to export beer, though it is doubtful that he had anything to do with its production.[87] But many of them were so derived. And of course, as with all guildsmen in all jurisdictions, a member of a guild did not by any means always practise the titular occupation of his fellowship, so that a nominal identification as a 'painter' might not, in some cases, mean that this was a genuine occupation. However, this was much more likely in large urban areas than in small, where painters were less likely to have a powerful guild to join, and would be more likely to be known locally by their actual occupation.

We must also consider painters' widows who kept up the shop. Then as now, and assuming they survived the rigours of childbirth, women tended to live somewhat longer than their spouses. Painters' wives were no exception, and

[80] Even by 1552, for example, John Hethe was able to leave bequests to the poor of Pinner, Middlesex, and to the universities of Oxford and Cambridge; money and a grinding stone for grinding pigments to his apprentices; money for a banquet at the Painter-Stainers' Hall; and a garden, cattle, and several tenements in and around London. TNA, PROB 11/36/91–2.

[81] Chester MSS. ZG 17/1 at 1567 and ZM AB/1/fo. 151^{v}.

[82] Margaret Pelling and Frances White (eds), *Physicians and Irregular Medical Practitioners in London, 1550–1640* (2004), 131 n. 140, and *ODNB*, vide 'Wisdom, Robert'.

[83] *Letters and Papers Foreign and Domestic of Henry VIII*, V (1880), item 952.

[84] Nesta Evans (ed.), *Wills of the Archdeaconry of Sudbury, 1636–1638* (Suffolk Record Society 35, 1993), 223. In Newcastle, for example, the painters and glaziers were listed together without any distinction between them in an amalgamated guild in which the other crafts—Goldsmiths, Pewterers, and Plumbers—were listed separately; Court Books, 'Goldsmiths, Pewterers, Plumbers, Painters and Glaziers' Company of Newcastle, 1598–1671', TWAS, MS. GP2/1 (microfilm 1273/8), fos. 4–6.

[85] *ODNB* vide 'Hickes, Francis'.

[86] Francis Collins (ed.), *Register of the Freemen of the City of York, 1559–1759* (1900), 21 and 48.

[87] Erna Auerbach, *Tudor Artists: A Study of Painters in the Royal Service and of Portraiture on Illuminated Documents from the Accession of Henry VIII to the Death of Elizabeth* (1954), 170.

painters' widows who did not remarry depended on an inheritance or family support to see them through their remaining years. Many of them inherited their husbands' stock and equipment. Some of them, as noted earlier, did try to keep the shop running, and were at least legally entitled, as freemen's widows, to do so. Seven such inheritances took place in Chester during the period at hand, and several of those widows kept the business going until their own presumed demise.[88]

But how much such widows actually knew about painting itself apart from its business side, and how much of a role they might have played in the production of paintings prior to their husband's demise, remain problematical. The assumption that a widow who inherited her husband's equipment and stock was thereby *necessarily* a painter, much less an 'artist', in her own right, cannot be sustained.[89]

Yet some widows undeniably did keep workshops going, usually, as with the Widow Dewsbury and Thomas Leigh of Chester, with the help of a journeyman or advanced apprentice. Numerous examples have been cited for London, and some have been identified in provincial centres.[90] The painters' workshop run by three generations of Hallewoods in Chester, for example, from the mid-1580s, on the part of what seem to be the brothers Nicholas, Ralph, and Richard through the career of Christopher, which extended beyond the 1650s, had a lot to do with Nicholas's widow keeping it up in the years between his death in 1629 and her own in 1638, by which time the next generation could take it over.[91]

The widow's role also appears in the tendency, recorded with particular frequency in Bristol, for painters taking on apprentices to draw up indentures listing both the master *and his wife* as the party contracting with the apprentice's parent.[92] No doubt this respected the wife's role in providing for the bed, board, and some other of the apprentice's domestic requirements. But it may also have embraced the understanding of legal responsibility for training in the workshop itself: a presumption that assumes her expertise in the craft.[93] A more explicit reference to a widow as painter comes in the patent of denization granted to the Antwerp-born Katherine Maynor [a.k.a. 'Maynour'] in November 1540 as 'Katherine Maynor, widow, painter, born at Antwerp in Brabant. Denization, Ampthill, 13 Sept. 32 Hen.

88 Widows of Edward Dewsbury, Nicholas Hallewood, William Handcock, Robert Leech, Thomas Pulford, John Thorpe, and William Welsh or Welch, none of whom are cited by their first names. Based on an analysis of Chester Record Office MS. ZG 17/1 and /2, *passim*. See also Keith Wrightson, *Earthly Necessities: Economic Lives in Early Modern Britain* (London and New Haven, 2000), 47, 63–4.

89 A recent summary of scholarship on these questions may conveniently be found in Danielle van den Heuvel and Elise van Nederveen Meerkerk, 'Partners in Business? Spousal Cooperation in Trades in Early Modern England and the Dutch Republic', *Continuity and Change*, 23/2 (2008), 209–16. See also Susan James, *The Feminine Dynamic in English Art, 1485–1603* (Farnham, Surrey, 2009), 233–42.

90 James, *Feminine Dynamic, loc. cit.*

91 Chester MS. ZG 17/1 and /2, unpaginated.

92 See, for example, Elizabeth Ralph (ed.), *Calendar of Bristol Apprenticeship Books* (Bristol Record Society, 43, 1992): John, son of Thomas Colman of Bristol, apprenticed to John Heming, *alias* Hetyghtman and his wife, Margaret, 1555 (p. 54); Richard, son of William George of Newnham, Gloucestershire, apprenticed to William Danyell, 'painter', and his wife, Katherine, 1563 (p. 111); and William, son of John Mathos of Bristol, to John Phillippes, 'painter', and Elizabeth, his wife (p. 126).

93 I. K. Ben-Amos, 'Woman Apprentices in the Trades and Crafts of Bristol', *Continuity and Change*, 6/2 (1991), 238–42.

VIII'.[94] The specification that Maynor was described as a painter as well as a widow suggests that she may have been considered a painter in her own right.

In cases where a widow kept a workshop going until a son or other relative could take it over, such successors may have apprenticed outside the family or within it. Outside the tight knit and relatively insular communities of foreign-born painters in London, where multi-generational family dynasties were particularly common,[95] the practice of painters apprenticing their sons to painters other than themselves (assuming they were apprenticed to painters at all) seems the more common option. In very small communities, there was sometimes no choice for those unwilling or financially unable to send their sons for apprenticeship elsewhere. The enormous number of painters working at any one time in London simply allowed London painters much more choice of masters for their sons. But we certainly find family dynasties, whether trained from father to son or not, established in provincial towns and cities as well. Several extended to three generations, including the Barnards of Chichester,[96] Johnsons of Canterbury,[97] and Hallewoods of Chester.[98] It follows from these examples that the likely role of widows grew with each passing generation.

Finally, though they were by no means numerous, we also know that some few women were painters, and even portrait painters, in their own right and were both recognized and employed as such. Some of them were widows; others were not. Most of them, including Katherine Maynor, Sofonisba Anguissola (1532–1625),[99] Alice Carmyan (fl. 1512–47),[100] Artemesia Gentileschi (1593–1652/3),[101] and the well-known Levina Teerlinck (1510/20–1576),[102] were foreign-born, linked to fathers or spouses who were also painters, and who enjoyed court or aristocratic patronage. But Alice Herne, wife of the Sergeant Painter William Herne (d.1580),

[94] James Gairdiner and R. H. Brodie (eds), *Letters and Papers of Henry VIII*, 16 (1898), item 305, no. 25.

[95] Mary Edmund, 'Limners and Picture-Makers: New Light on the Lives of Miniaturists and Large-Scale Portrait Painters Working in London in the Sixteenth and Seventeenth Centuries', *Walpole Society*, 47 (1978–80), 60–242; James, *Feminine Dynamic*, 232–36.

[96] Lambert Barnard (d.1567), his son Anthony (d.1619), and Anthony's son Mark (b.1581); Stewart and Cutten, *Dictionary*, 86; Witt Library, Courtauld Institute of Art, *Checklist of British Artists in the Witt Library* (1991), 12; West Sussex Record Office MSS. Ep/IV/3/1, fo. 27 and A1/1/5, 93.

[97] William Johnson (fl. 1523–52), his son John I (fl. to 1580s), and his grandson, John II (admitted freeman painter 1582); Canterbury City Archives, Account Books, CCA/FA 15, fo. 31^{v}; CCA/FA 18, fos. 102^{r} and 242^{r}; Canterbury Cathedral Archives, Bond of 1582, CCA-DCc-BB/77/102/a; J. M. Cowper, *Lives of the Deans of Canterbury* (1900), cols. 49 and 131; Waterhouse, *Dictionary*, 146.

[98] Though the precise relationships amongst them remain unclear, the Hallewoods obviously comprised an extended painter clan, active in Chester for more then half a century from *c.*1588 to after 1650. It included Richard (d.1592/3); Nicholas (who apprenticed with Thomas Pentney from 1574 and died 1629) and his wife, who carried on his workshop until her death in 1638; Ralph (fl. *c.*1588–d.1596/7); and Christopher (fl. 1619 ff. and d.post-1650).

[99] Heinz Archive, 'painters' files', vide 'Anguissola'.

[100] *ODNB*, vide 'Carmeliano, Pietro'; Auerbach, *Tudor Artists*, 157.

[101] *ODNB*, vide 'Gentileschi'; Heinz Archive, vide 'Gentileschi'.

[102] *ODNB*, vide 'Teerlinck'.

may have been a painter, as were a small handful of other women in London.[103] The King's Lynn miniaturist Margaret Clarke (fl. 1620s)[104] and the London-based court painter and copyist Joan Carlile, née Palmer (*c.*1606–79),[105] operated on their own with some considerable success, both of them anticipating the illustrious career of Mary Beale a generation later.

Especially if they were also freemen of their town or city, master artisans of this era might be seen as enjoying a golden age of independence and autonomy. They owned their own shops and the tools of their trade, they kept their own hours, and they hired journeymen and took on apprentices as they wished and as their economic circumstances allowed. Their craftsmanship earned them respect amongst their fellows and set them off from less skilled labourers. These advantages cannot but have lent dignity to their metier and social station.[106]

Yet even when provincial painters became prominent in their craft and reasonably affluent from its practice, their social status had its limits. It remained a commonplace throughout this period that all but the elite painters of the metropolis—dedicated portrait painters and/or senior liverymen of the Painter-Stainers' Company—were regarded by the 'middling' and 'better sort' of people as artisans or craftsmen, perched on the social ladder below, and often well below, the ranks of gentility.

Sir George Buck, writing in 1615, decried the fact that, although painters were once praised by ancients like Pliny, they were 'now accounted base and mechanaicall and a more mestier of an artificer and handy craftysmen'. 'No gentleman', he continued, 'or genrous and liberal person will adventure of practising this art'.[107] Knowing what we now do about, e.g., Nathaniel Bacon and others who followed Henry Peacham's recommendation that the gentleman take up painting, Buck was not entirely correct, but he was certainly expressing a common sentiment of his time. Even by 1685, in the age of the celebrated Sir Peter Lely and well after the triumphs of Rubens and Van Dyck, the writer on art and artists William Aglionby could complain that, in contrast to the Dutch, 'the World here . . . has a Notion of Painters little nobler than of Joyners or Carpenters, or of any of the Mechanick'.[108] The chief exception to this general verdict concerned heralds who painted portraits

[103] Auerbach, *Tudor Artists*, 147, and James, *Feminine Dynamic*, 239, though James, in her strenuous effort to make her case, relies on Auerbach while conveniently omitting the latter's cautionary qualifier, and dubs Herne ('Heron') not a mere painter, but actually an 'artist'.

[104] Mary Edmund, 'Bury St Edmunds, a Seventeenth Century Art Centre', *Walpole Society*, 43 for 1987 (1989), 111.

[105] *ODNB*, vide 'Carlile, Joan'.

[106] Keith Thomas, *The Ends of Life: Roads to Fulfilment in Early Modern England* (Oxford, 2009), 100.

[107] Sir George Buck, 'The Third Universite of England or a Treatise on the Foundation of all the Colleges', printed as an appendix to John Stow, *The Annales or General Chronicles of England* (1615 edn, *STC* no. 23,338), 987–8.

[108] William Aglionby, *Painting Illustrated in Three Dialogues* (1785), 23–4 and 98, as cited in Eric Jan Sluijter, 'The English Venture: Dutch and Flemish Artists in Britain 1550–1800', in Juliet Roding, Eric Jan Sluijter, Bart Westerweel, Marijke van der Meij-Tolmsa, and Eric Domela Nieuwenhuis (eds), *Dutch and Flemish Artists in Britain, 1550–1800* (Leiden, 2002), 11.

as well as arms, as many of them did. Buck noted this, too,[109] and we will see more of the herald's role both as gentlemen and as painters in an ensuing chapter.

Native-English painters had long borne the onus of being considered mere workmen. William Harrison did not name them specifically along with the 'tailors, shoemakers, carpenters, brick makers, masons, etc.' who 'have neither voice nor authority in the commonwealth, but are to be ruled and not to rule the other'.[110] Yet his contemporaries would nevertheless have placed most painters in that company. When the earl of Worcester referred to 'my paynter' as a workman,[111] he was therefore merely reflecting contemporary usage. Whomever entered the occupation, even at the highest levels, must at some time or other have wrestled with that burden. Though many must have taken pride in their own work, few thought of it as a genteel pursuit. Hilliard was certainly one who did, making an implicit plea for painters of his ilk to be considered gentlemen, and Gower another. Gower's claims to gentility have been noted earlier, his self-portrait and its eight line inscription arguing that brief.[112] Gower was exceptional amongst English painters for his gentle birth, and perhaps this allowed him the social confidence to assert this claim to gentility as a painter by such visual representation. Yet the real surprise is not that he felt obliged to make such a statement in 1579, but that he might, judging from Aglionby's verdict, still have felt the same need had he lived a century later.

As well as Sergeant Painter to Elizabeth from 1581 Gower must have earned a pretty penny for his portraits of the courtly and social elite. The combination of office, income, and gentle birth must surely have allowed him some social access to members of the court circle whose portraits he painted. Some few London-based painters of his standing could anticipate the sort of court patronage that would bring affluence and acclaim, and even, in the extreme cases of Rubens and Van Dyck, actual knighthood. Yet such hopes were never remotely in the cards for most London painters or almost any of their country cousins.

Judging by the sundry painters' wills that survive and the legatees and executors whom they name, many London Painter-Stainers left substantial estates in the early seventeenth century, but not the substantial, five-figure sums left by senior brethren of, e.g., the Merchant Taylors, Goldsmiths, or Mercers. Estates of the twenty London Painter-Stainers that were inventoried and recorded in the Court of Orphans in the late sixteenth and early seventeenth centuries, including such prominent brethren as John Gomershall, Richard Scarlett, and William Herne, averaged (before deductions for funeral expenses, debts, and so forth) £855.[113] No such comparable, single, and manageable source exists for provincial freemen

[109] Buck, 'The Third Universite', 987–8.

[110] William Harrison, *The Description of England*, ed. George Edelen (Ithaca, NY, 1968), 118. He did, however, acknowledge that men of this rank did hold local office in towns, villages, and parishes.

[111] See above, p. 60.

[112] *ODNB*, vide 'Gower, George'.

[113] City of London Court of Orphans, Common Sergeants' Book, LMA MS. CLA/002/01/001, fols. 12^{v}, 73^{r}, 88^{r}, 94^{r}, 106^{v}, 129^{v}, 169^{r}, 209^{r}, 218^{r}, 226^{r}, 272^{r}, 279^{r}, 293^{v}, 304^{v}, 307^{r}, 316^{v}, 326^{r}, 364^{r}, and 390^{v}, covering the years 1586–1613.

painters and painter-stainers. Yet scattered surviving inventories suggest that most would have left less than 10 per cent of that sum in the same period while some, as noted earlier, would have left far less.

The Holmes of Chester, Randle the elder (d.1655) and his son and namesake (d.1659), were probably as successful as painters could become without moving to London. Their additional role as deputy heralds and herald painters considerably enhanced both their status and their income. The father of Randle I, Thomas Holme, also of Chester, was a blacksmith from an otherwise well-established and sometimes minor gentry Cheshire family. Not being the eldest son, Randle would have known from an early age that his brother Thomas and not he would inherit his father's smithy. That event came to pass at the father's death in 1608. Instead, Thomas the elder apprenticed young Randle to the herald and herald painter Thomas Chaloner. Randle rapidly earned his master's confidence, and saw his apprenticeship to the end. Soon thereafter, in a remarkably fortuitous series of career-building events, he married Chaloner's widow and took on his son Jacob Chaloner as his own apprentice.[114]

That marriage must have added considerably to any start-up funds already on hand for Holme to embark upon a successful career, but it will not have launched him into what he might have enjoyed in London in the same years. Holme was able to take on a total of only seven apprentices and five journeymen over the course of a career spanning more than half a century.[115] Nevertheless, their assistance allowed him to take on time-consuming duties well beyond painting the sword rest for the Chester guildhall or patching up and gilding furnishings in his parish church: duties that included civic and guild office as well.[116] Holme's acolyte John Souch was a sufficiently prolific regional portrait painter as to have had (depending on the accuracy of modern attribution) as many as fifteen or sixteen of his portraits survive to the present. Yet he registered only three apprentices and a single journeyman in all during a career which stretched from 1617 to 1645.[117]

Still, Holme did very well for himself by substantially broadening his activities to active involvement in both Chester city and regional affairs. He served as deputy herald for several surrounding shires, as an official in his guild, as caretaker of the earl of Derby's picture collection, and eventually as Sheriff (1615–16) and Mayor

[114] *ODNB*, vide 'Holme, Randle'. Ormerod, *History of Chester*, II.456–7; Armitage and Rylands (eds), *Visitation of Cheshire*, 131–2.

[115] Apprentices included his step-son Jacob Chaloner (1601), his own sons William (1617) and Randle the younger (1617), probably his grandson Randle III (1644), the future portrait painter Edward Bellen (1624), the future engraver Daniel King (1630), and the most successful of all, the portrait painter John Souch (1607). Journeymen included Jacob de Villegrande (1598), Edward Salford (1605 and 1606), Samuel Harmer (1609), Edward Poyser (1629), and Humphrey Benet (1629 and 1630). Chester MS. ZG 17/1 and /2, (unpaginated) *passim*.

[116] C. P. Lewis and A. T. Thacker (eds), *A History of the County of Chester*, 5 vols (Woodbridge, Suffolk, 1987–2005), II, *The City of Chester*, 147 [hereafter *VCH Cheshire*]; J. P. Earwaker (ed.), 'The Four Randle Holmes of Chester, Antiquaries, Heralds, and Genealogists', *Journal of the Chester Archaeological and Historic Society*, NS 4 (1890/1), 115.

[117] Apprentices included Randle Johnson (1621 ff.), Thomas Pulford (1627 ff.), and John Sidall (1627), the last two becoming freemen painters of Chester in their turn, and the journeyman was the well-travelled Thomas Leigh the elder in 1618 and again in 1619. Chester MS. ZG 17/2, unpaginated.

(1633–4) of Chester. In addition to the various and considerable incomes that these activities would have produced, he collected rents on properties that he came to possess in and around his native city.[118] Fairly early in his career he acquired a substantial dwelling on the central thoroughfare of Bridge Street, on the corner of Castle Lane and just below St Mary-at-Hill Church. It devolved successively as the residence of at least three successive generations of the family.[119] Though no will or inventory has been found that might indicate his wealth at death, it is obvious that the family dynasty established by the elder Holme rested through the generations on much more than any combination of reproductive success and sheer dumb luck. Despite some difficulties arising from his suspected loyalties during the Civil Wars, Holme ended his exceptional life as a well-regarded member of both city and county community.

Painters seem to have held office in some other communities as well, but very rarely to the rank of mayor or sheriff, and also rarely in such larger and more complex places as Chester. Several Canterbury painters, including Robert Bettes, a relative to the Bettes dynasty of London painters, served as tax collectors for particular wards in that city over the course of the mid-sixteenth to the early seventeenth centuries.[120] That was probably a more typical level of civic engagement for a well-established, provincial freeman painter.

Aside from local office holding as a fillip to personal status, a painter's association with heraldry, as a herald painter or even an official deputy herald who painted, also proved a powerful boost to his reputation, status, and estate. This will obviously have been a factor in the reputation of the Holmes, but as we will see in a subsequent chapter, theirs was not by any means a unique case.

For the present, suffice it to say that, though the painters' occupation in London and the provincial scene had many things in common, they also remained distinct in a number of ways, some of which will have had a direct effect on the work produced by each. Like the works that they produced, we may think of their sophistication, training, and success as falling onto a broad continuum, ranging from the great court painters of the day to the small town painter-stainer whom, as now becomes clear, one might find at work almost anywhere in the realm. Amongst the distinctions that have not been discussed are those concerning differing access to materials, to formal training in contemporary fashions, and to the world view that informed the painter of each camp as he (or sometimes she) brought brush to panel. It is to these considerations which we now turn.

[118] *ODNB*, vide 'Holme, Randle'; *VCH Cheshire*, II.314; Ormerod, *History of Chester*, II.456–7; the earl of Derby to Randle Holme, 16 September 1624, Chester Record Office MS. ZM L/6/166.

[119] *ODNB*, vide 'Holme, Randle'.

[120] Canterbury City Archives MS. CCA/FA 16, fols. 49^r, 92^r, 134^{r-v}, 174^v, 175^r, 215^r, 258^r, 302^r, 345^r, 385^r, 424^r, etc.; CCA/FA 17, 18, and 19, *passim*.

5

Painters' Resources: Material and Cultural

Part of a painter's ability to pass on the trade to the next generation included the opportunity to bequeath essential equipment and materials to successors. The fact that such bequests appear so often in painters' wills affirms their value and the need to keep them in the family or at least in the hands of apprentices and journeymen of a particular workshop. Given the frequently greater difficulty of acquiring preferred materials in provincial England than in London or few of the larger urban places, the value of such bequests generally existed in something of an inverse proportion to one's access to such centres. Even if one had the good fortune to inherit some of the tools of the trade, painters working further afield had often to make do with a more limited range of pigments, brushes, panels or canvasses, pattern books, and other essential supplies that were more readily, and less expensively, on hand in London.

Instruction in the use and even the manufacture of some of those materials will also have depended considerably on one's proximity to the workshops of the more sophisticated and cosmopolitan painters of the day. Those same workshops, especially in London, will likely have exposed the apprentice painter to a richer decorative vocabulary and a more cosmopolitan cultural environment than could be experienced anywhere else in the realm. In consequence, some of the more affluent and ambitious parents apprenticed their offspring to masters of London workshops for their training. Other apprentices, as we've seen in the previous chapter, remained closer to home and gained what they could from the inevitably narrower and more traditional range of instruction and cultural outlook. A closer look at the tools and materials of the trade, and of the educational opportunities available to those who aspired to paint, reveals further contrasts between at least the extremes of the polite versus vernacular continuum.

One of the few technical advances in easel painting in this era consisted of the transition from the virtually exclusive use of wood panel, especially oak, to the increasingly frequent use of fine canvas. Both materials came in a wide range of qualities, and a similarly wide range of access and cost, all of which placed the more affluent and London-based painter at an additional advantage in obtaining the most appropriate materials for his work.

The best oak came from the eastern Baltic, where trees grew more closely together, trunks shot straight up in the competition for sunlight, and the grain grew naturally straighter and more even. Long planks of such wood would then be exported, often through Danzig, to Dutch workshops or even directly to London.

In either venue, panels would be cut from those planks, riven (rather than sawn) along the grain, smoothened, and then primed with one or another combination of chalk and animal-hide glue before being sent on. By 1617 the city of Antwerp issued complex regulations governing the control and inspection of that manufacture, ensuring that Antwerp panels remained the very best of their time.[1] Whether from London directly or from Antwerp through London, some such panels went on to east coast ports like Hull and Newcastle, Ipswich and King's Lynn.[2]

Recent dendrochronological research on panel paintings done by mostly foreign-born or -trained painters for the court circle or upper landed elites has now shown that many panels may have remained for tens or even scores of years before they were painted. These findings also suggest that the elite painters of the day could choose their panels, probably acquired from specialist, London-based, timber-sellers, with care.[3] While factors of cost have effectively prohibited similar testing on many provincially painted panels, it is unlikely that they would as often been similarly aged or expertly prepared. Provincial workshops or individual craftsmen would less commonly have had the luxury of local timber specialists from whom to acquire such materials, the clientele willing to pay for the extra cost, or the steady demand for portraits, amongst other sorts of work, as were available to their London counterparts.

In addition, and with the exception of those working in or near London and the greater east coast ports, the provincial painter would likely have had less access to the finer Baltic oak, having mostly to make do with the less even-grained English oak or even other, less suitable woods. The difference proved significant to the technical quality of the painting. Well-primed oak in general allows finer and more controlled work, and probably served better for depicting such contemporary fashions as the finely detailed lace work on collars of the late sixteenth and early seventeenth centuries. The straighter and more even grain of Baltic oak allowed the finest surface preparation, resulting in a smoother surface and better adhesion of sizing, ground, and paint to the panel.

The structural treatment of the panels to be painted also mattered in the appearance and durability of the finished product. Most portraits of any size were painted on two or three joined panels fixed vertically together. Such an arrangement allowed each piece to stabilize its neighbour, so as to reduce the chances of a single,

[1] Jo Kirby, 'The Painter's Trade in the Seventeenth Century: Theory and Practice', *National Gallery Technical Bulletin*, 20 (1999), 17–22; Ian Tyers, 'On Panel Making and the Later Holbein Panels', talk presented at the National Portrait Gallery Workshop, 'After Holbein and Beyond: Techniques, Practices and Findings', National Portrait Gallery, 5 December 2008. I am grateful to Ian Tyers for explaining to me the preparation of oak panels.

[2] Kirby, 'The Painters' Trade', 17–19; Ralph Davies, *The Trade and Shipping of Hull, 1500–1700* (Yorkshire Local History Society, 17, 1964), 11 and 15; Henry Zins, *England and the Baltic in the Elizabethan Era* (Manchester, 1972), 239–46 and esp. 242.

[3] In exceptional cases the time between the felling of a tree and the painting of a portrait on its wood could be as long as 60 years, as was the case with the portrait of baron Berbers, *c.*1520–6 (NPG no. 4953), painted on a panel dating to 1460. This research has been carried out as part of the 'Making Art in Tudor Britain' project directed at the NPG by Dr Tarnya Cooper. I am greatly indebted to her, to Sophie Plender, and Ian Tyers, for enhancing my understanding of these issues and for allowing me to cite this data.

large panel, warping. Joining could be done by carefully drilling holes at the same point in the facing edges of adjacent panels, inserting dowels in each hole, and glueing the edges of the two panels together once joined by those dowels. The resulting joined panel could then be beveled around the edges to fit snugly into a frame, while a wooden cradle ran along the back from side to side and/or top to bottom so as to hold the joined panel in place. Panels could also be glued together without dowels and held firmly in a well-cut frame and cradle. Smaller paintings required but a single panel, and occasionally a single piece of wood sufficed for both painting surface and frame, so that no such additional structures were required.

The skill with which these several techniques were employed could well determine the physical stability of the final painting. Like all woods, oak lives a life of its own: a naturally open-grained wood, it readily expands, contracts, and warps according to humidity and temperature and the nature of the grain. If cradles or frames are too rigid or restricting, they can work against this natural movement, often causing the wood to warp or split, and the paint (which does not always move in the same ways or to the same extent) to flake off as the surface shifts beneath it.[4] In consequence of all these concerns, well-prepared panels were hard to come by and often reused, and the appearance of under-drawings or previous paintings can readily be seen by the use of infrared reflectophotography.

A cradle of supports could presumably be constructed by any good local carpenter or joiner. At least until they became more intricate and ornately carved in the early seventeenth century, the same could be said of frames. But successful panel-making and preparation required distinctive and particular skills. London certainly hosted at least a few specialist frame-makers by the mid-sixteenth century if not before, and presumably panel-makers as well. In provincial towns the work could be done by carvers and joiners.[5] But it is doubtful that most provincial towns hosted those skilled in the preparation of panel surfaces for fine painting. The poor preparation of all these components undoubtedly accounts for the lower survival rate of paintings that are recorded archivally, or the poorer condition of those that have survived.

'Canvas' is a generic term for a variety of linen-based materials of various weights and weaves, ranging in its use from sail-cloth to painters' 'canvases'. Linen weaving was a major industry in sixteenth-century England, practised by native-English guildsmen and foreign settlers alike, the latter especially in towns like Sandwich, Southampton, Norwich, and London. In addition, a great deal continued to be imported and sold, especially by mercers, throughout the era at hand. Its use as a painting surface allowed a much looser and freer working of pigments with the

[4] An excellent example of an over-rigid support restricting the movement of a panel causing the paint to flake may be observed in the portrait of John and Joan Cooke in the Gloucester City Museum.

[5] One Ewens, a 'carver, gilder and pictureframe-maker' of East Taunton, Somerset (hardly a metropolis), is listed in a deed of 1618. 'Pearson the joiner', probably of Bristol, made frames for several pictures for Thomas Smyth's new seat at Ashton Court, Bristol, in 1633. Somerset Record Office, Creech St Michael and Rushton deeds, MS. DD/GC/6; J. H. Bettey (ed.), *Calendar of the Correspondence of the Smyth Family of Ashton Court, 1548–1642* (Bristol Record Society, 35, 1982), 192.

brush, though it was not always quite as useful for the fine detail that often characterized Tudor or early Stuart era paintings.[6]

The transition to its use cannot have been as dramatic, sudden, or late as has sometimes been assumed.[7] Linen canvas had been widely used in England for cloth banners, including portrait banners, well before it came into wider use in easel portraits in the latter decades of the sixteenth century. It had been widely employed in northern Europe by the 1520s, and was therefore a familiar surface to the foreign painters who came to England. Both Holbein and the prolific Chichester painter Lambert Barnard used it in England in the 1520s and 1530s.[8]

Canvas bore many practical advantages over oak. It required but stretching and simple sizing with a hide-based glue, processes that many painters could undertake themselves. Its lighter weight allowed it to be easily rolled up and transported. It came in a much wider variety of textures and sizes, and could provide the painter with much larger surfaces without the risks, costs, and skills required in the process of joining wood panels. The potential for larger surfaces facilitated the much larger paintings that came into fashion by the end of the sixteenth century. Properly primed canvas might tear or puncture with improper handling, but it did not warp, split, or shrink and it required little or no cradling to support it.[9]

Given that the principle exponents for painting on canvas were foreigners, and that most foreign painters settled in London, the use of canvas in easel painting came later to provincial painters in general than to their London counterparts. (In this as in several other respects, Barnard's work in Sussex proved an exception to the rule, though he may well have been foreign-trained.) Foreign-trained painters in London will likely have retained sources in their homelands for acquiring good canvas, affording easier access to it. All these factors will have had an obvious significance for the quality and refinement of the finished work. They mark one more distinction in the production of portraiture between metropolitan and provincial England.

Brushes were also critical tools to which access and quality may well have varied with locale. Broad and coarse brushes of pig bristles were employed to apply grounds and primers to the raw and/or rough surfaces and for painting backgrounds and other large, flat surface areas.[10] Other brushes will have had to span a broad range of fineness and quality. Brushes of a meaner sort could be and undoubtedly were made locally, even by painters themselves. But the finer quality brushes were traditionally imported from abroad. In places like Augsburg and

[6] Kirby, 'The Painters' Trade', 17. I am grateful to Jo Kirby for her further explanation of this issue.

[7] See letters by Katherine Duncan-Jones in *TLS* of 17 March and 7 April 2006, and responses in the 'Letters' page of the same publication by Tarnya Cooper, 31 March 2006, and myself, 3 May 2006.

[8] Susan Foister, *Holbein and England* (New Haven and London, 2004) 41, and, for Barnard, see esp. the 'Heroines of Antiquity' series now at Pallant House Gallery in West Sussex, done *c.*1526 in oil and tempura on canvas. Anon., *Oil Paintings in Public Ownership in West Sussex* (2005), 14 and 16.

[9] Maria Hayward, 'The London Linen Trade 1589–1641, and the Use of Linen by Painters in the Royal Service', in Jo Kirby, Susie Nash, and Joanna Cannon (eds.), *Trade in Artists' Materials: Markets and Commerce in Europe to 1700* (2010), 375–85.

[10] John Chenevix Trench, 'John Abbott's Manual of Limming (sic)', *Association for Studies in the Conservation of Historic Buildings, Transactions*, 2 (1986), 21.

Antwerp the craft became so specialized by the latter decades of the sixteenth century as to allow for distinctions to be made between those who made the coarser, bristle brushes and the finer 'pencil' brushes.[11]

When brush-making became a dedicated occupation in England, it also became a prime candidate for royal patents of monopoly. Such patents became sources of parliamentary concern in 1621 and 1624, but some of them had been hotly opposed even in Elizabeth's reign. In 1601 the Queen bowed to those pressures and removed monopolies on a number of items including brushes.[12] By the 1620s their manufacture seems to have become a full-time occupation for at least a small number of London craftsmen, perhaps an offshoot of the painter's trade itself. A 'Mr Smyth, brushmaker' and member of the Painter-Stainers' Company of London, was well enough established in his craft to take on Thomas Eggllfeyld as his apprentice in August of 1630.[13]

However, notwithstanding these milestones in the history of English brush-making, many painters continued to make their own brushes: both the coarser bristle brushes and the finer 'pencils' made with the tail hairs of squirrel, sable, or fitch and fixed in the quill of a duck, goose, or other large bird.[14] Only such finer brushes permitted the more delicate and refined work we see in the more subtly blended flesh tones or in the intricate workings of, e.g., lace collars which came into fashion in the late sixteenth and early seventeenth centuries. They therefore became essential for the very most skilful painters, who also relied on them both to draw thin and delicate outlines and to build up the subtly toned contours of flesh, fabric, and shadow that characterized their work. Some of the brush-strokes used in outlining in Holbein's work, or in Cornelius Johnson's, may only be seen with the aid of a low-powered microscope and seem to have been produced with brushes of a very few fine hairs. To the naked eye facial contours in these works produce a tonal shading of colour and shadow with no obvious outline at all.[15]

Most native-English painters relied more heavily on more prominent outlines 'pencilled' or drawn onto the primed surface, and not necessarily made with a brush. Instead, some employed a black lead or a sharpened piece of coal or charcoal, all of which were widely and readily obtainable.[16] They would then fill in the

[11] Roland Krischel, 'The Inventory of the Venetian *Vendecolori* Jacopo de' Benedetti: The Non-Pigment Materials', in Kirby *et al.* (eds), *Trade in Artists' Materials*, 53–66; Ursula Haller, 'The Purchase and Distribution Book of Wolk Pronner (1586–1590)', in Kirby *et al.* (eds), *Trade in Artists' Materials*, 332.

[12] Joan Thirsk, *Economic Policy and Projects: The Development of a Consumer Society in Early Modern England* (Oxford, 1978), Chs. 2 and 3 and esp. 98 and 182.

[13] LMA MS. 5667/1/55.

[14] Kirby, 'The Painter's Trade', 15–16.

[15] As demonstrated in a paper entitled 'Holbein's Drawing Processes' by Victoria Button at the National Portrait Gallery Research Workshop on 'English Portraiture: Holbein and Beyond', 5 December 2008. Use of both delicate and heavier handed outlining has been innovatively explored by the technical analysis of Tudor paintings by the 'Making Art in Tudor Britain' project at the National Portrait Gallery.

[16] See, e.g., the description of John Abbott which, though produced a generation after our period of interest, described a time-worn technique: 'John Abbott's Manual', 22.

colours as best they could, often leaving outlines that remain clearly visible to the naked eye.

The question of accessibility applied as well to pigments, and thus to the potential range of colours that a painter might employ. Over the European continent as a whole, cities like Venice and Antwerp continued to offer the greatest range and quality of dyestuffs and pigments. They served as centres of manufacture and distribution for a hinterland extending to other large cities throughout much of Europe. London served in similar capacities for the rest of England.

Some pigments and other painters' supplies came to provincial ports directly from the Continent as they had long done. But the predominance of London over other ports became so considerable by the late sixteenth century, and so many of the provincial ports along the south and southeast coast had silted up by that time, that London came to dominate England's import trade to an unprecedented extent.[17] Once manufactured in or imported through London, pigments could be trans-shipped coastally or by road to other English destinations. These shipments cannot be traced, as such trade crossed no customs barriers and required no record-keeping. But the infrequency with which pigments and other painting supplies turn up as foreign imports in the records of provincial ports suggests that London must have been the port of entry for most of those not manufactured there to begin with. A methodical survey of all the recorded customs accounts from *c.*1520 to 1565, and of their bureaucratic successor, the port books, from 1565 to the 1630s, for the south coast ports of Lyme Regis, Plymouth, Poole, Southampton, and Weymouth, turn up only three such shipments: red ochre from Malaga to Poole in 1618/19, turpentine from London to Poole in 1618/19, and varnish from London to Lyme Regis in 1604.[18] This evidence pales by comparison with what came through London in the same years.[19]

Shipping records of east coast ports, albeit more proximate to Dutch sources of supply, yield little more. Single shipments of a few barrels each of white lead and yellow ochre came in through Boston in the first four decades of the seventeenth century. Small shipments of cochineal, that most costly dyestuff from which carmine and (from about 1640) scarlet were made, derived from crushed insects, are recorded as being brought into Ipswich from France, though that well-travelled cargo will have originated in South America via Spain.[20] Lapis lazuli, the brilliant

[17] Lawrence Stone, 'Elizabethan Overseas Trade', *Economic History Review*, NS 2/1 (1949), 39; Brian Dietz, *The Port and Trade of Elizabethan London* (London Record Society, 8, 1972), Introduction.

[18] This comprehensive survey has been carried out by the author in 1982/3 but never published. References to these shipments are as follows: TNA, E.190/872/3; E.190/872/4; E.122/207/8; and E.190/869/1. Ochres were both mined locally in several areas of England and also imported from abroad; Jo Kirby, 'Trade in Painters' Materials in Sixteenth Century London', in Kirby *et al.* (eds), *Trade in Artists' Materials*, 342. The reference to 'chromae' is intriguing. Jo Kirby has indicated in personal correspondence that its use as a pigment was unknown in England before *c.*1800.

[19] Kirby, 'Trade in Painters' Materials', 342–9.

[20] T. S. Willan, *Studies in Elizabethan Foreign Trade* (Manchester, 1959), 70, 74–5, 77 and 81; R. W. K. Hinton (ed.), *The Port Books of Boston, 1601–1640* (Lincolnshire Record Society, 50, 1956), 229, 235 and 243.

blue mineral that served as the base for the equally costly ultramarine, also came from abroad, often from present-day Afghanistan.

In contrast to what has conventionally been assumed, and at least through the early decades of the seventeenth century, the inventories of many, perhaps most, provincial apothecaries and grocers yield no such pigments at all or very few and of the most common sort.[21] One could have obtained a fair sampling of the less exotic pigments in one of the half-dozen or so larger and more sophisticated provincial centres from the early Stuart years. But even then the range of stocked pigments could rarely have been as wide as those available in London.

Thomas Bowes of Newcastle, the biggest and most commercially important centre of the north-east, had what must have been for the times an enormous stock of general goods, much of it no doubt imported coastally from London or by sea directly to Newcastle from abroad. But of pigments and other painters' supplies, he held at his death in 1593 only two pounds of red lead, a hundred weight of ochre—both amongst the commonest and least expensive of all pigments—and half a barrel of turpentine: hardly a full range of supplies.[22] More than a generation later the extensive stock of the Stockport apothecary William Simkin included at his death 'gumes' of various sorts (including gum arabic, widely used in watercolour), fourteen ounces of verdigris, a quart of linseed oil, and sixteen pounds of white lead.[23] And the 1633 inventory of the Chester apothecary Robert Blease similarly held a few pigments and other painters' supplies, though nothing like a full range.[24] These examples are even more striking when it is considered that both Newcastle and Chester, if not necessarily Stockport, served as major regional centres for painting in these years. Painters in both operated within formal, amalgamated guilds; their numbers allowed them considerable influence in the local government and economy.

Few as they may be, the painting supplies stocked by these provincial merchants, all three of whom seem to have been the largest stockists of their region at the time of their death, are probably typical for the times. Vermilion, saffron, ceruse, the difficult-to-use (and poisonous) orpiment, ultramarine, azurite (also known as 'bice'), and cochineal-derived red lake, much less gold and silver leaf, were simply not as readily available outside London and the larger centres. As goods traded in small quantities and often from quite distant sources, many were also extremely costly.[25]

[21] The role of London grocers and apothecaries in the trade of painters' supplies is treated in Kirby, 'Trade in Painters' Materials', esp. 339–41.

[22] Anon., *Wills and Inventories from the Registry at Durham*, part II (Surtees Society, 38, 1860), 237.

[23] C. S. Phillips and J. H. Smith (eds.), *Stockport Probate Records, 1620–1650* (Record Society of Lancashire and Cheshire, 131, 1992), 180–1.

[24] Inventory post-mortem of Robert Blease, 1633, Cheshire Record Office MS. 1633 Blease.

[25] Jo Kirby, 'Fading and Colour Changes of Prussian Blue: Occurrences and Early Reports', *National Gallery Technical Bulletion*, 14 (1993), 63; Jo Kirby and Raymond White, 'The Identification of Red Lake Pigment Dyestuffs and a Discussion of Their Use', *National Gallery Technical Bulletin*, 17 (1996), 66; National Art Library MS. 86.EE.69, fo. 35^{r}; Ann Rosalind Jones and Peter Stallybrass, *Renaissance Clothing and the Materials of Memory* (Cambridge, 2000), 43–5.

In consequence of all these factors, one would have had to deal with a number of such provincial merchants in order to obtain a full range of colours, to have sent or gone to London to obtain them, or—in a few cases where raw materials could be found locally—manufactured them from scratch. The same conditions applied to the sundry other supplies, including, e.g., linseed or 'painters' oil, primed oak panels and linen canvas, and various gums and glues. Provincial retailers could thus have acquired much of their stock on buying trips to London, adjusting their prices to reflect the costs of transport.[26] Visiting merchants might have purchased their supplies at wholesale directly from a merchant-importer. They were more likely to have done so from a London apothecary or other retailer as if they were drugs or dyes or, in some cases by around 1600, from a specialist pigment-maker.

And, of course, many painters made their own purchasing trips to London when their commissions required them to do so, circumventing the local retailer altogether. Some patrons even paid the painter extra for his pigments and for the expense of going to London to obtain them when they couldn't be obtained locally. This was certainly true for many of those working within the Home Counties. In providing pigments for his painters at Dulwich and London in the late 1610s, for example, Edward Alleyn, who came and went between Dulwich and London almost every week during that time, paid a penny an ounce each for umber and for lamp-black, tuppence an ounce for a quart for 'pink', four pence an ounce for masticot, and five pence for two pounds of red lead. He also paid 1s. 8d for an ounce of vermilion and 14s. for seven small leaves of gold.[27] It will also have been the case for painters situated further afield. Philip Cornish ('Cornish the paynter'), working at Wulf Hall in Wiltshire in 1539, received from the household coffers 31s. 8d for 'divers colours by him bought . . . and for his cost in being sent to London for the same colours'.[28]

Of course not all provincial painters could or did go or send to London for their paints. Cornish, after all, was the household painter of Edward Seymour, earl of Hertford and later Protector Somerset, and was helping on that occasion to prepare for the wedding at Wulf Hall of Henry VIII to Jane Seymour. Other, less enterprising or affluent provincial painters, and those commissioned by patrons of a less affluent or discerning stripe, will have found such trips too difficult and costly to be undertaken regularly. A great many of them will not, as we have seen, have been full-time portrait painters to begin with. They will not have found it economically viable to keep a wide range of pigments on hand from earlier or occasional forays to the metropolis. When a portrait commission came along, they

[26] Shipments of 'painters' oil' invariably came from Antwerp in the early Elizabethan period, though it is not clear how well this trade held up after the outbreak of the Dutch revolt and the Spanish sack of that city in 1576. Brian Dietz (ed.), *The Port and Trade of Early Elizabethan London* (London Record Society, 8, 1972) items 18, 154, 210, 309, 465.

[27] Edward Alleyn's Diary and Account Book, Dulwich College Library MS. IX, fos. 8^{v}, 10^{r}, and 15^{r}.

[28] Cited from an unidentified manuscript account book of Edward Seymour, earl of Hertford, in Rev. Canon J. E. Jackson, 'Wulfhall and the Seymours', *Wiltshire Archaeological and Natural History Magazine*, 15 (1875), 145.

will have tended to make do with whatever pigments they could acquire locally, frequently resorting to less costly choices and inferior quality materials. For other painters, even some of those based in London, many pigments simply lay out of their financial reach. Nicholas Hilliard tells the cautionary tale of John Bossam,

> whose work in that kind are comparable with the best whatsoever . . . whoe being very poore, and belyke wanting to buy faier cullors, wrought therefore for the most part in whit and black.[29]

In general, the wide variety of materials available in London made for an equally wide range of quality and cost: two essential components in the commissioning and painting of a portrait. The most skilful painters of the age knew this all too well. As we see in Hilliard's and other technical treatises of the era, they chose their pigments with consummate care and took great pains to master the often complex techniques of mixing, blending, and applying them. Such complex procedures as were required in the preparations of some pigments were far less likely to be passed down from master to apprentice in the traditional provincial workshop than exchanged in such treatises, many of them in manuscript form, which circulated amongst the more sophisticated patrons and painters.[30] These factors undoubtedly added to the distinctions between the type and technical quality of paintings produced by the more affluent and elite painters working in or around London (not to mention their foreign-trained neighbours), and those less sophisticated or affluent painters typically working there or elsewhere. The former will have been able to construct their palette from a much wider range of colour and quality, and to blend and employ them in more complex ways, than their country cousins or even some of their poorer London neighbours like Bossam.[31]

The question of what pigments were used in particular paintings and in particular provincial locales will long remain difficult and expensive to determine with any technical precision. Thus far technical analysis of particular paintings from this era has been carried out almost exclusively by major national institutions like the National Gallery, the National Portrait Gallery, Tate Britain, and the Courtauld, mostly using works in their own collections for their samples. Almost none of it has been done on the myriad vernacular paintings typical of provincial portraiture at this time. Yet a visual inspection of such works and a consideration of written evidence nevertheless yields a number of observations about choices of pigments and colours.

[29] *Nicholas Hilliard's Arte of Limning*, transcr. A. F. Kinney, ed. Linda Bradley Salamon (Boston, MA, 1983), 18.

[30] Jo Kirby traces the circulation of such manuscript treatises amongst a circle including the court intellectual Theodore de Mayerne, the herald and painter Edward Norgate, the country gentleman and skilled painter Sir Nathaniel Bacon, and the fashionable, London-based limners Peter and Isaac Oliver: Jo Kirby, 'Sir Nathaniel Bacon's "Pinke"', *Dyes in History and Archaeology*, 19 (2003), 38–40; Edward Norgate, *Miniatura of the Art of Limning*, ed. Jeffrey M. Muller and Jim Murrell (London and New Haven, 1997), 256–7; BL. Harleian MS. 6376.

[31] My thanks to Klaas Jan van den Berg of the Conservation Institute of the Netherlands for clarifying this point for me.

Blacks and whites were indeed extremely common, especially in backgrounds and in depictions of clothing. They remained so as much for the inexpensive pigments that could be used to produce them by painters like Hilliard's friend Bossam as for the dictates of contemporary fashion. Though blacks could be produced from a wide range of pigments and combinations, some of them quite costly, they could also be obtained inexpensively from such ubiquitous sources as charred and powdered wood or lamp-black. The impressively large number of contemporary portraits, especially of males, that show their sitter in black dress may have reflected contemporary fashion. As we'll see in Chapter 7, the more expensive sources of black also characterized the much-prized, Flemish dyed clothes preferred by wealthy merchants of the Tudor era. But at the more provincial and less affluent end of the scale, it may have simply reflected the ubiquitous availability and low cost of some of the pigments that produced that colour. The same may be said for some whites, which could be made if necessary from a simple chalk base.

Given the knowledge of how to process them, provincial painters could often turn to other locally available raw materials as sources of pigments. Amongst the plant-based sources was the pigment range of yellow lakes known as 'pinke', which could be made from plants known as 'dyers' broom', and weld or, more commonly in the seventeenth century, unripened berries of the buckthorn. It was widely used by painters of all levels of skill and sophistication, from Van Dyck and Rubens on down to the local painter-stainer. But like most locally available, plant-based dyestuffs, it was not especially stable, fading or changing colour over time.[32] Verdigris, easily made from copper plates and vinegar, yellow pigments like yellow lake and 'masticot', and red lakes were also manufactured in certain areas. In his *Description of England*, William Harrison noted that both red and yellow orpiment were common, though both were arsenic based and therefore highly poisonous.[33] Earth-based pigments like the ochres, especially including browns, oranges, reds, and yellows, were also locally available in areas like Gloucestershire. Easily and cheaply prepared, they were used in the local and regional vernacular of their indigenous areas.[34]

Some of these pigments were commonly utilized at all levels of painting. But others had qualities that ruled out their use as pigments of first choice for those who could obtain better and/or more expensive ones. Many, especially those derived from plants, were inherently unstable, fading in their intensity or changing colour over time. Blues, associated symbolically with affluence and conspicuous display, had often to be comprised of the inexpensive and widely available but also unstable and impermanent smalt, or of the relatively inexpensive blue verditer or indigo,

32 Kirby, 'Sir Nathaniel Bacon's "Pinke"', 37–42.

33 William Harrison, *The Description of England* (1577, 1587), in *Holinshed Chronicle*, I (1877), III.x.

34 Andrea Kirkham, 'Pattern and Colour in Late 16th and 17th Century Wall and Panel Paintings in Suffolk', in Robert Gowring and Robin Pender (eds), *All Manner of Murals: The History, Techniques, and Conservation of Secular Wall Paintings* (2007), 34–6; National Art Library MS. 86.EE.69, fol. 35^{r}; Kathryn Davies, *Artisan Art, Vernacular Wall Paintings in the Welsh Marches, 1550–1650* (Almeley, Herefordshire, 2008), 61–4.

rather than of such much more costly but also more reliable alternatives such as ultramarine, made from lapis lazuli, or azurite.[35]

Because the raw materials for many pigments will also have occurred locally in some areas but not others, regionally specific palettes may sometimes be observed. This has been demonstrated with respect to wall paintings, whose greater survival rate makes for more confident conclusions than for easel portraits.[36] But it does seem likely to apply in some provincial areas to panel paintings as well. The prevalence of red and yellow ochres in the locally produced portraits of the twelve benefactors of Gloucester, for example, must reflect the local availability of such raw materials. Ochres are quarried in Gloucestershire even to the present day.

Whatever the relative availability of particular pigments, painters in both provincial and metropolitan England ground or otherwise produced some of their own colours. The London Painter Stainer John Hethe left grinding stones ('mullers') to his apprentices in 1552 for that purpose. His fellow Painter-Stainer Harry Blankstone (d. *c.*1540) left a quantity of colours already ground and also mullers and other supplies to his son-in-law to-be.[37] Richard Flint left a grinding stone to the young painter John Kimby, along with brushes and patterns, in 1572.[38] Their provincial counterparts also left grinding equipment for making colours. The widow Alice Gammedge of Walden, Essex, passed on in 1591 the grinding stones and other painters' supplies that her husband had left to her.[39] The Norwich painters Richard Edmonds (in 1611–12) and John Cock (in 1613–14) both passed on grinding stones at their deaths.[40] And at his death in 1636 the Newcastle herald-painter William Robinson left an estate worth but £10 1s. 10d, but it included '2 stones & povells for grinding colours' worth 2s.[41] Such bequests seem virtually ubiquitous for the age.

Early in this same era, however, some, mostly London-based, painters came to manufacture certain pigments as a by-employment of its own, selling them to others in London and, eventually, at wholesale to merchants there and elsewhere. The prominent Painter-Stainer Andrew Wright had come by his death in 1541 to produce 'pink' by the barrelful for wholesale and retail sale, and he seems to have specialized in this to the exclusion of other colours.[42] The manufacture of smalt

[35] Rica Jones, 'The Methods and Materials of Three Tudor Artists: Bettes, Hilliard and Ketel', in Karen Hearn (ed.), *Dynasties: Painting in Tudor and Jacobean England, 1530–1630* (1995), 235; Kirkham, 'Pattern and Colour', 33 and 40; Kirby, 'The Painter's Trade', 36.

[36] Kirby, 'The Painter's Trade', 30; Kirkham, 'Pattern and Colour', 34–6; Davies, *Artisan Art*, 61–6. I am grateful to Jo Kirby for suggesting the latter two studies, and to Kathryn Davies for discussing her work with me.

[37] TNA, PROB 11/29/160 and PROB 11/28/290.

[38] *Wills and Inventories in the Commissary Court of London*, LMA, microfilm no. 9051/4/11.

[39] Susan James, *The Feminine Dynamic in English Art, 1485–1603* (Farnham, Surrey, 2009), 47.

[40] Norwich and Norfolk Record Office MSS. DN/INV24/170 and DN/INV26/87.

[41] I am grateful to Professor Keith Wrightson for this reference, to be found in the Durham University Library, Special Collections, MS. DPR I/1/1636/1-2. 'Povells' were the stone surfaces on which pigments were placed to be ground by the hand-held mullers.

[42] TNA, PROB 11/36/91-2; PROB 11/29/160.

came to be monopolized in 1605 for potential distribution to anyone who would buy it.[43]

By 1640 the production of some common pigments had become even more highly commercialized. Some such productions were carried on outside the metropolis and proximate to the raw materials involved. Though the outcome of the bequest remains unknown, the London Painter-Stainer Jeremy Crew left a hundred pounds in his will of 1637 to employ poverty-stricken members of that company in a veritable factory for the manufacture of painters' colours.[44] In 1626 the crown granted by letters patent a monopoly on the production of red and burnt brown ochre in the Forest of Dean.[45]

In sum, given the costs and difficulties of technical, scientific analysis of the pigments employed in the provincial paintings of this era, much of what we know has had to be based on visual inspection and a close reading of the recipe books and treatises that circulated, mostly in manuscript, and mostly amongst people who travelled in courtly or culturally sophisticated circles. One such treatise, unpublished in its time but copied several times over, has been traced within a circle including the polymath Thomas de Mayerne, the herald and painter Edward Norgate, the amateur painter and country gentlemen Sir Nathaniel Bacon, and the painters Isaac and Peter Oliver in the early seventeenth century.[46] Such circulation seems likely to have been reasonably common amongst men of that social and intellectual milieu.

Even if archivally rather than technically based, this closer investigation brings into serious question some standing assumptions. The conclusion that even in Holbein's time 'similar pigments and [painters'] materials were available in England to those used in the rest of Northern Europe'[47] may have applied to London and to the more elite, sophisticated, and affluent clientele of the age. It cannot, on the other hand, be taken as an accurate assessment of what was accessible over most of the rest of England, and to myriad non-elite patrons and painters, at that time or for some time thereafter.

Of course even ready access to the full range of pigments and other materials that might have been available to the London-based painter did not ensure production of refined work. The knowledge of what to do with those pigments and materials, and the training and experience that imparted that knowledge, made all the difference. And obvious as it may seem, training at the highest levels of expertise and sophistication, that which drew confidently on the decorative vocabulary and sophisticated techniques then current across most of western continental Europe,

[43] Kirby, 'The Painter's Trade', 31; Nicola Costaras, 'Early Modern Blues: The Smalt Patent in Context', in Kirby *et al.* (eds), *Trade in Artists' Materials*, 401–14; R. D. Harley, *Artists' Pigments c. 1600–1835: A Study in English Documentary Sources*, 2nd edn (1982), 197–201.

[44] TNA, E.214/365; TNA, PROB 11/174/fos. 423–4.

[45] Kirby, 'The Painter's Trade', 31. I am grateful to Nigel Cox, Curator of the Gloucester Folk Museum, for this information.

[46] Kirby, 'Sir Nathaniel Bacon's "Pink"', 38–40.

[47] Susan Foister, *Holbein in England* (2006), 14.

was but rarely available in England outside the workshops of the foreign-born or -trained painter or the most experienced and well-travelled native-born painter, almost all of whom maintained their workshops in the London metropolis.

Many of the foreign-born and/or -trained painters who flocked to England will have had extensive experience in, and exposure to, that continental visual culture in which the practice of painting had become a quasi-academic discipline of the liberal arts, governed by certain widely taught theories and principles, exemplified by widely circulated models, and inspired especially by classical examples. Many such painters enjoyed at least some foundation in the theoretical writings, inspired by the likes of Euclid and Vitruvius and articulated by humanist writers like Leon Battista Alberti and Leonardo Bruni in the fifteenth century and many others in the sixteenth. Those theoretical works will not only have pertained to painting, but also to visual media running the gamut from architecture, medals, and sculpture to such academic subjects as geometry and even to ideas about optics and the nature of vision itself.

Painters at that level of accomplishment often belonged to the transnational and virtual fraternity of virtuosi who moved from country to country and court to court as equally sophisticated and very well-heeled patrons vied for their services. Many of them must be counted as intellectuals in their own right, commanding a cultural breadth and depth that left almost all native-English and especially provincial craftsman in their dust. Their production mightily challenged and often overwhelmed the sundry provincial vernaculars of continental Europe, driving them out of fashion and compelling their makers to keep up or give way.

Only a very few native-born painters, virtually all of them working in London and most of them having trained or travelled abroad, had the opportunity to taste of these waters. In consequence, and despite such efforts to keep up as were exemplified by, e.g., the circulation of various pattern books and writings, by the 'album' of foreign prints and drawings collected by the two Randle Holmes,[48] by Robert Peake's efforts to disseminate an English translation of Serlio,[49] or by Paul Isaacson's adaptation of drawings from Karl van Mander at Knole,[50] most native-English painting of this era remained insular, naive, and un-theoretized by continental standards of the day.

True artists, as Lucy Gent reminds us, could produce 'the illusion of three dimensions in a plane surface by means of shading and perspective' so that, for example, the depiction of open windows does actually make them look open.[51] Native-English painters certainly painted windows in their portraits. Gent cites the two windows in George Gower's 'Armada' portrait of Elizabeth. The anonymous

[48] Robert Tittler and Anne Thackray, 'Print Collecting in Provincial England Prior to 1650: The Randle Holme Album', *British Art Journal*, 9/2 (Autumn 2008), 3–11.

[49] See above, Ch. 4.

[50] Anthony Wells-Cole, *Art and Decoration in Elizabethan and Jacobean England: The Influence of Continental Prints, 1558–1625* (London and New Haven, 1997), 211–12.

[51] Lucy Gent, '"The Rash Gazer": Economies of Vision in Britain, 1550–1660', in ead. (ed.), *Albion's Classicism: The Visual Arts in Britain, 1550–1660* (London and New Haven, 1995), 377–94, esp. 383.

1603 portrait of the London Merchant Taylor George Benson in St Johns College Oxford offers another;[52] that of the sea captain John Hunnynge, a third.[53] But none of these offer the illusions of openness, distance, or space. Instead they remain framed vignettes, paintings within paintings, all on the same flat surface.

Even by 1640 (virtually a century after Holbein's death), few provincial craftsmen will have caught up with that 'Republic of Letters', whose various preoccupations will have come by then to dominate English as well as European intellectual life. This will have left them with an impoverished world view and an insular decorative vocabulary compared with some of their London-based confreres, whether foreign-trained or not. It would have cost them the patronage of those increasingly sophisticated patrons who therefore had to look elsewhere for their portraiture.

The best an aspiring provincial painter could do was to apprentice with an experienced, industrious, and well-established master open to current ideas. Such a person would ideally have assembled a reliable collection of patterns, model or pattern books, or even, by the latter decades of the period, perhaps a random collection of prints and drawings taken from books or purchased as single copies from stationers. Not many of them were likely to have acquired Peake's Serlio, Haydocke's Lomazzo, or English manuals on technique by the likes of Henry Peacham, Edward Norgate, or Nicholas Hilliard. In any event, most of these few pre-1640 treatises on painting, written in England and for an English audience, were directed as much to the gentleman amateur as to any working craftsman.[54] Probate inventories of native-English and especially provincially based painters sometimes contain published books, but very rarely treatises as these.

On the other hand, simple pattern and models books, or individual patterns, had become reasonably common possessions of the working painter in many urban centres by *c.*1600.[55] Patterns might be nothing more than modest collections of prints, either single sheets or pages clipped from books, or collections of drawings of particular bodily features or decorative motifs. The Norwich painter John Cock's possession of 'certen prynts and patterns of paper' pretty well sums up this sort of resource.[56] Books, often of a religious nature and intended for ecclesiastical venues,

[52] Gent, 'The Rash Gazer'; oil on panel, 43" × 32¾", R. L. Poole (ed.), *Catalogue of Portraits in the Possession of the University, Colleges, City and County of Oxford*, 3 vols (Oxford Historical Society Publications, 1912–26), III.165–6.

[53] Anon., oil on panel, 1585; Victoria and Albert Museum, no. 176–1880.

[54] Anon., *A Very Proper Treatise Wherein is Briefly Sett Forthe the Arte of Limming* (1573); an anonymous and a more technical work of *c.*1582 and attributed to Edmonde Barton, National Art Library MS. 86.EE.69; Nicholas Hilliard, *A Treatise Concerning the Arte of Limning* (*c.*1600), ed. R. K. R. Thornton and T. G. S. Cain (1981); Richard Haydocke, *A Tracte Containing the Artes of Curious Paintinge, Carvinge & Buildinge* (1598): a translation of part of Giovanni Paolo Lomazzo's *Trattoro dell'arte della pittura, sculptura ed architettura* (1584); Henry Peacham, *The Art of Drawing with a Pen* (1606) and its later version, *Graphica, or the Most Auncient and Excellent Art of Drawing and Limning* (1612) or the same book under a different title, *The Gentleman's Exercize* also of 1612, and *The Compleat Gentleman* (1622); and Norgate, *Miniatura, or the Art of Limning.*

[55] Phillip Lindley, 'The "Artist": Institutions, Training and Status', in Tim Ayers (ed.), *The History of British Art, 600–1600* (London and New Haven, 2008), 164.

[56] Norfolk and Norwich Record Office MS. DN/INV 26/87, p. 2, 1613/14.

had long been employed to offer models of pre-Reformation painting. But we know that pattern books, both published and unpublished, were both widely employed by known painters, and even by some of the more sophisticated patrons, of the post-Reformation period as well.[57] Painters and certainly herald painters, along with practitioners of other visual crafts, frequently bequeathed them as coveted items to their successors.[58] Richard Hossell of Bicester, may have left an 'estate' worth but £2 8s. 4d at his death in 1587, but that sum included 'certen Pattens' and other implements 'belonginge to the painters trade' which were collectively worth 2s.[59] And despite the strenuous wear and tear they must have endured on the workshop bench, a few even of manuscript sources have survived to the present.[60] Yet in the smaller and often remote communities, there cannot have been many even of these. The same may be said for prints and engravings, which remained relatively scarce in provincial portraiture of the same era.

In these circumstances, innovations of almost any kind moved deliberately. Native-English approaches, including some that were distinctly regional, took on continental influences but gradually and without abandoning some of their more deeply rooted characteristics. One such root lay in the prominent role played by heraldry, itself forcefully driven by the social competition and fluidity of the era, and its influence on the ambient visual imagery. It is to this which we now turn.

[57] Wells-Cole, *Art and Decoration*, 5, 9; Francis Ames-Lewis, 'Modelbook Drawings and the Florentine Quattrocento Artist', *Art History*, 10/1 (March 1987), 1–16.

[58] See Malcolm Airs, *The Tudor and Jacobean Country House: A Building History* (Stroud, 1995), 51–4; Ann Payne, 'Sir Thomas Wriothesley and His Heraldic Artists', in Michelle P. Brown and Scott McKendrick (eds), *Illuminating the Book: Makers and Interpreters: Essays in Honour of Janet Backhouse* (1998), 147–8; will of John Multon, 1546, as cited in W. J. Williams (ed.), 'Wills of Masons and Freemen', *The Masonic Record*, 16 (1936) 204; will of the herald painter Richard Scarlett (1608), TNA, PROB 11/109 (unpaginated); will of William Robinson, painter and deputy herald of Newcastle-upon-Tyne, 1635: Durham University Library MS. DPRI/11/1636 1-2; will of Thomas Playne, citizen and painter of London and Ludlow, GH MS. 9171/18/395 (1596), etc.

[59] M. A. Havinden (ed.), *Household and Farm Inventories in Oxfordshire, 1550–1590* (Historical Manuscripts Commission, Joint Series, 10, 1965), 250.

[60] Jim Murrell, 'John Guillim's Book: A Heraldic Painter's *Vade Mecum*', *Walpole Society*, 57 (1995), 1–52, *passim*; Epiphanius Evesham's pattern book of heraldic drawings, National Art Library MS. MSL/1982/29; the anonymous manuscript sometimes attributed to Edmonde Barton, National Art Library MS. 86.EE.69.

6

Heraldry and Portraiture

In England as well as in sundry continental societies, the relationship between painters and heralds, and portraiture and heraldry, go well back in time. In creating what may well be the first family portrait gallery in England, Eleanor de Clare, wife of Hugh Dispenser and grand-daughter of Edward I, commissioned sometime in the 1330s painted glass portraits of eight knights with blazoned cloaks to be set in the clerestory windows of her 'family church' of Tewkesbury Abbey. These glass paintings, of Clare's two husbands and six close relatives buried in the Abbey, are not portraits in the sense of the contemporary term *contrefois al vif*: imitations or 'counterfeits' from real life.[1] That would probably have been beyond the capability of their anonymous glass painter, and he would have been mightily challenged in any event to depict lifelike facial features on such helmeted figures. But they were nevertheless representations of real people, in which heraldic description provided the identities that artistic skill could not. From that time on, the relations of portraiture and heraldry, and of painters and heralds, remained tightly entangled, and they did so as much or even more in England than in most other areas of Europe.

In considering the place of heraldic imagery in English portraiture of the Tudor and early Stuart era three questions seem especially germane. This chapter will discuss the social context that made heraldic devices so important in the England of this era; the sort of craftsmen who painted the devices themselves; and the portraits that featured them. It will conclude by suggesting the significance of heraldic painting for the native-English school of portraiture at this time.

The distinctive predominance of heraldic imagery in English provincial portraiture owes more to the social context in which those portraits were commissioned than to any other factor. As noted in greater detail in Chapter 2, that context lay especially in the distinctive social dynamic that pertained in England at that time. The extremely fluid nature of Tudor and early Stuart society, the rapid population growth, and the unprecedented opportunities to acquire land and office, opened the gateway to individual advancement wider than ever before. With those factors came fierce competition for individual recognition and status.

To those in the upper ranks, the fear of encroachment from below loomed as a constant reality, spawning sundry efforts to maintain customary social barriers or erect new ones. At the same time, those below them, whether of the landed or

[1] Andrew Martindale, *Heroes, Ancestors, Relatives, and the Birth of the Portrait* (The Hague, 1988), 16–20; *ODNB*, vide 'Dispenser, Hugh'.

urban communities, strove to climb upwards, grasping as they did so for property, material possessions, and similar talismans of status and legitimacy. The turf on which gentle but untitled families stood proved especially contentious. Those residing at higher elevations on the social pyramid had the social and legal certification that came with knighthood or peerage. A 'mere' gentleman, including the rank of 'esquire', had no such designation on which to rest. According to contemporary opinion, a gentleman was one who could afford the lifestyle of that status, and therefore be considered worthy of that status by others. In the oft-quoted words of the Elizabethan observer William Harrison,

> Whosoever studieth the lawes of the realme, who so studieth in the Universitie or professeth Physicke and the liberall Sciences, or beside his service in the rowme of a capitaine in the warres, can live ydely and without manuell labour, and thereto is able and will beare the port, charge, and countenance of a gentleman, he shall be called Master, (which is the title that men give to Esquires and Gentlemen and reputed for a Gentleman . . .).[2]

Gentility was, in other words, largely a standing defined by a person's appearance, reputation, and behaviour in the eyes of his contemporaries. And given the long-standing and ambient resentment, for example, by the landed elite of the merchant figure and his urban milieu, or by the armigerous sorts of people of the middling, the urge for enhanced social respectability and acceptance remained especially acute throughout the period at hand.

Given those characteristics, social stability depended considerably on a legal and administrative system of certification and governance by which claims of gentility, and the assertions of lineage that supported such claims, could be closely observed, managed, and controlled. The system of heraldry, administered by the College of Arms at the request and instigation of the crown, evolved to do precisely that.

The very nature of their job required the heralds to remain in close and continuing contact with the armigerous and would-be armigerous families, and with the civic institutions, of each shire. By the early fifteenth century the unwarranted assumption and display of armorial bearings had become so common, and so unregulated, that the crown gave the College the task of reforming and supervising it. Such efforts were only sporadically effective over the next century. But in 1530, a royal commission authorized the Clarenceux King of Arms, one of the three kings of arms serving under the Earl Marshall, to carry out systematic heraldic visitations of each of the shires under his jurisdiction, all of which lay south of the River Trent. Clarenceux engaged heralds, deputy heralds, and other officers of the College, along with county sheriffs, bailiffs of hundreds, and lesser officials, in the task.[3] Together,

[2] William Harrison, *An Historicall description of the iland of Britaine* (1587), I.128; also commonly attributed to Sir Thomas Smith, who copied it in his *de Republica Anglorum*; Mary Dewar, 'A Question of Plagiarism: The "Harrison Chapters" in Sir Thomas Smith's "De Republica Anglorum"', *Historical Journal*, 22/4 (December 1979), 927.

[3] Anthony Wagner and George Squibb, 'Deputy Heralds', in Frederick Emmison and Roy Stephens (eds), *Tribute to an Antiquary: Essays Presented to Marc Fitch by Some of his Friends* (1976), 229–33 and Appendix III, 252–63; Adrian Ailes, 'The Development of Heralds' Visitations in

these officials set out to inspect every use of arms they could find, affirming and recording the legitimate ones, destroying the rest, and fining those who had illicitly assumed unauthorized arms. In the years 1580, 1620, and 1666, major rounds of visitations were held not just in the area within Clarenceux's jurisdiction but nation-wide, though visitations of particular shires were carried out from time to time in other years as well.[4]

In addition to carrying out visitations of this sort and certifying the legitimacy of existing arms where appropriate, the heralds and their deputies received, vetted, and adjudicated new requests for arms from the socially mobile families of that era. They designed the actual arms for those whose requests they approved. They also arranged public processions, so as to maintain strict order of precedence amongst participants. They presided at the weddings and funerals of armigerous families, so as to keep straight the implications of those generational comings and goings for family pedigrees. They awarded and designed new arms for each successive generation of armigerous families, helped design armorial displays for funeral monuments, and carried out sundry similar chores as part of their regular work.[5] Critically, if more generally, they were obliged, in the words of a 1609 manual on the duties of a herald, 'to keep the seacrettes of Knights, Esquires, Ladyes and gentlemen as a confessor of Arms and not to discover [e.g., 'disclose'] them in noe wise'.[6]

In addition, heralds performed similar functions for chartered civic institutions, including grammar schools, charitable institutions, university colleges, and trade guilds (including the London liveries), which were frequently being re-established or founded anew in the decades following the Henrician and Edwardian dissolutions, and even entire boroughs, many of which were first incorporated in this era.[7]

In these circumstances, officers of the College of Arms and their deputies were obliged to became intimately familiar with the leading families and institutions in each area of their jurisdiction. Their task required expertise in genealogical research and close working relations with officials of the county, hundred, borough, and parish. They had to be able to provide accurate drawings and paintings of the various armorial devices that were the visual product of their work. The results of those extensive efforts were recorded in thousands of field notes, in the form of armorial sketches or 'tricks', genealogical charts, and explanatory prose, before they were recorded in the visitation records held in the College itself.

England and Wales, 1450–1600', *The Coat of Arms*, 3rd ser., 5 (2009), 7–23; id., 'Artists and Artwork of the Heralds' Visitations in England and Wales, 1530–1687', unpublished essay as of this writing. I am grateful to the author for permission to read and cite it.

4 Stephen Friar, *The Sutton Companion to Heraldry* (Stroud, Gloucestershire, 1992 and 2004), 9–11.

5 Summarized succinctly in Friar, *Companion to Heraldry*, 8–10; G. D. Squibb, 'Deputy Heralds of Chester', *Journal of the Chester Archaeological and Historic Society*, 56 (1969), 24–8.

6 'A Collection on Heraldry', Society of Antiquaries MS. 213, fo. 3^{r}.

7 Robert Tittler, *The Reformation and the Towns in England, Politics and Political Culture, c. 1540–1640* (Oxford, 1998), esp. 87–96. An excellent example of what a herald did in a visitation to a particular town may be found in the records of the Burghmote Court of Maidstone, in which the 1619 visitation of the herald Richard Phillipot, and his thorough search of the arms and mottos of the borough, are closely described: Centre for Kentish Studies, Maidstone, MS. MD/ACM1/2.

Visitations, and the armigerous status that they verified or bestowed on individuals and their families, definitively affirmed the very gentility to which the landed classes of the day so earnestly and famously aspired. The award or certification of arms served, along with what Lawrence Stone has described as the 'genealogical trees and sumptuous tombs as symptoms of the frenzied status-seeking and ancestor worship of the age', as the common coinage of social status.[8] In consequence, anyone who felt he could fulfil the expectations of gentility, or who could claim the lineage to affirm it, looked to heraldic display as a visual certification of those status claims. The award of arms to institutions, providing political legitimation for the institution rather than social legitimation for the family, had much the same effect.[9]

Given these differences between England's social structure and dynamic and those more rigidly constrained societies that pertained over most of Europe, the prominence of heraldic display loomed as much more important in the former than elsewhere. By the same token, the importance of heraldic imagery weighed much less heavily in the mindset of French and even Netherlandish painters working in England. They will not often have been trained in its intricacies or have had the same cause to incorporate it into their portraiture. Even when they were called upon to use their skills to celebrate the social arrival of their English patrons, as they often were, they could usually call on more subtle and refined ways of fulfilling that role than by the laconic provision of a coat of arms. Most native-English painters, as we have seen, were not so skilled or culturally well-rounded. As provincial portraiture, in both senses of that term, was almost exclusively carried out by the native-English, it is here perhaps even more than in the formal, polite portraits of the landed elite where we see the most extensive use of heraldic devices.

An excellent example of the use of heraldic portraits by contemporary social climbers lies in the experience of the London Mercer cum Northamptonshire squire John Isham of London and Lamport Hall (1525–96), and in the evidence supplied by his portrait done in 1567. Isham's career presents a striking example of upward social mobility. A fourth son of a Northamptonshire squire who received only £3 6d in his father's will, he apprenticed to a London mercer, married upwards both socially and financially, became a leading member of the Mercers' Company of London, and purchased a country estate at Lamport in his native shire from Sir William Cecil in 1560, at a cost of £610. In subsequent years he expanded his holdings by purchase and enclosure, converted a former rectory into what became his seat at Lamport Hall, and successfully adopted to life as a country gentleman. By 1576 he served as JP for Northamptonshire, and by 1581 as sheriff.[10]

8 Lawrence Stone, *The Crisis of the Aristocracy, 1558–1641* (Oxford, 1965), 715.

9 For social legitimation, virtually a commonplace, see Stone, *loc. cit*. For religious legitimation, see Tarnya Cooper, '*Memento Mori* Portraiture: Painting, Protestant Culture and the Patronage of the Middle Elites in England and Wales', unpublished PhD thesis, Sussex University (2001) and ead., 'Predestined Lives? Portraiture and Religious Belief in England and Wales, 1560–1620', in Tara Hamling and Richard L. Williams (eds), *Art Re-Formed, Re-assessing the Impact of the Reformation on the Visual Arts* (Newcastle, 2007), 49–64. And for civic legitimation, see Robert Tittler, *The Face of the City: Civic Portraiture and Civic Identity in Early Modern England* (Manchester, 2007), esp. Chs. 4–5.

10 *ODNB*, vide 'Isham, John'; G. D. Ramsay, *John Isham, Mercer and Merchant Adventurer* (Gateshead, 1962).

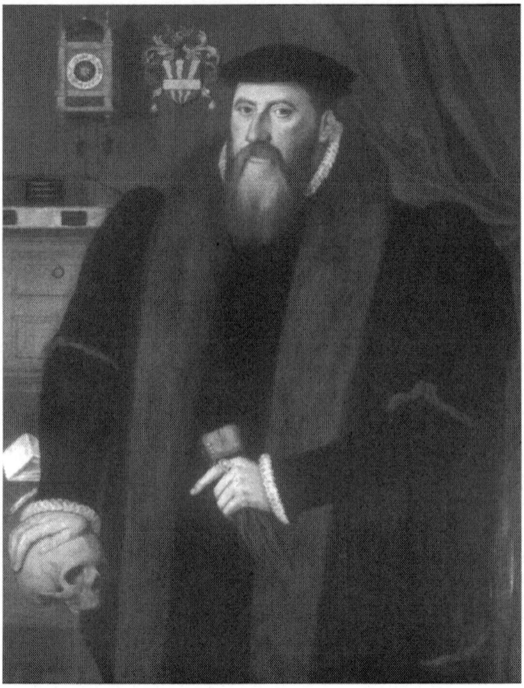

Fig. 6.1. Anon., *John Isham of Lamport Hall* (1567). Lamport Hall Preservation Trust, Lamport Hall, Northampton, Northamptonshire.

The single surviving portrait of Isham, still hanging over a Lamport mantlepiece, reflects much of this success, and reveals, under close scrutiny, even more about its sitter (Fig. 6.1). Done anonymously in 1567, it seems to have been commissioned to mark a critical juncture in the sitter's life. That year marked his election as renter warden of the Mercers' Company. The enormous and very costly feast that he hosted to celebrate that milestone seems likely to have been the occasion of its unveiling to the Company brethren. But it was destined to hang at Lamport, and in the following year Isham began the conversion of the former rectory that would become Lamport Hall itself.

The portrait serves as a virtual catalogue of symbolic props, most of them referring in one way or another to Isham's mercantile career. Isham dressed for his sitting in an elegant robe typical of a successful Mercer. He holds what must be considered freemen's gloves in his left hand,[11] and rests his right hand on a skull, a memento mori device symbolizing the transitory nature of life on earth and the importance of seizing opportunities at hand. Over his shoulder we see a clock: another memento mori device but also a reminder of the time discipline associated

[11] Robert Tittler, 'Freemens' Gloves and Civic Authority: The Evidence from Post-Reformation Portraiture', *Costume*, 40 (2006), 13–20.

with mercantile and urban life: 'In cities and townes', as a contemporary writing put it, 'men rule theym by the clocke'.[12]

On a shelf over Isham's shoulder we find a strange looking rectangular form, which, on closer examination, proves to be two of Isham's ledger books stacked atop each other. Others of that set, though not the ones actually portrayed, may still be found in the Isham Papers in the Northamptonshire Record Office. It is uncommon for a merchant's portrait to refer to the tools of the trade that permitted its subject's success. The social reputation of merchants in general remained controversial in the still-dominant landed society of the day, so that those who followed a career path like Isham's almost always preferred to demonstrate how they spent their money, in charitable bequests especially, rather than how they had earned it.[13] But Isham obviously took pride in his origins as well as in his newfound gentility, and a portrait done to commemorate his advancement in his livery could hardly deny that identity.

Finally, we come to the coat of arms, placed as if on the wall between Isham's head and the clock. Here is much more, or perhaps much less, than meets the eye. Investigation in the records of the College of Arms tells us that Isham was never formally awarded such a device,[14] leaving us to presume that it is entirely of his own invention. He had it displayed in the portrait, and elsewhere in and about the hall, to trumpet the gentility he claimed in setting up as a country squire. An adjacent room at Lamport holds an embroidered device displaying the same arms, along with the same date of 1569.[15] Three years later, Isham felt the need to extend those images elsewhere in and about his seat, and so paid a herald painter 'for makynge the pyctures in plat and the Merc[er]s armys and in gravynge them w[i]t[h] settynge them on a ston' for a total of £7 3s.[16]

It was obviously extremely important to Isham, and absolutely integral to his quest for gentility, to secure a coat of arms, just as it seemed essential to him to commission a portrait that displayed them. A closer consideration of what a coat of arms looked like, and how its elements served the purpose to which men like Isham put it, reveals a lot about how portraiture of the middling sort of people at this time so frequently brought together the skills of both herald and painter.

12 *Dives et Pauper* (1536 edn) fo. 30^{v}. My thanks to Michael Berlin for bringing this citation to my attention. For a fuller explanation of this symbolic meaning, see Robert Tittler, *Architecture and Power: The Town Hall and the English Urban Community, c. 1500–1640* (Oxford, 1998), 136–9.

13 On the negative or ambiguous image of the merchant in this period, see, e.g., Alexander Leggatt, *Citizen Comedy in the Age of Shakespeare* (Toronto, 1973); Laura Stephenson O'Connell, 'Anti-Entrepreneurial Attitudes in Elizabethan Sermons and Popular Literature', *Journal of British Studies*, 15 (1976), 2–20; John McVeagh, *Tradeful Merchants: The Portrayal of the Capitalist in Literature* (1981), *passim*; Keith Wrightson, *English Society, 1580–1680* (1982), 27–31; Richard Grassby, *The Business Community of Seventeenth Century England* (Cambridge, 1995), 29–36; and Lawrence Manley, *Literature and Culture in Early Modern London* (Cambridge, 1995), Ch. 2.

14 I am grateful to Peter O'Donoghue, Bluemantle Pursuivant, for searching the records at the College of Arms and affirming this for me.

15 These observations were made on a visit to Lamport Hall with Dr Tarnya Cooper in 2007. I am most grateful to Dr Cooper for inviting me along to inspect the portrait, for her observations on it, and for alerting me to the survival of the ledger books in the Northamptonshire County Record Office.

16 Entry dated 14 June 1572, cited in Ramsay, *John Isham*, 147.

The central component of the entire device is the shield, in which the juxtaposition of particular images and colours assigned and registered to that family identified the current generation and its immediate forebears. Each succeeding generation enjoyed the right to its own version of that combination, added in the form of additional quarterings, so that intermarriages and births could also be represented. In that sense, the shield represented a concise visual genealogy that established the lineage of the family. In addition, the very shape and name for this element conjured up, and was meant to conjure up, the notion of feudal military service in 'olden days', when that service could be much more than ceremonial in nature. Whether the family had ever engaged in such service remained irrelevant.

Amongst the other elements in the coat of arms were the helmet on top of the shield; the crest, often in animate form, which sat atop both shield and helmet; the motto, which usually lay across the bottom and articulated the family's moral aspirations; and the 'supporters', dexter and sinister, which supported the shield on each side. Coats of arms were certainly intricate devices, and malleable ones as well. In order fully to fulfil their intended functions they would have to be amended with each passing generation of the family. And in order specifically to fulfil their social function of affirming the legitimacy of those who possessed them, they did of course often appear on easel portraits.

Taken together, the successful production of a coat of arms, and its maintenance over time, required considerable kinds of skill. Creators of such devices required expertise in genealogical research and intimate familiarity with the armigerous families of a particular jurisdiction. They had to be able to carry out the composition and painting of the device. And they had to have mastered the complex law and lore of heraldry itself that governed the whole system. Though sometimes all these skills rested in a single person, several such people could also be involved, each contributing his own expertise to the whole. Given the nature of the task at hand, all of them could be and often were closely associated with the production of portraiture. In this context, the affinities amongst those who worked as heralds, herald painters, and portrait painters, and the relations of all three with their patrons, bear further exploration.

At first glance, the institutional relations between painters and heralds make this occupational intimacy a little surprising. Jurisdictional conflict between the Painter-Stainers' Company of London and the heralds and other officials of the College of Arms remained almost as frequent and hard-fought as those famously contested between the Painter-Stainers and foreign interlopers.[17] But in practice, both painter-stainers and herald painters painted a wide variety of heraldic devices on

[17] W. A. D. Englefield, *The History of the Painter-Stainers Company of London* (1923), and Alan Borg, *The History of the Worshipful Company of Painters, Otherwise Painter-Stainers* (Huddersfield, 2005); J. H. Parker Oxspring, 'The Painter-Stainers and Their Dispute with the Heralds', 3 vol. typescript (College of Arms MS. Her/BH, n.d.); Susan Foister, 'Foreigners at Court: Holbein, Van Dyck and the Painter-Stainers Company', in David Howarth (ed.), *Art and Patronage in the Caroline Court: Essays in Honour of Sir Oliver Millar* (Cambridge, 1993), 32–50; 'Accounts of the Company of Painter-Stainers, Glaziers, Embroiderers and Stationers of Chester', Chester Record Office MS. ZG 17/1–2, unpaginated, *passim*; and Squibb, 'Deputy Heralds of Chester', 27–8.

an equally wide variety of objects and surfaces. Both required training in many of the same techniques; both employed most of the same materials and tools of the trade. It was inevitable that their expertises should overlap and that members of the two groups should vie for control of such work. And, indeed, competition between them ensued on a frequent and continual basis throughout this era.

And yet the activities of heraldry and portraiture were also closely and often collaboratively linked in the sixteenth and early seventeenth centuries.[18] One component of the Painter-Stainers' Company of London consisted of those trained specifically in herald painting or arms painting.[19] For their part, some members of the College of Arms were sufficiently skilled in the visual arts as to be able to respond fully to these needs themselves. Some heralds or deputy heralds even enjoyed parallel careers as painters, and especially portrait painters, at the highest level of skill and patronage to be found at least amongst the native-born English practitioners of the day.

The most prominent of this latter number was undoubtedly William Segar (*c.*1564–1633), probably born in England of Dutch heritage. Though initially trained as a scrivener, another skill appropriate to the herald's (and often the portraitist's) work, Segar landed the post of Portcullis Pursuivant in his twenty-first year (1585), moving up the ladder of College offices to Somerset Herald (1589), Norroy King of Arms (one of three kings of arms, the highest position in the College under the Earl Marshall himself) in 1597, and then to Garter King of Arms in 1604. Though he came into disfavour and was briefly imprisoned for granting arms to a bogus claimant, he was eventually restored to James I's good graces and knighted in 1616.[20] Along with George Gower, Robert Peake, William Larkin, and Nicholas Hilliard, Segar must be counted amongst the most prominent English-born portrait painters of his generation. Amongst works confidently attributed to him are portraits of the earl of Leicester; the earl of Essex; Francis, the countess of Essex; and Queen Elizabeth herself.[21]

Another herald/portraitist, Edward Norgate (1581–1650) was something of a polymath, also being highly skilled in music and calligraphy, serving as an agent in the purchase of paintings abroad for Queen Henrietta Maria and the earl of Arundel, and as tutor to Arundel's sons. His broad skills brought him to the attention of the court circle under Charles I, and to an appointment in the College of Arms, first as Rouge Croix Pursuivant and then Windsor Herald. It is some sign of his prominence amongst other painters that he was an invited guest in November

[18] Jim Murrell, 'John Guillem's Book: A Heraldic Painter's *Vade Mecum*', *Walpole Society*, 57 (1995), 4; Foister, 'Foreigners at Court', 34–8; Squibb, 'Deputy Heralds of Chester', 23–8.

[19] Mary Edmond, 'Limners and Picture-Makers: New Light on the Lives of Miniaturists and Large-Scale Portrait Painters Working in London in the Sixteenth and Seventeenth Centuries', *Walpole Society*, 47 (1978–80), 163–70, 64–5.

[20] *ODNB*, vide 'Segar, William', though this entry remarkably fails even to mention Segar's career as a painter of considerable note. See also Erna Auerbach, *Nicholas Hilliard* (London and Boston, MA, 1961), 271–81.

[21] Karen Hearn, *Dynasties: Painting in Tudor and Jacobean England, 1530–1630* (1995), 77, 91; Auerbach, *Hilliard*, 271–81; D. T. Piper, 'The 1590 Lumley Inventory: Hilliard, Segar and the Earl of Essex', *Burlington Magazine*, 99 (1957), 299–303.

1637, when the London Painter-Stainers entertained Van Dyck, Inigo Jones, and Jan de Critz in their hall in Queenhithe. Van Dyck had stayed with Norgate upon first coming to London in 1632 before settling into his own accommodations.[22] Along with these sundry occupations and appointments, Norgate also painted miniatures, and wrote a treatise on the subject, *Miniatura*, which is both important and frequently cited.[23]

However, those heralds who lacked these skills, or whose extraordinary workload simply necessitated putting other hands to the task, had to rely on others outside the official ranks of the College: painter-stainers, herald painters, arms painters, and similarly designated craftsmen. In and around London and the court circle such commissions comprised a major employment for the hierarchy of painter-stainers working under the jurisdiction of the Sergeant Painter to the Crown, where such jurisdiction was formally laid out in the patent for that office.[24] But elsewhere throughout the realm as well, painter-stainers were commonly employed to paint or 'refresh' the arms of individual people as well as towns and boroughs, or the royal arms that came frequently to be displayed in buildings like town halls, parish churches, and market halls. To facilitate their help in visitations, some of them were formally deputized as officers of the College of Arms in their own right. Other painter-stainers were employed as ad hoc deputies for such work, without ever becoming members of the College. Still others simply took commissions from patrons with neither official standing or training in heraldic work. We have no evidence to suggest, for example, that the Norwich painter Henry Eives was in any official sense a herald painter or that he received specific training appropriate to that metier. Yet his probate inventory of 1599 included 'ii boockes of armes with patterns of paper', which can only have been employed in painting heraldic devices for his clients.[25] As the socially driven clamor for heraldic services reached flood-tide from the late sixteenth century, some deputy heralds (though probably not complete freelancers like Eives) were even permitted to carry out entire visitations on their own.[26]

Most of these deputy heralds will have been locally based painters or painter-stainers with particular training or experience as herald painters. 'A Herald Painter', we read in Randle Holme III's *The Academy of Armory*, 'is such as Paints Coats of Armes on Escochions, Shields, Tables, Penons, Standarts and such like'.[27] The items on this list bear close attention. While 'escochions' and shields are familiar parts of the coat of arms, a 'table' was a common contemporary synonym for a framed painting or portrait,[28] while 'penons'—e.g., pennants—and standards were

[22] Jo Kirby, 'The Painter's Trade in the Seventeenth Century: Theory and Practice', *National Gallery Technical Bulletin*, 20 (1999), 9, and Painter-Stainers' Company Minute Book, LMA MS. 5667/1, 124.

[23] Edward Norgate, *Miniatura, or, the Art of Limning*, ed. J. M. Muller and Jim Murrell (London and New Haven, 1997); Auerbach, *Hilliard*, 282–5.

[24] Noted in Foister, 'Foreigners at Court', 36.

[25] Norwich and Norfolk Record Office MS. DN/INV 16/176, p. 2.

[26] Wagner and Squibb, 'Deputy Heralds', 232–3.

[27] Randle Holme, *The Academy of Armory* (1688), pt. III, 147.

[28] On the contemporary meanings of 'table' in this context, see Tittler, *Face of the City*, 93 n. 70.

commonly painted on cloth by painter-stainers or stainers. In short, this description brings even closer together the work of the herald painter and the painter-stainer of that time. Whether formally deputized or not, painter-stainers ranged in prominence from the Henrician Sergeant Painter John Browne and the prominent London painter-stainer Richard Scarlett to such provincial painters as Jacob Chaloner of Chester, Peter Henson of Oundle, and William Robinson of Newcastle. All of them kept books of arms and extensive notes on heraldic devices of families in particular areas just like the heralds whom they assisted.[29]

Notwithstanding the complex and even litigious relations that often pertained between the two occupations,[30] this sort of interdependence, and the collaboration to which it led, remained equally common and sometimes quite extensive. Evidence of professional ties sometimes includes tokens of gratitude from painter-stainers to particular heralds who had provided patronage. Not all painter-stainers went as far as Robert Greenwood, who left in his 1585 will bequests to the heralds Edmund Knight (Norroy King of Arms), Richard Lee (Richmond Herald), Robert Coke (Clarenceux King of Arms), Edmund Coke (deputy herald for Chester), and Robert Glover (Somerset Herald),[31] but these gestures were not by any means unique.

Such matrices of employment, apprenticeship, family, and influence were also often specific to a particular region. They could extend to virtually all the sundry activities involving painting in that region. The model for this sort of close-knit and even inbred local artisan community remains the complex matrix of foreign-derived artisan families of sixteenth- and seventeenth-century London so closely described by Mary Edmond.[32] But similar family and occupational matrices, albeit on a smaller scale, may also be found in some provincial areas.

Something of the sort has been described in Norwich, where foreign-born painter-stainers and other 'stranger'-craftsmen settled in considerable numbers in the Elizabethan era. Restricted in a variety of ways from full entry into local life, and sharing a common language and heritage, they intermarried, took on each other's children as apprentices, and sustained their ethnic identity for several generations thereafter. Part of that continuity extended to occupational continuity in the visual arts,[33] though this is not to suggest an absence of such craftsmen within the native-

[29] See the manuscript volume of such drawings and sketches kept 'By me Peter Henson of Owndell [Oundle] Painter' in the early years of the seventeenth century; National Art Library MS. 86.H.H.62 L.29-1982; Brown's early-sixteenth-century books of heraldic drawings; TNA PROB 11/30/14; Chaloner's volumes of heraldic notes in the British Library as BL. Harleian 1091, Add. MS. 26,704, Add. MS. 47,185, and Scarlett's collection of 'pedigrees, draughters and writings', left to his son and namesake by his will of 1607: TNA PROB 11/109, BL. Harleian MSS. 1354, 1366, and 2021. Robinson, who listed himself at various times as a painter and embroiderer and as a 'deputy to the office of armes', left six books of arms at his death in 1636; Durham University Archives MS. DPRI/1/1636/R9/2.

[30] Wagner and Squibb, 'Deputy Heralds', esp. 235–6; Foister, 'Foreigners at Court', 32.

[31] TNA, PROB 11/68/372r, 16 June 1585.

[32] Edmond, 'Limners and Picture Makers', *passim*.

[33] Virginia Tillyard, 'Civic Portraits Painted for, or Donated to, the Council Chamber of Norwich Guildhall, before 1687, with Documentary Evidence Relating to the Artistic Background of the City,

born population. The usual rivalry between native and foreign workmen ensued, sometimes even to the point of violence, before the two groups began to blend together into one over the first half of the seventeenth century.

Though far less populous, affluent, or favoured as a place of settlement by 'strangers' from abroad, the west coast port of Chester provides a similar but as yet undocumented case of occupational and familial intermingling. Chester served as the jurisdictional focal point of a particular office in the College of Arms, the Chester Herald of Arms in Ordinary, probably created to serve the needs of the County Palatine of Chester.[34] It also hosted from well back in the fourteenth century its own guild association representing the interests of local painters. Chiefly in order to share expenses in producing the City's annual Shepherds' Play, the Painter-Stainers formally merged with the Glaziers, Embroiderers, and Stationers in 1536, gaining a charter from the mayor of that City, Henry Gee, under that rubric.[35] The performance of the play would shortly be proscribed by a puritan mayoral regime,[36] but the guild itself endured well into the eighteenth century, with the painter-stainers remaining its largest and most influential occupational component over most of that time.

The Company charter specifically licensed its painter-stainer members to practise 'the arts of painting, hatching, lymninge, staining and seeling', all but the last of which specifically echoed requirements of the herald painter. Hatching, or the drawing of fine, parallel lines to indicate shading, was particularly essential to heraldic painting. Different patterns of hatching were employed in heraldic sketches, or 'tricks', both to represent the different colours of the arms and as vital elements in the design of a coat of arms itself.[37] 'Lymning' usually referred to the painting of miniatures, but it became very useful to the herald commissioned to do family trees for his clients, in which small portraits of particular members were often 'limned', apple-like, onto particular branches. Staining, or painting on cloth, proved an essential skill in the frequent production of heraldic banners.

An important Chester figure for the point at hand was Thomas Chaloner (d.1598), poet, painter-stainer, and a valued aid to the leading magnate in the area, Henry Stanley, fourth earl of Derby. Chaloner had long been engaged in painter-stainer work in and around Chester and in several sorts of work for the earls

the Artists and the Sitters', unpublished MA thesis, Courtauld Institute of Art, London (1978); ead., 'Painters in Sixteenth and Seventeenth Century Norwich', *Norfolk Archaeology*, 37 (1980), 315–18; Victor Morgan, 'The Dutch and Flemish Presence and the Emergence of an Anglo-Dutch Provincial Artistic Tradition in Norwich, *c.* 1500–1700', in Juliette Roding, Eric Jan Slutter, Bart Westerweel, Marijke van der Meiji-Tolmsa, and Eric Domela Nieuwenhuis (eds), *Dutch and Flemish Artists in Britain, 1550–1800* (Leiden, 2002), 57–72, esp. 63–8.

34 Friar, *Companion to Heraldry*, 17; Squibb, 'Deputy Heralds of Chester', 23–36.

35 BL. Harleian MS. 2054, fos. 88^r–9^v, 91^r, and 156 b; *Victoria History of the County of Chester*, V, pt 2 (Woodbridge, Suffolk, 2005), 115–16, 200.

36 Lawrence M. Clopper (ed.), *Records of Early English Drama, Chester* (Toronto, 1979), 198; Robert Tittler, 'Henry Hardware and the Face of Puritan Reform in Chester', in id., *Townspeople and Nation: English Urban Experiences, 1540–1640* (Stanford, CA, 2001), 140–55.

37 The latter usage applied especially to what was known as the Petra Sancta system of hatching; Friar, *Companion to Heraldry*, 188–9.

of Derby. He had performed with the earl's players, and had been commissioned to paint an elaborate screen for the earl's residence.[38] But in his heraldic capacity he became deputy to the Norroy King of Arms in 1598 and had carried out seven years earlier, as an ad hoc deputy, a visitation of the city of Chester in 1591.[39] As we've seen in Chapter 4, Chaloner took on as one of his apprentices the next key figure who would sustain the link between heralds and painters in the Chester area, Randle Holme (1570/1–1655). And though Chaloner could little foresee it, his new apprentice would succeed him in more than the narrow occupational sense.

Having trained in Chaloner's workshop, married Chaloner's widow, Elizabeth (née Alcock), and taken on Chaloner's son Jacob as an apprentice, Holme launched a long and illustrious local career as a painter-stainer, city and county office-holder, and deputy herald. But several of his other achievements are also important to us. He established the direct line of his male descendants as herald painters and painter-stainers for three generations to follow, all of those successors in turn taking his forename as well as his occupation: Randle Holme II (1601–59); Randle Holme III (1627–99/1700), and Randle Holme IV (d.1707). Holme the elder remained actively involved in heraldic painting and other aspects of the herald's work for a good many years. Though his own father was a blacksmith, some of Holme's ancestors had served as heralds in the fifteenth century, and he may well have thought of this as a deeply rooted family tradition which it was his familial obligation to revive.[40]

Holme's first recorded act in that capacity came in 1591, when he made extensive additions to Chaloner's 1580 visitation of Chester. This will have counted heavily in earning him his first appointment as deputy to the Norroy King of Arms for Cheshire, Lancashire, and North Wales in 1600. His appointment lasted until 1618, and was redefined in the following year to include Cheshire and North Wales.[41] The fact that he was obliged to report each Easter to the College of Arms itself further certifies that this was no mere casual, part-time appointment.[42]

[38] Thomas Hughes, 'On Chester Literature, its Authors and Publishers during the Sixteenth and Seventeenth Centuries', *Journal of the Architectural, Archaeological and Historic* [*sic*] *Society of Chester*, 2 (1864), 21–30; Joy Hancox, *Kingdom for a Stage: Magicians and Aristocrats in the Elizabethan Theatre* (Stroud, Gloucestershire, 2001), 15–17; BL. Harleian MS. 1927, fos. 13–14. My thanks to Professor Lawrence Manley and Dr Sally-Beth MacLean for the last two references.

[39] Wagner and Squibb, 'Deputy Heralds', 233. Chaloner's genealogical investigation of the city has been partly appended to Robert Glover, *The Visitation of Cheshire, 1580*, ed. John Paul Rylands (Harleian Society, 18, 1882), 261–72.

[40] An earlier Randle Holme left a book of 'arms in trick' c. Henry VI, and a Thomas Holme served as Clarenceux King of Arms until his death in 1493. Ormerod, *Chester, loc cit.*; *ODNB*, vide 'Holme, Randle'; Louise Campbell and Francis Steer (eds.), *A Catalogue of the Manuscripts in the College of Arms, Collections* I (1988), 41 and 567.

[41] Glover, *Visitation of Cheshire*, 260; *ODNB*, vide 'Holme, Randle'; George J. Armitage and J. Paul Rylands (eds.), *Pedigrees Made at the Visitation of Chester, 1613* (Harleian Society, 59, 1909), 1; Walter H. Godfrey, *The College of Arms, Queen Victoria Street, Being the Sixth and Final Monograph of the London Survey Committee* (1963), 86; Wagner and Squibb, 'Deputy Heralds', 237; Squibb, 'Deputy Heralds of Chester', 27–9.

[42] *ODNB*, vide 'Holme, Randle'; Rev. Canon S. Cooper Scott, 'Cotes Monument: Once Set Up in St John's Church, Chester', *Journal of the Architectural, Archaeological and Historic* [*sic*] *Society of Chester*, NS 8 (1902), 13; Godfrey, *College of Arms*, 86.

Holme himself may or may not have painted portraits. The portrait of Thomas ap Ieuan ap David of Arddynwent, now held by the National Museum of Wales, has been tentatively attributed to him, and it certainly offers ample evidence of heraldic imagery.[43] But we do know that Holme established a family-based workshop of painter-staining and herald-painting that would extend to successive generations of Cestrians who would carry on and expand upon that trade. They included his own sons William (1599–1623), Randle the younger, and his stepson Jacob Chaloner. They extended to Edward Bellen (d.1650), at least one of whose signed portraits has survived,[44] and to John Souch. Randle Holme the younger apprenticed the well-known mid-century engraver Daniel King, who went on to work with the antiquary and herald William Dugdale and the engraver Wenceslaus Hollar.[45] In his early years as master of his own shop, as we've seen in Chapter 4, Souch employed Thomas Leigh the elder as his journeyman, Leigh then proceeding to a long career as a well-documented itinerant portrait painter.[46] Later on Souch apprenticed Thomas Pulford, whose portraits of the puritan radical William Prynne formed the focal point of a local riot of Prynne's puritan supporters in 1637.[47]

All of these men and others like them were members of the Chester company at one time or another, some also serving as its officers. Most of them also maintained an active presence in heraldry. Randle Holme the younger served as deputy herald.[48] Jacob Chaloner may or may not had an official appointment as a deputy herald himself, but he took a serious interest in, and derived much of his income from, heraldic work. At least two volumes of his heraldic sketches may still be found

[43] Randle Holme (attrib.), oil on panel, 1610, 67.5 cm × 54.3 cm; National Museum of Wales, no. A 3691. Though the prominence and intricacy of the coat of arms suggests authorship by someone of Holme's expertise, and though he was certainly active in that era and area, much of the attribution derives from the reading of a small monogram in the lower right corner of the work which has struck some, but not others, as reading 'RHF': Randall Holme *fecit*. Having examined the painting at length, through the generous invitation and courtesy of Stephanie Roberts of the NMW, I remain amongst the sceptics. The monogram looks to me to read TR or TRF, which might well point to Holme's contemporary and fellow Cestrian painter, Thomas Robinson.

[44] 'Unknown Man of the Family of Edwards of Rhual', dated 1636; current location uncertain; Heinz Archive painters' files, vide Bellen, Edward.

[45] *ODNB*, vide 'King, Daniel'.

[46] Some sixteen portraits have been at least tentatively identified as Leigh's, some of them signed and dated. But much confusion has sprung from the failure to realize until very recently that there were two Thomas Leighs, father and son, who were itinerant portrait painters in the early seventeenth century. See Stephanie Roberts and Robert Tittler, 'Tracking the Elusive Portrait Painter Thomas Leigh through Caroline England and Wales', *British Art Journal*, 11/1 (2010), 1–9.

[47] Ormerod, *Cheshire*, II.456–7; Brian Stewart and Mervyn Cutten (eds), *The Dictionary of Portrait Painters in Britain up to 1920* (1997), 432; Rev. Canon Blomefield, 'Puritanism in Chester in 1637: An Account of the Reception of William Prynne by Certain Inhabitants of the City of Chester', *Journal of the Architectural, Archaeological and Historic [sic] Society of Chester* III (1885), 281–3; R. C. Richardson, 'Puritanism and the Ecclesiastical Authorities: The Case of the Diocese of Chester', in Brian Manning (ed.), *Politics, Religion and the English Civil War* (1973), 24–5.

[48] Wagner and Squibb, 'Deputy Heralds', 258.

in the British Library, consisting largely of the 'tricks' of heraldic devices of families in several northwest counties.[49]

In sum, and for almost anyone with serious social aspirations in Tudor or early Jacobean England, or for any civic institution seeking to identify and legitimize itself, the affinity between portraits and arms, and the importance of obtaining both, will have been patently obvious. Portraits were constructed tableaux of personal presentation, offering up the image of the sitter in the pose, raiment, and situation in which he or she chose to be seen and remembered. And if the sitter's image showed what he or she looked like, and other props showed what the sitter did, thought about, or stood for, the coat of arms announced his or her lineage (whether contrived, as many famously and outlandishly were, or genuine), thus fulfilling an essential requirement for claims of gentility.

One other, usually overlooked, portrait category in which the heraldic device looms large is the civic portrait: the painting, for example, of the London liveryman, the founder or major benefactor of the grammar school or university college, the mayor of the provincial borough or city or even the lord mayor of London, and other such civic leaders. It is in civic portraits of London figures, usually commissioned by London-based institutions and displayed in the great livery company halls of the day, where the more refined and sophisticated painter, including some of the foreign-born elite, will most often have been required to include an heraldic device. Such great institutions need not have settled for the country craftsman painter, but they did have a very similar need to display such icons of legitimacy and authority as the country gentleman. Civic portraits done outside of London, in the universities, the towns and boroughs, the endowed grammar schools, and similar institutions, were more likely to have their portraits done by local, native-English craftsmen. If anything, they will have been even more likely to require an heraldic device to certify the authority of the sitter and/or his institution.

This last point presents an obvious twist to the civic portrait that we do not find in other types. Civic portraits were not intended to celebrate the sitter in his or her own right so much as to celebrate him or her for service rendered to the institution with which he or she had been associated. Symbolic objects in the scene tend, as we will see at greater length in Chapter 7, therefore to dwell on such civic and institutional associations as were suggested by, e.g., the freeman's gloves or the scrolled foundation charter. Towards the same end, the use of heraldry sometimes extended beyond the arms of the sitter to those of the institution as well.

Interesting forerunners of this tradition may be found in the mid-fifteenth-century series of depictions on paper of the aldermen of London done by Roger

[49] BL. Add. MS. 26,704, 'A book of arms, crests, quarterings and mottos of the Irish nobility, done by Jacobus Chaloner, anno 1634', and BL. Add. MS. 47,185, a book of heraldic tricks and sketches done by Chaloner ('Chaloner the tricker of this book') for the herald Henry Lilly. A third volume, BL. Harleian MS. 1091, contains tricks and sketches for the visitation of Devonshire taken by William Harvey, Clarenceux King of Arms, in 1564. Chaloner's name appears at the bottom of the title page, but the early date of this manuscript suggests that this was a mark of Chaloner's ownership rather than of his authorship.

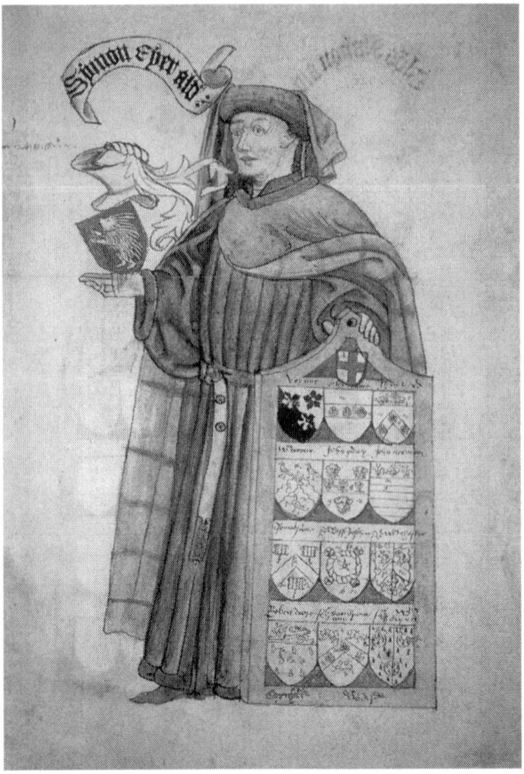

Fig. 6.2. Roger Leigh, *Simon Eyre* (mid-15th c.). City of London, London Metropolitan Archives.

Leigh (Fig. 6.2), or the image, also on paper,[50] of a generic mayor of Bristol being sworn in to his office in Robert Ricart's late-fifteenth-century instruction book for the governance of that city (Fig. 6.3),[51] or even in the illuminated initial letters of the annual plea rolls of the Court of King's Bench, in which figures of the ruling monarch of the day sit enthroned as a visual reminder of whose authority empowered that court (Fig. 6.4).[52]

The Leigh images are especially interesting in this regard. All but one employ exactly the same outline of the figure and dress, as if a single woodblock had been used for the outline again and again, with the colours and details filled in, and the identifying inscription added, to distinguish one from another. All these generic figures face to our left and lean with their left arm on what looks like a sign-board. Each sign-board bears twelve shields, each representing the personal arms of a

[50] Guildhall Library Print Collection, London Aldermen Series, nos. 32,132–52 and 32,170–3.

[51] Robert Ricart, *The Maire of Bristowe Is Kalendar,* (*c.*1484), Bristol Record Office MS. 04720(1), fo. 152.

[52] Public Record Office, *Royal Portraits from the Plea Rolls, Henry VIII to Charles II* (1974), *passim.*

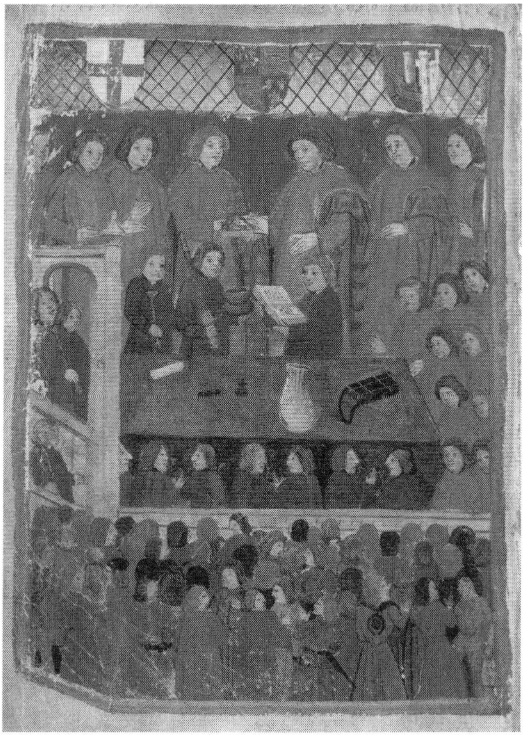

Fig. 6.3. Anon., *Swearing the Mayor* from Robert Ricart, *The maire of Bristowe . . .* (*c.*1484). Bristol Record Office MS. 04720(1). By kind permission of the Bristol Record Office.

previous alderman who represented the particular ward being celebrated in the image. At the very top centre of this board we find the contemporary coat of arms of London itself: the cross of St George with a red sword in the canton. Though each alderman has been named, no effort has been made to indicate individual facial features, so that each remains but a 'virtual' or imaginary portrait. Yet the connection between the office and the individual has been made by the heraldic device, and thus these images stand near the beginning of what became a long and well-respected tradition.

Given the strong affinity between heraldry and both civic and personal portraiture, and the close interaction of heralds and painters, it remains to ask what influence that relationship might have borne for native-English portraiture itself. As we have seen, a great many more native-English portraits of this era include heraldic imagery than those painted by the foreign-born and -trained. But can we see other sorts of heraldic influence in English portraits of this era even when no such heraldic devices appeared? Were native-English, especially provincial, portrait painters influenced at all by the techniques and visual characteristics of heraldic painting, and can we see suggestions of that influence in some of their work beyond the appearance of coats of arms?

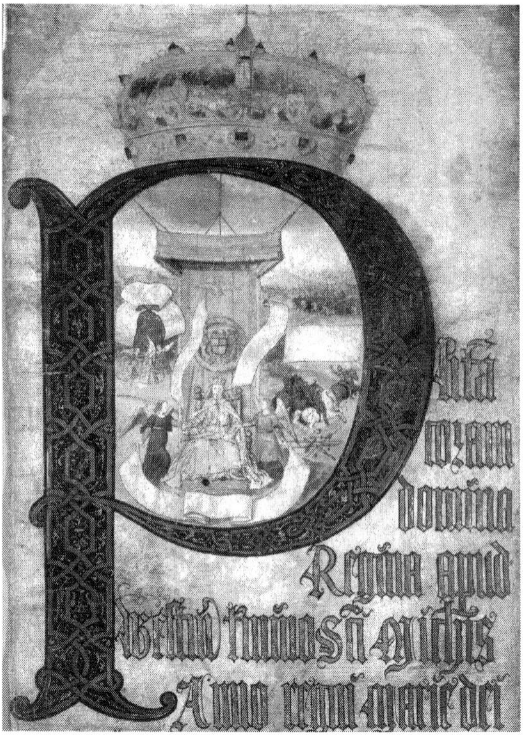

Fig. 6.4. Anon., Illumination of Mary I, King's Bench Plea Roll (Michelmas term, 1553). The National Archives MS. KB 27/1168. By permission of The National Archives.

Sticking with the Chester region as a point of focus, two portraits come to the fore as plausible and representative responses to the question. Only one includes a coats of arms, but both seem highly likely to have been done by regionally based painters who will have drawn heavily on heraldic tradition in their work. One is the highly distinctive and much discussed double portrait of the *Two Ladies of the Cholmondeley Family,* which hangs in Tate Britain (Fig. 6.5). The other is John Souch's distinctive and somewhat cryptic family portrait of *Sir Thomas Aston at the Deathbed of his Wife*, held at the Manchester City Art Gallery (Fig. 6.6).

The *Chomondeley Ladies* is a famously distinctive work: a starkly painted, intriguingly enigmatic, and obviously vernacular version of the family group portrait so fashionable in that era. It has been persuasively dated to the opening years of the seventeenth century.[53] Though the precise identity of the actual subjects remains uncertain, it incontrovertibly derives from one of the two branches

[53] The painting has been described, and its context explored, with particular thoroughness in J. T. Hopkins, '"Such a Twin Likeness There was in the Pair": An Investigation into the Painting of "The Cholmondeley Sisters"', *Transactions of the Historic* [*sic*] *Society of Lancashire and Cheshire*, 144 (1991), 1–37, and esp. 2–6.

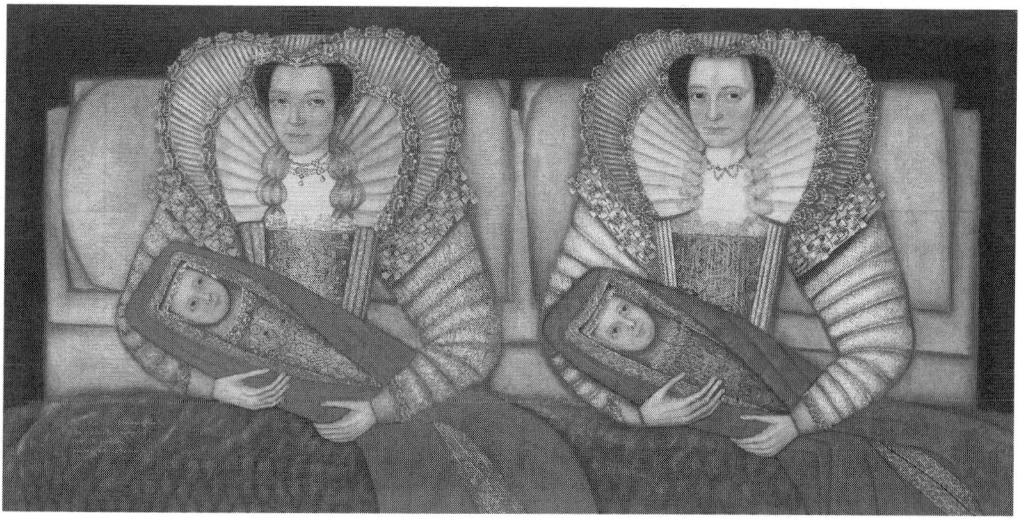

Fig. 6.5. Anon., *Two Ladies of the Cholmondeley Family* (*c.*1600–20), oil on panel, 88.6 cm × 172.3 cm. © Tate, London, 2011.

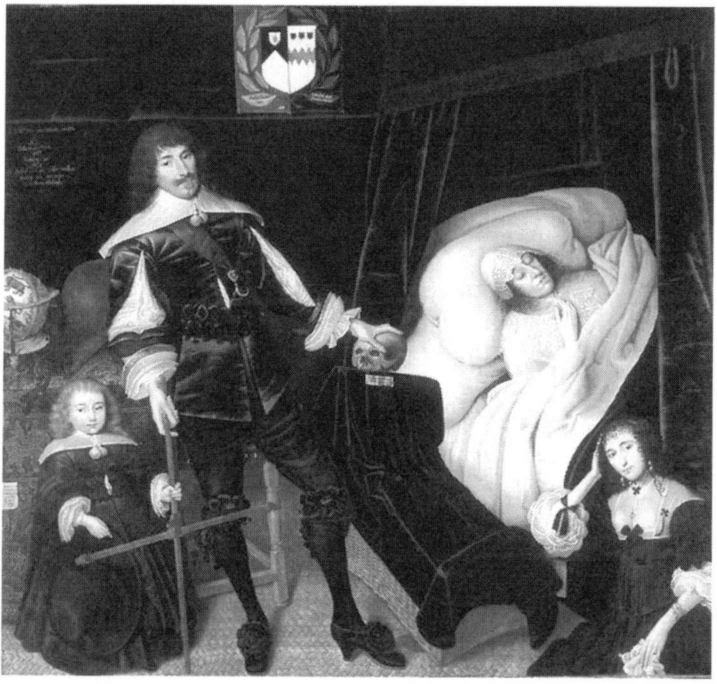

Fig. 6.6. John Souch, *Sir Thomas Aston at the Deathbed of his Wife* (*c.*1635), oil on canvas, 203 cm × 215.1 cm. Manchester City Art Gallery no. 1927.150.

of the Cholmondeleys of Cheshire: an extended and well-known middling gentry clan.

The picture shows two nearly identical young women reclining next to each other against pillows on a bed, each holding an infant diagonally across her lap. Both women are fashionably dressed in silvery white, which stands out dramatically against the black hair of each figure and the dark background of the whole scene. A brownish coverlet and splashes of bright crimson round out the principal palette of the whole. Though there is some intricate figuring of the lace work in the elaborate collars and dress worn by each figure, the workmanship of all else remains schematic. Flesh is modelled, to the extent that it is modelled at all, in a flat monotone; ornate sleeves are modelled in an equally schematic and wholly unnatural manner. Save for the strikingly direct stare of each woman, emotional depth has entirely eluded the painter. The painting remains strictly two-dimensional: figures resemble cardboard cut-outs pasted against the panel.

True to heraldic painting in general, the colours are few: white standing for cleanliness, purity, and joy; black, for prudence and humility; and red (in this case probably vermilion) a symbol of blood—much in evidence in childbirth—and of bravery.[54] In their most common, pure, and unblended form the six colours permitted in heraldic painting comprised a complex and widely understood symbolic language. Lacking the need or ability to convey emotional characteristics in any more direct manner,[55] heraldic painters and those influenced by them used particular and pure colours to signal particular human emotions or personal characteristics. Many vernacular portraits also deployed colours in this fashion, refraining from blending them as freely as the fashionable continental painters of the day, which would literally have diluted their symbolic meaning. Whether painters followed or created contemporary English fashion in such stark use of colour remains an open question, and an important one. But such usage was not uncommon in English School portraits of the era, whether court or provincially based.

Another factor to contemplate is the prominent use of outlining that characterizes much of native-English portraiture of this era. Foreign-trained portrait painters were more inclined to create their shapes and facial features by the subtle building up of tonality on the board or canvas, or were at least characteristically subtle in their use of outlining with chalk, charcoal, or similar materials. English portraits typically reveal more prominent outlining, which is also an obvious characteristic of heraldic work: in the latter case it often amounts to little more than filling in an outline with unblended and/or unshaded colour. Such outlining is especially emphatic in some of the cruder vernacular work of the time, including most of the portrait series known as the *Twelve Worthies of Gloucester* and in

[54] J. Gage, *Colour and Culture: Practice and Meaning from Antiquity to Abstraction* (1993), 82–4. Vermilion, producing a rich, clear red, was a costly pigment but often favoured by arms painters for heraldic use; Kathryn Davies, *Artisan Art: Vernacular Wall Paintings in the Welsh Marches, 1550–1650* (Almeley, Herefordshire, 2008), 62.

[55] A theme pursued in Robert Tittler, 'Portraiture and Character in Shakespeare's England', *Dalhousie Review*, 86/1 (Spring 2006), 7–26.

virtually all of that alternative vernacular form of the wall-painting portrait on plaster or wood. We also see it, albeit more subtly, in the Cholmondeley painting and many other accomplished provincial works.

The lack of natural shading or anything resembling naturalistic modelling, the two-dimensional perspective, the limited palette of colours (each of which nevertheless carried substantial symbolic weight), and the schematic definition of form and gesture, all read directly from the heraldic playbook. They yield little inkling of contact with the polite, formal portraiture of contemporary Netherlandish or other continental traditions. This cannot be anything but a thoroughly naive work carried out by a local painter with extensive familiarity and experience in heraldic painting. It undoubtedly did, as has been suggested, come from any one of that small number of painter-stainers specializing in arms painting in the Holme circle,[56] or even (as has somehow not been considered) by Randle Holme I himself.

In many of these respects, the painting's heraldic elements come quite naturally. The family in all its branches would have been well known to the heralds and herald painters of the region. Cholmondeleys were thick on the ground throughout Cheshire, they find their place in all the major heraldic visitations of the shire during the sixteenth and seventeenth centuries, including those on which herald painters collaborated.[57] The scene itself, marking the birth of a succeeding generation of the family, would have been of particular, indeed obligatory, interest to heralds carrying out such visitations, and to the family wishing to have its genealogical succession recorded in that manner.

John Souch's *Sir Thomas Aston at the Deathbed of his Wife*, certainly lacks the exotic quality of *The Cholmondeley Ladies*. Its workmanship and general appearance lie closer to the conventional, essentially polite, portraiture of its time. We also know who most of the subjects are: Sir Thomas (1600–46), a minor courtier and Cheshire gentleman, his first wife, Magdalene, née Poultney (d.1635), probably his second wife, Anne, and two children presumably of the first marriage.[58] We know (because he signed it) that Souch painted it, and that he did so around 1635, some three decades after *The Cholmondeley Ladies*. And we know a fair bit about Souch. We may take the work itself to represent local and regional portraiture at a more advanced stage of assimilation of the formal polite mode and with the techniques required by that mode.

And yet, a closer investigation shows the two works share a very similar social and geographic context, and the latter as well as the former reveal some distinctively heraldic footprints. At least in its conventional readings, Souch's scene offers a clear genealogical record of a complex family. It has often been interpreted to show the

[56] Hopkins, '"Such a Twin Likeness"', 25–7.

[57] Glover, *Visitation of Cheshire, passim*; Armitage and Rylands, *Pedigrees Made at the Visitation of Cheshire, passim*; and Arthur Adams (ed.), *Cheshire Visitation Pedigrees, 1663* (Harleian Society, 93, 1941), *passim.*

[58] *ODNB*, vide 'Aston, Sir Thomas'. An unresolved question remains about the assigned date of the painting, 1635, and the identity of the second woman, as Aston's second marriage did not take place until 1637. One version has both women identified as Aston's first wife shown before and after death. Both marriages produced children, though those of the first marriage all died young.

death of one wife, the marriage with another, the two children whom we may presume resulted from the first marriage, all revolving around Aston himself as the paterfamilias. His family also figures in contemporary heraldic visitations. He, too, will have known, and been known by, regional heralds and herald painters. In fact, both correspondence and genealogical records tell us that branches of the Aston and Cholmondeley families remained in close and frequent touch with each other throughout the years in which both paintings appeared, and may well have intermarried.[59]

If Souch avoids the laconic use of colour in the heraldic idiom, he still makes ample use of symbolic objects—the cross, globe, skull, the watch depending from Aston's waistband, the coat of arms itself—to represent elements of character or emotion which his still only partially developed 'artistic' skills kept him from depicting in any more subtle or direct ways. He makes an honest effort at naturalistic modelling of his figures, their flesh and clothing; and he does at least present his figures in something approaching real space. But his sense of gesture, anatomy—witness Aston's oddly bent left leg—and especially perspective, remain insecure, and his figures bear little emotional or even conscious relationship with each other. The whole scheme of the work suggests the distorted perspective of a country fair fun-house.

All this fits with what we know and have seen of John Souch (1594–1645).[60] His father, an Ormskirk draper, apprenticed young John to Randle Holme the elder in 1607 for ten years. As noted in Chapter 4, Souch became a freeman of Chester as a member of his master's Chester Company of Painters, etc., shortly thereafter. He soon became a well-established portrait painter, catering mostly to the mostly Anglo-Catholic and Royalist gentry of Cheshire and surrounding counties. As many as sixteen surviving portraits have been attributed to him, six of them signed. He also served in local office, and, most important, he served as well as deputy to the College of Arms for Cheshire, Shropshire, and North Wales:[61] precisely the region in which he found his patronage. Holme would have trained Souch in heraldic as well as other forms of painting, probably helped him secure his post as deputy herald, and played an active role in steering potential patrons to his star pupil. Most significantly, it was almost certainly the senior Holme, in his heraldic capacity, who would have presided over the funeral of Magdalene Aston in 1635, just as he had over that of Thomas Aston's father and namesake, whose funeral certificate he actually signed in 1613 and examined again in 1640.[62] In addition, Holme would almost certainly have afforded Souch free and frequent

[59] See letters and other references scattered through the Aston Papers, BL. Add. MSS. 36,901-36,927. A letter from one of the Cholmondeleys to Sir Thomas Aston refers to the recipient as his 'verie lovinge kinsman Sir Thomas Aston'; BL. Add. MS 36,914 fo. 199^{r}.

[60] The following based on Julian Treuherz, 'New Light on John Souch of Chester', *Burlington Magazine*, 139/1130 (May 1997), 300–7; Weiss Gallery Collection, *Icons of Splendour: Early Portraiture, 1530–1700* (2004), 15; Heinz Archive, NPG, 'British Painters 1625–1650' file; Witt Library, Courtauld Institute of Art, 'Souch' file.

[61] Treuherz, 'New Light', 301.

[62] Weiss Gallery, *Icons of Splendour*, 15; J. P. Rylands (ed.), *Cheshire and Lancashire Funeral Certificates, 1600–1670* (Record Society of Lancashire and Cheshire, 6, 1882), 9.

access to the extensive and important collection of contemporary prints and drawings that Holme and his son were collecting in these years: a collection geared to the understanding of contemporary continental figurative art.[63]

This sort of training, and the obvious friendship which it spawned, gave Souch a considerable edge of refinement over whomever painted *The Cholmondeley Ladies*, in the very same region, a generation earlier. The contrast between the two works, and the training that would have produced them, marks the development of a native-English, and regional portraiture emerging over that time span, and of the influence of heraldic traditions in that story.

One final example demonstrates the influence of heraldic painting even at court. Robert Peake was one of the most prominent court painters of his time. He trained with the London Goldsmith Lawrence Woodham rather than with anyone directly connected to heraldry. There is little to suggest that he ever worked closely with heralds in his work. As Sergeant Painter to James I from 1607, a post he shared with Jan de Critz the elder, he will have enjoyed extensive exposure to the latest continental ideas about pictorial representation as conveyed both on panel or canvas and on the printed or engraved page. He was particularly interested in the latest theories of geometry and perspective as expressed by the likes of Inigo Jones and Sebastian Serlio, even distributing the first English edition of Serlio's *Five Books of Architecture* in 1611 from his shop. And yet notwithstanding all these attainments, a compelling case has been made for the consistent influence of heraldic tradition in his portraits, and even in those portraits in which no actual heraldic devices appear. His division of panels into geometric quarterings, his two-dimensional figures (contrasting with the striking three-dimensionality of some of his backgrounds), and his use of particular, vivid, and unmodulated colours, all point in that direction.[64]

In conclusion, the very nature of English vernacular portraiture as produced by sundry painter-stainers, herald painters, and similar craftsmen makes it impossible to attribute all but a very few specific portraits to their creators. We can only speculate at whomever may have painted *The Cholmondeley Ladies*. We are fortunate that John Souch and a few others like him signed some of his paintings and/or are identified in written documentation.

Until roughly the end of the sixteenth century native-English painters working outside of metropolitan London, the Home Counties, and southern- or eastern-facing coastlines will at first have had very little contact with continental, even Netherlandish, techniques or models from which to learn. They were unlikely to have travelled much abroad or to have apprenticed with those who had. But by the early seventeenth century, just about the time when *The Cholmondeley Ladies* appeared on the scene, they will have come more often to observe formal and

[63] Robert Tittler and Anne Thackray, 'Print Collecting in Provincial England Prior to 1650: The Randle Holme Album', *British Art Journal*, 11/1 (2008), 23–30.

[64] *ODNB*, vide 'Peake, Robert'; Ellen Chirelstein, 'Lady Elizabeth Pope: The Heraldic Body', in Lucy Gent and Nigel Llewellyn (eds), *Renaissance Bodies: The Human Figure in Renaissance Culture, c. 1540–1660* (1990), 47–53.

polite portraiture in the country houses of regional gentry and aristocracy or in occasional trips to London, and to have seen prints and engravings of the sort collected by the Holmes. Like Souch, many such painters came in time to try and emulate the more formal, continentally driven styles that the imperatives of social competition led their potential patrons more frequently to demand.

Yet earnest attempts to assimilate the new styles and techniques did not entirely eradicate the old ways. English provincial painters and even some native-born court painters of the same era produced a portraiture often distinctive for its fine, literal, and intricate detail; its extensive deployment of symbolic objects; its limited palette and laconic deployment of colours; and its concern for the genealogical record and other heraldic preoccupations. It is not, on the other hand, characterized by the emotional range, spatial dimension, naturalistic modelling, or complex and subtly blended colours typical of the mainstream of contemporary court painters, and especially foreign-born or -trained court painters, who comprised the elite ranks of the profession.

We see these lingering influences of heraldry and other traditional influences even in the better known native-English portraitists of the era: in the incomplete understanding of perspective in Souch's *Sir Thomas Aston* or in William Larkin's *Richard Sackville, third earl of Dorset* of 1613,[65] or in some of the work of Robert Peake. Larkin in particular also exemplifies the penchant for creating contours with firmly drawn outlines, which were then filled in with colour, rather than by building such contours up tonally, with subtly shaded layers of paint so as to create a chiaroscuro effect.[66] The former technique, along with the flat, two-dimensional, and poorly modelled applications of colour and the common inclusion of detailed pattern work that it encouraged, remained characteristic of both an heraldic and an English approach; the lack of chiaroscuro, or (as in *The Cholmondeley Ladies*) its clumsy application, distinguished it from mainstream continental portraiture, as did the still crude and laconic language of gesture. Peake, like John Browne, Andrew Wright, Nicholas Lyzard, George Gower, and others before him, served as Sergeant Painter,[67] a post that, amongst its considerable breadth of required expertise, might well have included heraldic work and even portraiture.

If the term 'English School' is to mean much more than merely work completed in England and presumably by an English painter, then these are the elements most likely to characterize it in the period at hand, and to distinguish it from formal, polite, and contemporary portraiture as it was produced elsewhere over most of Europe.

[65] *Richard Sackville, third earl of Dorset*, (1613), oil on canvas, 206.4 cm × 122.3 cm, depicted in Hearn, *Dynasties*, 199.

[66] Sir Roy Strong, 'William Larkin, Icons of Splendour', in id., *The Tudor and Stuart Monarchy: Pageantry, Painting, Iconography*, 3 vols (Woodbridge, Suffolk, 1998), III.7–9.

[67] Appointed in 1607; *ODNB*, vide 'Peake, Robert'.

7

The Provincial Vocabulary: 'Props' and Their Meaning

If provincial English painters often worked with a more constricted range of materials, shared a narrower world view, and received a less sophisticated training than their elite counterparts, what sort of portraits did they paint? What, aside from the figure itself and the frequent heraldic device, did they depict? What sort of content might we expect of provincially produced portraits during this era? These questions invite a discussion of portrait content as a reflection both of what patrons required and what painters could comfortably provide.

A portrait serves as a tableau in which the patron and the painter collaborate in determining and arranging the content so that it conveys the desired narrative. Most of the elite portrait painters of the day could bring their artistry to reproduce inner emotion and workings of the mind, or the appearance of figures, objects, and landscapes as if they existed in naturalistic, three-dimensional space. For the most sophisticated and affluent patrons, the painter's ability to do this, along with his reputation, represented key qualifications for employment. Nicholas Hilliard came to appreciate this in an exchange with Sir Philip Sidney, surely one of the most sophisticated English patrons of his time. As Hilliard tells the story, Sidney quizzed him on whether and how he could create the illusion of naturalistic perspective on the flat plane of his primed surface, or, to put it more essentially, whether he could paint the truth about the natural world. Hilliard's long and measured response, drawing partly on Lomazzo, showed at least some awareness of the principles of perspective and how they might be applied to the painted surface.[1]

However, to most other patrons, Sidney's criteria and standards were far less important than those of an essentially utilitarian nature. In responding to the sorts of motivations described in Chapter 2, the painting needed first, foremost, and often only to represent the subject in an appropriate light and setting. Few painters of Hilliard's time, almost none of them provincially based, could satisfactorily have met Sidney's criteria. Many would not have understood the question. The difference between Hilliard and those provincial contemporaries brings us to the depiction of windows in contemporary paintings: either as opening out to a distant scene so as realistically to convey the illusion of space and distance, or as a mere

[1] A. F. Kinney and Linda Bradley Salamon (eds), *Nicholas Hilliard's Art of Limning* (Boston, MA, 1983), 27–8. See also Clark Hulse, *The Rule of Art: Literature and Painting in the Renaissance* (Chicago and London, 1990), 120–2.

suggestion of such a scene which nevertheless remains visually on the surface plane of the painting, as if it were a painting within a painting.[2]

At one time or another, virtually all portrait painters of the era depicted in their work such ambient devices as material objects, inscriptions, armorial bearings, and physical settings in their effort to describe the sitter. Such content serves as a form of vocabulary. Generally lacking the ability to describe the sitter's interior life, provincial painters particularly relied on such a vocabulary to describe the sitter's exterior life instead. These elements at least narrated information *about* the sitter. Though allegory was not entirely unknown in provincial portraits, most painters employed their vocabulary in a laconic and therefore more readily accessible manner. Hilliard himself engaged in this sort of strategy in his very careful and extensive depiction of his sitters' clothing, jewels, and other details. Some have even considered that in Hilliard's miniatures, those accouterments were more important, and more carefully depicted, than the sitters' faces.[3]

As noted in Chapter 2, Maurice Howard has identified some paintings in which the sitters' figures have been drawn more uni-dimensionally than the backgrounds or other elements within the frame, suggesting that some contemporary painters could paint more naturalistically if they chose to do so. He has usefully suggested that protestant sensibilities may have felt threatened by images that were too realistic and life-like, such verisimilitude being seen as idolatrous to the biblically minded.[4] As the range of protestant attitudes towards portraiture throughout this period remained quite wide, this is by no means implausible. To some of the most fervent amongst them, the whole notion of portraiture violated the Second Commandment and therefore had to be proscribed. But the point remains that few if any provincial painters could rival in this regard the sort of painters whom, for example, someone like Sidney would have commissioned. Provincial, native-English painters in general really did lack the skills for persuasively naturalistic representation, and the frequent absence of precise verisimilitude in their works was most often unintentional.

The burden of describing the subject became particularly onerous in paintings whose subjects' faces were unfamiliar or unrecognizable on their own: those, for example, who were mythological, long deceased, or otherwise not personally known to the patron or painter. When the borough council of Coventry wished in the 1580s to commission a portrait of their semi-mythical champion, Lady Godiva, literal verisimilitude remained irrelevant (Fig. 7.1). An image of a nude woman riding her horse through city streets was all that mattered, though the urban background of the resulting portrait is said to depict the city of Coventry. The

[2] Lucy Gent, '"The Rash Gazer": Economies of Vision in Britain, 1550–1660', in ead. (ed.), *Albion's Classicism: The Visual Arts in Britain, 1550–1660* (London and New Haven, 1995), 383. See above, pp. 99–100.

[3] Ann Rosalind Jones and Peter Stallybrass, *Renaissance Clothing and the Materials of Memory* (Cambridge, 2000), 35, citing Patricia Fumerton, *Cultural Aesthetics: Renaissance Literature and the Practice of Social Ornament* (Chicago, 1991), 79–80.

[4] Maurice Howard, 'Art and the Reformation', in Tim Ayers (ed.), *The History of British Art 600–1600* (New Haven and London, 2008), 234.

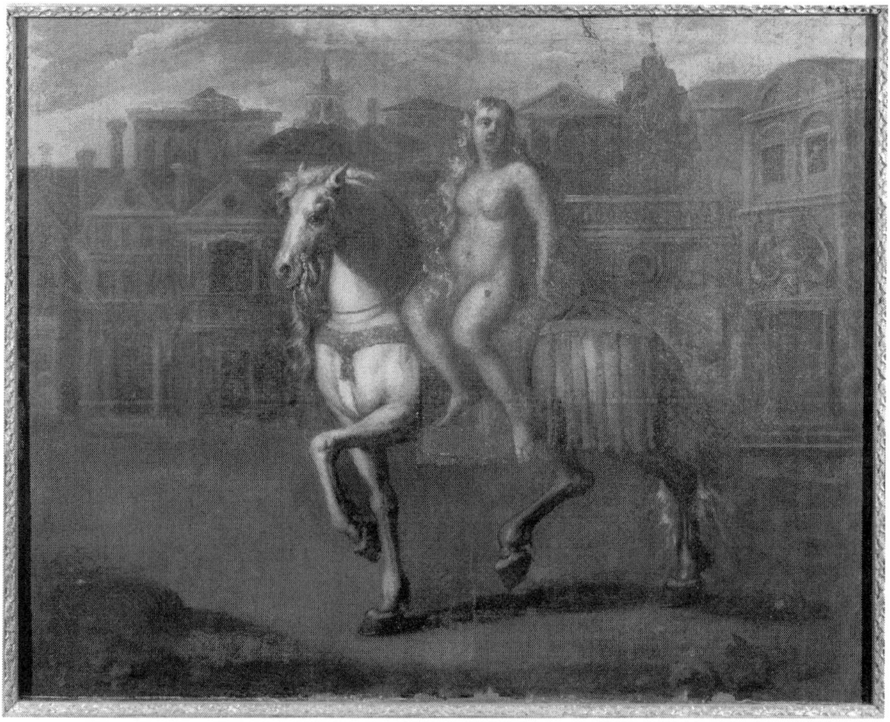

Fig. 7.1. Adam van der Noort (attributed), *Lady Godiva* (*c.*1586), oil on panel. © Bridgeman Art Library. Herbert Art Gallery, Coventry, no. 161/50 CH 1.

finished painting can only be considered a symbol rather than an accurate depiction of Godiva, but that was its purpose.[5]

Paintings of English kings and queens often reflected an iconic image of the monarch's visage as it appeared on the coins of the realm. But when paintings were required of living people who were not known to the patron, they could be either based on borrowed copies of likenesses or, failing that possibility, simply made up and labelled with the name of the desired subject: an emphatic form of painting as symbol. Most of the twenty or more extant portraits of the London Merchant Taylor and generous benefactor Sir Thomas White look very much alike because they were copies of only one or two originals. Exceptionally, those in Chester and Gloucester bear no resemblance to the rest. Officials of both cities felt they should have a portrait of White, who had generally endowed each city, along with twenty-one other towns and one London livery, with a lucrative, perpetual charity. But for some reason they failed to go to the trouble or expense of borrowing one of

[5] See also R. A. Clarke and P. A. E. Day, *Lady Godiva: Images of a Legend in Art and Society* (Coventry, 1982).

the other White portraits from which to make a copy. They simply had a generic portrait made up locally and added a label identifying the subject as White.

For paintings of most living people verisimilitude did of course matter, especially when the purpose of the painting was to create a record of the subject's appearance. This was important to patrons like Thomas Whythorne, who, as noted in Chapter 2, wanted to create a record of his appearance over time for both himself and his descendants.[6] Whythorne certainly practised what he preached, sitting at least four times for his portrait at different stages of his adult life.

Virtually all painters could create at least a reasonable 'counterfeit' of the subject's appearance when they could paint from life or copy from another image. But at one time or another most employed additional elements within the picture frame to help describe the sitter to the viewer. The use of such 'props' applied to portraits at all levels of sophistication. Antonis Mor could produce one of the most naturalistic portraits of his time in his *Sir Henry Lee* of 1568,[7] but even for one of his consummate talent and skill, props still mattered. Joanna Woodall's close reading of Mor's 'wedding portrait' of Mary I aptly exemplifies the point.[8]

If we think of portraits as texts to be read by the viewer, it stands to reason that some sitters and patrons had different sorts of things to say in such texts than others. Especially by the opening of the seventeenth century elite patrons enjoying or aspiring to courtly status might choose from a vocabulary of material objects that Woodall has described as 'the courtly console tables, wooden chairs, curtains, columns, helmets, and handkerchiefs'. They might include such animate figures as 'dogs, dwarfs, servants, jesters, and black attendants'.[9] And they might well include classical or biblical allusions of the sort that Holbein pioneered in portraying Henry VIII as Solomon on his throne or as David taking aim at Goliath.[10] This approach reached its apogee under Elizabeth and the first two Stuarts. The culture of those courts imaginatively mixed prose, music, poetry, and drama along with visual imagery to celebrate the monarch in myriad allegorical ways: Elizabeth as Deborah or Judith, as Tuccia the Virgin, as Diana, as Cynthia, as Belphoebe, as Astraea, and so forth.[11] Though English portraiture in general probably reflected fewer elements of classical design than other visual genres of that time,[12] such

[6] James M. Osborne (ed.), *The Autobiography of Thomas Whythorne* (Oxford, 1961), 134 (spelling modernized).

[7] Antonis Mor, *Sir Henry Lee* (1568), oil on panel, 64.2 cm × 53.3 cm, NPG.

[8] Joanna Woodall, '"An Exemplary Consort": Antonis Mor's Portrait of Mary Tudor', *Art History*, 14/1 (June 1991), 192–224.

[9] Joanna Woodall (ed.), *Portraiture: Facing the Subject* (Manchester and New York, 1997), 2.

[10] Christopher Lloyd and Simon Thurley, *Henry VIII: Images of a Tudor King* (1990), 30–1.

[11] Classically expounded in E. C. Wilson, *England's Eliza* (Cambridge, MA, 1939), but see also, amongst myriad works on the same theme, Lloyd and Thurley, *Henry*; David Howarth, *Images of Rule: Art and Politics in the English Renaissance, 1485–1649* (Berkeley and Los Angeles, 1997), 28, 27, 90, 111; Frances Yates, 'Queen Elizabeth as Astraea', *Journal of the Warburg and Courtauld Institutes*, 10 (1947), 27–82; and Elizabeth W. Pomeroy, *Reading the Portraits of Queen Elizabeth I* (Hamden, CT, 1989).

[12] Inferred from Anthony Wells-Cole, *Art and Design in Elizabethan and Jacobean England: The Influence of Continental Prints, 1558–1625* (London and New Haven, 1997), 12 and Ch. 12.

elements will nevertheless also have figured prominently in a good many such portraits.

However, as we've seen in Chapter 5, provincial portraits done for middling and lesser patrons reflected a simpler and more insular mental world. In consequence, they displayed a more restricted vocabulary and one informed by a native-English rather than a particularly sophisticated, more classically informed outlook. Here allegorical allusions almost disappear (while somehow remaining common in wall paintings), and material objects become much more mundane. The common run of provincial imagery extends to items like books, gloves, swords (as opposed, for example, to lances or armour), hourglasses, clocks, skulls, scrolls, and distinctive (but not always elaborate) forms of dress. We also more often find in these works than in those produced for the court circle and landed elites (and also more often than portraits produced elsewhere in Europe) written inscriptions and heraldic devices meant literally to be read.

This is not to suggest an absence of vocabulary which could readily be shared by both ends of the patronal continuum, but rather that the sharing necessarily remained one-sided. The more sophisticated painters and patrons certainly drew from the more mundane elements of their subordinates' portraits, but their own more sophisticated references often lay beyond the cultural or pragmatic reach of many middling status provincial patrons or of the native-English painters whom they employed.

Still, the purpose of such elements remained the same throughout. They helped convey the sitter's identity and self-image, communicating as best they could such qualities as his/her beliefs, moral bearings, religious affiliations, occupational and intellectual attainments, social status, fecundity, emotional states, and other biographical distinctions. When a successful and upwardly mobile merchant or craftsman commissioned a portrait, for example, he often wanted it to proclaim his achievement as a major benefactor or his arrival into the ranks of the country squirarchy, distancing himself from what was still often considered the morally dubious life of commerce and the city in which he had gained his fortune. As noted in Chapter 2, he more often commissioned a portrait showing what he did with his money rather than how he earned it. Of course there are exceptions to this. The merchant George Benson has his ships on view through a window in his portrait at St John's College, Oxford; the London Mercer John Isham has his ledger books shown in a shelf behind him in his portrait at Lamport Hall (Fig. 6.1); William Portington, Master Carpenter to the Crown, has his calipers and ruler in hand.[13] And, as noted in Chapter 4, George Gower was so proud of his painter's occupation that he displayed his calipers weighing more heavily on a balance scale than his family's arms.[14] But the exceptions are so few as to support the general rule.

[13] Oil on panel, 43" × 32¾"; R. M. Poole (ed.), *Catalogue of Portraits in . . . the University, Colleges, City and County of Oxford*, 3 vols (Oxford Historical Society Publications, vols 57, 1912; 81, 1926; and 82, 1926), III.165; Heinz Archive, NPG, vide 'Isham, Portington'.

[14] George Gower, oil on panel, 23¾" × 19½" (1579), private collection.

Props must be considered in the context of the subject, time, and place. Even when the same material object may be found in different paintings, it may not bear the same connotations from one to another. Particularly for those of lesser status, such props do more than place the sitter in his or her material world. They possess an agency in and of themselves effectively to define the sitter. No one blinks on seeing a portrait of the earl of Leicester wearing a sword round his waist. We expect him to wear one: if he is the earl of Leicester of course he wears a sword. But one certainly does take note when a sword graces some more obscure figure. Here the assumption becomes that if he wears a sword, he must be part of the landed gentry, with the additional connotations of military service and even chivalric ideals that accrued to that status. The Yorkshire esquire John Kaye (Fig. 4.2) was neither entitled by contemporary sumptuary laws to wear a sword nor did he quite possess the effrontery to have one shown on his portrait.[15] But he does have a knife sheathed at his belt as if it were a sword: a similar violation of those laws, but not as much of an affront to their spirit. In the eye of the beholder, it is in this case the suggestion of a sword that makes the man.

The depiction of gloves makes for an interesting example of an object whose meaning in a portrait depended at least in part on the identity of the sitter. In some circumstances, gloves also possess an agency of their own in forging the sitter's identity. We find gloves in all sorts of portraits: of men and women, of the courtly and the non-courtly, of landed gentry and urban tradesmen. We find them in various states: worn, lying on a table, and, most often, as a pair held together in one hand. We also see them in various states of finery and embellishment, from the relatively mundane to the extraordinarily ornate.

In paintings of the landed classes and courtly circle, gloves had long been taken as a sign of gentility.[16] After all, they were expensive items, often delicately laced or embroidered, and they were costly both to clean and to repair. In the early years of our period only the reasonably well-off could afford leather gloves of any sort, much less the long-cuffed and embroidered varieties that became fashionable later on. Then, too, gloves protected the hands from manual labour, which remained well below the dignity of the landed classes to perform. Gloves figure very frequently and prominently in the courtly portraits of both men and women throughout the period at hand, becoming more elaborately designed and decorated up to about the 1620s and 1630s.[17] All of this made gloves prime objects for conspicuous display in the socially mobile society of that time.

And yet, despite their frequent signification of gentility, we find them as well in portraits of sitters who were not only below the status of the landed elites, but were also urban people like merchants and craftsmen. This begs a question. How would contemporaries have interpreted the appearance of gloves in the

[15] Tolson Museum, Huddersfield, ref. nos. KLMUS 1990/399; KLMUS 1990/398; KLMUS 1990/398a; and KLMUS 1990/399a. My thanks to Kathryn White, Museum and Galleries Collection Manager, for shedding light on these works.

[16] Lorne Campbell, *Renaissance Portraits* (London and New Haven, 1990), 99; David R. Smith, *Masks of Wedlock: Seventeenth Century Dutch Marriage Portraiture* (Ann Arbor, MI, 1982), 74–81.

[17] Valerie Cumming, *Gloves* (1982), 21–7.

urban, non-courtly, context? Would townspeople viewing such portraits have seen them as pretensions to gentility, or would they have read them with alternative or additional meanings? The preliminary answer must of course be that different sorts of people would have seen them in different ways. While a member of the landed aristocracy might see them as pretentious claims to higher status, a townsperson would indeed have read quite different things in that image.

The first meaning that gloves will have held for the townsperson and citizen would have been a signification of the subject's full membership in the civic body: the freemanry, or a particular guild or livery company. In some such cases the guild or company might even be referred to as 'the gloverie': hence the London Painter-Stainer Thomas Tottey left in his will of 1630 five pounds 'to the poor of the gloverie'.[18] In many towns throughout the realm, a newly elected freeman signified his election, and his new status as a member of those inner circles, by giving pairs of gloves as gifts to his newly acquired brethren. In many towns and cities this practice extended back to pre-Reformation usage. It signified gratitude for admission to the ranks, submission to the collective will of the corporate body, and a willingness to share in its burdens and costs. In the Somerset town of Wells the very recording of new freemen's admissions in the town book, the Great Assembly Book, included a glove—clearly not a hand—drawn in the margin of the page next to the record of that admission.[19] Gloves would also have represented a sign of friendship: a figurative or symbolic shaking of the hands with new colleagues. In some cases it also meant that one had clean hands in the sense of being uncorrupted.[20] In paintings that employ gloves in this way, the glove helps make the guildsman or (in London) the liveryman.

Interestingly, and though the number of portraits that can be discovered of urban women remains quite limited to begin with, it is extremely unusual for urban women to be shown with gloves in such civic paintings, just as it remained extremely unusual for a woman to enter the freemanry in her own right. This stands in marked contrast to the increasingly frequent depiction of gentlewomen of the same era wearing gloves: another distinction in the social symbolism of gloves in civic and courtly contexts.

As is often the case, a prominent exception proves the rule. A double portrait of John and Joan Cooke, Mayor and Mayoress of Gloucester, shows Joan rather than John holding the gloves (Fig. 7.2). There is a reason for this. This is a posthumous portrait, probably done in the early years of the seventeenth century, of a married couple long deceased. John Cooke, four-time Mayor of Gloucester, died in 1528. He willed a substantial sum to be employed in the founding of a grammar school in the Gloucester parish church of St Mary Crypt. He named his wife, Joan, as his chief executor, making her responsible for establishing that foundation. Joan took

[18] TNA, PROB 11/157/35.

[19] David Gary Shaw, *The Creation of a Community: The City of Wells in the Middle Ages* (Oxford, 1993), 157, 198–9.

[20] Anon., *Brewer's Dictionary of Phrase and Fable*, 2nd edn (1952), 403.

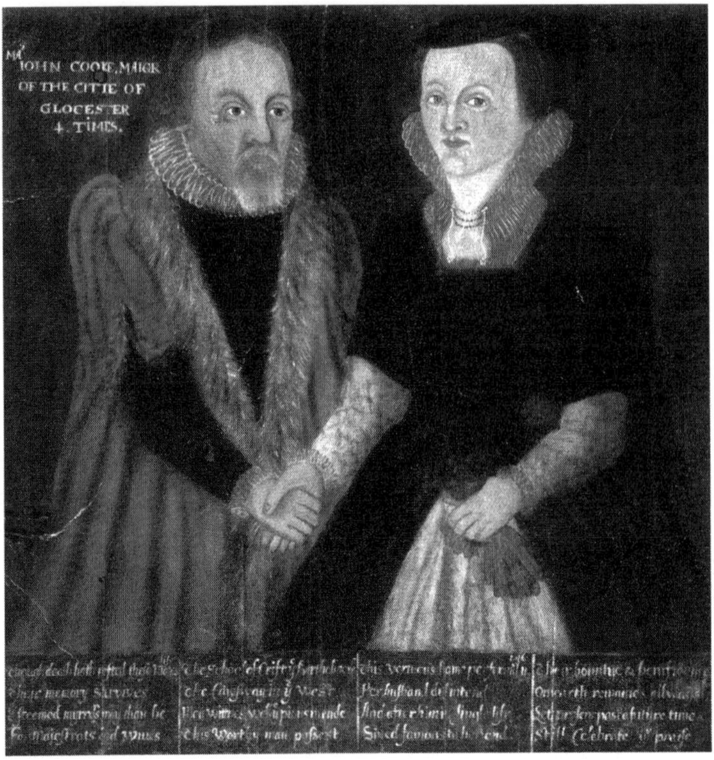

Fig. 7.2. Anon., *John and Joan Cooke, Mayor and Mayoress of Gloucester* (*c.*1600–20). © Gloucester City Museum and Art Gallery.

that responsibility very seriously, adding to John's bequest in her own will and effecting the actual establishment of the school by the time of her death in 1544.[21]

The portrait narrates this story in several semiotic ways. John is pictured in a passive, wooden, and trance-like state, indicating his demise. Joan, by contrast, with her lively eyes looking straight at the viewer and still very much alive, leads John's figure (and hence, his legacy) forth with her right hand while clutching the gloves—the sign of his freeman's status now devolved upon her—in her left. She now 'wears the gloves', if not the proverbial trousers, and has utilized the status that they symbolize to carry out the intentions of his will. The organization of these elements within the picture frame places the gloves front and centre: they are the most important element in the story.

A second connotation borne by glove-holding in civic and urban portraits is also at least indirectly connected to the notion of the freemanry; it also has links with the symbolism of gloves amongst the landed classes. This usage concerns the traditional

[21] Robert Tittler, 'John and Joan Cooke: Civic Portraiture and Urban Identity in Gloucester', in id., *Townspeople and Nation: English Urban Experiences, 1540–1640* (Stanford, CA, 2001), 81–99.

and perhaps most essential role of the freemanry, which was to regulate the market and, by extension, virtually all economic activities in the town. Most markets began as perquisites of feudal lordship, in which the lord of the town served, with royal sanction, as the immediate authority over that place of meeting and exchange. He either ran the market himself, through his bailiff or steward, or permitted selected townsmen to do it on his behalf. Directly or, in most cases, indirectly, he thus exercised the judicial authority over its activities. To reflect this responsibility, the custom arose in many towns whereby the erection of a leather glove or carved wooden hand on a long pole signalled the opening of the market day. The lowering of the gloved pole signalled its close. The hand or glove represented the hand of that lord under whose protection the market proceeded, and under which buyers and sellers could be assured of that jurisdiction. When the hand came down, that protection, and the market itself, came to an end for the day.[22]

Finally, in English as well as Dutch portraits of the time, gloves bore two additional implications that helped define their wearer's identity or character. They were often given at weddings both to the bride and groom and to guests. And second, they were taken as signs of friendship when removed from the hand and held, just as one removes one's glove today to shake hands. In both cases they were signs of good will and good wishes.[23]

Other commonly employed props were religious in nature, affirming and/or defining the nature of personal belief in these decades of religious upheaval and uncertainty. They appear in portraits of both Catholics and protestants, but not always in the same forms. Protestant sitters had to be careful about portraiture to begin with, making sure that a portrait of, for example, a biblical figure or prominent reformer didn't come across as an object of veneration as would have been the case with, e.g., saints' portraits prior to the Reformation. But portraiture as commemoration or in other secular guises passed muster with all but the very most strenuous puritan critics.[24]

In view of such negative attitudes towards portraits on the part of the extremists, there is some irony in the need felt by some other protestants to use portraiture in a positive manner to affirm their religious identity. Certainly the shifting sands of religious belief in these years created ample imperative for such a need. Resulting portraits celebrated piety by frequent inclusion of a Bible in the scene, by depiction of modest, often black, dress, and by a frequent inclusion of memento mori

[22] Robert Tittler, 'Freemen's Gloves and Civic Authority: The Evidence from Post-Reformation Portraiture', *Costume*, 40 (2006), 15 and n. 10. The custom endured in some towns into the 19th century: Joseph Gribble, writing in 1830, observes its use in announcing the annual fair in his native Barnstaple even then: Joseph B. Gribble, *Memorials of Barnstaple: A History of That Ancient Borough* (Barnstaple, 1830), 292.

[23] Smith, *Masks of Wedlock*, 75–8.

[24] The copious literature on this is succinctly summarized in Daniel Woolf, *The Social Circulation of the Past: English Historical Culture 1500–1700* (Oxford, 2003), 189–200. See also Margaret Aston, *England's Iconoclasts*, Vol. I: *Laws against Images* (Oxford, 1988), *passim*; Tessa Watt, *Cheap Print and Popular Piety, 1550–1640* (Cambridge, 1991), 131–40, 159–68, 185–6; and Patrick Collinson, *The Birthpangs of Protestant England: Religious and Cultural Change in the Sixteenth and Seventeenth Centuries* (Basingstoke, 1988), 117–19.

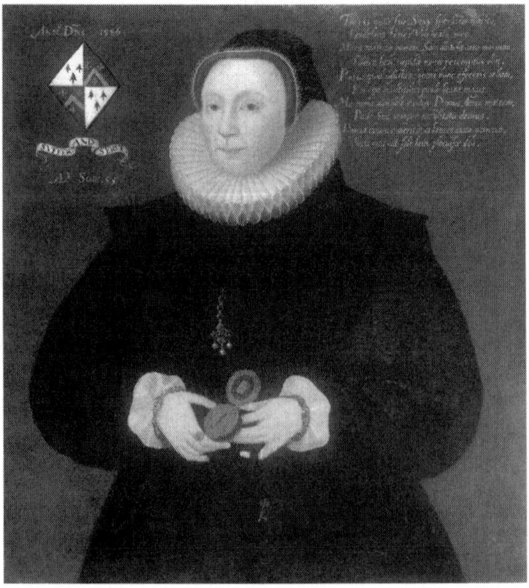

Fig. 7.3. Anon., *Joyce Frankland* (*c.*1586/7), oil on panel, 25" × 20½". By permission of the Principal and Fellows of Brasenose College, Oxford.

imagery, including skulls, hourglasses, and sometimes clocks. The Elizabethan portrait of Francis Windham of Norfolk covers as many of these bases as possible within a single frame. It features a skull (inscribed, lest the point should somehow be missed, '*Cogita Mori*'!), hourglass, and Bible, and depicts the sitter in black dress.[25]

The depiction of clocks or watches in such imagery tells us that memento mori imagery—intended to emphasize man's mortality, the fleeting nature of life on earth, and the imminence of death—continued to evolve over the Reformation divide. It may even be seen as following technological developments in the creation of such time-keeping devices over the course of that era. We see small clocks in the *c.*1616 portrait of Hester Crispe,[26] and in at least two of the portraits of Joyce Frankland (Fig. 7.3). Frankland in particular certainly had occasion to contemplate the fleeting passage of time and her own mortality on the occasion of those paintings. By 1577 this London merchant's wife had been widowed a second time, and had only her son, William, remaining. When he was thrown from a horse and tragically killed in 1581 she is said to have been beside herself with grief. According to the story associated with the portraits, her very close friend, the dean of St Paul's, Alexander Nowell, came to her side and suggested that she could extend her largesse to other young men of her son's approximate age by making endowments to university colleges. Frankland proceeded accordingly, making generous

[25] Anon., oil on panel, Norwich Castle Museum and Art Gallery, civic portrait no. C60.

[26] Anon., oil on canvas, private collection. I am grateful to Melissa Hamnett, Victoria and Albert Museum, for bringing this portrait to my attention.

endowments to four colleges plus the Grammar School of Newport, Essex.[27] The inscription on the Brasenose version tells of her loss, and asks, 'Fate, why do you insult me?' The image of the clock, held open to the viewer so as better to see the time, conveys the full force of memento mori imagery: life's fleeting and uncertain nature obliges us to act charitably while we can.[28] Many other portraits of the era employ clocks, hourglasses, wilted or withered foliage, skulls, and even full skeletons to convey the same message.

Memento mori images also emphasized the subject's humility in the face of time's passage, the fragile and finite quality of life on earth, and the potential terrors of what followed. Portraits devoted to such imagery tended to mark threshold occasions in the life of the sitter or the family. Their common appearance in tomb imagery often marked periods of intense spiritual reflection. Tarnya Cooper has found this imagery particularly common amongst the middling elites—lesser gentry, merchants, and urban professionals—and amongst those of protestant inclination.[29] The fact that so many of the surviving civic portraits from Norwich, an early and fervent hotbed of Protestantism, display such imagery adds weight to this suggestion.[30]

Of course not all portraits with religious content were either memento mori portraits or commissioned for protestant patrons. Catholic recusants continued to commission portraits long after the break from Rome and the proscription of purgatorial belief. Some of them even depicted their sitters in the act of prayer. Others found alternate means of recording or even flaunting their loyalty to the old faith. Though anti-Catholic sentiment will have led them to be commissioned and displayed with great care, enough of these recusant portraits survive for us to treat them as a distinct class.

A useful example, noted above in Chapter 2, may be found at Towneley Hall: a portrait of *c.*1601 depicting two generations of the Towneley family at prayer (Fig. 2.4). At the start of Elizabeth's reign John Towneley (d.1607) was but a steward of Ightenhill Manor, with the minor gentry status of 'esquire'. By 1601 he had gained important connections through marriage, amassed considerable wealth, and worked his way into the middling ranks of the Lancashire gentry. But though his social status changed (and though he could claim Alexander Nowell, the very

[27] *ODNB*, vide 'Frankland'; W. K. Jordan, *The Charities of London* (1969), 263–4; Robert Tittler, 'Thomas Heywood and the Portrayal of Female Benefactors in Post-Reformation England', *Early Theatre*, 11/1 (June 2008), 44–6.

[28] Poole, *Catalogue of Oxford Portraits*, II.247; Tarnya Cooper, '*Memento Mori* Portraiture: Painting, Protestant Culture and the Patronage of the Middle Elites in England and Wales, 1540–1630', unpublished PhD thesis, University of Sussex (2001), 336–7. I am very grateful to Dr Cooper for allowing me to read and cite this thesis.

[29] Cooper, '*Memento Mori* Portraiture', 2–3 *et passim*; Nigel Llewellyn, *Funeral Monuments in Post-Reformation England* (Cambridge, 2000), esp. 337–9; Peter Sherlock, *Monuments and Memory in Early Modern England* (Aldershot, 2008), esp. 77–84.

[30] These would include portraits of John Marsham (with skull), Robert Jannys (with skull and skeleton), Augustine Steward (skull), Sir Edward Coke (skull), Robert Yarham (skull), Thomas Layer (skull), Thomas Anguish (skull), and Wyndham (skull and hourglass), all done before 1611. Conveniently depicted in Andrew Moore and Charlotte Crawley (eds), *Family and Friends: A Regional Survey of British Portraiture* (1992), 196–8.

protestant dean of St Paul's, as his brother-in-law) his faith remained steady throughout. Towneley experienced continual persecution for his recusancy, including long spells in prison. Yet he remained one of the stalwarts of Lancashire Catholicism throughout his life.[31]

The Towneley family portrait has two prominent themes. First, it records the family and its lineage in heraldic detail. We see four small coats of arms on the left-hand side, representing John's family, and three coats of arms on the right side, representing his wife's. A large coat of arms in the top centre of the picture frame shows both sides combined: eight coats of arms in all. And second, it is intended as an explicit celebration of the family's continued adherence to the old faith. Both John and his wife, the central figures, kneel in an attitude of prayer at a prie-dieu in the very centre of the picture frame. The male children on the left and female on the right line up behind them in similar poses. It is, in all, a prime example of what must have been, in Lancashire and other notoriously Catholic areas of the realm, a widespread affirmation of continuing Catholic identity through successive generations of a single family.

Most such flagrantly Catholic portraits were intended to be seen by the family and members of the household, and by those who came for social visits or even the celebration of religious rites. Many of them were kept within the house, and the family, from generation to generation. One suspects that many remain there still, undiscovered outside that closed family circle. Others lacked an association with a family and are less likely to have been preserved: the picture of the Holy Trinity left by John Baxter of Newcastle in 1597 to his friend and fellow alderman William Jenison, for example, has vanished.[32]

A few such portraits were more publicly accessible right from the start. The still extant portrait of John Alcock (1430–1500), Bishop of Ely and founder of Jesus College, Cambridge, done as late as 1598 though probably based on an earlier copy, would have been visible within the College's walls where it may be seen today (Fig. 7.4).[33] Alcock has what we must assume is his prayer book spread out before him, next to his mitre, resting on his prie-dieu. The books in this and similar portraits would have been service books: books of hours, missals, breviaries, and so forth.

The inclusion of books as shown in the Towneley family portraits or in Alcock's, or—for that matter—in the famous copy of 'The Family of Thomas More' by

[31] David George (ed.), *Records of Early English Drama, Lancashire* (Toronto, Buffalo, and London, 1991), 99 and 182; Christopher Haigh, *Reformation and Resistance in Tudor Lancashire* (Cambridge, 1975), 251, 260–1.

[32] Durham University Library MS. DPR I/1597/B3/2.

[33] The image looks in every way as if it had jumped off the page of a late medieval, Gothic manuscript, but a payment for a portrait of Alcock is recorded in the College archives in 1598. I am grateful to Ms Frances Willmouth, College Archivist, to Dr Rod Mengham, College Fellow and Curator of Pictures, and Professor Keith Wrightson, all of whom helped me track this down. Robert Tittler, *The Face of the City, Civic Portraiture and Civic identity in Early Modern England* (Manchester, 2007), 38–9 and n. 5.

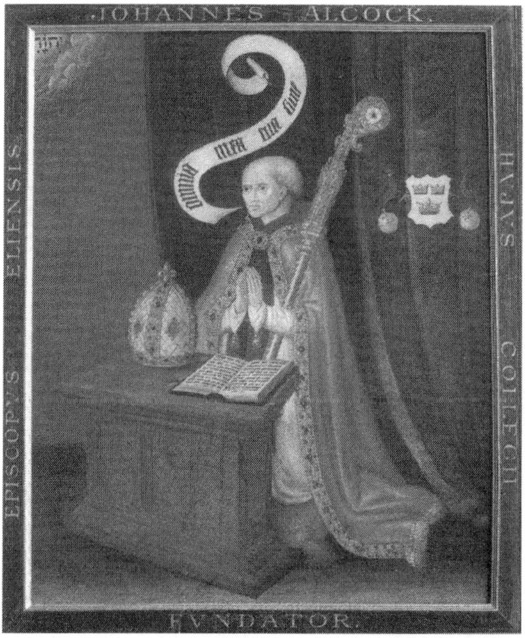

Fig. 7.4. Anon., *Bishop John Alcock, founder, Jesus College, Cambridge* (1598?). By permission of the Masters and Fellows, Jesus College, Cambridge.

Rowland Lockey, show their use in portraits of Catholic and Catholic families.[34] But of course it is protestantism that we think of as the religion of the word, and we find books included more commonly here than elsewhere. In portraits of those not principally engaged in intellectual activity, books represented the attainment of literacy itself: a new achievement for many at this time, and one that marked the sitter's identity as laying outside the traditional and still highly valued context of knighthood, chivalry, and military service. For those whose literacy might readily be assumed, the inclusion of books often spoke to the importance of scripture and/or to the burgeoning humanist learning of the day.

Examples of this usage abound at several levels of the social pyramid. At the top end, we see this early in our period in Holbein's famous 1523 portrait of Erasmus[35] and his first (1527) portrait of archbishop William Warham;[36] in the foreigner Gerlach Flicke's 1545 or 1546 portrait of Thomas Cranmer;[37] in the anonymous

34 Rowland Lockey, *Sir Thomas More, His Father, His Household, and His Descendants* (1593), oil on canvas, 89½" × 130"; NPG no. 2765.

35 Paul Ganz, *The Paintings of Hans Holbein* (1950), plate 64, catalogue no. 34 (Longford Castle, Salisbury).

36 Ibid. plate 81, cat. 46 (Lambeth Palace, London).

37 Karen Hearn (ed.), *Dynasties: Painting in Tudor and Jacobean England, 1530–1630* (1995), plate 12 (National Gallery, London).

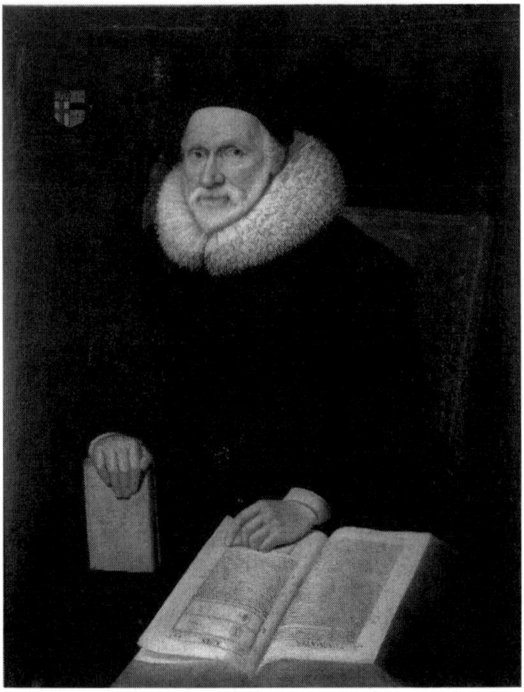

Fig. 7.5. Anon., *William Camden* (presented 1622), oil on canvas, 43" × 32". By permission of the Provost and Fellows of Worcester College, Oxford.

portrait of archbishop Matthew Parker done in Norwich;[38] and in most of the Peterhouse, Cambridge, portraits of its founder and benefactors.[39] One version of Lockey's large 'More Family' paintings of *c.*1593 shows no fewer than seven members of this learned dynasty, three of them women, holding books.[40] Books appear in a great many university and college portraits, as we would expect, and in portraits of school officials and benefactors like Sir Richard Dobbs, founder of Christ's Hospital (now in Horsham), Lady Mary Ramsay, benefactress to the same,[41] and Richard Platt, founder of Aldenham School in 1599.[42]

Sometimes sitters are shown holding books that they have written themselves, in which cases the painting means to celebrate the sitter's reputation as an author. Worcester College, Oxford's portrait of William Camden shows him with two books, one of which is a copy of his *Britannia* (Fig. 7.5).[43] Brasenose College,

[38] Now located in the Castle Museum of that City, but presumably done for the Guildhall as one of the Norwich civic series.

[39] See listing in Tittler, *Face of the City*, 169–72.

[40] Lockey, *Sir Thomas More*, NPG, no. 2765.

[41] Both portraits are still in the possession of the Hospital, are displayed on the walls of its buildings, and are fully identified in their inscriptions. My thanks to Ms Rhona Mitchell for guiding me through this collection.

[42] Nicholas Carlisle, *A Concise Description of the Endowed Grammar Schools of England and Wales*, 2 vols (1818), I.528–30.

[43] Poole, *Catalogue*, III.256.

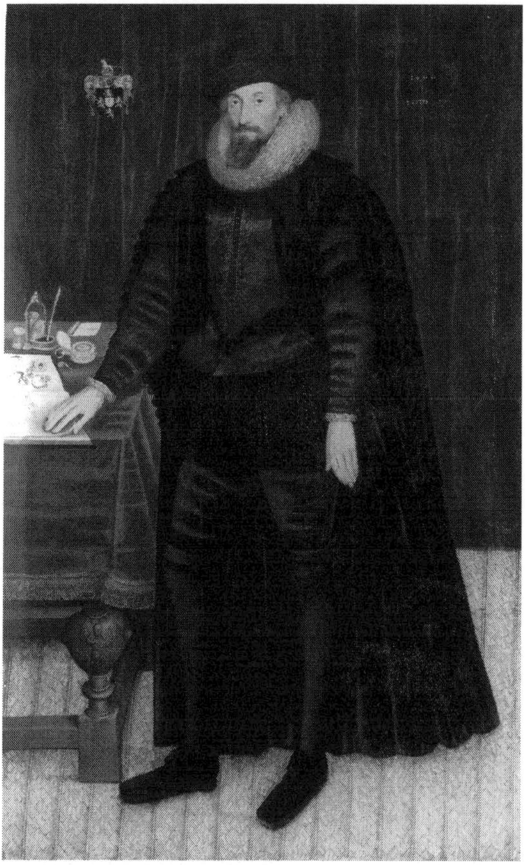

Fig. 7.6. Marcus Gheeraerts the younger (?), *Sir William Paddy* (*c.*1600), oil on panel, 83" × 51". The President and Fellows of St John's College, Oxford.

Oxford's portrait of its fellow and benefactor Alexander Nowell (putative host, in Thomas Heywood's play *If You Know Not Me, You Know No Body*, in his London picture gallery) engages in a rare and playful recognition of both his vocation and his avocation in displaying both books and fish-hooks, with a flyrod on the wall behind him.[44] And St John's, Oxford's portrait of Sir William Paddy, BA and Fellow of the College and also president of the Royal College of Physicians, shows him with an opened book of anatomical drawings to celebrate his erudition in that field (Fig. 7.6).[45] Those few surviving portraits depicting lawyers and judges also tend to include books as testaments to the sitter's learning in the law. The

[44] Oil on panel, 34¾" × 27¼" (Brasenose College, Oxford), Poole, *Catalogue*, II.249–50; Tittler, 'Thomas Heywood', 33–52.

[45] Poole, *Catalogue*, III.163–4.

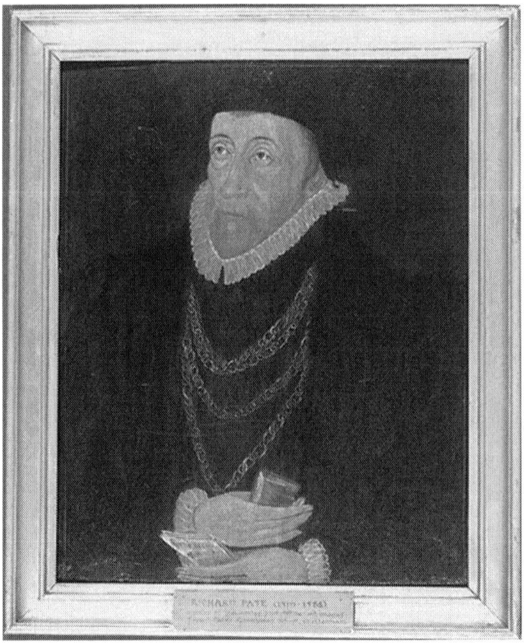

Fig. 7.7. Anon., *Richard Pate* (*c.*1610–20). © Gloucester City Museum and Art Gallery.

Gloucester portrait of Richard Pate, who was both a barrister and a school-founder and perhaps the most important Gloucester citizen of his time, touches several of these bases at once (Fig. 7.7).[46]

That huge Oxford portrait series of this era known as 'the Bodley Frieze' does not show any of its 202 subjects actually holding books. But most of the subjects owed their fame, and their portrait image, to the books they had written. This has led one authority to interpret the series itself as a celebration of the authors represented in the Bodley collection at the time of its foundation.[47]

On the other hand, we find fewer depictions of books in portraits of courtly or aristocratic subjects—especially the men of those groups—for whom book learning in general took longer to become the virtue that it had become for others, and who were often still largely bound up in a chivalric and patently non-literary culture. Nor do they frequently appear in mayoral or livery company portraits save when a prominent liveryman also founded a school or college. Such middling status urban dwellers were usually literate by this time, but literacy did not serve as their claim to fame.

[46] Brian Frith, *Twelve Portraits of Gloucester* (Gloucester, 1972), 12–13; History of Parliament Trust, *The House of Commons, 1509–1558*, ed. S. T. Bindoff, 3 vols (1982), III.69–70, and *The House of Commons, 1558–1603*, ed. P. W. Hasler, 3 vols (1981), III.185–6.

[47] J. N. L. Myers, 'Thomas James and the Painted Frieze', *Bodleian Library Record*, 4 (1952–3), 30–51.

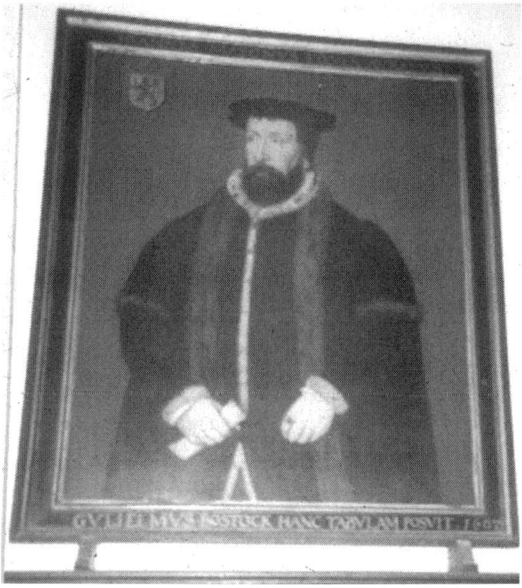

Fig. 7.8. Sampson Strong, *Sir John Mason* (1607). With the kind permission of Christ's Hospital of Abingdon.

Scrolls, on the other hand, do play a frequent role in civic portraits, and their meaning is both less mysterious and more precise. Many civic portraits, especially those done for schools and charitable institutions, were produced to commemorate the founder and the foundation of an institution or the acquisition of a charter. The few extant 'charter presentation' group portraits show charters in their scrolled form, as in Edward VI's presenting the charter to Christ's Hospital (now in Horsham) and to Bridewell Hospital.[48] As documentation for the act of foundation, and also as very large paintings, these representations were important to render in their full and complete form. But in individual portraits of founders themselves, there was neither room nor need to be quite so literal in displaying the document. The tightly rolled and fairly small bundle of paper or parchment we so frequently see in such portraits thus served symbolically to represent such documents, but their meaning can hardly have been lost on the viewer.

We see just this implication of a held scroll in the portrait of Sir John Mason commissioned for, and still displayed at, Christ's Hospital, Abingdon (Fig. 7.8). A national figure as a member of Mary Tudor's Privy Council in any event, Mason was also a loyal native son of Abingdon. He was educated in its grammar school, from which he then matriculated at Oxford. He was one of two petitioners for the refounding of Christ's Hospital in 1553 after it had been dissolved and thus helped

[48] Heinz Archive, vide 'Christ's Hospital', 'Bridewell Hospital'; L. M. N. Surrey (ed.), *The Portraits of Edward VI* (Portsmouth, n.d.), 89–90.

to secure its charter. When the petition succeeded, Mason served as the Hospital's first lay governor.[49]

The portrait was commissioned by the governors, and especially by one of their number named William Bostock, to be copied from a personal portrait of Mason that had been done for his family.[50] Mason wears clothing that seems unrelated to the office, but the meaning of the scroll in his right hand, often seen and understood as the hand of power and authority, seems clear. The same may be said for the scroll-bearing figure of Robert Thorne of Bristol, founder of its Grammar School,[51] while the scroll held by John Vowell, alias Hooker, probably marks the new charter for the Merchant Adventurers of Bristol which Hooker helped to secure as one of many civic acts in a long and illustrious career.[52]

Though they are not props in the sense of material objects, the frequent use of inscription either on the picture frame or, more commonly, on the surface of the picture itself, must also be considered as a descriptive device. In a visual sense, these inscriptions on the picture itself further detract from any sense of a naturalistic scene. Though they appear in the same tableau as the subject and on the same, flat, picture plane, they are not part of the sitter's clothing, or the background, or furnishings. They operate something like a Shakesperian soliloquy, perceived by the portrait viewer but not by the figures in it. With some obvious exceptions, including Holbein's familiar portrait of the future Edward VI with his rattle/sceptre,[53] such inscriptions may well appear more frequently in provincial portraits than in London-based, polite portraiture. They certainly appear more frequently in the former than in continental European portraits of the same era.

The briefest type of inscription was also the most common, typically offering the sitter's name and/or age or date: e.g., 'John Jones, *aet suae* 63' or 'John Jones, a.d. 1565', or simply, e.g., '*anno domini* 1565'. A great many portraits offer more. Inscriptions on civic portraits, as noted elsewhere, tended to speak of the virtues of civic office or the primacy of the law.[54] But on 'personal' portraits inscriptions often conveyed religious content, as in the doggerel on the portrait of the Ipswich preacher Samuel Ward: 'Watch, Ward, and keep thy garments tight | For I come thief-like at Midnight | All-seeing, never slumbering Lord | Be thou my watch; I'll

[49] Bindoff (ed.), *House of Commons, 1509–1558*, II.582–4; Hasler (ed.), *House of Commons, 1558–1603*, III.29–31; Arthur F. Preston, *Christ's Hospital, Abingdon* (Oxford, n.d. [*c.*1929]), 40–5; *ODNB*, vide 'Mason, Sir John'. I am grateful to the late Nigel Hammond, Hon. Archivist of Christ's Hospital, for his hospitality and expertise on my visit of 24 June 2002.

[50] Preston, *Christ's Hospital*, 44–5.

[51] Carlisle, *Endowed Grammar Schools of England and Wales*, II.404; Jean Vanes, *Education and Apprenticeship in Sixteenth Century Bristol* (unpaginated pamphlet, Bristol, 1982); C. P. Hill, *A History of the Bristol Grammar School* (Gloucester, 1951), frontispiece. My thanks to Ms Sheena Stoddart, Curator of the Bristol Museum, for guiding me through the relevant holdings in her care.

[52] Hasler (ed.), *House of Commons, 1558–1603*, II.333–5. The painting hangs in the Exeter Guildhall.

[53] Hans Holbein, *Edward, Prince of Wales* (1538), oil on panel, National Gallery of Art, Washington, DC.

[54] Tittler, *Face of the City*, 131–8.

be thy Ward'.[55] They described benefactions, as in several of the twenty-four portraits of Sir Thomas White.[56] Latin mottos conveyed moral sentiments or aspirations in a conspicuously learned manner. And some texts offered detailed biographical information. In most cases the sitter will have determined his or her own inscription, but unless the pigments or handwriting can be effectively analysed, some caution must be exercised in assuming this. Some were obviously added later, often after death, by other parties.

Some inscriptions could be very long indeed. The remarkable portraits of John Kaye and his wife Dorothy of Woodsome, near Huddersfield, must surely have two of the longest inscriptions (and also the crudest workmanship) of any contemporary portraits (Figs. 4.2 and 4.3).[57] Amateurishly painted, extensively inscribed (the text on Dorothy's portrait takes up at least half the surface), and genealogically rich, these tableaux present Kaye as a hard-working, morally upright, but still minor figure who nevertheless exhibited many of the attributes of gentility and candidly aspired to even more. As if the pretensions offered in a possibly bogus coat of arms and a Latin inscription on the frame itself, not to mention a presentation of sixty-six other family coats of arms on an accompanying panel, were insufficient, the very opening lines of one of the three lengthy inscriptions on his portrait set the tone for the rest: 'I lyve at home in husbandrye | Without Office or fee trulye | As servithe myne abilitie | I maintain hosspitalytie'.

Kaye (*c.*1530–94) would have been a striving figure of thirty-seven when these paintings were completed. He lived on another twenty-seven years: long enough to set himself and future generations of his family on the path he so earnestly desired for himself. From his modest start as a Woodsome esquire, he twice married upwards into the county gentry, purchased the manor of Honley, built fulling mills both there and in nearby Burton, and set up his family as entrepreneurs. His son Robert (*c.*1550–1620) built further on these foundations; his grandson John (1616–62) propelled the family further still and gained a baronetcy for his toil.[58]

Finally, we come to clothing. In the sixteenth as well as in the early twenty-first century, 'clothes do maketh the man', and the woman as well. It has become a central corollary of current scholarship on material culture that clothing, like many

[55] Reproduced in John Blatchley, *The Town Library of Ipswich, Provided for the Use of the Town Preachers in 1599: A History and Catalogue* (Woodbridge, Suffolk, 1989), opp. p. 9. The portrait itself hangs in Christchurch Museum.

[56] Leicester's portrait of White contains a twelve-line poem; the Merchant Taylors' *White* only seven lines; others are shorter still. See the full text of the former in Tittler, *Face of the City*, 120, and of the latter in F. M. Fry (ed.), *A Historical Catalogue of the Pictures, Herse-Cloths, and Tapestry at Merchant Taylors' Hall* (1907), 93.

[57] See n. 15 above. These are accompanied by a panel of the Kaye family tree in which portrait busts of family members hang like fruit from the foliage (Tolson Museum no. KLMUS.1990.398a), and a panel of 56 coats of arms showing the putative origins and branches of the family (Tolson Museum KLMUS 1990.399a). All appear to have been done by the same hand and in the same year of 1567.

[58] Joseph Foster (ed.), *The Visitation of Yorkshire, 1584/5 to which is added the Subsequent Visitation made in 1612* (1875), 201, 320–1; William Flower (ed.), *The Visitation of Yorkshire, 1563 and 1564* (Harleian Society, 16, 1881), 175. See also J. T. Cliffe, *The Yorkshire Gentry from the Reformation to the Civil War* (1969), 97; Bradfer Lawrence MSS., Yorkshire Archaeological Society, MD 335/15/1/34 (a licence to alienate properties to Kaye in 1574).

other material forms, does more than reflect social activity and identity. It possesses agency of its own, helping to forge social—even political—identities and to mediate social activity. Some painters of the era seem even to have privileged clothing over faces as descriptors of their sitters.[59] Though this doesn't necessarily apply to the same extent in middling and provincial portraits of the day as to their upmarket counterparts, the thought reminds us to take careful note of the role of clothing in all portraits of the time.

The social agency of clothing at this time had such force, and such potential for subversion in the eyes of the ruling sort, that Crown and Parliament felt obliged repeatedly to regulate what sorts of clothing could be worn by what sorts of people.[60] And when a portrait painter possessed sufficient skill to depict a particular style of dress, portraits offered a way for clothes to perform their function for a particular sitter in perpetuity. Save for the few painted bust portraits, often in oval frames, which obviated the depiction of clothes altogether (a particular speciality of Cornelius Johnson amongst the fashionable painters of the day), clothes formed an obvious and important defining element in the picture. If gloves, as we have seen, had the ability to define their wearer or holder, other forms of clothing did so as much or even more. Here again the differences between one sort of sitter and another come readily to the fore.

A plethora of current scholarship tells us that for patrons who enjoyed or aspired to courtly status, showing the latest and most costly styles and materials formed part and parcel of contemporary self-fashioning. Portrait sitters chose the clothes for their sittings with care. Some hardly missed any bodily surface on which to display the fur, jewellery, gold thread-trimmed satins, elaborate embroidery, and other such luxurious accouterments to make a point about the sitter. More restrained displays could also be shown without loss of elegance, and styles of course changed frequently. The fashion for fur, for example, though common in Holbein's time, waned after the middle of the sixteenth century.[61] Intricately worked lace collars came in shortly thereafter. Though this risked a degree of censure from those who considered it un-English, members of the social and political elite, along with those who could afford to ape them, indulged freely in the purchase and display of clothes that were of foreign origin and style, or domestically made from conspicuously foreign fabrics: silks, satins, and velvets.[62]

The rapidity of change in sartorial fashion has often allowed an otherwise undocumented portrait to be dated by the cut of the sitter's clothing. But clothing is not always a reliable indicator of a painting's date. Clothing styles came later

[59] Jones and Stallybrass, *Renaissance Clothing and the Materials of Memory*, 34–8.

[60] See esp. N. B. Harte, 'State Control of Dress and Social Change in Pre-Industrial England', in D. C. Coleman and A. H. John (eds), *Trade, Government and Economy in Pre-Industrial England* (1976), 132–65, and Maria Hayward, *Rich Apparel: Clothing and the Law in Henry VIII's England* (Farnham, Surrey, 2009), Ch. 1.

[61] Hayward, *Rich Apparel*, 162.

[62] Ruth Hentschell, 'Treasonous Textiles: Foreign Cloth and the Construction of Englishness', *Journal of Medieval and Early Modern Studies*, 32/3 (September 2002), 543–70, and 'A Question of Nation: Foreign Clothes on the English Subject', in Catherine Richardson (ed.), *Clothing Culture, 1350–1650* (Aldershot, 2004), 49–62.

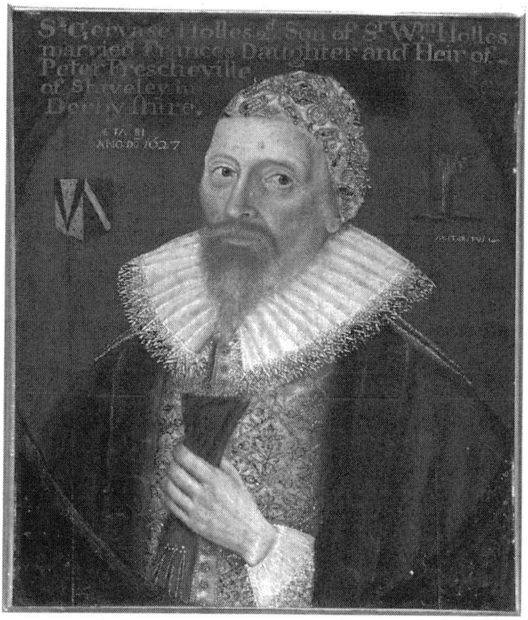

Fig. 7.9. Anon., *Sir Gervase Holles* (1626). Private Collection.

to more isolated parts of the realm than to London, and so the sitter and/or painter's geographic location and access to models of fashion must also be considered. Then, too, second-hand clothing abounded, even amongst quite respectable people, so that older styles could enjoy a prolonged life well beyond their fashionable 'best before' date.[63] And some, especially elderly male, sitters sometimes intentionally chose to appear in clothes that associated them with past glories rather than current fashions. When in 1626, at the age of 80, the Lincolnshire gentleman Sir Gervase Holles finally succumbed to the fervent pleadings of his grandson and namesake to have his portrait painted, he clung to one condition. As the younger Holles described it,

> taking a key out of his pocket he gave it me and bid me to take out of such a trunke a white sattin doublet embroidered with flowers of silke and golde, saying withall that he did not like theis fooleries but seeing we would have it so, and that he could be drawne with no better face, he would be drawne in a good doublet.

The painting (Fig. 7.9), carried out by an anonymous local painter ('the best yt was then in the country'), is not a particularly refined work. Holles's phrase that he could be drawn 'with no better face' may not refer only to the sitter's advanced years. But it does show the old, cherished doublet, fashionable in its time, as

[63] Hayward, *Rich Apparel*, 110.

accurately and prominently as Holles could have wished.[64] Most portraits of the age were meant to show what the sitter had amounted to at the time and/or, often by heraldic device, the lineage that had brought him to that point. Holles's showed what the sitter had once been, and of which he was still very proud.

A patron's choice of the colour and design of clothing to be worn for a portrait undoubtedly contributed greatly to his or her self-image. Gloria Kury has characterized the long-prevalent view of Tudor painting as being 'flat and decorative', and consisting of 'firmly delineated areas of vivid colour'.[65] But while 'flat' accurately characterizes most painting of this era and nearly all provincial paintings, 'vivid' and 'decorative' have their limitations as accurate descriptions beyond the polite end of the portrait continuum, as produced largely in London for the court circle, the landed elites, and those who aspired to their ranks. Such a stereotype may well reveal more about the elite and canonical traditions of scholarship on the subject than they do about the whole of English portraiture at this time.[66]

Especially from the Elizabethan years onwards, court culture certainly did encourage ostentation, wrought in part by the ample and varied use of bright coloured and expensive clothing, and by clothing that was often foreign in its provenance, fabric, or design. Sir Keith Thomas has pointed out that the sumptuary laws of the era exempted soldiers because ostentatious, brightly coloured clothing was considered a component of manly 'bravery', and soldiers were permitted to dress accordingly even if their social status had not permitted it.[67] Many courtiers also had their painters employ this strategy so to indicate their associations with the chivalric revival of the Elizabethan years. Subsequent imagery in male portraits spoke to their service and loyalty to the monarch, their military prowess, their valour, bravery, and self-sacrifice. In many of their commissions fashionable court painters of the time became particularly adept at 'decorating' their sitters, both male and female, as colourfully and lavishly as they could. Along with that particular attribute of courtly portraiture went the tendency, from the 1620s especially, to depict the male sitter in an active, athletic, often contrapposto pose. This entailed the frequent painting of male sitters in tights, and/or the placement of those sitters outdoors.

However, when we consider provincial portraiture and those of lesser placed sitters, the role of clothing sometimes needs to be qualified as a critically defining element of Tudor/early Stuart portraiture in general. Some provincial sitters, like

[64] A. C. Wood (ed.), *Memorials of the Holles Family, 1493–1656* (Camden Society, 3rd series, 55, 1937), 125.

[65] Gloria Kury, '"Glancing Surfaces": Hilliard, Armour, and the Italian Model', in Gent (ed.), *Albion's Classicism*, 395.

[66] Though a great many treatments of the subject cover a later period and/or deal with clothing in the context of consumerism, see, e.g., Valerie Cumming, *A Visual History of Costume: The Seventeenth Century* (1984); Janet Arnold, *Patterns of Fashion: The Cut and Construction of Clothes for Men and Women c. 1580–1620* (1985) and *Queen Elizabeth's Wardrobe Unlock'd* (Leeds, 1988); Jane Ashelford, *Dress in the Age of Elizabeth* (1988); Jones and Stallybrass, *Renaissance Clothing and the Materials of Memory*; and Susan Vincent, *Dressing the Elite: Clothes in Early Modern Europe* (Oxford, 2002).

[67] Keith Thomas, *The Ends of Life: Roads to Fulfilment in Early Modern England* (Oxford, 2009), 60.

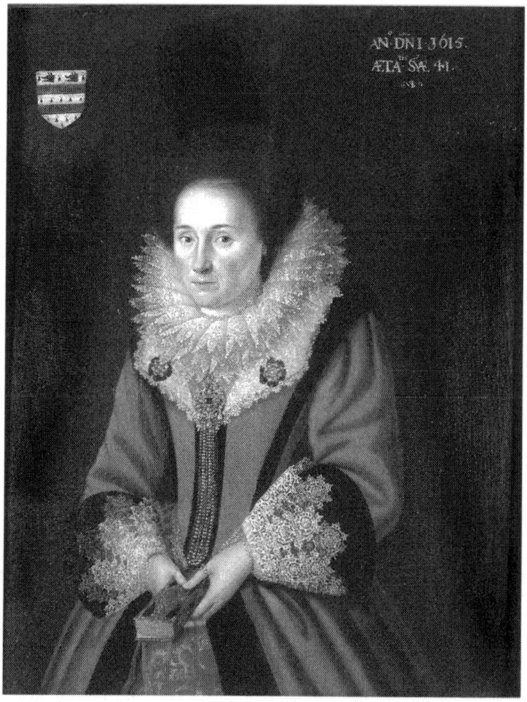

Fig. 7.10. Anon., *Sarah Jones, Mayoress of Shrewsbury* (1615). By kind permission of the Shrewsbury Museum and Art Gallery (Shropshire Museum Service), UK.

Sarah Jones, wife of the Shrewsbury Mayor Thomas Jones, succeeded in having a very skilful painter depict her in a red over-gown (suggesting a mayor's robe) with elaborate, intricately worked cuffs, collar, and jewellery to stake her claims to a substantial social standing (Fig. 7.10).[68] But for those from lower down the ladder, the desire to claim social standing through dress had to be tempered with the expectations placed by others upon their provincial setting and middling status, the cost and availability of the latest clothing, the full range of desirable pigments, and the availability of painters who could carry off the desired effect. Rapid changes in the intricacies of fashion as they spread outwards from London, and the sumptuary laws that pertained at least through the sixteenth century, imposed other barriers to such sartorial aspirations. The challenge for many middling sitters was to select clothing that indicated status without the potentially contentious suggestion of excessive ostentation. Taken together, these factors made it ever more difficult, literally in this case, to keep up with the Joneses.

Some middling and provincial sitters had no such aspirations anyway. The more strenuous protestants, clergy especially but also many laypeople, avoided lavish and colourful clothing out of choice. They carried out their lives far from the

68 See also Mark Girouard, 'Farringdon House, Berkshire, II', *Country Life*, 139 (May 1966), 1247.

ostentatious and neo-chivalric culture of the court and its imitators. They remained well aware of the distance between that cultural ethos and their own more pious sobriety. While some clergy added brighter colours to their wardrobes, even those more reform-minded clergy who opposed clerical vestments altogether in the Elizabethan years and after stuck to more sombre and dignified hues.[69] And, like their lay puritan contemporaries, they certainly avoided the manly pose and dress worn by courtiers and their gentry imitators in the latter decades of our period.

Whether 'strenuous protestants' or not, a great many urbanites—lawyers, civic officials, merchants, entrepreneurs, and master craftsmen, whether in provincial cities or London itself—also chose to avoid the flashier, often foreign-made clothing or fabrics. They could hardly have been unaware that many contemporaries considered such displays unacceptably garish, patently un-English, and even immoral.[70] At a time when the entire urban environment still struck many as morally dubious, and tinged with a reputation for avaricious, licentious, and disorderly behaviour,[71] these sorts of men aimed for sober respectability and trustworthiness. Those same choices also extended to some urban women, whose portraits therefore stand in sharp sartorial contrast to the socially striving Sarah Jones and her ilk. Some, of course, will have dressed soberly to indicate their status as widows, but married women did so as well.

Some urbanites of course had different perspectives, wearing sombre clothes for different reasons, and not necessarily eschewing foreign clothing or fabrics. Thomas Gresham, for example, may well have been influenced by Dutch styles and fabrics, for that was certainly the most prominent tendency of the Dutch burgher world in which he spent a good part of his career.[72] From what we can tell of his portraits, his wardrobe remained sombre in colour, but apparently rich in its fabrics and tailoring.

Few Englishmen of the time will have enjoyed as close an affinity for Dutch culture as Gresham, who fathered a child of a Dutch woman and spent much his working life on those shores. But especially in the most fervently protestant eastern and southern areas of England, many townspeople will have been familiar with Dutch and other northern European cultural models. Even at home they were the most likely to feel the effects of Dutch culture, and to have access to foreign-born or -trained painters in their midst. Taken together, religious inclinations and cultural contexts may have contributed to a sartorial sobriety in those more cosmopolitan

[69] For a general discussion, see Hayward, *Rich Apparel*, 263–73.

[70] Hentschell, 'A Question of Nation: Foreign Clothes on the English Subject', 49–62, citing copiously from writers like Ben Jonson, Thomas Dekker, Philip Stubbes, and Robert Green.

[71] See esp. Lawrence Manley, *Literature and Culture in Early Modern London* (Cambridge, 1995) esp. Ch. 2; John McVeagh, *Tradeful Merchants: The Portrayal of the Capitalist in Literature* (1981); Alexander Leggat, *Citizen Comedy in the Age of Shakespeare* (Toronto, 1973); and Laura Stephenson O'Connell, 'Anti-Entrepreneurial Attitudes in Elizabethan Sermons and Popular Literature', *Journal of British Studies*, 15 (1976), 2–20.

[72] *ODNB*, vide 'Gresham, Thomas'; see also Joanna Woodall, 'Sovereign Bodies: The Reality of Status in Seventeenth-Century Dutch Portraiture', in ead., *Portraiture, Facing the Subject* (Manchester and New York, 1997), 91–4.

reaches of provincial England in East Anglia and elsewhere along the east and southeast coasts.

In view of these several influences, black proved the most common colour in the provincial portraitist's palette, employed for both clothing and backgrounds. There is some irony in this observation. Black, followed by white, were the principle colours of choice in the wardrobe of Henry VIII, and was therefore employed as well by the well-to-do or politically influential through most of the sixteenth century.[73] And of course the King and his sartorial imitators would have had the most refined and expensive black dyes in their clothing and pigments in their portraits. But both pigments and dyes of black could be comprised of a variety of components, some cheaper and more readily obtainable than others. One must assume that these latter were in more frequent use in paintings done in the more distant corners of the realm and for those of more modest means. Such choice also conformed with the heraldic tradition that associated black with prudence and humility:[74] both widely cherished values.

As noted in previous chapters, both heraldic tradition and local availability of pigments will have played considerable roles in the palettes of provincial paintings, especially in those parts of the realm least accessible to foreign influence or trade. The black, white, and red palette of the Cheshire-produced *Cholmondeley Ladies* and the prominence of red, yellow, and orange ochres in the twelve highly vernacular civic portraits of Gloucester, to cite two examples, may in large measure be attributed to such local conditions.

Civic portraits of course usually carried their own conventions of dress so as to invoke the sitter's civic role. The aldermanic or mayoral gown, instantly recognizable for what it was, provides the most obvious example of such dress, and remains the most striking feature of many such portraits. Its length and general shapelessness saved the painter from any more demanding burden of depiction and the patron from any more imaginative choice.[75] The anonymous, early-seventeenth-century portrait of John Falkner, mayor of Gloucester (Fig. 7.11), presents a typical example of this well-established type. The painter had an obvious lack of skill overall. He would have found it very difficult persuasively to depict delicate ornament, jewellery, lace, or other such refinements. But there is no mistaking the red robe as an icon of civic authority, instantly recognizable to anyone who saw the painting. One of a long line of Gloucester mayors who will have worn similar robes, Falkner seems hardly alive. His shapeless figure serves as little more than a dress dummy on which to display his official raiment. To the city fathers who commissioned this portrait, it is that which mattered in the end. This was a time of urban decay and social stress in Gloucester, and the portraits of the *Twelve*

[73] Hayward, *Rich Apparel*, 158, 184–5, 192–4.

[74] John Gage, *Colours and Culture, Practice and Meaning from Antiquity to Abstraction* (1993), 84.

[75] Tittler, *Face of the City*, 104–6 and 118–23; Llewellyn Jewitt and W. H. St John Hope, *The Corporate Plate and Insignia of Office of the Cities and Corporate Towns of England and Wales*, 2 vols (1895), II.138–45.

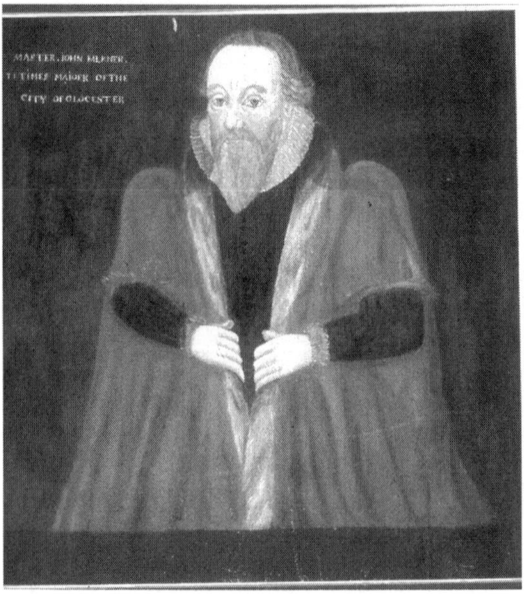

Fig. 7.11. Anon., *John Falkner, Mayor of Gloucester* (*c.*1600–20), oil on panel. © Gloucester City Museum and Art Gallery.

Worthies, as they are known, served as much-needed models of benevolence and civic responsibility when they were most needed.

Here as well as in 'personal' portraits, clothing possessed an agency appropriate to a particular task. Just as placing the crown and royal mantle marked the coronation of the monarch, so did the civic livery serve to transform the layman into the civic official, and thus to invoke the mystery and memory—certainly the identity—of the institution. As the London writer John Earle remarked about a London alderman in 1628, 'He is venerable in his gowne, . . . wherein he setts forth *not his owne* so much as the face of a *City* . . . his scarlet gowne is a monument, and it lasts from generation to generation'.[76] In portraits like this the notion of character has been transferred from the potential subtleties of expression and pose to the raiment itself, a symbolic but effective communication of the portrait's intent. Much the same may be said of other professionals entitled to official dress: lawyers like Sir Edmund Anderson, barrister of the Inner Temple, in his distinctive cap and robe, might well be added to the same list.[77]

Though mayors' wives bore no particular official responsibilities beyond partaking in the occasional civic ceremony, their portraits sometimes signalled their status as 'mayoress' by exhibiting variations on the theme of the (usually) red mayoral

[76] John Earle, *Microcosmography, or a Piece of the World Discovered in Essays and Characters* (1628), ed. Edward Arber (1895), 26–7.

[77] English School (1592), oil on canvas, presented to the Inner Temple, where it may still be seen, in 1871.

robe that signalled their husband's status. Some towns, including Bristol, Salisbury, and Southampton, actually required mayors' wives as well as mayors to wear red gowns for the duration of their spouse's term in office.[78] In some other towns, mayoresses sitting for portraits used their imagination in incorporating their husband's red robe into a spousal version. Sarah Jones chose a particularly ornate variation on this theme in Shrewsbury while Joan Tuckfield of Exeter[79] opted for a similar version. But both built around the symbolically important red mayoral robe as the basic element in their portrait costume. (In addition, some towns allowed mayors' wives to wear a distinctive kerchief as a sign of her status, but we cannot be certain that any of these have been recorded in portraits.)

Taken together with the heraldic elements described in a previous chapter, all these devices contributed to the common vocabulary of the English provincial portrait in the period at hand, and many of them may be found in the elite portraiture of the day as well. We see several of these devices so much more frequently in English portraits than in portraits painted abroad as to allow us to consider it at least a distinctively, if not uniquely, English vocabulary.

[78] Tittler, *Face of the City*, 120 and nn. 15–16.
[79] English School (*c.*1560), oil on panel, 75.8 cm × 59.8 cm.

8

Varieties of Regional Experience

If we look carefully at the provincially produced paintings from this era we begin to notice some visual distinctions from region to region. Portraits on the more formal and polite end of the stylistic continuum certainly evolved over time, but as their evolution remained driven by models and theories that were international in scope and derivation, they did so without particularly pronounced regional variations. As for the vernacular end of that continuum, there may be insufficient surviving examples of provincial paintings to offer anything like a comprehensive overview of distinctive regional styles. Yet there do seem to be enough surviving portraits to permit us to observe regional distinctions in some areas of the country from which inferences about the wider scene may confidently be drawn. Distinctively regional patterns of patronage as well as painting also seem to have been at work. They, too, influenced the appearance of paintings from one region to another.

The strength of regional expressions in other respects has been familiar for so long as to make it a little surprising that they have yet to be explored at much depth for portraiture. We see such regionalism in distinctive patterns of landscape and settlement, lordship and loyalty, custom and belief, production and consumption, and certainly in speech and mimetic expression.

For aspects of the visual arts, seminal investigations of regionality in this era have been carried out by, for example, Nigel Llewellyn for funeral monuments and monumental sculpture,[1] Edward Croft-Murray for the decorative arts,[2] Anthony Wells-Cole for the impact of prints,[3] and myriad scholars for regional vernacular building.[4] Yet no such substantial work has appeared for the study of regional portraiture. Small-scale and specific studies of local portrait activity have broached the subject in valuable ways.[5] But they have tended more to identify painters than

[1] Nigel Llewellyn, *Funeral Monuments in Post-Reformation England* (Cambridge, 2000).

[2] Edward Croft-Murray, *Decorative Painting in England 1537–1837*, I (1962).

[3] Anthony Wells-Cole, *Art and Decoration in Elizabethan and Jacobean England: The Influence of Continental Prints, 1558–1625* (London and New Haven, 1997).

[4] Surveys of vernacular in general, implicitly or explicitly observing the regional vernacular, include Alec Clifton-Taylor, *The Pattern of English Building* (London and Boston, MA, 1972); and three works by R. W. Brunskill: *Traditional Buildings of Britain: An Introduction to Vernacular Architecture* (1985), *Illustrated Handbook of Vernacular Architecture* (London and Boston, MA, 1971, 1978), and *Vernacular Architecture of the Lake Counties: A Field Handbook* (1974, 1987).

[5] These include Mary Edmond, 'Bury St Edmunds: A Seventeenth Century Art Centre', *Walpole Society*, 43 for 1987 (1989), 106–18; Virginia Tillyard, 'Civic Portraits Painted for, or Donated to, the Council Chamber of Norwich Guildhall before 1687 . . . ', MA thesis, Courtauld Institute (1978), and ead., 'Painters in Sixteenth and Seventeenth Century Norwich', *Norfolk Archaeology*, 37 (1980), 315–19; Victor Morgan, 'The Norwich Guildhall Portraits: Images in Context', in Andrew Moore and

to connect them to their patrons or to observe regionally distinct elements in their painting.

Observing the evidence for regional portrait activity in this era proves a lot easier than providing an interpretive framework for it. One of the most suggestive efforts at constructing such a framework has been provided by Charles Phythian-Adams. Drawing on concepts from the fields of cultural anthropology and historical geography, and working in the supportive ambience of the Centres for Urban History and for Local History at the University of Leicester, Phythian-Adams has long championed the idea that English history in general, and by implication English cultural history as well, could and should be perceived from a regional as well as a national perspective. In seminal essays of 1987 and 1993 he stated the essentials of his case, suggesting especially in the latter work the notion of pre-industrial England as a collection of eleven 'cultural provinces', bounded especially by such geographic factors as watersheds, and manifested in a variety of social, political, and cultural characteristics. In subsequent essays he has expanded and refined the notion of regional distinctions while sustaining his initial emphasis on the regionality of economic, social, and cultural activity.[6]

The fragmentary nature of the evidence for the geographic distribution of portraiture makes it impossible to apply this model very closely. Our ability to observe the patronage and production of portraits in a few specific areas seems more likely to contribute to such efforts than to draw from them. Yet the geographic context for social and cultural activity can no longer be overlooked. As Henry French recently put it,[7]

> Clearly, the physical environment affected the distribution of wealth, social interaction and cohesion in a village, hamlet or town. The geography of settlement, land quality, access to common resources, the consequent profitability and stratification of farming and farm sizes, the authority of landlords and institutions (of manor and parish) and the demographic experience of a community all influenced the speed and trajectory of its social and cultural development.

Within what have been variously termed cultural 'provinces', or 'hinterlands', or 'neighbourhoods' it appears, as Mary Blackstone has noted with regard to literary

Charlotte Crawley (eds), *Family and Friends: A Regional Survey of British Portraiture* (1992), 21–30, and id., 'The Dutch and Flemish Presence and the Emergence of an Anglo-Dutch Provincial Artistic Tradition in Norwich, *c.* 1500–1700', in Juliette Roding, Eric Jan Sluijter, Bart Westerweel, Marijke van der Meji-Tolmsa, and Eric Domela Nieuwenhuis (eds), *Dutch and Flemish Artists in Britain, 1550–1800* (Leiden, 2002), 57–72; Roy Strong, 'Forgotten Faces: Regional History and Regional Portraiture', *Historical Research*, 78/199 (February 2005), 42–57.

[6] Charles Phythian-Adams, *Rethinking English Local History* (Leicester, 1987); and 'Introduction: An Agenda for English Local History', in id., *Societies, Cultures and Kinship, 1580–1850: Cultural Provinces and English Local History* (Leicester, 1993), 1–23. See also the refinements of these initial efforts to be found in Phythian-Adams's 'Environments and Identities: Landscape as Cultural Projection in the English Provincial Past', in Paul Slack (ed.), *Environments and Historical Change: The Linacre Lectures 1998* (Oxford, 1999), 118–46; and id., 'Differentiating Provincial Societies in English History: Spatial Contexts and Cultural Processes', in Bill Lancaster, Diana Newton, and Natasha Vall (eds), *An Agenda for Regional History* (Northumbria University, 2007), 3–22.

[7] H. R. French, *The Middling Sort of People in Provincial England, 1600–1750* (Oxford, 2007), 31.

traditions, that people within such areas seem often to have been 'drawn together by a shared vocabulary of dramatic texts and current events as well as alliances and allegiances arising out of the ties of kinship, patronage, educational background, religious loyalties, business interests and politics'.[8]

This chapter explores the possibility of regional distinctions, and the varieties of regional activity, in both paintings and patronage as they may have pertained in provincial England in the years at hand. None of it is meant to masquerade as the comprehensive, seminal work on the regionality of provincial portraiture that we need to have. Given the more ephemeral nature of this material object compared to many other cultural artefacts, the anonymity of most portrait painters, the uncertainty about where most were painted, and the very spotty survival of the written record, that would be a daunting task indeed. But the following is meant to broach the subject and suggest the contours that such a work might take.

The discussion is less preoccupied with determining precise geographic boundaries of particular regions and more concerned with observing both the patronage and production of portraiture that they hosted. Additionally, it seeks (as far as the sources allow) to identify the social, economic, and geographic varieties of such activity. It suggests a tripartite model for locating those activities. First it observes relatively small and local 'circles' of patrons and painters operating in particular areas and at specific times. Here patrons of similar social status and cultural interests, often sharing interpersonal ties as well as geographic proximity, typically engaged a particular painter or group of painters to do their portraits, often over a relatively short period of time. Second, it observes the geographic framework provided by the operation of such circles within a number of wider cultural provinces or 'hinterlands'. Each of these larger areas remained anchored by a major provincial urban centre and was characterized at least in general terms by the elements described by Phythian-Adams, French, and Blackstone. Here we may detect regional characteristics of patronage and production, though they will be of a broader and more general nature than in any particular circle. Finally, we have the emerging public for portraiture which can be seen as a nation-wide phenomenon, taking in the activities of both hinterlands and the social and cultural circles operating within them.

None of these constructs remained static or rigidly defined entities. As the smallest and most localized unit of cultural activity, circles coalescing around particular painters or patrons prove most ephemeral of all. They appeared and disappeared sometimes in matters of months, sometimes in a few decades, as the objects of their coalescence transformed, disappeared, or were—or were not—superceded by others.[9] Cultural hinterlands remain more enduring as geographic

[8] Mary A. Blackstone, 'Lancashire, Shakespeare and the Construction of Cultural Neighbourhoods in Sixteenth Century England', in Richard Dutton, Alison Findlay, and Richard Wilson (eds), *Religion, Politics and Patronage, Lancastrian Shakespeare* (Manchester and New York, 2003), 188–9.

[9] On the frequently ephemeral nature of particular publics, and of the social and geographic units that comprise them, see Craig Calhoun, 'Imagining Solidarity: Cosmopolitanism, Constitutional Patriotism, and the Public Sphere', *Public Culture*, 14/1 (2002), 162, and Bronwen Wilson and

constructs. Yet depending on such factors as the broader development of fashion, the mastery of new techniques or styles of painting, and sundry other economic and social factors, the patronage and production of portraiture within them also evolves, albeit more gradually than in individual circles. Even the burgeoning English portrait public, nation-wide though it seems to have been, retained its fluidity as new social or economic groups joined in; as fashions and circumstances changed; as vernacular traditions clashed both with each other and with the emerging, 'polite' mainstream; as certain technological advances, like the use of canvas surfaces, gained traction; and as great national events (including such episodes as the Reformation or the Civil Wars) powerfully intruded.[10]

This tripartite framework for cultural activity appears more vividly on the provincial scene than on the metropolitan. Many aspects of portrait activity may of course be found in both provincial and metropolitan scenes. The term 'court circle', though far more complex and extensive than any local circle, certainly bears meaning when applied to portraiture. But the concentration of patronage and production within its porous but still restricted social and political boundaries made the London metropolis a unique and enormously fertile environment for cultural activity, unmatched even closely by any other in the British Isles. It is, uniquely, both a local and a national unit of patronal activity.

When we seek further to root these notions in the firmament of archival and visual evidence, four regional examples prove particularly apposite to the task. None of them can offer the full range of evidence, either visual or archival, which would describe every facet of their indigenous portrait activity. At best one or the other of them allows us to flesh out particular aspects of the whole: e.g., the impact of geographic, social, and economic factors; the operation of a particular 'circle' of painters or patrons; or the visual characteristics of paintings in particular regions. Risky though it may be to do so, we have little choice but to take each of these well-documented vignettes as representative of a larger, and only partly retrievable, picture of the whole of provincial England.

The four areas are the eastern part of the county of Kent, and the areas that might be considered the hinterlands surrounding the cities of Norwich, Gloucester, and Chester. All four were anchored by an ecclesiastical centre that will have served as a source of patronage for decorative work from well back before the Reformation and continued to do so through the era at hand. Each functioned as a regional centre for all sorts of political and economic activity; each might be considered the 'capital' city of its region. Norwich was by far the largest; its population of around 12,000–13,000 in the 1580s, probably more than doubling by the 1620s, made it

Paul Yachnin (eds), *Making Publics in Early Modern Europe: People, Things, Forms of Knowledge* (New York and Abingdon, 2010), 18–19.

[10] Linda Levy Peck has recently argued that the impact of the Civil Wars and Interregnum was not as deleterious on the consumption of material goods as we have assumed. But her comments on the production and consumption of portraiture remains restricted to the court circle and senior aristocracy, largely overlooking the provincial scene. Peck, *Consuming Splendor: Society and Culture in Seventeenth Century England* (Cambridge, 2005), 162–83.

the second largest city in England after London.[11] Gloucester, Canterbury, and Chester came in the second rank of provincial cities, with populations probably in the range of 6,000 to 9,000 by the 1620s. Each of them dominated a region of smaller market towns that were more numerous and wealthier in Gloucestershire and Kent, and much poorer and less numerous in the hinterland of Chester.[12]

Most of these areas demonstrate a range of patronage and portraiture, more sophisticated and technologically advanced in some areas than in others, as will have typified provincial England as a whole. At one end of that spectrum we find the wealthier patrons, leading gentry, and aristocracy or even ecclesiastical magnates, whose affluence and sophistication led them to seek out the 'finer' sort of contemporary painters. They will typically have engaged painters working in the more formal and polite modes of contemporary 'Renaissance' painting, often based in London or elsewhere outside the region and sometimes even working abroad. At the other end we have the less affluent and sophisticated patrons: lesser gentry and even some yeomen, clergy of the middling ranks, leading provincial urban merchants and professionals, and civic institutions. These patrons will typically have patronized the local and regional craftsmen located in provincial centres and working more distinctly in the traditional, regional vernacular. A look at these factors in each of the four regions affirms the essential regionality of much of English painting at this time, and suggests the varieties of portrait patronage and production in provincial England.

Areas like Kent were most likely of all to enjoy the broadest spectrum of patronage and expertise. The rich soils and temperate climate favouring most of the shire made for some of the best agricultural lands in all of England. The ease of bringing its produce to the populous London and Home County markets further favoured its producers and landlords, making them amongst the most prosperous in the realm. Its geographic location included some of the most direct routes between London and the Continent, allowing it close and sustained contact with those two vibrant poles of cultural activity. Thousands of migrants and merchants will have traversed those routes on their way to and from London. Hundreds at a time will have settled in Kentish towns like Maidstone, Sandwich, Canterbury, Faversham, and Dover.

The landed elites of Kent, most of whom undoubtedly knew each other and many of whom undoubtedly shared their ideas and experiences with the visual arts, consisted by 1640 of some 'twenty or thirty related "county" families'. Along with their subordinate branches, they comprised the heart of what Alan Everitt famously

[11] John T. Evans, *Seventeenth Century Norwich: Politics, Religion, and Government, 1620–1690* (Oxford, 1979), 4–5, estimates approx. 20,000, but A. Hassell Smith's estimate of approx. 32,000 seems more likely; A. Hassell Smith, *County and Court: Government and Politics in Norfolk, 1558–1603* (Oxford, 1974), 10.

[12] Though the two shires are roughly the same size, Alan Everitt's classic map and listing of English market towns in this era shows 34 such towns in Gloucestersire and only 13 in Cheshire: Everitt, 'The Marketing of Agricultural Produce', in Joan Thirsk (ed.), *The Agrarian History of England and Wales*, IV: *1500–1640* (Cambridge, 1967), 470–1.

and controversially referred to as a 'county community'.[13] As a group, they were also as well or better connected at court than their counterparts in almost any other shire.[14] Most will have sat together on the county commission of the peace as JPs. They also came to know the sundry court figures who bought lands and settled in Kent.

These factors allowed Kent to boast some of the most culturally sophisticated English men and women in all provincial England, both ready and able to afford the best hands available to do their bidding.[15] The same of course may be said for the senior ecclesiastical figures of the shire, the bishops of Rochester and especially the archbishops of Canterbury, who joined their lay compatriots in looking to London for most of their portrait painters.[16] (Contemporary portraits of the deans of Canterbury, by contrast, are largely vernacular in nature, and almost certainly painted locally.[17]) Some Kentish families even sent to London for decorative painters to adorn their country houses, as did the Sackvilles in bringing the prominent London painter-stainer Paul Isaacson, amongst others, to work at Knole.[18]

The evidence of such elite authorship of Kentish paintings, and of close cultural ties to London, is not far to seek. In such families as, e.g., the Sidneys of Penshurst and the Sackvilles of Knole, Kent could boast by the early decades of the seventeenth century some of the country's great collectors of paintings and other visual

[13] Alan Everitt, *The Community of Kent and the Great Rebellion, 1640–1660* (Leicester, 1973), 35 and Ch. 2.

[14] S. T. Bindoff (ed.), *The House of Commons, 1509–1558*, 3 vols (History of Parliament Trust, 1982), I.113; Peter Clark, *English Provincial Society from the Reformation to the Revolution: Religion, Politics and Society in Kent, 1500–1640* (Hassocks, Sussex, 1977), *passim*; Michael Zell (ed.), *Early Modern Kent, 1540–1640* (Woodbridge, Suffolk, 2000), 26–8.

[15] Hence the traditional rhyme, to which there was much truth:

> A Knight of Wales
> A gentleman of Cales
> A laird of the North countree
> A yeoman of Kent
> With his yearly rent
> Will buy them out all three

cited in J. H. L. de Vaynes (ed.), *A Kentish Garland*, 2 vols (Hertford, 1881), I.139. For the structure and affluence of Kentish society in these years, see esp. Peter Laslett, 'The Gentry of Kent in 1640', *Cambridge Historical Journal*, 9/2 (1948), 148–64; Everitt, *The Community of Kent*, and Clark, *English Provincial Society*.

[16] Rochester is poorly documented, but for Canterbury inventories of 1584 (confirmed in 1586) and 1634 list over 30 paintings, most of them portraits of the archbishops, hanging in the Great Chamber. J. Wickham Legg (ed.), *Inventories of Christchurch, Canterbury, with Historical and Topographical Introductions and Illustrative Documents* (1902), 242, 261. See also G. M. Bevan (ed.), *Portraits of the Archbishops of Canterbury* (1908); J. Ingamells, *The English Episcopal Portrait, 1559–1835* (Guildford, 1983), *passim*; and BL. Add. MS. 6391, fos. 88–9^{v}.

[17] Sir William Musgrave, *Painted Portraits in many of the Publick Buildings and Capital Mansions of England Ranged Alphabetically*, 7 vols (1796), BL. Add. MS. 6391, I, fo. 88^{r}; Sir Roy Strong, 'Portraits of the Deans of Canterbury Cathedral', *Canterbury Chronicle*, 65 (1970), 102–11

[18] E.g., Paul Isaacson, one of a well-known and accomplished family of London painter-stainers and a member of its Painter-Stainers' Livery, was employed to do the 'Four Ages of Man', after the engraving by Maartin de Vos, for the Sackvilles' staircase at Knole in the opening years of the seventeenth century (Wells-Cole, *Art and Decoration*, 112).

imagery outside the immediate court circle. Such magnates freely commissioned portraits of their own family members, but they also purchased portraits—of religious figures, English aristocrats, and heads of state both English and foreign—from home and abroad, employing reliable agents to make their purchases.[19]

Not all gentry families took up collecting for its own sake, but a great many assiduously commissioned family portraits. Sir Edward Dering of Surrenden Dering proves fairly typical of this sort of patronage. In 1626 Dering had the London painter-stainer George Cottington paint his portrait and those of his deceased first wife, second wife, and brother. Both Cottington and Dering seem to have been closely connected to the courtly circle of the duke of Buckingham. It is most likely through that circle that Dering came to know of Cottington and bring him to Kent.[20] Cottington may have been a well-connected portrait painter of his time and a senior member of the Painter-Stainers' Company of London, but he was no Daniel Mytens or Cornelius Johnson. Dering came to understand this and, as he rose in both prominence and affluence, he sought to move up market in his choice of family painters as well.

He had before him choices in both London and within the county, thus illustrating the tiers of painterly expertise available in Kent. On the one hand his mother-in-law, Frances, countess of Thanet, wrote in 1636 urging him to consider the Maidstone-based Kentish painter and limner John Cawarden. 'If you shall have any occasion to use a limner', she wrote, Cawarden was 'an able man by the report of ye Countrye (and in parte I can speake by experience) to take the face of my daughter Elizabeth'.[21] But Dering demurred, aspiring to do better than to take the 'report of ye Countrye'. In 1636, ten years after he had commissioned Cottington, he settled on Johnson to do another portrait of himself.[22] Though we think of Johnson, a longtime resident of Blackfriars, as a London painter, he had close ties to Kent, as we'll see, and these ties would also have counted heavily in Dering's choice of him in 1636.

The Dering portraits are especially well documented, and they show clearly the close cultural relations between Kent and London during this entire era. Dering recorded in his account book that 'Mr Cuddington', as he rendered George Cottington, came down to the family seat at Surrenden Dering to take preliminary drawings or sketches of his sitters, probably using an earlier portrait of the first Lady Dering as a model for hers, and then finished them up in his London workshop.

19 See, e.g., Musgrave, *Painted Portraits*, BL. Add. MS. 6391, I, fos. 88–93; Centre for Kentish Studies, Maidstone, De L'Isle MSS. CKS U 1475/A 64/1-35 and/E 49, the latter examined with the gracious consent of the Viscount De L'Isle.

20 Dering owed his knighthood to Buckingham in 1619, married his second wife in Buckingham's house in 1625, and possessed at least one portrait of the duke at his seat at Surrenden Dering. Cottington was related to Sir Francis Cottington, an influential courtier and close Buckingham associate. *ODNB*, vide 'Dering, Sir Edward', and 'Cottington, George'; Robert Tittler, 'George Cottington and the Dering Family Portraits of 1626', *Burlington Magazine*, 151 (April 2009), 208–11; BL. Add. MS. 47787, fo. 14^{v}.

21 Francis, countess of Thanet to Sir Edward Dering, 1636, BL. Stowe MS. 243, fo. 121, as cited in Daphne Foskett, *A Dictionary of British Miniature Painters* (1972), 197.

22 Tittler, 'George Cottington', 210.

This was almost certainly a common practice in Kent and elsewhere in the Home Counties, whose patrons readily utilized their proximity to London for that purpose.[23] It was undoubtedly pursued not only by Cottington, but also by other London-based painters who took commissions from Kentish patrons. We know that all of them had workshops in London, and that certainly de Critz, Marcus Gheeraerts the younger, and undoubtedly others of his ilk employed numerous journeyman and apprentices to share the work. The same pattern accrued in commissioning copies of portraits held in London. The city of Canterbury fulfilled its wish to have a portrait of its benefactor, Sir Thomas White, for its guildhall in 1607/8 by having a copy made of the Merchant Taylors' de Critz portrait of White and sent down from London via Herne Bay.[24]

The Knatchbulls of Maidstone and Mercham Hatch and the Oxendens of Dene and elsewhere have been described as 'ordinary' rather than elite gentry families of Kent.[25] Yet like the Derings they, too, were 'families of ancient standing, local outlook and moderate fortune',[26] and their portrait patronage typifies that of other Kentish gentry families. Despite claims to the contrary, the Knatchbulls began their patronal activities by commissioning work from the likes of Paul Van Somer (of Susan Knatchbull and Sir Norton Knatchbull), Jan de Critz the elder (of Richard Knatchbull), and Marcus Gheeraerts the younger (of Susan, wife of Sir Richard Knatchbull), around the start of the seventeenth century.[27]

The Oxendens turned at one time or another to Gheeraerts the younger and Daniel Mytens,[28] but seem to have been especially fond of Cornelius Johnson and quickly took advantage of his temporary residence in the county in 1636. Johnson was far too enterprising and prolific to be tied for long to any one circle of patrons. In 1636 he accepted an invitation to stay with the Dutch émigré merchant Sir Arnold Braemes, who had bought Sir Edward Parthericke's home at Bridge in East Kent.[29] The Braemeses, who were also cousins to the Derings,[30] will undoubtedly have brought Johnson further to Sir Edward Dering's attention so that he became Sir Edward's choice in that year.

[23] The same pattern pertained throughout the Home Counties. Sometime between 1572 and 1576 William More of Losely Park in Surrey had a London painter take images at Losely itself. But that (unfortunately unnamed) painter then preferred to complete this and other portrait work in his London studio and send the finished work to More. Letter from Charles Bradshaw to William More at Losely, *c.*1572–6; More Molyneux Family of Losely Park, Historical Correspondence, vol. 9 (1420–1642), Surrey Record Office MS. 6729/7/138.

[24] Canterbury City and Cathedral Archives [hereafter CCA], City Chamberlains' Accounts, MS. CC/FA 21; Heinz Archive, NPG, vide 'Canterbury Corporation'; Edward Hasted, *The History and Topographical Survey of the County of Kent*, 12 vols (Canterbury, 1797–1801), XII.642.

[25] Clark, *English Provincial Society*, 219.

[26] A. M. Everitt, *The Community of Kent and the Great Rebellion, 1640–1660* (Leicester, 1973), 44.

[27] Anon., *Oil Paintings in Public Ownership in Kent* (2004), 115–19. [Hereafter *Oil Paintings, Kent*]. A 1562 portrait here listed as *Gentleman of the Knatchbull Family* proves instead to be of the London lord mayor Sir Martin Bowes.

[28] Dorothy Gardiner (ed.), *The Oxenden Letters, 1617–1642* (1933), 34 and pl. opp. p. 6.

[29] Ibid. xvii, 168.

[30] Everitt, *Community of Kent*, 72.

Johnson also used those connections to paint portraits for several associated and neighbouring families amongst the middling shire gentry: the Auchers of Losenham, Hammonds of Nonnington, Peytons of Knowlton Court, Knatchbulls of Maidstone, and Oxendens of Dene, improving his host Braemes's standing with his new neighbours as he did so. For the Oxendens he painted Henry of Barham and Henry's first wife, Anne, née Peyton; Henry's son Thomas; and Henry Oxenden of Dene and also Anne, daughter of Sir James Oxenden, who had married Sir Richard Master of Canterbury and East Langdon.[31] Like the Braemeses at Bridge, most of these families held their seats in a closely circumscribed area of East Kent: the Oxendens, Hammonds, Peytons, and Braemeses all dwelt within six to eight miles east of Canterbury and even closer to each other, with the Derings and Knatchbulls a mere twenty miles or so to the southwest. Some of these families were connected by marriage and even by political outlook.[32]

Taken as a whole they constituted a small and informal circle of closely associated, geographically proximate, and generally like-minded patrons of portraiture in general and of Johnson in particular. Some continued to commission Johnson after he left Braemes's home; others turned to painters of similar stature. In all such choices the rich agricultural lands upon which their fortunes rested, and their proximity to London, allowed these Kentish families to commission the very best painters of their time. Their proximity to Dutch and Flemish émigrés also seems to have imparted a taste for Netherlandish painting, so that Johnson, Gheeraerts the younger, de Critz the elder, and Van Somer were widely employed in that area.

This pattern of gentry patronage at this time left local Kentish craftsmen-painters to find their portrait commissions amongst patrons of a distinctly lesser social and economic status: the lesser gentry or even yeomanry, urban merchants, and professionals. Patrons of this sort would include William Lovelace, sergeant-at-law and steward of the Liberties of Canterbury Cathedral, who possessed nearly twenty panel portraits and nearly the same number of painted hangings in his Canterbury abode at his death in 1577.[33] Urban patrons of lesser status included 'Penne the painter' cited in 1573,[34] John Robins of Dover prior to 1580, John Curtop of Faversham by 1582, and William Crisp of Sandwich by 1592.[35] Though none of their portraits are known to have survived, we may assume them to have been largely vernacular works of a sort that have sometimes found their way to local museums.[36]

[31] Gardiner, *Oxenden Letters*, xvii, 168, and pl. opp. pp. 66, 80, 180, and 210; A. J. Finberg, 'A Chronological List of Portraits by Cornelius Johnson, or Jonson', *Walpole Society*, 10 (1922), 25 and pl. 65.

[32] Everitt, *Community of Kent*, 42–4, 72, 278–80.

[33] TNA, PROB 2/404B (1577); I am grateful to Dr Tarnya Cooper for bringing this reference to my attention. Lovelace married into the Canterbury city elite, served as legal counsel for the Cinq Ports and for Faversham, and sat in Parliament for Canterbury (1562/3, 1571, and 1572), where he is buried in the Cathedral nave. P. W. Hasler (ed.), *The House of Commons, 1558–1603*, 3 vols (History of Parliament, 1981), II.491–3; BL. Harleian MS. 1366, fo. 27^{v}.

[34] Duncan Harrington and Patricia Hyde (eds), *The Early Town Books of Faversham*, 2 vols (Folkstone, 2008), II.332.

[35] I am grateful to Dr Catherine Richardson of the University of Kent, Canterbury, for this inventory-derived information.

[36] *Oil Paintings in Kent*, see the holdings of the Canterbury Museums; the Dover Collections; the Kent County Collection at County Hall, Maidstone; the Maidstone Museum and Bentlif Gallery; the Margate Local History Museum; and the Tenterden Town Council.

In addition, civic institutions like the city of Canterbury have left a number of contemporary vernacular portraits that will also have been locally produced. Civic portraits inevitably brook large in any study of regional portraiture. For one, as civic institutions tend to last longer and be less likely to disperse their possessions than individual families, both their portraits and their financial accounts are often more likely to have survived than those kept in gentry households.[37] And because civic institutions commissioned portraits for different purposes than did individual patrons, the skill and reputation of the painter remained less important than the display of civic raiment or symbols of civic office and benefaction. Most civic portraits fall decidedly on the vernacular end of the scale of portraiture in general, and thus are more likely to reflect local and regional characteristics.[38]

Those civic portraits that survive for Canterbury include vernacular depictions of the mayors and/or benefactors Sir John Boys (1612), Joseph Colfe (*c.*1620), and John Cogan (early seventeenth century).[39] Save for one exception, virtually all surviving civic portraits from Canterbury and elsewhere in Kent seem to have been produced locally and in the vernacular mode. The odd one out is Canterbury's portrait of the London Merchant Taylor and philanthropist Sir Thomas White, a major benefactor to that city and to twenty-three other cities and towns. Canterbury's civic government paid £5 in 1608 to have this large and imposing work copied from the de Critz original in the Merchant Taylors' Hall, an additional 6s. 8d to have it brought to Canterbury by water via Whitstable, and still another 22s. 6d to have it hung with a curtain to protect it, for total cost of £6 2s. 6d.[40] As we shall see, this particular White portrait makes an interesting comparison with Chester and Gloucester portraits of the same man. It also suggests that those patrons who had no access to the elite painters of the day, or who couldn't afford their services, could sometimes commission copies from competent painters instead.

Though it proves impossible to identify who painted any of the locally produced portraits, thirty-three painters of one sort or another have been identified as working and residing in Canterbury between 1500 and 1640.[41] In addition there

[37] The dispersal of estate collections and archives has been especially emphasized in Strong, 'Forgotten Faces', 43–5, *passim*.

[38] See Robert Tittler, *The Face of the City: Civic Portraiture and Civic Identity in Early Modern England* (Manchester, 2007), *passim*.

[39] *Oil Paintings in Kent*, 27 and 33. Two other paintings of Canterbury figures of this era in the Museum, those of John Watson and Leonard Cotton, have also been taken for portraits of the early seventeenth century. But the former now appears to be an 18th-century copy, and the latter an entire painting of the 18th century, probably based on an earlier original. I am grateful to Dr Tarnya Cooper for her interpretation of these works on our visit to the Museum in April 2008, and to Mr Ken Reedie, Curator of the Museum, for access to these paintings.

[40] Canterbury City Archives, Canterbury Cathedral, MS. CC/FA/21, fo. 290^{v}.

[41] Based on a search of the Canterbury City Chamberlains' Accounts (Canterbury City Archives MS. CC FA vol 15–24); J. M. Cowper (ed.), *Canterbury Marriage Licenses,* 1st ser., *1568–1618* (Canterbury, 1892), and 2nd ser., *1619–1660* (1894); and id., (ed.), *Rolls of the Freemen of the City of Canterbury* (1903); 'The Diary of Thomas Cocks', Canterbury City Literary MS. E.31.

were at least four in Dover,[42] two in Maidstone,[43] and one each in Faversham,[44] Rochester,[45] and even in relatively remote Wealden Cranbrook.[46] It seems safe to assume that other towns of some importance, like Folkestone, Sandwich, and Deal, probably had at least one or two per generation to carry out the broad local range of decorative work.

Then, too, itinerant English painters of no particular renown also came through the shire now and again from elsewhere, and not always en route to London from abroad. Thomas Sprye, identified as a painter from Plymouth, came before Dover's mayor's court in August of 1621 for having unlawfully left his wife and children in Plymouth in order to work in Dover. He had obviously found work, for the court permitted him to complete it before returning to his family.[47]

Some of these painters did quite well at their occupation and a few, like the Johnsons of Canterbury (no obvious relation to Cornelius Johnson, though the proximity of time and place is intriguing!), were able to sustain a family business over two or three generations. Others held properties, diversified their economic activities, and took on minor-to-middling civic offices. Robert Bettes of Canterbury, probably related to the renowned Bettes family of London painters, held minor city office between 1561 and 1579.[48] But in contrast, for example, to painters in Chester or Newcastle, none served as mayors or aldermen,[49] and most failed to climb beyond the status of skilled craftsmen.

It is impossible to tell which or how many of these painters might have turned their hands to portraiture. Yet nearly any one of them could have done so, and the survival of numerous vernacular portraits in the shire strongly suggests that a number of them did. Of course the city of Canterbury wasn't the region's only significant centre for portrait production during the era at hand, though it brooked very large amongst the 'men of Kent' east of the Medway. The overall wealth and sophistication, population density, and number of substantial urban places in that shire allow Kent to stand out from most other shires in those ways. It would be hard to find a more dispersed distribution of portrait production within any similarly sized region . . . save perhaps for Norfolk.

42 William Allen, fl. 1605 (Dover Chamberlains' Accounts, East Kent Record Office, Dover [hereafter EKRO], MS. DO/FCA 4 (1603–15), fos. 55^{v}, 84^{v}, and 89^{v}); John Wyman, fl. 1606 (DO/FCA 4, fos. 117^{v} and 119^{v}); Thomas Sprye, fl. 1621 (Dover Borough Assembly Book, EKRO, MS. A/DO/AAM 2, fo. 172^{r}); and John Edwards, fl. 1623–39 (EKRO MS. A/DO/AAM/2, fos. 38^{v} and 186^{r}). I am grateful to Dr Helen Wicker for the last reference.

43 John Cawarden, 'Limner [which often meant portrait painter and/or miniaturist] and picture-drawer', fl. 1637–59; Maidstone Burghmote Book, KSC, MS. MD/ACM1/2, fos. 167^{v}, and 169^{r}; Foskett, *Dictionary*, 197; and a 'Mr' Virgoe, fl. 1570s; KSC MS. FA1/1579, fo. 7^{r}.

44 'Penne the painter'; fl. 1573. Harrington and Hyde, *Early Town Books of Faversham*, II.332.

45 Richard Kelly, fl. 1533–8; TNA MS. C.1/834/8.

46 Thomas Phillips, d.1597; Centre for Kentish Studies, Maidstone, MS. QM/SRc/1597/43.

47 EKRO, MS. A/DO/AAM 2, fol. 172^{r}.

48 CCA, MS. CC/FA 16–17, *passim*.

49 In Norwich both Randle Holme the elder and younger served as aldermen, mayors, and sheriffs; *ODNB*, vide 'Holme'.

Fortunately for us, Norfolk's portrait history from this era remains as well or better documented than any other shire in the realm.[50] The region anchored by the cathedral city of Norwich shared many of the characteristics of the Kentish scene.[51] Excluding the fenlands on its western edge, Norfolk's rich agricultural lands and the investment in trade and industry in Norwich, King's Lynn, and Great Yarmouth produced a politically powerful and affluent merchant community and regional gentry. A number of Norfolk figures held substantial office at Westminster throughout the era, dividing their time between the two regions. They were quick to catch on to contemporary cultural fashions through their close links with London, the Netherlands, and other European centres.[52]

Norwich anchored an even larger hinterland than Canterbury: one that extended in one way or another to much of the rest of East Anglia as well. It served as a much more powerful magnet for gentry activity and the consumption of material goods than the smaller Canterbury could do for Kent. The population of Norwich also remained several times that of Canterbury, reaching an estimated 32,000 inhabitants by 1622, including over 4,000 Dutch and Flemish settlers.[53] Though obviously further removed from the metropolis than their Kentish counterparts, the great families and wealthy landowners of Norfolk freely commissioned portraits in London or had them done abroad, tending to seek out the more fashionable and better known painters of the day just like their Kentish contemporaries. These included John Hoskins the elder, Robert Peake the elder, George Gower, and probably Cornelius Johnson. Some of the resulting paintings were subsequently copied, probably for regional consumption and possibly by local painters.[54] As in Kent, lesser patrons and civic bodies resorted to locally based painters working in larger towns like King's Lynn as well as Norwich itself.

Both Norwich and Canterbury remained rich in civic tradition and ceremonial after the break with Rome as before. Norwich worked particularly hard to sustain a secular civic ceremonial, commissioning numerous portraits of its civic officials and benefactors as part of that process.[55] The fruits of that effort constitute the largest surviving civic portrait collection of any town or city in England, with somewhere between nineteen and twenty-two (depending on attribution and imprecise dating) portraits of mayors and benefactors completed before 1640.[56] Considering the long-standing and close ties between Norfolk and the Netherlands, this profusion

[50] See, for example, Prince Frederick Duleep Singh, *Portraits in Norfolk Houses*, ed. Edmund Farrer, 2 vols (Norwich, 1928); Moore and Crawley (eds), *Family and Friends*; Tillyard, 'Civic Portraits of Norwich Guildhall'; and The Public Catalogue Foundation, *Oil Paintings in Public Ownership, Norfolk* (2006).

[51] The following is based largely on Smith, *County and Court*, Chs. 1 and 5.

[52] See particularly ibid. Chs. 1 and 2.

[53] Ibid. 10.

[54] Portraits by Hoskins of Sir Hamon Le Strange (1617); by Johnson (tentative attribution) of Sir Henry Spelman (n.d.); by Peake of Elizabeth D'Oyley (*c.*1608), and of Elizabeth Buxton, née Kemp (*c.*1588–90); and by Gower of Sir William Drury (*c.*1575); *Oil Paintings in Norfolk*, 73, 151, 174, 285.

[55] Morgan, 'Norwich Guildhall Portraits', 21–9; Muriel McClendon, *The Quiet Revolution: Magistrates and the Emergence of Protestantism in Tudor Norwich* (Stanford, CA, 1999), 91–109.

[56] Moore and Crawley, *Family and Friends*, Appendix I; *Oil Paintings in Norfolk*, 243–7.

of civic portraiture in Norwich may well reflect the rich Netherlandish tradition of celebrating civic authorities in portrait imagery as well as the Calvinist emphasis on civic responsibility. Though they do not by any means represent all of Norfolk's vernacular portraiture they do nicely exemplify the stylistic range of such work. In general they depart from the distinctive East Anglian, Gothic-oriented, figurative painting of pre-Reformation days. Instead they draw heavily on contemporary Dutch and Flemish painting, though not always of the most sophisticated variety.

Almost all these Norwich civic portraits display a very limited palette of black, white, gray, red, and occasionally gold. Along with blue, these were five of the most common colours in heraldic painting, and their use here points again to the strong influence of that tradition in the vernacular portraiture of the era. Yet there are many other influences at work here as well. Some of the modelling of the clothing and flesh in these paintings also remains distinct from the other regions studied so far. Nor is there much of the delicate rendering of lace or other finely detailed work that we commonly see elsewhere. Clothing has frequently been modelled as though it were made of thin sheets of foam rubber, folding stiffly and hanging in broad, unwrinkled swathes.[57] The figures themselves have been noted for their 'starkness of outline' and 'rigidity of gesture'.[58] Most have expressions that are more than usually grave and dour, though this is not inappropriate for civic leaders. Reflecting the region's early investment in protestantism, memento mori devices like skulls and hourglasses are particularly common here.[59]

Some, as we'll see, may well have been done by Dutch or Flemish painters who had settled in Norwich with several thousand of their compatriots by the 1580s, but the constant and long-standing ebb and flow of people between East Anglia and the Low Countries in general will in any event have sustained that influence as an active presence in virtually all forms of its art and architecture.

Of course the civic portraits of Norwich cannot speak for all the contemporary regional portraiture of Norwich or Norfolk. The region's size, diversity, and affluence permitted portraiture of virtually every contemporary type and refinement. But this large group of civic portraits offers a fair indication of vernacular characteristics to be found in Norwich and its extensive cultural hinterland. Much cruder vernacular portraits may be found elsewhere in the region as well, of which two civic portraits in King's Lynn offer striking evidence. Here, in addition to the much more refined *c.*1630 image of the mayor Joshua Green, we find the distinctive images of William Atkin (Fig. 4.1) and Thomas Snelling, mayors both, done *c.*1619 and *c.*1622 respectively, and probably by the same hand. They contain a

[57] Especially in the portraits of Sir Edward Coke (1587); Augustine Steward (late 16th c.); John Marsham (late 16th c.); Sir John Pettus (1612); Robert Jannys (early 17th c.); and Sir Thomas Richardson (*c.*1620–35). Respectively catalogued as Norwich Civic Portrait Collection numbers 81: F, 75: F; 70: F; 71: F; 68: F; and 109: F.

[58] Tillyard, 'Civic Portraits', 3.

[59] Skulls especially abound. They appear in portraits of Sir Edward Coke (collection number 81: F); Robert Yarham (84: F); Francis Wyndham, who also has an hourglass (60: F); Augustine Steward (75: F); John Marsham (70: F); Thomas Layer (63: F); and Robert Jannys, who is also being pulled off the scene by a skeleton (68: F).

striking mix of finely wrought and intricate detail on the ruff collars and cuffs with much more crudely wrought faces and clothing. Both paintings have their sitters' merchant's marks in an upper corner. Each remains strongly suggestive of heraldic influence, though it is also possible that Snelling himself, though not known to be an *heraldic* painter, may have done them both.[60]

As is often the case, it proves impossible to attribute particular works to individual painters, but it is not difficult to suggest what type of painter they would have been. Local civic and parish records establish the presence of a large community of painters who could also have turned their hands to portraits when asked to do so. Virginia Tillyard has identified twenty-five painters at work in Norwich alone between 1554 and 1640, most of them native-English but a few of them of Dutch or Flemish birth or recent ancestry.[61] Augustine Isbourne and George Trewe have been identified as the most likely to have done some of the portraits, but several other hands have obviously been at work as well.[62] A smaller number of painters have been identified for King's Lynn, but it has also been considered a centre for local portraiture.[63]

The areas anchored by Canterbury and Norwich represent some of the most affluent, sophisticated, and cosmopolitan in all of provincial England at this time. Taken together, they make a striking contrast to many other parts of England whose potential patrons were far less affluent, sophisticated, well-travelled, or proximate to continental influences. As noted in previous chapters, patrons in most of provincial England will have had less practical access to the prestigious or more sophisticated painters of the day, or to those areas of the realm, London especially, where such skilled painters largely worked. Local painters will have had more difficulty finding the range of supplies—pigments, well-seasoned Baltic oak, or fine linen canvas especially—available in places like London, Kent, or Norwich.

The experience of the Holles family in commissioning a portrait of their paterfamilias (see above, Ch. 7 and Fig. 7.9) speaks to a great many patrons in such areas. When the elder Sir Gervase Holles came in his old age to be persuaded by his son and grandson to have his portrait painted, he was living near the small and impoverished fishing port of Grimsby in Lincolnshire. Having persuaded him, they obtained the services of what the grandson's memoires described as 'a workeman (the best yt was then in the country)' to do the job. Observing the finished portrait, the grandson noted that 'that peice [*sic*] though performed but by an ordinary hand was very like him and representes a most comely and venerable

[60] King's Lynn Town Hall reference numbers 1 (Atkins), 2 (Snelling), and 3 (Green), depicted in *Oil Paintings in Norfolk*, 71. My thanks to David Pitcher of King's Lynn for showing me these paintings on site.

[61] Virginia Tillyard, 'Painters in Sixteenth and Seventeenth Century Norwich', *Norfolk Archaeology*, 37 (1980), 315–18. One more, Richard Edmonds (d.1611–12), may be added to the list; Norwich and Norfolk Record Office MS. DN/inv24/170.

[62] Morgan, 'Norwich Guildhall Portraits', 28.

[63] Five painters are known to have worked in King's Lynn in these years: Margaret Clark and her husband, Robert Snelling (both known to have done portraits), Robert Trewe (possibly a migrant from Norwich), Robert Lexham, and Richard White; Edmond, 'Bury St Edmunds', 111–12; Norfolk and Norwich Record Office MSS. DN/INV 21/12 and KL C50/157.

countenance'.[64] And so it does . . . but not with much trace of sophistication.[65] If Holles had lived out his last years in London, Kent, or Norwich, his experience would almost certainly have been different.

Little else has been learned of portraiture on the Lincolnshire coast. But two other areas, anchored by the cities of Gloucester and Chester, seem more typical of the contemporary regional experience. Though the nature of the surviving evidence is again not precisely comparable, these two examples round out a representative sampling of regional portraiture prior to 1640.

The Gloucester evidence reveals less than Chester about local painters and patrons or of a wider hinterland. But it does tell us more about the characteristics of local portraiture itself. The principal sources here are the twelve surviving portraits of that city's civic benefactors, known as the *Twelve Worthies*. All were painted some time between 1600 and 1618; all share common elements of content and technique that are distinctively local.[66] Taken together, they suggest some interesting observations about the appearance of local portraiture both in these cases and in general.

Save perhaps for Sir Thomas Bell's portrait (Fig. 8.1), which is larger than the rest and has a coat of arms, all twelve appear to have been part of a series of civic portraits heralding the past and present worthies of the community. They are all thinly painted images on oak panel, and they share a common palette dominated by shades of yellow, brown, and red ochres, and with a great deal of inexpensive, granular, carbon black used for both backgrounds and clothing. All are crudely worked, vernacular pieces done with little subtlety and no background imagery. All but Richard Pate's (Fig. 7.7) have inscriptions, and those by a similar hand. The figures themselves share common and distinctly idiosyncratic characteristics of modelling and perspective. Limbs are distinctly foreshortened in all but two (Pate and William Goldston) of the twelve. Eyes in most of the twelve appear large, almond shaped, heavily outlined, and framed by prominent and highly arched brows. While none of the figures may be said to have naturalistically drawn flesh or fingers, six of them—John Falkner (Fig. 7.11), John and Joan Cooke (Fig. 7.2), Thomas Hayden, John Thorne, Sir Thomas White (Fig. 8.2), and Gregory Wilsheire—show fingers with a distinctly rubbery, tube-like appearance. Only

[64] A. C. Wood (ed.), *Memorials of the Holles Family, 1493–1656* (Camden Society, 3rd ser., 55, 1937), 125.

[65] Richard W. Goulding and C. K. Adams (eds), *Catalogue of the Pictures Belonging to his Grace the Duke of Portland* (Cambridge, 1936), 354, catalogue no. 586 and, for the sake of comparison, see an earlier portrait of Holles, ibid. no. 585.

[66] There were initially eighteen civic portraits, as recorded in an account of 1635/6. Portrait subjects include John and Joan Cooke (double portrait), John Falkner, Sir Thomas Bell, Richard Pate, Sir Thomas White, John Haydon, William Goldston, Joan Goldston, Gregory Wilsheire, Isabel Wetherstone, Thomas Poulton, and John Thorne. A brief description of each may be found in Brian Frith, *Twelve Portraits of Gloucester* (Gloucester, 1972). Images of the paintings themselves may be seen on the City of Gloucester website: http://www.livinggloucester.co.uk/search/collection. The following paragraph is based on personal observation over several visits to Gloucester, and by the invaluable observations of Dr Tarnya Cooper, who examined them with me on 7 May 2009. I am also grateful to Nigel Cox of the Gloucester Folk Museum and both Louise Allen and David Rice of the Gloucester City Museum for facilitating these visits.

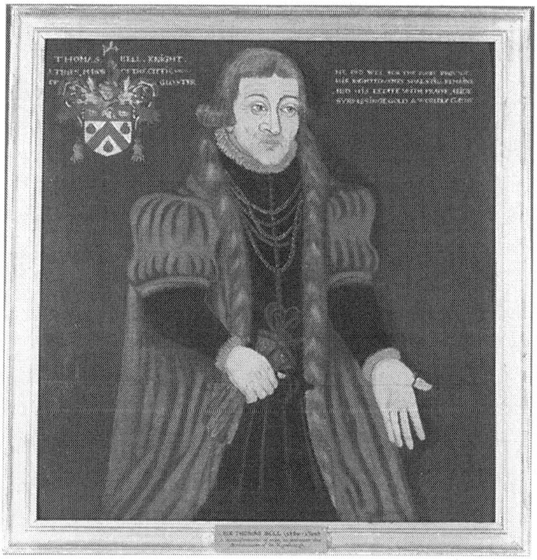

Fig. 8.1. Anon., *Thomas Bell of Gloucester* (*c.*1600–20). © Gloucester City Museum and Art Gallery.

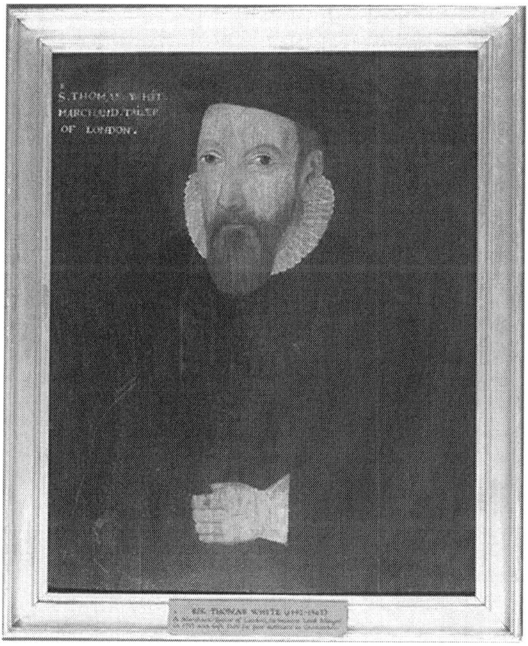

Fig. 8.2. Anon., *Sir Thomas White* (*c.*1600–20). © Gloucester City Museum and Art Gallery.

the Bell portrait, crude though it may be, even strives towards three-dimensionality in the shadows suggested behind the figure on one side. Along with Pate's portrait it is slightly more accomplished than the rest, though these all remain crude works.

The portrait of Sir Thomas White (d.1567) proves particularly revealing. As an eminent and famous benefactor who established a self-perpetuating loan-fund to journeymen clothiers in twenty-three different towns plus the Merchant Taylors' Company of London, White was one of the most widely portrayed urban figures of his time. Virtually every one of the twenty-four recipient bodies, including Canterbury and Gloucester, eventually commemorated his benefaction with a portrait. Nearly all survive. But almost all the other White portraits derive from one or two models (one by Jan de Critz done for the Merchant Taylors itself), which are skilfully done in a formal, polite idiom, with fine furniture, rich drapery, and appropriately fashionable dress serving to dignify the whole. They depict a serious, clean-shaven, and astute figure with well-modelled features, sometimes shown full-length and always naturally posed.[67]

Gloucester's White looks nothing like this, showing instead a haggard, crudely drawn, bearded figure against a black, featureless background devoid of any furniture or drapery. It does, however, somewhat resemble some of the others of the Gloucester series in its limited palette, rubbery fingers, foreshortened limbs, and almond-shaped eyes. We can only conclude that it must have been carried out locally, perhaps by one of the painters responsible for others of the twelve, and without any resort to other White portraits that might have served as a model. The objective was to have a talisman of the benefactor and his benefaction, but not necessarily to strive for any verisimilitude: an aim frequently replicated in civic portraits the realm over.

Despite these similarities, scholarly consensus has these twelve portraits produced by four or five different hands,[68] suggesting a common training or the use of a common, locally accessible pattern book or books from which features could be modelled. Certainly their similarities would rule out the suggestion[69] that they may have been done at different times by itinerant painters passing through. The names of only five Gloucester-area painters from this period have come to light in local archives,[70] but there must surely have been more painters than this at work in a cathedral centre with the decorative work and restoration entailed in such places.

[67] Robert Tittler, 'Sir Thomas White of London: Civic Philanthropy and the Making of the Merchant Hero', in id., *Townspeople and Nation: English Urban Experiences, 1540–1640* (Stanford, CA, 2001), 100–20; id., 'Three Livery Company Portraits by Jan de Critz', *Burlington Magazine*, 147/1228 (July 2005), 141–4.

[68] Frith, *Twelve Portraits*, 5, as confirmed on site by Dr Cooper.

[69] Ibid. 7.

[70] Richard Harrison, John Johnson, Richard Kinges, Thomas Pritchard, and George Mitchell. Kinges was probably a Tewkesbury man and formally a glazier, but he is also known to have painted, as many glaziers did. Gloucestershire Record Office MS. GBR B/3/1, fo. 76^{v}; John Smith (ed.), *The Names and Surnames of all the Able and Sufficient Men in Body fit for His Majesty's Service in the Wars within the County of Gloucester* (1902), 2; Kathryn Davies, *Artisan Art: Vernacular Wall Paintings in the Welsh Marches, 1550–1650* (Almeley, Herefordshire, 2008), 68; Jill Barlow (ed.), *A Calendar of the Registers of Apprentices of the City of Gloucester, 1595–1700* (Bristol and Gloucestershire Archaeological Society Record Series, 14, 2001), 55, 81, and 93.

It also remains possible that these crude images were carried out not by those specifically trained as painters at all, but rather by, e.g., masons, glaziers (which would explain the heavily outlined facial features), or even plasterers. All such occupations entailed some painting from time to time. The few surviving court books of painter-stainers' companies, especially in London and Chester, are full of complaints about men in such occupations painting without licence. Ironically, the contemporary panel portraits on the funerary monument of John and Anne Bower in Gloucester Cathedral, *c.*1615, which one might expect in such a venue to have been done by a mason or glazier, are sufficiently skilful to suggest a trained craftsman/painter at work instead.[71]

There is also insufficient evidence to indicate whether these visual characteristics might be found in paintings done over a wider region around the city of Gloucester. But the main point is that these twelve portraits, all done within about ten years in and around that city, represent the work of several hands and yet are much of a type in their naive modelling of facial features, palette, and technique. They remain very distinctive amongst the general run even of contemporary English vernacular portraiture. They represent local and deeply rooted craft-based traditions of figurative imagery. Like their Norfolk counterparts they may reflect something of the protestant and particularly Calvinist emphasis on civic involvement amongst the laity: both Gloucester and Norwich, along with several centres in Kent, were amongst the earliest urban centres to embrace a protestantism of this stripe.

Having drawn on Chester evidence so heavily in earlier chapters, less need be said about it here save to point out its distinctive regional nature and to compare it with the other three examples discussed above. The evidence from Chester and its surrounding region, including the rest of the shire of Cheshire, southern Lancashire, and the northern Welsh counties of Flintshire and Denbighshire, proves especially strong for the painters and only slightly less so for patrons. The former, as noted in Chapter 4 above, formed the largest component in an amalgamated Chester Guild of Painter-Stainers, Embroiderers, Glaziers, and Stationers, established in 1533. At least three painters in that company—John Souch, Edward Bellin, and Thomas Pulford—are known to have painted portraits prior to 1640.[72] At least three more, Randle Holme the elder and the younger and Thomas Robinson, may possibly have done so.[73] After apprenticing with the younger

[71] Located in the west side of the north transept and observed 5 and 7 May 2009.

[72] Souch must have been quite prolific, as sixteen and (depending on the veracity of attribution) perhaps as many as twenty of his paintings have survived. One of Bellin's has survived. Pulford is recorded as having painted five portraits of the puritan William Prynne as he passed through Chester to exile in 1637. All were confiscated and destroyed by the ecclesiastical authorities. Both Souch and Bellin apprenticed with one or the other Randle Holmes. *ODNB*, vide 'Souch, John'; Heinz Archive, painters' files, vide 'Bellin, Edward'; Rev. Canon Blomefield, 'Puritanism in Chester in 1637: An Account of the Reception of William Prynne by Certain Inhabitants of the City of Chester', *Journal of the Architectural, Archaeological and Historic Society of Chester*, 3 (1885), 271–88. David Cressy, *Travesties and Transgressions in Tudor and Stuart England* (Oxford, 2000), 226–9; P. Graunt, 'William Prynne's Reception at Chester, 1637', *Cheshire History*, 37 (1997), 26–35.

[73] The claim that one of them may have painted Thomas ap Ieuen ap David, now in the National Museum of Wales, remains unsubstantiated. In fact, the mysterious monogram that has suggested that attribution may well point to another Chester painter, Thomas Robinson (d.1642), instead.

Holme even the prominent engraver Daniel King may also have painted portraits, albeit probably after 1640.[74]

The context for regional patronage is more readily retrievable here than for Gloucester and strikingly different than that which pertained in Kent or Norfolk. Though the port of Chester certainly remained active throughout the period at hand, campaigns to Ireland took up much more of its shipping, and contacts with northwestern Europe much less, than was the case with those ports on the eastern or southern coast.[75] Even the interior of the shire and its surrounding areas were more isolated in almost every sense—socially, politically, culturally, and geographically—than Kent or Norfolk. Obviously further from the London centre, most of this extended area had poor soil, limited agricultural production, and little industry aside from the salt wells of Nantwich, Northwich, and Middlewich.[76] Save for the Stanley earls of Derby and other great men who took turns running the Palatinate of Chester (though not necessarily living there), few of the landowning families of this whole area held affluent estates, or enjoyed the same sort of court connections as their Kentish or Norfolk counterparts.

It is also the case that protestantism came later to most of this hinterland, and that the emphasis on civic portraits that it seems to have encouraged elsewhere did not play much of a role in this religiously more traditional area. Insofar as they can be identified, the regional patrons to whom Souch, Bellin, and Thomas Leigh the elder catered in this era were Catholic or Anglo-Catholic royalists; none of this trio are known to have done civic portraits.

Those locational circumstances also produced a regional gentry that was isolated socially as well as culturally, so that perhaps a greater number than elsewhere married within rather than beyond the region. As anxious as gentry anywhere to establish their legitimacy and reputation by the display of material goods, they were nevertheless less able conveniently to do so by building great country houses or patronizing the more fashionable painters of the day. In consequence, and with few exceptions, the regional gentry therefore relied on local talent, based in Chester, and received the sorts of imagery which that talent could produce.

That is not to say that the patrons or painters of the region remained completely ignorant throughout the entire era of the more sophisticated styles and techniques being practised elsewhere. And it is not to overlook the increasing refinement of painting done in this era in the very last decades of our period. Merchants and others did of course pass through the city of Chester from other parts of England or even from abroad; even royal officials passed through en route to or from the Irish Wars from the 1590s especially. Some influence of continental prints has been identified in the decorative work of a few isolated and relatively modest, if still

[74] Following his apprenticeship, King (*c.*1616–61) joined the Chester Company of Painter-Stainers, etc., in 1639, and knew enough about painting later to have written a manuscript treatise on limning. *ODNB*, vide 'King, Daniel'; *Miniatura, or the Art of Limning*, BL. Add. MS. 12461.

[75] D. M. Woodward, *The Trade of Elizabethan Chester* (Hull, 1970), 1–52.

[76] Joan Thirsk, 'The Farming Regions of England', in ead., *Agrarian History*, 80–8.

interesting, Cheshire country houses in the Elizabethan years and after.[77] But the most important source for continental, classically derived models of visual culture seems to have been the collection of prints and drawings being assembled from about the 1610s by the Holmeses, elder and younger, which has come to be known as the 'Holme Album'.[78] Though the heraldic influence remained particularly strong in these regions as we have seen in Chapter 4, this 'Album' throws some light on the more cosmopolitan and sophisticated visual idiom that came into the area from about the 1630s.

These two influences, the heraldic and the polite, and the movement in fashion from the former to the latter, may be seen in the contrasts described in Chapter 6 between the two most familiar Cheshire paintings of their time. The stylistic and technical distance between the naive and strongly heraldic *Cholmondeley Ladies* of the 1610s and Souch's *Sir Thomas Aston* of a short generation later marks the transition towards a more polished, cosmopolitan, and polite approach in a relatively isolated area of the realm. In that short space Chester painters, and presumably their patrons, had begun to take note of such models as would have been accessible to them at least through such sources as the Holmes's collection. Souch's painting pales by comparison with anything Cornelius Johnson was producing in Kent at the very same time. It still shows some heraldic roots in its imagery and in its limited palette. It fails utterly to obtain a naturalistic perspective. But in its striving to produce a more polite imagery overall it begins to close the gate on the regional vernacular, and anticipates the more polite and sophisticated work to come, both from Souch himself and from his regional contemporaries like Edward Bellin.[79]

Given the fragile and therefore often ephemeral nature of the archival and visual evidence for portraiture, the observations that can be drawn from these four areas can neither address the same questions for each nor give us a complete picture of all forms of portrait activity in any one. Yet they do serve to identify regionally specific characteristics of both patronage and production. They identify many of the social, economic, and cultural contexts for both these activities. They certainly support the view of an English portraiture in which regional distinctions must be recognized and acknowledged.

The social and geographic structure of portrait activity in these years will often have consisted of definable circles like those briefly coalescing around Cornelius Johnson in East Kent or the gentry of Chester's hinterland as it revolved, at greater

[77] Such houses include Lyme Park (1570), Brereton Hall (1586), Grafton Hall, Malpas (*c.*1609), and Crewe Hall (*c.*1615–36). Wells-Cole, *Art and Decoration*, 22, 34, 64, 66, 68, and 208–9.

[78] BL. Harleian MS. 2001; Robert Tittler and Anne Thackray, 'Print Collecting in Provincial England Prior to 1650, the Randle Holme Album', *British Art Journal*, 11/2 (Autumn 2008), 3–10.

[79] Edward Bellin, *Unknown Man of the Family of Edwards of Rhual* (1636), oil on canvas, 29" × 21½", private collection; John Steegman, *A Survey of Portraits in Welsh Houses*, 2 vols (Cardiff, 1957), I.207, pl. 37A. I am grateful to Stephanie Roberts of the National Museum of Wales for this reference. Like Souch, Bellin (b.1609) apprenticed with Randle Holme the elder (1624 ff.), was admitted to the Chester Company in 1634, and became prominent in its ranks thereafter. Chester Record Office MS. ZCR 63/2/131, fos. 29^r, 36^r, 39^r, and 40^r, and MS. ZG 17/1 (unpaginated, vide minutes for 1624).

length, around the Holmes, Souch, Bellin, and others of their milieu. Members of these patronal circles and denizens of these hinterlands shared similar social, financial, cultural, sometimes even religious characteristics. Their members were often known to each other and not infrequently related by marriage or descent. Their affluence and sophistication, and thus the characteristics of their patronage, remained broadly linked to the productivity of their lands or, as with merchants, their businesses, and to their physical proximity to provincial centres, to London, and to the Continent. They almost certainly shared ideas about favoured painters, and we may presume that they visited each other often enough to have been familiar with paintings held by their friends and neighbours. Some of these areas prove larger and more geographically contiguous than others: the one surrounding the Chester painters extended to a hinterland of several counties with similar characteristics, all revolving around a single urban centre. Those east Kentish families patronizing Johnson in 1636 dwelt in two areas not far from each other within a distinctive region of a single shire.

Groups of painters working from a common location, including those in Chester and Gloucester, will likely have apprenticed in the same guild, perhaps with one or two dominant masters within that guild, and therefore have acquired similar approaches to their craft. Such guilds also existed in Newcastle, briefly in Exeter, and probably elsewhere as well, though we have insufficient evidence of the portraits produced by their members. They will have shared access to whatever pigments and other materials were available in a particular area, and to pattern books in local circulation.

The evidence of portrait activity from the area anchored by Chester is also as near as we are likely to get to a rounded picture of a single and distinctive cultural hinterland in this era. Yet it seems just as likely that, had we only the luxury of surviving evidence to flesh them out, we would find similar regions operating at the same time and in the same ways as this one. Some unique features, such as allegiance to a particular painter, will have been diluted into the richer mix, but factors like location and physical environment, the dominance (or lack of it) of a particular great landlord or figure of state, geographic proximity, and access to critical resources, remain defining features of provincial portraiture at this time.

9

Conclusion

Taking its cue from the notion of the public sphere, and from subsequent scholarly efforts to observe, record, or even imagine the roots of such a construct in European society, this book has described the growing affinity for secular portraiture in sixteenth- and early-seventeenth-century England. It has sought to understand the content and dynamic of that emerging affinity, to consider what it might tell us about the making of a 'public' form of cultural activity, and thus to illuminate the early stages of the putative public sphere itself. It has sought to do so not in the theoretical or imagined terms of what could or might have been, but in the empirical context of social, economic, and cultural activity of a specific time and place.

The phenomenon of 'public making' has recently been described as:

> the active creation of new forms of association that allowed people to connect with others in ways not rooted in family, rank, or vocation, but rather founded in voluntary groupings built on the shared interests, tastes, commitments, and desires of individuals. By creating new forms of public association, cultural producers and consumers in effect challenged dominant ideas about just who could be a public person, greatly expanded the resources of public life for ordinary people in their own time, and developed ideas and practices that have helped to create the political culture of modernity.[1]

The cultural producers in this study have been the painters. The 'consumers' included those who literally consumed these 'products' through patronage and purchase, but they have also been defined more broadly here to include those who also engaged in some non-commercial manner with the portraiture, or idea of portraiture, of their time. That takes in those who may also have expressed their affinity in other ways: by observing, discussing, collecting, displaying, or exchanging portraits, or even by producing portraits themselves as an avocation. All of those activities contributed to an emerging public for, and discourse regarding, that particular cultural genre: a discourse that does not seem, at least in England, to have been much in evidence in the same guise prior to about the latter half of the reign of Henry VIII.

None of this is to claim a uniformity amongst the makers or partakers of this emerging public: in their social or political or economic status, in their tastes and

[1] Bronwen Wilson and Paul Yachnin (eds), *Making Publics in Early Modern Europe: People, Things, Forms of Knowledge* (2010), 1.

motives, in their level of wealth, or in their geographic situation. Rather it exhibits quite the opposite. The public emerging here remained patently diverse in all such respects. Its members ranged from kings, queens, courtiers, and the landed elites, to some lesser gentry, even the occasional yeomen, along with sundry professionals, merchants, and craftsmen. As paintings remained relatively inexpensive material objects at least until about the 1610s or 1620s, people of relatively modest means could and did obtain them. And if consumers were not as likely to have lived in the remote corners of the realm as in, e.g., the London metropolis, they may still be found in such corners, and with increasingly frequency over the time at hand.

In the social and geographic diversity of this activity, socially well beyond the crown and court circle and geographically well beyond the London metropolis, those who shared this growing affinity did indeed expand both the resources for public life and the range of those engaging in it. Hard though it may to imagine a king or queen having much in common with, e.g., a Somerset yeoman, such diverse people did still broadly share some of the same objectives in their engagement with portraiture. From the very early years of secular easel portraiture in England these will have included a view of portraiture as an affirmation of personal or official legitimacy, religious belief, political loyalty, intellectual or cultural engagement, personal friendship, and/or as a memorial for posterity.

Those who catered to, and therefore facilitated, these concerns took in an equally wide swathe of people. As we have long known, they included London-based virtuoso painters, many of them foreign-born and/or -trained, and London-based painter-stainers reared in, protected, and possibly constrained by the Painter-Stainers' livery. But they also included itinerant journeymen and provincially based guildsmen who served the clientele of particular regions throughout the realm. Failed apprentices and such occupational interlopers as, e.g., masons, carvers, embroiderers, plasterers, and even heralds, also played their part despite myriad formal constraints on such activity.

The products of these labours were by no means uniform in their sophistication or craftsmanship, or in the success with which they met their patrons' expectations. During most of the era at hand, what we think of as sophistication or indeed 'art' itself will have had little to do with what contemporaries perceived as the function of a painting. When applied to portraits of this time our notion of quality has traditionally been based on how closely an image conformed to the classical ideal in such respects as its figurative proportions, tonal subtlety, perspective, and other elements of naturalistic representation.

Those concepts of 'art'—that which Habermas saw as a key component of his public sphere[2]—came into the English public consciousness only gradually during the period at hand. Its progress would surely have been slower still were it not for the influence of foreign-born or -trained painters on the one hand, the sophisticated foreign-born queens, Anne of Denmark and Henrietta Maria, or the lifting of constraints on foreign travel under the early Stuarts. The latter two factors, if not

[2] Jürgen Habermas, *The Structural Transformation of the Public Sphere: An Inquiry into a Category of Bourgeois Society*, trans. Thomas Berger (Cambridge, MA, 1989), 39–40.

necessarily the former, were phenomena of the early seventeenth century. These helped encourage the notion of portraiture and other forms of painting as 'art', a luxury item valued for its aesthetic quality, the skill and (when known) reputation of its creator, thus to be sought, purchased, and displayed.

The increasing frequency with which formal and polite rather than vernacular portraits came to be produced certainly provides a barometer of social change and cultural sophistication. We see this not only at the metropolitan centre, but also at the provincial periphery, where painters like John Souch of Chester were encouraged by the increasingly sophisticated tastes of their clientele to explore (often with but mixed success) equally sophisticated forms of representation. We see it in the rapid acceleration in the price of the painted portrait which accrued, after a century of relative stagnation, first in the courtly environment and then more widely, from the 1610s and 1620s onwards. We see it in the fervour and increasing number of contemporary collectors, as most emphatically exemplified in Lucy Harrington's desperate effort to add the Bacons' Holbeins to her collection. We see it in the dedicated residential spaces that emerged for public display, not only in the long galleries of the Hatfields, Knoles, and Longleats of the day, but also in the sitting room of Heywood's Alexander Nowell or perhaps even in the parlour of precocious strivers like John Kaye. And we see it in the notoriety symbolized in the knighting of Rubens and Van Dyck.

These events helped create, and certainly reflected, a world of increased disposable income, social opportunity, cultural sophistication, foreign travel, and conspicuous material consumption. Taken together, these characteristics have rightly been seen as the harbinger of the putative consumer revolution conventionally placed at the beginning in the Restoration era.[3] They also identify for us an early stage in the formation of a public sphere, and of the increasingly public nature of the portrait genre.

[3] Especially, e.g., in Linda Levy Peck, *Consuming Splendor: Society and Culture in Seventeenth Century England* (Cambridge, 2005).

Bibliography

Place of publication for all works is London unless otherwise specified.

UNPUBLISHED SOURCES

Birmingham Public Library

Aylesford Collection.

Bristol Record Office

MS 04720(1). Robert Ricart, 'The Maire of Bristowe Is Kalendar', [*c.*1484].

British Library

Additional MS 6391. Sir William Musgrave, *Painted Portraits in many of the Publick Buildings and Capital Mansions of England Ranged Alphabetically*, 7 vols (1796 ff.).

Additional MS 12461. *Miniatura, or the Art of Limning.*

Additional MS 26,704. Chaloner's Heraldic drawings.

Additional MSS 36,901–36,927. Aston Family Papers.

Additional MS 47,185. Chaloner's Heraldic drawings.

Additional MS 47,787. Sir Edward Dering's Letter Book.

Egerton MS 784. William Whiteway's Diary.

Harleian MS 1091. Chaloner's Heraldic Drawings.

Harleian MS 1354. Heraldic notes.

Harleian MS 1366. Papers of Richard Scarlett.

Harleian MS 1927. Thomas Chaloner's Book.

Harleian MS 2001. Randle Holme Papers.

Harleian MS 2021. Richard Scarlett's Heraldic Book.

Harleian MS 2054. Holme Papers.

Harleian MS 6376.

Lansdowne MS 20. Miscellaneous papers.

Stowe MS 243. Stanhope Letterbooks.

Cambridge University Library

MS Dd.xi.73. William Whiteway's Commonplace Book.

Canterbury City and Cathedral Archives

MS CCA Literary MS./E 31. 'Diary of Thomas Cocks'.

MS CC/FA 9-24. City Chamberlains' Accounts, 1505–1640.

MS Dcc-BB/77/102/a. Bond, 1582.

Centre for Kentish Studies, Maidstone

MS CKS MD/ACM 1/2. Maidstone Burghmote Book.

MS CKS FA1/1579.

MS CKS QM/SRc/1597/43.

MS CKS U 350/E4. 'Edward Dering's Book of Expenses'.
MS CKS U 1475/A 64/1–35 and /E 49. De L'Isle MSS. Penshurst Household Accounts.
MS MD/ACM1/2. Heraldic Visitation, 1619.

Cheshire and Chester Record Office, Chester
MS 1633 Blease. Will of Robert Blease.
MS ZCR 63/2/131. Rough Minute Book of the Company of Painter-Stainers, Embroiderers, Glaziers, and Stationers.
MS ZG 17/1. Minute Book, Company of Painter-Stainers, Embroiderers, Glaziers, and Stationers, 1575–1621.
MS ZG 17/2. Minute Book, Company of Painter-Stainers, Embroiderers, Glaziers, and Stationers, 1621 ff.
MS ZM/AB/1. City Assembly Book, 1539 ff.
MS ZM/AB/2. City Assembly Book, 1624–89.
MS ZM/L/6/166.

College of Arms
MS Her/BH. J. H. Parker Oxspring, 'The Painter-Stainers and their Dispute with the Heralds', 3 parts, typescript (no date).

Courtauld Institute of Art
Rees Jones, S. 'Five Portraits from Peterhouse', Cambridge Research Report no. 152 [typescript] (1951).

Courtauld Institute of Art: Witt Library
Various files.

Devon County Record Office, Exeter
'Exeter Corporation Act Book no. 5'.

Durham University Archives
DPR I/1/(various). Consistory Court of Durham Probate Inventories.

East Kent Record Office, Dover
MS DO/FCA 4. Dover Chamberlains' Accounts (1603–25).
MS A/DO/AAM 2. Dover Borough Assembly Book (1603–73).

East Suffolk Record Office, Ipswich
MS W61. Wills.

Gloucestershire Archives, Gloucester
MS GBR B/3/1. Gloucester Corporation Minute Book, 1565–1632.

Guildhall Library
MS 16,967/2. Ironmongers Company, Quarter Court Minutes.
Print Collection, London Aldermen Series, nos. 32132–52 and 32170–3.

London Metropolitan Archives

MS CLA/002/01/001 and CLA/002/03/001. City of London Court of Orphans, Common Sergeant's Books from 1586.

MS 5667/1 and 2. Court Minute Books, Painter-Stainers' Company of London.

Microfilms 9051. Wills and Inventories, Commissary Court of London.

Microfilm 9171. Registers of wills, Commissary Court of London.

National Art Library, Victoria and Albert Museum

MS 86.EE.69. [Edward Barton, attrib.] instruction book on painting, *c.*1582.

MS 86.HH.62 L.29-1982. Peter Henson's drawings.

MS MSL/1982/29. Epiphanius Evesham's pattern book of heraldic drawings.

National Portrait Gallery

Heinz Archive, Various files.

Norwich and Norfolk Record Office, Norwich

MS DN/INV 21/12. Inventory.

MS DN/INV 24/170. Inventory.

MS DN/INV 26/87. Inventory.

MS KL C50/157.

Society of Antiquaries of London

MS 213. 'A Collection on Heraldry'.

Somerset Record Office, Taunton

MS DD/GC/6. Creech St Michael and Rushton deeds.

Surrey Record Office, Woking

MS 6729/7/138. More Molyneux Family of Losely Park, Historical Correspondence (1420–1642).

The National Archives, Kew

C.1. Early Chancery Proceedings.

C.115. Chancery, Master Harvey's Exhibits, Duchess of Norfolk's Deeds.

C.131. Chancery, Extents for Debts.

C.239. Chancery, Extents for Debts, Series II.

E.122. Exchequer: King's Remembrancer: Customs Accounts.

E.190. Exchequer: King's Remembrancer: Port Books.

E.210. Exchequer, King's Remembrancer: Ancient Deeds, Ser. D.

E.214 Exchequer, King's Remembrancer: Modern Deeds, Ser. D.

LC.5. Lord Chamberlain's Department, Miscl. Accounts

PROB 2. Prerogative Court of Canterbury Inventories.

PROB 11. Prerogative Court of Canterbury Will Registers.

STAC 5. Proceedings, Elizabeth I.

Tyne and Wear Archives Service, Newcastle

MS GU.GP1/1. Charter, Company of Goldsmiths, Pewterers, Plumbers, Painters, and Glaziers of Newcastle, 1536.

MS GP2/1 (microfilm 1273/7). Court Books, Company of Goldsmiths, Pewterers, Plumbers, Painters and Glaziers of Newcastle, 1598–1671.
MS NC/F/1/1/10-13. Newcastle Chamberlains' Accounts.

West Sussex Record Office, Chichester
MS A1/1/5. Barnarde Genealogy, Cutton manuscripts.
MS Ep/IV/3/1. Deposition Book.

Yorkshire Archaeological Society
Bradfer Lawrence MS MD 335/15/1/34. License to alienate (1574).

THESES

Cooper, Tarnya, '*Memento Mori* Portraiture: Painting, Protestant Culture and the Patronage of Middle Elites in England and Wales', PhD thesis, University of Sussex (2001).
Tillyard, Virginia, 'Civic Portraits Painted for, or Donated to, the Council Chamber of Norwich Guildhall before 1687', MA thesis, Courtauld Institute (1978).

PUBLISHED SOURCES

Adams, Arthur (ed.), *Cheshire Visitation Pedigrees, 1663* (Harleian Society, 1941).
Ailes, Adrian, 'Artists and Artwork of the Heralds' Visitations in England and Wales, 1530–1687', in *Proceedings of the XVI Colloquium of the Academie Internationale d'Heraldique* (Verviers, Belgium, 2011).
—— 'The Development of Heralds' Visitations in England and Wales, 1450–1600', *Coat of Arms*, 3rd ser., 5 (2009), 7–23.
Airs, Malcolm, *The Tudor and Jacobean Country House: A Building History* (Stroud, 1995).
Allen, Marion E. (ed.), *The Wills of the Archdeaconry of Suffolk, 1625–1626* (Suffolk Record Society, 37, 1995).
Ames-Lewis, Francis, 'Modelbook Drawings and the Florentine Quattrocento Artist', *Art History*, 10/1 (March 1987), 1–16.
Anon., *Dives et Pauper* (1536 edn).
Anon., *Oil Paintings in Public Ownership, Kent* (2004).
Anon., *Oil Paintings in Public Ownership, Norfolk* (2006).
Anon., *Oil Paintings in Public Ownership in West Sussex* (2005).
Anon., *Queen Elizabeth's Entertainment at Mitcham* (1598).
Anon., *William Whiteway's Diary* (Dorset Record Society, 12, 1991).
Anon., *Wills and Inventories from the Register at Durham*, II: *1580–99* (Surtees Society, 38, 1860).
Armitage, George J., and John P. Rylands (eds), *Pedigrees Made at the Visitation of Cheshire, 1613* (Record Society of Lancashire and Cheshire, 58, 1909).
Arnold, Janet, *Patterns of Fashion: The Cut and Construction of Clothes for Men and Women c. 1580–1620* (1985).
—— *Queen Elizabeth's Wardrobe Unlock'd* (Leeds, 1988).
Ashelford, Jane, *Dress in the Age of Elizabeth* (1988).
Ashmore, Owen (ed.), *Household Inventories of the Lancashire Gentry, 1500–1700* (Transactions of the Historic Society of Lancashire and Cheshire for 1958, 1959).

Aston, Margaret, *England's Iconoclasts*, I: *Laws against Images* (Oxford, 1988).
—— 'Puritans and Iconoclasm, 1560–1660', in C. Durston and J. Eales (eds), *The Culture of English Puritanism, 1560–1700* (Basingstoke, 1996), 92–121.
Atkinson, J. A., *et al.* (eds), *Darlington Wills and Inventories, 1600–1625* (Newcastle, 1993).
Auerbach, Erna, *Nicholas Hilliard* (London and Boston, MA, 1961).
—— *Tudor Artists: A Study of the Painters in the Royal Service and of Portraiture on Illuminated Documents from the Accession of Henry VII to the Death of Elizabeth* (1954).
Barlow, Jill (ed.), *A Calendar of the Registers of Apprentices of the City of Gloucester, 1595–1700* (Bristol and Gloucestershire Archaeological Society Record Series, 14, 2001).
Barry, Jonathan, 'Review and Commentary: The State of the Middle Classes in Early Modern England', *Journal of Historical Sociology*, 4 (1991), 75–86.
—— and Christopher Brooks (eds), *The Middling Sorts of People: Culture, Society and Politics in England, 1550–1800* (1994), 28–51.
Bateson, Mary (ed.), *Records of the Borough of Leicester*, III (1905).
Batho, Gordon (ed.), *The Household Papers of Henry Percy, ninth earl of Northumberland* (Camden Society, 3rd ser., 93, 1962).
Belsey, Andrew, and Catherine Belsey, 'Icons of Divinity, Portraits of Elizabeth I', in Lucy Gent and Nigel Llewellyn (eds), *Renaissance Bodies* (1990), 11–35.
Ben-Amos, Ilana Kraus, *Adolescence and Youth in Early Modern England* (London and New Haven, 1994).
—— 'Failure to Become Freemen: Urban Apprentices in Early Modern England', *Social History*, 16/2 (May 1991), 41–65.
—— 'Woman Apprentices in the Trades and Crafts of Bristol', *Continuity and Change*, 6/2 (1991), 227–52.
Bendall, Sarah (ed.), *Dictionary of Land Surveyors and Local Cartographers*, 2nd edn, 2 vols (1997).
Berry, Elizabeth K. (ed.), *Swaledale Wills and Inventories, 1522–1689* (Yorkshire Archaeological Society Record Series, 152, 1998).
Bettey, J. H. (ed.), *Calendar of the Correspondence of the Smyth Family of Ashton Court, 1548–1642* (Bristol Record Society, 35, 1982).
Bevan, G. M. (ed.), *Portraits of the Archbishops of Canterbury* (1908).
Bindman, David (ed.), *The History of British Art*, 3 vols (London and New Haven, 2008).
Bindoff, S. T. (ed.), *The House of Commons, 1509–1558*, 3 vols (History of Parliament Trust, 1982).
Blackstone, Mary A., 'Lancashire, Shakespeare and the Construction of Cultural Neighbourhoods in Sixteenth Century England', in Richard Dutton, Alison Findlay, and Richard Wilson (eds), *Religion, Politics and Patronage, Lancastrian Shakespeare* (Manchester and New York, 2003), 186–204.
Blackstone, William, *Commentaries on the Laws of England*, 4 vols (1765–9).
Blank, Paula, *Broken English: Dialectics and the Politics of Language in Renaissance Writing* (New York and London, 1996).
Blatchley, John, *The Town Library of Ipswich* (Woodbridge, Suffolk, 1989).
Blomefield, Rev. Canon, 'Puritanism in Chester in 1637: An Account of the Reception of William Prynne by Certain Inhabitants of the City of Chester', *Journal of the Architectural, Archaeological and Historic Society of Chester*, 3 (1885), 271–88.
Borg, Alan, *The History of the Worshipful Company of Painters, Otherwise Painter-Stainers* (Huddersfield, 2005).
Borsay, Peter, *The English Urban Renaissance: Culture and Society in the Provincial Town, 1660–1770* (Oxford, 1989).

Bradshaw, Henry, 'On the Collection of Portraits belonging to the University before the Civil War' [1872], *Collected Papers of Henry Bradshaw* (Cambridge, 1889).
Brears, Peter C. D. (ed.), *Yorkshire Probate Inventories, 1542–1689* (Yorkshire Archaeological Society Record Series, 134, 1972).
Brigden, Susan, 'Religion and Social Obligation in Early Sixteenth Century London', *Past and Present*, 103 (May 1984), 67–112.
Brunskill, R. W., *Illustrated Handbook of Vernacular Architecture* (London and Boston, MA, 1971, 1978).
—— *Traditional Buildings of Britain: An Introduction to Vernacular Architecture* (1985).
—— *Vernacular Architecture of the Lake Counties: A Field Handbook* (1974, 1987).
Buck, Sir George, 'The Thirde Universitie of England or a Treatise on the Foundation of all the Colleges', published as an Appendix to John Stow, *The Annales or General Chronicles of England* (1615, *STC* 23,338).
Bullard, M. R. A., 'Talking Heads: The Bodleian Frieze and Inspiration, Sources, Design and Significance', *Bodleian Library Record*, 14 (April 1994), 461–83.
Burn, Richard, *Ecclesiastical Law*, 6th edn, 4 vols (1797).
Calendar of State Papers Foreign for the Reign of Elizabeth, ed. R. B. Wernham, 22 (1936).
Calhoun, Craig, 'Imagining Solidarity: Cosmopolitanism, Constitutional Patriotism, and the Public Sphere', *Public Culture*, 14/1 (2002), 147–71.
Campbell, Lorne, *Renaissance Portraits* (London and New Haven, 1990).
Carlisle, Nicholas, *A Concise Description of the Endowed Grammar Schools of England and Wales*, 2 vols (1818).
Carlton, Charles, *The Court of Orphans* (Leicester, 1974).
Chamberlain, Mary, *Fenwomen: A Portrait of Women in an English Village* (1975).
Chirelstein, Ellen, 'Emblem and Reckless Presence: The Drury Portrait at Yale', in Lucy Gent (ed.), *Albion's Classicism: The Visual Arts in Britain, 1550–1660* (London and New Haven, 1995), 287–312.
Christoferson, John, *An Exhortation to all Menne* (1554), sig. Uiii.
Clark, Peter, *English Provincial Society from the Reformation to the Revolution: Religion: Politics and Society in Kent, 1500–1640* (Hassocks, Sussex, 1977).
—— and Jean Hosking, *Population Estimates of English Small Towns 1550–1851*, rev. edn (Leicester, 1993).
Clarke, R. A., and P. A. E. Day, *Lady Godiva: Images of a Legend in Art and Society* (Coventry, 1982).
Cliffe, J. T., *The Yorkshire Gentry from the Reformation to the Civil War* (1969).
Clifton-Taylor, Alec, *The Pattern of English Building* (London and Boston, MA, 1972).
Clopper, Lawrence M. (ed.), *Records of Early English Drama, Chester* (Toronto, 1979).
Coates, Ben, 'Poor Relief in London during the English Revolution Revisited', *London Journal*, 25 (2000), 40–58.
Collins, Francis (ed.), *Register of the Freemen of the City of York, 1559–1759* (1900).
Collinson, Patrick, *The Birthpangs of Protestant England: Religious and Cultural Change in the Sixteenth and Seventeenth Centuries* (Basingstoke, 1988).
Cooper, Alix, *Inventing the Indigenous: Local Knowledge and Natural History in Early Modern Europe* (Cambridge, 2007).
Cooper, Tarnya, '"Frail Flesh, as in a Glass": The Portrait as an Immortal Presence in Early Modern England and Wales', in Mary Rogers (ed.), *Fashioning Identities in Renaissance Art* (Aldershot, 2000), 197–212.

Costaras, Nicola, 'Early Modern Blues: The Smalt Patent in Context', in Jo Kirby, Susie Nash, and Joanna Cannon (eds), *Trade in Artists' Materials: Markets and Commerce in Europe to 1700* (2010), 401–14.

Cowper, J. M. (ed.), Canterbury Marriage Licenses, 1st ser., *1568–1618* (Canterbury, 1892), and 2nd ser., *1619–1660* (1894).

—— *Lives of the Deans of Canterbury* (1900).

—— *Rolls of the Freemen of the City of Canterbury* (1903).

Cressy, David, *Travesties and Transgressions in Tudor and Stuart England* (Oxford, 2000).

Croft-Murray, Edward, *Decorative Painting in England 1537–1837*, I (1962).

—— 'Lambert Barnard: An English Early Renaissance Painter', *Archaeological Journal*, 113 (1957), 108–25.

Cumming, Valerie, *Gloves* (1982).

—— *A Visual History of Costume: The Seventeenth Century* (1984).

Cust, Lionel, 'The Lumley Inventories', *Walpole Society*, 6 (1917–18), 15–35.

Davidson, Clifford, and Anne Elizabeth Nicholas (eds), *Iconoclasm in Art and Drama* (Kalamazoo, MI, 1989).

Davies, J. C., *A History of Borlase School* (Aylesbury, 1932).

Davies, Kathryn, *Artisan Art: Vernacular Wall Paintings in the Welsh Marches, 1550–1650* (Almeley, Herefordshire, 2008).

Davies, Ralph, *The Trade and Shipping of Hull, 1500–1700* (Yorkshire Local History Society, 17, 1964).

Davis, Nathalie Z., *The Gift in Seventeenth Century France* (Madison, WI, 2000).

Dietz, Brian, *The Port and Trade of Elizabethan London* (London Record Society, 8, 1972).

De Vaynes, J. H. L. (ed.), *A Kentish Garland*, 2 vols (Hertford, 1881).

Dewar, Mary 'A Question of Plagiarism: The "Harrison Chapters" in Sir Thomas Smith's "De Republica Anglorum"', *Historical Journal*, 22/4 (December 1979), 921–9.

Doolittle, Ian, *The Mercer's Company* (Leeds, 1994).

Doran, Susan, 'Virginity, Divinity and Power: The Portraits of Elizabeth I', in S. Doran and Thomas S. Freeman (eds), *The Myth of Elizabeth I* (Basingstoke, 2003).

Douglas, Audrey, and Sally-Beth MacLean (eds), *REED in Review: Essays in Celebration of the First Twenty-Five Years* (Toronto, 1976).

Duffy, Eamon, *The Stripping of the Altars: Traditional Religion in England, c. 1400–1580* (London and New Haven, 1992).

Earle, John, *Microcosmography, or a Piece of the World Discovered in Essays and Characters* (1628), ed. Edward Arber (1895).

Earle, Peter, *The Making of the English Working Class: Business, Society and Family Life in London, 1660–1730* (1989).

Earwaker, J. P. (ed.), *An Index to Wills and Inventories at Chester*, 2 vols (Record Society of Lancashire and Cheshire, 2, 1879 and 4, 1881).

—— *East Cheshire Past and Present or, a History of the Hundred of Macclesfield in the County Palatine of Chester*, 2 vols (1877 and 1880).

—— 'The Four Randle Holmes of Chester, Antiquaries, Heralds, and Genealogists', *Journal of the Chester Archaeological and Historic Society*, NS 4 (1890/1).

Edmond, Mary, 'Bury St Edmunds: A Seventeenth Century Art Centre', *Walpole Society*, 43 for 1987 (1989), 106–18.

—— 'Limners and Picture-Makers: New Light on the Lives of Miniaturists and Large-Scale Portrait Painters working in London in the Sixteenth and Seventeenth Centuries', *Walpole Society*, 47 (1978–80), 60–242.

Edwards, A. C. (ed.), *English History from Essex Sources* (Chelmsford, 1952).

Elyot, Sir Thomas, *The Book Named the Governor* (1531), ed. S. E. Lehmberg (New York, 1962).

Englefield, W. A. D., *The History of the Painter-Stainers' Company of London* (1923).

Evans, John T., *Seventeenth Century Norwich: Politics, Religion, and Government, 1620–1690* (Oxford, 1979).

Evans, Nesta (ed.), *Wills of the Archdeaconry of Sudbury, 1636–1638* (Suffolk Record Society 35, 1993).

Everitt, Alan, *The Community of Kent and the Great Rebellion, 1640–1660* (Leicester, 1973).

—— 'The Marketing of Agricultural Produce', in Joan Thirsk (ed.), *The Agrarian History of England and Wales*, IV: *1500–1640* (Cambridge, 1967), 466–592.

Farrer, Edmund, *Portraits in Suffolk Houses (West)* (1908).

Finberg, A. J., 'A Chronological List of Portraits by Cornelius Johnson, or Jonson', *Walpole Society*, 10 (1922), 1–37.

Fisher, F. J., 'The Development of London as a Centre of Conspicuous Consumption in the Sixteenth and Seventeenth Centuries', *Transactions of the Royal Historical Society*, 4th ser., 30 (1948), 37–50.

—— 'London as an Engine of Economic Growth', in J. S. Bromley and E. H. Kossman (eds), *Britain and the Netherlands*, IV: *Metropolis, Dominion and Province* (The Hague, 1971), 3–16.

Flower, William (ed.), *The Visitation of Yorkshire, 1563 and 1564* (Harleian Society, 16, 1881).

Foister, Susan, 'Edward Alleyn's Collection of Paintings', in Aileen Read and Robert Maniure (eds), *Edward Alleyn, Elizabethan Actor, Jacobean Gentleman* (Dulwich, 1994), 33–61.

—— 'Foreigners at Court: Holbein, Van Dyck and the Painter-Stainers Company', in David Howarth (ed.), *Art and Patronage in the Caroline Court: Essays in Honour of Sir Oliver Millar* (Cambridge, 1993), 32–50.

—— *Holbein and England* (London and New Haven, 2004).

—— *Holbein in England* (London and New Haven, 2006).

—— 'Humanism and Art in the Early Tudor Period: John Leland's Poetic Praise of Painting', in Jonathan Woolfson (ed.), *Reassessing Tudor Humanism* (Basingstoke, 2002), 129–50.

—— 'Paintings and Other Works of Art in Sixteenth Century English Inventories', *Burlington Magazine*, 123 (1981), 273–82.

—— 'Sixteenth-Century English Portraiture and the Idea of the Classical', in Lucy Gent (ed.), *Albion's Classicism: Visual Arts in Britain 1550–1660* (London and New Haven, 1995).

Foskett, Daphne, *A Dictionary of British Miniature Painters*, 2 vols (New York and Washington, 1972).

Foster, Joseph (ed.), *The Visitation of Yorkshire* (1875), 320–1.

French, H. R., *The Middle Sort of People in Provincial England, 1600–1750* (Oxford, 2007).

Friar, Stephen, *The Sutton Companion to Heraldry* (Stroud, Gloucestershire, 1992 and 2004).

Frith, Brian, *Twelve Portraits of Gloucester* (Gloucester, 1972).

Fry, F. M. (ed.), *A Historical Catalogue of the Pictures, Herse-Cloths, and Tapestry at Merchant Taylors' Hall* (1907).

Gage, J., *Colour and Culture: Practice and Meaning from Antiquity to Abstraction* (1993).

Gairdner, James, and R. H. Brodie (eds), *Letters and Papers, Foreign and Domestic, Henry VIII*, 15 1689 (1896).

Ganz, Paul, *The Paintings of Hans Holbein* (1950).
Gardiner, Dorothy (ed.), *The Oxenden Letters, 1617–1642* (1933).
Geertz, Clifford, 'Centers, Kings and Charisma: Reflections on the Symbolics of Power', in Joseph Ben-David and Terry Nicholas Clark (eds), *Culture and Its Creators* (Chicago, 1977).
Gent, Lucy (ed.), *Albion's Classicism: The Visual Arts in Britain, 1550–1660* (London and New Haven, 1995).
—— '"The Rash Gazer": Economies of Vision in Britain, 1550–1660', in ead. (ed.), *Albion's Classicism: The Visual Arts in Britain, 1550–1660* (London and New Haven, 1995), 377–94.
George, David (ed.), *Records of Early English Drama, Lancashire* (Toronto, Buffalo, and London, 1991).
George, Edwin, and Stella George (eds), *Bristol Probate Inventories*, Part I: *1542–1650* (Bristol Record Society, 54, 2002).
Girouard, Mark, *Elizabethan Architecture, Its Rise and Fall* (London and New Haven, 2009).
—— 'Farringdon House, Berkshire, II', *Country Life*, 139/3611 (May 1966), 1246–50.
Glover, Robert, *The Visitation of Cheshire, 1580*, ed. John Paul Rylands (Harleian Society, 18, London, 1882).
Goldsmith, Oliver, *The Vicar of Wakefield* (1834 edn).
Goodison, J. W. (ed.), *Catalogue of the Portraits in Christ's, Clare, and Sidney Sussex Colleges* (Cambridge, 1985).
Goulding, Richard W., and C. K. Adams (eds), *Catalogue of the Pictures Belonging to his Grace the Duke of Portland* (Cambridge, 1936).
Grassby, Richard, *The Business Community of Seventeenth Century England* (Cambridge, 1995).
Graunt, P., 'William Prynne's Reception at Chester, 1637', *Cheshire History*, 37 (1997), 26–35.
Graunt, William, *A Concise History of English Painting* (New York, 1964).
Grazeberooke, H. S. (ed.), *The Heraldic Visitations of Staffordshire Made by Sir Richard St George and Sir William Dugdale* (1885).
Greenblatt, Stephen, *Renaissance Self-Fashioning from More to Shakespeare* (London and Chicago, 1980).
Gribble, Joseph B., *Memorials of Barnstaple: A History of that Ancient Borough* (Barnstaple, 1830).
Griffiths, Paul, *Youth and Authority: Formative Experiences in England, 1560–1640* (Oxford, 1996).
Habermas, Jürgen, *The Structural Transformation of the Public Sphere: An Inquiry into a Category of Bourgeois Society*, trans. Thomas Burger (Cambridge, MA, 1989).
Haigh, Christopher, *Reformation and Resistance in Tudor Lancashire* (Cambridge, 1975).
Haller, Ursula, 'The Purchase and Distribution Book of Wolk Pronner (1586–1590)', in Jo Kirby, Susie Nash, and Joanna Cannon (eds), *Trade in Artists' Materials: Markets and Commerce in Europe to 1700* (2010), 325–35.
Hamling, Tara, and Richard L. Williams (eds), *Art Re-Formed: Re-Assessing the Impact of the Reformation on the Visual Arts* (Newcastle, 2007).
Hancox, Joy, *Kingdom for a Stage: Magicians and Aristocrats in the Elizabethan Theatre* (Stroud, Gloucestershire, 2001).
Harley, R. D., *Artists' Pigments c. 1600–1835: A Study in English Documentary Sources*, 2nd edn (1982).

Harrington, Duncan, and Patricia Hyde (eds), *The Early Town Books of Faversham*, 2 vols (Folkstone, 2008).

Harris, Mary Dormer (ed.), *The Register of the Guild of the Holy Trinity, St Mary, St John the Baptist, and St Katherine of Coventry* (Dugdale Society, 13, 1935).

Harrison, William, *The Description of England* (1577), ed. George Edelen (Ithaca, NY, 1968).

Hart, John, *An Orthographie, conteyning the due order and reason, howe to write or paint thimage of mannes voice* . . . , 2nd edn (1569, *STC* 12,890).

Harte, N. B., 'State Control of Dress and Social Change in Pre-Industrial England', in D. C. Coleman and A. H. Johns (eds), *Trade, Government and Economy in Pre-Industrial England* (1976), 132–65.

Hasler, P. W. (ed.), *The House of Commons, 1558–1603*, 3 vols (History of Parliament, 1981).

Hasted, Edward, *The History and Topographical Survey of the County of Kent*, 12 vols (Canterbury, 1797–1801).

Havinden, M. A. (ed.), *Household and Farm Inventories in Oxfordshire, 1550–1590* (1965).

Haydocke, Richard, *A Tracte Containinge the Artes of Curious Paintinge Carvinge & Buildinge* [a translation of part of Giovanni Paolo Lomazzo's *Trattoro dell'arte della pittura, sculptura ed architettura* (1584)] (Oxford, 1598; *STC* 16,698).

Hayward, Maria, 'The London Linen Trade 1589–1641, and the Use of Linen by Painters in the Royal Service', in Jo Kirby, Susie Nash, and Joanna Cannon (eds), *Trade in Artists' Materials: Markets and Commerce in Europe to 1700* (2010), 375–85.

—— *Rich Apparel: Clothing and the Law in Henry VIII's England* (Farnham, Surrey, 2009).

Hazlitt, Carew, *The Livery Companies of the City of London* (1892).

Heal, Felicity, 'Recoprocity and Exchange in the Late Medieval London Household', in B. A. Hanawalt and David Wallace (eds), *Bodies and Disciplines: Intersections of Literature and History in Fifteenth Century England* (Minneapolis, 1996).

Hearn, Karen, 'An English Gentleman Painter, Henry Gibbs', *Burlington Magazine*, 140 (February 1998), 99–101.

—— (ed.), *Dynasties: Painting in Tudor and Jacobean England 1530–1630* (1995).

—— 'Insiders or Outsiders? Overseas-Born Artists at the Jacobean Court', in Randolphe Vigne and Charles Littleton (eds), *From Strangers to Citizens: The Integration of Immigrant Communities in Britain, Ireland, and Colonial America, 1550–1750* (Brighton, Sussex, 2001), 117–26.

—— *Nathaniel Bacon, Artist, Gentleman, and Gardener* (2005).

—— 'A Question of Judgment: Lucy Harrington, Countess of Bedford as Art Patron and Collector', in Edward Chayney (ed.), *The Evolution of English Collecting* (London and New Haven, 2003), 221–39.

—— *Van Dyck and Britain* (2009).

Hentschell, Ruth, 'A Question of Nation: Foreign Clothes on the English Subject', in Catherine Richardson (ed.), *Clothing Culture, 1350–1650* (Aldershot, 2004), 49–62.

—— 'Treasonous Textiles: Foreign Cloth and the Construction of Englishness', *Journal of Medieval and Early Modern Studies*, 32/3 (September 2002), 543–70.

Hervey, Mary F. S., 'A Lumley Inventory of 1609', *Walpole Society*, 6 (1917–18), 36–50.

Hessels, J. H. (ed.), *Abrahami Ortelii . . . et virorum eruditoram ad candem et ad J. Colium Ortelianum . . . epistolae* (Cambridge, 1887).

Heywood, Thomas, 'If You Know Not Me, You Know No Body', 2nd edn (1623, *STC* 13,338).

Hill, C. P., *A History of the Bristol Grammar School* (Gloucester, 1951).

Hilliard, Nicholas, *A Treatise Concerning the Arte of Limning* (*c.*1600), ed. A. F. Kinney and Linda Bradley Salamon (Boston, MA, 1983).

—— *A Treatise Concerning the Arte of Limning* (*c.*1600), ed. R. K. R. Thornton and T. G. S. Cain (1981).

Hinton, R. W. K. (ed.), *The Port Books of Boston, 1601–1640* (Lincolnshire Record Society, 50, 1956).

Historical Manuscripts Commission, *Calendar of the Manuscripts of the Marquess (sic) of Salisbury preserved at Hatfield House*, ed. M. S. Giuseppi, 15 (1930).

Historical Manuscripts Commission, *Reports of the Percy MSS., Sixth Report*, Appendix I (1877).

Historical Manuscript Commission, *Seventh Report, Appendix* (1879); More/Losely Family of Losely Park, Historical Correspondence, vol. 9 (1420–1642).

Historical Manuscript Commission, *Twelfth Report*, Appendix V, vol. 4 (1905).

Hobbs, Mary (ed.), *Chichester Cathedral: An Historical Survey* (Chichester, 1994).

Holme, Randle, *The Academy of Armory* (1688).

Hopkins, J. T., '"Such a Twin Likeness There was in the Pair": An Investigation into the Painting of the Cholmondeley Sisters', *Transactions of the Historic* [*sic*] *Society of Lancashire and Cheshire*, 144 (1991), 1–37.

Howard, Maurice, 'Art and the Reformation', in Tim Ayers (ed.), *The History of British Art 600–1600*, 3 vols (New Haven and London, 2008), I.231–41.

—— 'Inventories, Surveys and the History of Great Houses', *Architectural History*, 41 (1998), 14–29.

—— *The Tudor Image* (1995).

Howarth, David, *Images of Rule: Art and Politics in the English Renaissance, 1485–1649* (Berkeley and Los Angeles, 1997).

Hughes, Thomas, 'On Chester Literature, Its Authors and Publishers during the Sixteenth and Seventeenth Centuries', *Journal of the Architectural, Archaeological and Historic* [*sic*] *Society of Chester*, 2 (1864), 21–30.

Hulse, Clark, 'Dead Man's Treasure: The Cult of Thomas More', in David Lee Miller, Sharon O'Dair, and Harold Weber (eds), *The Production of English Renaissance Culture* (Ithaca, NY, 1994), 190–225.

—— *The Rule of Art, Literature and Painting in the Renaissance* (Chicago and London, 1990).

Hunneyball, Paul, *Architecture and Image Building in Seventeenth Century Hertfordshire* (Oxford, 2004).

Ingamells, J., *The English Episcopal Portrait, 1559–1835* (Guildford, 1983).

—— *The English Episcopal Portrait 1559–1835: A Catalogue* (1981).

Ingram, R. W. (ed.), *Records of Early English Drama, Coventry* (Toronto, 1981).

Irvine, William F. (ed.), *A Collection of Lancashire and Cheshire Wills Not Now to be Found in any Probate Inventory, 1301–1752* (Record Society of Lancashire and Cheshire, 30, 1896).

—— *Marriage Licenses Granted within the Archdeaconry of Chester in the Diocese of Chester* (Record Society of Lancashire and Cheshire, 54, 1909).

Jackson, Rev. Canon J. E., 'Wulfhall and the Seymours', *Wiltshire Archaeological and Natural History Magazine*, 15 (1875), 140–207.

James, Susan E., *The Feminist Dynamic in English Art, 1485–1603: Women as Consumers, Patrons and Painters* (Farnham, Surrey, 2009).

Jervis, Simon, *British and Irish Inventories: A List and Bibliography of Published Transcriptions of Secular Inventories* (2010).

Johnson, Matthew, *English Houses 1300–1800, Vernacular Architecture, Social Life* (2010).

Johnston, Alexandra F., 'The Founding of the Records of Early English Drama', in Audrey Douglas and Sally-Beth MacLean (eds), *REED in Review: Essays in Celebration of the First Twenty-Five Years* (Toronto, 2006), 21–38.

Jones, Ann Rosalind, and Peter Stallybrass, *Renaissance Clothing and the Materials of Memory* (Cambridge, 2000).

Jones, Rica, 'The Methods and Materials of Three Tudor Artists: Bettes, Hilliard and Ketel', in Karen Hearn (ed.), *Dynasties: Painting in Tudor and Jacobean England, 1530–1630* (1995), 231–40.

Jordan, W. K., *The Charities of London* (1969).

Keene, Derek, 'National and Regional Identities', in Richard Marks and Paul Williamson (eds), *Gothic Art for England 1400–1547* (2003), 46–55.

Kingsford, Charles Lethbridge (ed.), *John Stow: A Survey of London Reprinted from the Text of 1603*, 2 vols (Oxford, 1908, with Additional Notes, 1927).

Kirby, Jo, 'Fading and Colour Changes of Prussian Blue: Occurrences and Early Reports', *National Gallery Technical Bulletion*, 14 (1993), 63–71.

—— 'The Painter's Trade in the Seventeenth Century: Theory and Practice', *National Gallery Technical Bulletin*, 20 (1999), 5–49.

—— 'Sir Nathaniel Bacon's 'Pinke', *Dyes in History and Archaeology*, 19 (2003), 37–50.

——, Susie Nash, and Joanna Cannon (eds), *Trade in Artists' Materials: Markets and Commerce in Europe to 1700* (2010).

—— and Raymond White, 'The Identification of Red Lake Pigment Dyestuffs and a Discussion of their Use', *National Gallery Technical Bulletin*, 17 (1996), 56–80.

Kirkham, Andrea, 'Pattern and Colour in Late 16th and 17th Century Wall and Panel Paintings in Suffolk', in Robert Gowring and Robin Pender (eds), *All Manner of Murals: The History, Techniques, and Conservation of Secular Wall Paintings* (2007), 33–42.

Krischel, Roland, 'The Inventory of the Venetian *Vendecolori* Jacopo de' Benedetti: The Non-Pigment Materials', in Jo Kirby, Susie Nash, and Joanna Cannon (eds), *Trade in Artists' Materials: Markets and Commerce in Europe to 1700* (2010), 53–66.

Kury, Gloria, '"Glancing Surfaces": Hilliard, Armour, and the Italian Model', in Lucy Gent (ed.), *Albion's Classicism: The Visual Arts in Britain, 1550–1660* (London and New Haven, 1995), 395–426.

Laslett, Peter, 'The Gentry of Kent in 1640', *Cambridge Historical Journal*, 9/2 (1948), 148–64.

Legg, J. Wickham, and W. H. St John Hope (eds), *Inventories of Christchurch Canterbury, with Historical and Topographical Introductions and Illustrated Documents* (Westminster, 1902).

Leggatt, Alexander, *Citizen Comedy in the Age of Shakespeare* (Toronto, 1973).

Leicester Museum and Art Gallery, *Catalogue of Local Portraits* ([Leicester], 1956).

Letters and Papers Foreign and Domestic of Henry VIII.

Lewis, C. P., and A. T. Thacker (eds), *A History of the County of Chester*, 5 vols (Woodbridge, Suffolk, 1987–2005), II: *The City of Chester.*

Lindley, Phillip, 'The "Artist": Institutions, Training and Status', in Tim Ayers (ed.), *The History of British Art, 600–1600* (London and New Haven, 2008), 141–65.

Livock, D. M. (ed.), *City Chamberlain Accounts in the Sixteenth and Seventeenth Centuries* (Bristol Record Society, 24, 1966).

Llewellyn, Nigel, *Funeral Monuments in Post-Reformation England* (Cambridge, 2000).

Lloyd, Christopher, and Simon Thurley, *Henry VIII: Images of a Tudor King* (1990).
Luders, A., T. E. Tomlins, and J. Raithby (eds), *Statutes of the Realm*, 11 vols (1810–28).
MacCaffrey, Wallace T., *Exeter, 1540–1640: The Growth of an English Country Town*, 2nd edn (Cambridge, MA, 1975).
McClendon, Muriel, *The Quiet Revolution: Magistrates and the Emergence of Protestantism in Tudor Norwich* (Stanford, CA, 1999).
MaClean, Sally-Beth, *Chester Art: A Subject List of Extant and Lost Art Including Items Relevant to Early Drama* (Kalamazoo, MI, 1982).
McVeagh, John, *Tradeful Merchants: The Portrayal of the Capitalist in Literature* (1981).
Malbon, Thomas, *Memorials of the Civil War in Cheshire and the Adjacent Counties* (Record Society of Lancashire and Cheshire, 48, 1889).
Manley, Lawrence, *Literature and Culture in Early Modern London* (Cambridge, 1995).
Martindale, Andrew, *Heroes, Ancestors, Relatives, and the Birth of the Portrait* (The Hague, 1988).
Mercer, Eric, *English Art, 1553–1625* (Oxford, 1962).
Moore, Andrew, and Charlotte Crawley (eds), *Family and Friends: A Regional Survey of British Portraiture* (1992).
Morgan, Victor, 'The Dutch and Flemish Presence and the Emergence of an Anglo-Dutch Provincial Artistic Tradition in Norwich, *c.* 1500–1700', in Juliette Roding, Eric Jan Sluijter, Bart Westerweel, Marijke van der Meij-Tolmsa, and Eric Domela Nieuwenhuis (eds), *Dutch and Flemish Artists in Britain, 1550–1800* (Leiden, 2002), 57–72.
—— 'The Norwich Guildhall Portraits: Images in Context', in Andrew Moore and Charlotte Crawley (eds), *Family and Friends: A Regional Survey of British Portraiture* (1992), 21–30.
Murrell, Jim, 'John Guillem's Book: A Heraldic Painter's *Vade Mecum*', *Walpole Society*, 57 (1995), 1–52.
Myers, J. N. L., 'The Painted Frieze in the Picture Gallery', *Bodleian Library Record*, 3 (1950–1), 82–90.
Norgate, Edward, *Miniatura, or the Art of Limning* (1627–8), ed. J. M. Muller and J. Murrell (London and New Haven, 1997).
O'Connell, Laura Stephenson, 'Anti-Entrepreneurial Attitudes in Elizabethan Sermons and Popular Literature', *Journal of British Studies*, 15 (1976), 2–20.
Orlin, Lena Cowen, 'Fictions of the Early Modern Probate Inventory', in H. S. Turner (ed.), *The Culture of Capital: Property, Cities and Knowledge in Early Modern England* (New York and London, 2002), 51–83.
—— *Locating Privacy in Tudor London* (Oxford and New York, 2007).
Ormerod, George, *The History of the County Palatine and City of Chester*, 2nd edn, 3 vols (1882).
Osborne, James M. (ed.), *The Autobiography of Thomas Whythorne* (Oxford, 1961).
Overton, Mark, Jane Whittle, Darron Dean, and Andrew Hann, *Production and Consumption in English Households 1600–1750* (2004).
Oxford Dictionary of National Biography, 61 vols (2004).
Page, William (ed.), *Letters of Denization and Acts of Naturalization for Aliens in England* (Publications of the Huguenot Society of London, VIII, 1883).
Painter, William, *Chaucer Newly Painted* (1623 edn, *STC* 19, 125–5).
Palliser, D. M., *The Age of Elizabeth: England under the Later Tudors, 1547–1603*, 2nd edn (1992).

Parry, Hugh Lloyd, *The History of the Exeter Guildhall and the Life Within* (Exeter, 1936).

Patterson, Annabel, 'Catholic Communities and their Art', in Nicholas Howe (ed.), *Visions of Community in the Pre-Modern World* (Notre Dame, IN, 2002), 108–49.

Payne, Ann, 'Sir Thomas Wriothesley and his Heraldic Artists', in Michelle P. Brown and Scott McKendrick (eds), *Illuminating the Book: Makers and Interpreters: Essays in Honour of Janet Backhouse* (1998), 143–61.

Peacham, Henry, *The Art of Drawing with a Pen* (1606).

—— *The Compleat Gentleman* (1622).

—— *The Gentleman's Exercize* (1612).

—— *Graphica, or the Most Auncient and Excellent Art of Drawing and Limning* (1612).

Peck, Linda Levy, *Consuming Splendor, Society and Culture in Seventeenth Century England* (Cambridge, 2005).

—— *Court Patronage and Corruption in Early Stuart England* (1990).

—— 'The Dutch and Flemish Presence and the Emergence of an Anglo-Dutch Provincial Artistic Tradition in Norwich, *c.* 1500–1700', in Juliette Roding, Eric Jan Sluijter, Bart Westerweel, Marijke van der Meiji-Tolmsa, and Eric Domela Nieuwenhuis (eds), *Dutch and Flemish Artists in Britain, 1550–1800* (Leiden, 2002), 57–72.

Pelling, Margaret, and Frances White (eds), *Physicians and Irregular Medical Practitioners in London, 1550–1640* (2004).

Pevsner, Niklaus, *Outline of European Architecture*, 7th edn (Harmondsworth, Middlesex, 1968).

Phelps Brown, E. H., and Sheila V. Hopkins, 'Seven Centuries of Prices of Consumables, Compared with Builders' Wage-Rates', *Economica*, NS 23/92 (November 1956), 296–314.

Phillips, C. B., and J. H. Smith (eds), *Stockport Probate Records*, 2 vols (Record Society of Lancashire and Cheshire, 124, 1985, and 131, 1992).

Phillips, John, *The Reformation of Images: Destruction of Art in England, 1535–1660* (Berkeley and Los Angeles, 1973).

Phythian-Adams, Charles, 'Differentiating Provincial Societies in English History: Spatial Contexts and Cultural Processes', in Bill Lancaster, Diana Newton, and Natasha Vall (eds), *An Agenda for Regional History* (Northumbria University, 2007), 3–22.

—— 'Environments and Identities: Landscape as Cultural Projection in the English Provincial Past', in Paul Slack (ed.), *Environments and Historical Change: The Linacre Lectures 1998* (Oxford, 1999), 118–46.

—— 'Introduction: An Agenda for English Local History', in id. (ed.), *Societies, Cultures and Kinship, 1580–1850: Cultural Provinces and English Local History* (Leicester, 1993), 1–23.

—— *Land of the Cumbrians: A Study in British Provincial Origins AD 400–1120* (Aldershot, 1996).

—— 'Local History and Social History', *Local Population Studies*, 51 (1993), 30–45.

—— *Rethinking English Local History* (Leicester, 1987).

Piper, David, 'The 1590 Lumley Inventory: Hilliard, Segar and the Earl of Essex', *Burlington Magazine*, 99 (1957), 299–303.

—— *The English Face* (1957, 2nd edn, 1992).

Pomeroy, Elizabeth W., *Reading the Portraits of Queen Elizabeth I* (Hamden, CT, 1989).

Poole, Rachel (ed.), *Catalogue of Portraits Exhibited in the Reading Room and Gallery of the Bodleian Library* (Oxford, 1920).

Poole, Rachel (ed.), *Catalogue of Portraits in . . . the University, Colleges, City and County of Oxford*, 3 vols (Oxford Historical Society Publications, vols 57, 1912; 81, 1926; and 82, 1926).

Porter, Stephen, *Destruction in the English Civil Wars* (Stroud, Gloucestershire, 1994).

—— 'The Economic and Social Impact of the Civil Wars upon London', in id. (ed.), *London and the Civil War* (Basingstoke, 1996), 175–204.

Preston, Arthur E., *Christ's Hospital, Abingdon: The Almshouses, the Hall, and the Portraits* (Oxford, 1929).

Prideaux, Sir Walter Shelburne, *Memorials of the Goldsmiths' Company*, 2 vols (1896).

Public Record Office, *Royal Portraits from the Plea Rolls, Henry VIII to Charles II* (1974).

Questier, Michael, *Catholicism and Community in Early Modern England: Politics, Aristocratic Patronage and Religion, c. 1550–1640* (Cambridge, 2006).

Ralph, Elizabeth, and Nora M. Hardwick (eds), *Calendar of the Bristol Apprenticeship Book*, I: *1532–1565 and* II: *1542–1552* (Bristol Record Society, 33, 1980).

Ramsay, G. D., *John Isham, Mercer and Merchant Adventurer* (Gateshead, 1962).

Rappaport, Steve, *Worlds within Worlds: Structures of Life in Sixteenth Century London* (Cambridge, 1989).

Rastell, John, *The Pastyme of People: the Chronycles of Dyvers realmys and most specyally of the realme of Englond brevely co[m]pylyd* (1529; *STC*, 20724).

Reed, Michael (ed.), *The Ipswich Probate Inventories, 1583–1631* (Suffolk Record Society, 22, 1981).

Richardson, Catherine, and Tara Hamling (eds), *Everyday Things in Early Modern England* (Farnham, Surrey, 2009).

Richardson, R. C., 'Puritanism and the Ecclesiastical Authorities: The Case of the Diocese of Chester', in Brian Manning (ed.), *Politics, Religion and the English Civil Wars* (1973), 3–33.

Roberts, Stephanie, and Robert Tittler, 'Tracking the Elusive Portrait Painter Thomas Leigh through Caroline England and Wales', *British Art Journal*, 11/1 (Summer 2010), 1–9.

Rostenberg, Leona, *English Publishers in the Graphic Arts, 1599–1700: A Study of the Printsellers and Publishers of Engravings* (repr., New York, 1963).

Rouse, E. Clive, 'Further Notes on the Painted Frieze and Other Discoveries in the Upper Reading Room and the Tower Room', *Bodleian Library Record*, 5 (October 1956), 290–308.

Rylands, John Paul (ed.), *Cheshire and Lancashire Funeral Certificates, A.D. 1600 to 1678* (Record Society of Lancashire and Cheshire, 6, 1882).

Salzman, L. F. (ed.), *Victoria History of the County of Sussex*, III (1935).

Schama, Simon, *Landscape and Memory* (1995).

Scott, Rev. Canon S. Cooper, 'Cotes Monument: Once Set Up in St John's Church, Chester', *Journal of the Architectural, Archaeological and Historic (sic) Society of Chester*, NS 8 (1902), 5–17.

Serlio, Sebastian, *The first booke of architecture, made by Sebastian Serly, entreating of geometrie*, Printed for Robert Peake (1611, *STC* 22,235).

Shammas, Carol, *The Pre-Industrial Consumer in England and America* (Oxford, 1990).

Sharpe, Kevin, *Selling the Tudor Monarchy: Authority and Image in Sixteenth Century England* (New Haven and London, 2009).

Sharpe, Thomas, *Illustrative Papers on the History and Antiquities of the City of Coventry* (Birmingham, 1871).

Shaw, David Gary, *The Creation of a Community: The City of Wells in the Middle Ages* (Oxford, 1993).
Shawe-Taylor, Desmond, *Dulwich Picture Gallery: A Visitor's Guide* (Dulwich, 2000).
Sherlock, Peter, *Monuments and Memory in Early Modern England* (Aldershot, 2008).
Shute, John, *The First and Chief Groundes of Architecture* (facsimile edition, 1912).
Singh, Prince Frederick Duleep, *Portraits in Norfolk Houses*, ed. Edmund Farrer, 2 vols (Norwich, 1928).
Sklaer, R. J., 'The Panel Portrait of Andrew Perne', *Peterhouse: A Record* (volume for 1997–8, published 1999), 38–41.
Sluijter, Eric Jan, 'The English Venture: Dutch and Flemish Artists in Britain 1550–1800', in Juliet Roding, Eric Jan Sluijter, Bart Westerweel, Marijke van der Meij-Tolmsa, and Eric Domela Nieuwenhuis (eds), *Dutch and Flemish Artists in Britain, 1550–1800* (Leiden, 2002), 7–30.
Smith, David R., *Masks of Wedlock: Seventeenth Century Dutch Marriage Portraiture* (Ann Arbor, MI, 1982).
Smith, John (ed.), *The Names and Surnames of all the Able and Sufficient Men in Body fit for His Majesty's Service in the Wars within the County of Gloucester* (1902).
Spufford, Margaret, 'The Limitations of the Probate Inventory', in J. Chartres and D. Hey (eds), *English Rural Society, 1500–1800* (Cambridge, 1990), 139–74.
Spufford, Peter, *et al.* (eds), *Index to the Probate Accounts of England and Wales, 'A to J'* (British Record Society, Index Library, 1999).
Squibb, G. D., 'Deputy Heralds of Chester', *Journal of the Chester Archaeological and Historic Society*, 56 (1969), 23–36.
Statham, Margaret (ed.), *Accounts of the Feoffees of the Town Lands of Bury St Edmunds, 1569–1622* (Suffolk Record Society, 46, 2003).
Steegman, John, *A Survey of Portraits in Welsh Houses*, 2 vols (Cardiff, 1957).
Stewart, Brian, and Mervyn Cutten (eds), *Chichester Artists, 1530–1900* (Canterbury, 1987).
Stocks, Helen, and W. H. Stevenson (eds), *Records of the Borough of Leicester*, II (Cambridge, 1923).
Stone, Lawrence, *The Crisis of the Aristocracy, 1558–1641* (Oxford, 1965).
—— 'Elizabethan Overseas Trade', *Economic History Review*, NS 2/1 (1949), 30–58.
String, Tatiana, *Art and Communication in the Reign of Henry VIII* (Aldershot, 2009).
Strong, Roy, *The Cult of Elizabeth: Elizabethan Portraiture and Pageantry* (Berkeley and Los Angeles, 1977).
—— *The Elizabethan Image: Painting in England, 1540–1620* (1970).
—— *The English Icon: Elizabethan and Jacobean Portraiture* (New York, 1969).
Strong, Roy, 'Forgotten Faces: Regional History and Regional Portraiture', *Historical Research*, 78/199 (February 2005), 43–57.
—— 'Hans Eworth, a Tudor Artist and his Circle', in id., *The Tudor and Stuart Monarchy, Pageantry, Painting, Iconography*, 3 vols (Woodbridge, Suffolk, 1995), I.93–134.
—— *Holbein and Henry VIII* (1967).
—— 'More Tudor Artists', *Burlington Magazine*, 108 (1966), 83–85 repr. in id., *The Tudor and Stuart Monarchy, Pageantry, Painting, Iconography*, 3 vols (Woodbridge, Suffolk, 1995), I.147–53.
—— 'Portraits of the Deans of Canterbury Cathedral', *Canterbury Chronicle*, 65 (1970), 102–11.
—— 'Portraiture and Character in Shakespeare's England', *Dalhousie Review*, 86/1 (Spring 2006), 7–26.

Strong, Roy, *Tudor and Jacobean Portraits,* 2 vols (1969).
—— *The Tudor and Stuart Monarchy,* 3 vols (Woodbridge, Suffolk, 1995–8).
—— 'William Larkin, Icons of Splendour', in id., *The Tudor and Stuart Monarchy, Pageantry, Painting, Iconography,* 3 vols (Woodbridge, Suffolk, 1998), III.1–68.
Sturt, George, [pseud. George Bourne], *Change in the Village* (1912).
—— *The Wheelwright's Shop* (Cambridge, 1923).
Surrey, L. M. N. (ed.), *The Portraits of Edward VI* (Portsmouth, n.d.).
Sutton, Anne, *The Mercery of London* (2005).
Talley, M. K., *Portrait Painting in England: Studies in the Technical Literature before 1700* (1981).
Thirsk, *Economic Policy and Projects: The Development of a Consumer Society in Early Modern England* (Oxford, 1978).
Thomas, Keith, *The Ends of Life: Roads to Fulfilment in Early Modern England* (Oxford, 2009).
—— *Man and the Natural World: Changing Attitudes in England, 1500–1800* (1983).
Thompson, James, 'The Herrick Portraits in the Guildhall, Leicester', *Transactions of the Leicestershire Architectural and Archaeological Society,* 2 (1870), 43–54.
Thwaite, Hartley (ed.), *Abstracts of Abbotside Wills, 1552–1688* (Yorkshire Archaeological Society Record Series, 130, 1902).
Tillyard, Virginia, 'Painters in Sixteenth and Seventeenth Century Norwich' *Norfolk Archaeology,* 37 (1980), 315–19.
Tittler, Robert, *Architecture and Power: The Town Hall and the English Urban Community, c. 1500–1640* (Oxford, 1991).
—— *The Face of the City: Civic Portraiture and Civic Identity in Early Modern England* (Manchester, 2007).
—— 'Faces and Spaces: Displaying the Civic Portrait in Early Modern England', in Catherine Richardson and Tara Hamling (eds), *Everyday Objects: Medieval and Early Modern Culture and Its Meanings* (Farnham, Surrey, 2010), 179–90.
—— 'Freemens' Gloves and Civic Authority: The Evidence from Post-Reformation Portraiture', *Costume,* 40 (2006), 13–20.
—— 'George Cottington and the Dering Family Portraits of 1626', *Burlington Magazine,* 151 (April 2009), 208–11.
—— 'Henry Hardware and the Face of Puritan Reform in Chester', in id., *Townspeople and Nation: English Urban Experiences, 1540–1640* (Stanford, CA, 2001), 140–55.
—— 'Henry Manship: Constructing the Civic Memory in Great Yarmouth', in id., *Townspeople and Nation: English Urban Experiences, 1540–1640* (Stanford, CA, 2001), 121–39.
—— 'The Incorporation of Boroughs, 1540–1558', *History,* 62/204 (February 1977), 24–42.
—— 'John and Joan Cooke: Civic Portraiture and Urban Identity in Gloucester', in id., *Townspeople and Nation: English Urban Experiences, 1540–1640* (Stanford, CA, 2001), 81–99.
—— *The Reformation and the Towns in England: Politics and Political Culture, c. 1540–1640* (Oxford, 1998).
—— 'Regional Portraiture and the Heraldic Connection in Tudor and Early Stuart England', *British Art Journal,* 10/1 (2009), 3–10.
—— 'Sir Thomas White of London: Civic Philanthropy and the Making of the Merchant Hero', in id., *Townspeople and Nation: English Urban Experiences, 1540–1640* (Stanford, CA, 2001), 100–20.

—— 'Thomas Heywood and the Portrayal of Female Benefactors in Post-Reformation England', *Early Theatre*, 11/1 (June 2008), 33–52.

—— 'Three Portraits by Jan de Critz for the Merchant Taylors' Company', *Burlington Magazine*, 147/1228 (July 2005), 491–3.

—— and Anne Thackray, 'Cultural Relations between London and the Provincial Towns: Portraiture and Publics in Early Modern England', in Bronwen Wilson and Paul Yachnin (eds), *Making Publics in Early Modern Europe: People, Things, Forms of Knowledge* (Abingdon and New York, 2010), 123–38.

—— 'Print Collecting in Provincial England Prior to 1650, the Randle Holme Album', *British Art Journal*, 11/2 (Autumn 2008), 3–10.

Trench, John Chenevix, 'John Abbott's Manual of Limming [sic]', *Association for Studies in the Conservation of Historic Buildings, Transactions*, 2 (1986), 19–26.

Treuherz, Julian, 'New Light on John Souch of Chester', *Burlington Magazine*, 139/1130 (May 1997), 299–307.

Tummers, Anna, and Koenraed Jonckheere (eds), *Art Market and Connoisseurship: A Closer Look at Paintings by Rembrandt, Rubens, and Their Contemporaries* (Amsterdam, 2008).

van den Heuvel, Danielle, and Elise van Nederveen Meerkerk, 'Partners in Business? Spousal Cooperation in Trades in Early Modern England and the Dutch Republic', *Continuity and Change*, 23/2 (2008), 209–16.

Vanes, Jean, *Education and Apprenticeship in Sixteenth Century Bristol* (unpaginated pamphlet, Bristol, 1982).

Victoria History of the County of Chester, V, pt. 2 (Woodbridge, Suffolk, 2005).

Vincent, Susan, *Dressing the Elite: Clothes in Early Modern Europe* (Oxford, 2002).

Wagner, Anthony, and George Squibb, 'Deputy Heralds', in Frederick Emmison and Roy Stephens (eds), *Tribute to an Antiquary: Essays Presented to Marc Fitch by Some of His Friends* (1976), 229–64.

Wanklyn, Malcolm (ed.), *Inventories of Worcestershire Landed Gentry, 1537–1786* (Worcestershire Historical Society, NS 16, 1998).

Waterhouse, Ellis K., *The Dictionary of 16th and 17th c. British Painters* (Woodbridge, Suffolk, 1988).

—— *Painting in Britain 1530 to 1790* (1953; 4th edn, Harmondsworth, Middlesex, 1978).

Watt, Tessa, *Cheap Print and Popular Piety, 1550–1640* (Cambridge, 1991).

Weaver, F. W. (ed.), *Somerset Medieval Wills (Third Series) 1531–1558* (Somerset Record Society, 21, 1905).

Weever, John, *Ancient Funeral Monuments* (1631).

Weiss Gallery Collection, *Icons of Splendour: Early Portraiture, 1530–1700* (2004).

Wells-Cole, Anthony, *Art and Decoration in Elizabethan and Jacobean England: The Influence of Continental Prints, 1558–1625* (London and New Haven, 1997).

—— 'Elusive Sources for Renaissance Wall Paintings', in Robert Gowing and Robyn Pender (eds), *All Manner of Murals: The History, Techniques, and Conservation of Secular Wall Paintings* (2007), 3–9.

Wetherill, Lorna, *Consumer Behaviour and Material Culture in Britain, 1660–1720,* 2nd edn (1996).

—— 'The Meaning of the Consumer Revolution in England and America in the Late Seventeenth and Early Eighteenth Centuries' in John Brewer and Roy Porter (eds), *Consumption and the World of Goods* (1993), 206–17.

Whiting, C. E., 'The Durham Trades Guilds', *Transactions of the Architectural and Archaeological Society of Durham and Northumberland*, 9, pt 2 (1941), 143–262.

Willan, T. S., *Studies in Elizabethan Foreign Trade* (Manchester, 1959).

Williams, Neville, *Thomas Howard Fourth Duke of Norfolk* (1964).
Williams, W. J. (ed.), 'Wills of Masons and Freemen', *Masonic Record*, 16 (August 1936), 204–5.
Willis, Robert, *The Architectural History of the University of Cambridge*, 3 vols (Cambridge, 1886, ed. John Willis Clarke, repr. 1988).
Wilson, Bronwen, and Paul Yachnin (eds), *Making Publics in Early Modern Europe: People, Things, Forms of Knowledge* (New York and Abingdon, 2010).
Wilson, E. C., *England's Eliza* (Cambridge, MA, 1939).
Witt Library, Courtauld Institute of Art, *Checklist of British Artists in the Witt Library* (1991).
Wood, A. C. (ed.), *Memorials of the Holles Family, 1493–1656* (Camden Society, 3rd ser., 55, 1937).
Woodall, Joanna, 'An Exemplary Consort: Antonis Mor's Wedding Portrait of Mary Tudor', *Art History*, 14/2 (June 1991), 192–224.
—— *Portraiture: Facing the Subject* (Manchester and New York, 1997).
—— 'Status Symbols: Role and Rank in Seventeenth Century Netherlandish Portraiture', *Dutch Crossing*, 42 (Autumn 1990), 34–68.
Woods-Marsden, Joanna, *Renaissance Self-Portraiture: The Visual Construction of Identity and the Social Status of the Artist* (London and New Haven, 1998).
Woodward, D. M., *The Trade of Elizabethan Chester* (Hull, 1970).
Woolf, Daniel, 'Senses of the Past in Tudor Britain', in Robert Tittler and Norman Jones (eds), *A Companion to Tudor Britain* (Oxford, 2004) , 407–29.
—— *The Social Circulation of the Past: English Historical Culture, 1500–1730* (Oxford, 2003).
Woolfson, J., and D. Lush, 'Lambert Barnard in Chichester Cathedral: Ecclesiastical Politics and the Tudor Royal Image', *Antiquaries Journal*, 87 (2007), 259–80.
Wrightson, Keith, *Earthly Necessities: Economic Lives in Early Modern Britain* (London and New Haven, 2000).
—— *English Society, 1580–1680* (1982).
—— 'Estates, Degrees, and Sorts: Changing Perceptions of Society in Tudor and Stuart England', in P. J. Corfield (ed.), *Language, History and Class* (Oxford, 1991), 30–52.
—— '"Sorts of People" in Tudor and Stuart England', in Jonathan Barry and Christopher Brooks (eds), *The Middling Sorts of People, Culture, Society and Politics in England, 1550–1800* (Basingstoke, 1994), 28–51.
Wrigley, E. A., 'A Simple Model of London's Importance in Changing English Society and Economy, 1650–1759', *Past and Present*, 37 (July 1967), 44–70.
—— and R. S. Schofield, *The Population History of England, 1541–1871* (1981).
Yates, Frances, 'Queen Elizabeth as Astraea', *Journal of the Warburg and Courtauld Institutes*, 10 (1947), 27–82.
Young, Sidney, *Annals of the Barber Surgeons of London* (1890).
Zell, Michael (ed.), *Early Modern Kent, 1540–1640* (Woodbridge, Suffolk, 2000).
—— 'The Social Parameters of Probate Records in the Sixteenth Century', *Bulletin of the Institute of Historical Research*, 57 (1984), 107–13.
Zins, Henry, *England and the Baltic in the Elizabethan Era* (Manchester, 1972).

Index

[References to figures are in italics.]

Printed and bound by CPI Group (UK) Ltd, Croydon, CR0 4YY